ELAINE EVANS

D1491930

COOKING EXPLAINED

COOKING EXPLAINED

Barbara Hammond

Teacher's Diploma of Battersea
Polytechnic Training College of Domestic Science
Formerly Deputy Principal and Principal Lecturer in Cookery at Battersea
Training College of Domestic Science

Longman

LONGMAN GROUP LIMITED
LONDON

*Associated companies, branches and representatives
throughout the world*

First published 1963
Seventh impression 1971

ISBN 0 582 32512 9

*Printed in Great Britain by
Butler & Tanner Ltd, Frome and London*

PREFACE

Cooking is a necessary part of everyday life. We must eat to live and most of our food must be cooked if we are to enjoy it and digest it. But cooking is much more than just a necessity of life, it is a fascinating and exciting occupation. The good cook probably gets as much enjoyment from the preparation of an excellent meal as do the diners and she has the great reward of knowing that she has given pleasure to others.

The great wealth of materials that are used in cooking makes it an exciting subject, all the more so when a little research is made into the source of these materials that come from all parts of the world and from all climates. The way in which many foodstuffs change and blend with each other during cooking is often surprising and usually interesting and leads to the beginnings of a scientific approach to food and cooking.

Science is important in many ways in the study of food and cooking; it has made us aware of the need for cleanliness to prevent disease; of the need for balancing our diet and it has removed much of the guesswork from cooking. Indirectly modern science may have made cooking more complicated by widening the choice of foodstuffs and the selection of materials for kitchen furnishing, but it has also improved the quality and freshness when marketed of many foods and produced equipment that makes the cook's work today much lighter and more enjoyable than it was even one generation ago.

To sum up the aims of this book, they are: to make cooking interesting; to make it an adventurous subject and one in which thought is required as well as action; to show that cooking needs skill and accuracy and, above all, to show the beginner that she is embarking upon an occupation that is infinitely varied, very wide and wholly enjoyable.

CONTENTS

Part One—Explanations

Part Two—Recipes

Part One

EXPLANATIONS

FOUNDATIONS OF SKILL
IN COOKING

Accuracy is a first essential to skill in cooking—it is essential in following a recipe, in measuring and weighing and in selecting and maintaining the right temperature in cooking.

Accuracy in following a recipe means reading it right through, checking that the measurements are intended to be level or rounded, that the size of dish or tin is stated and that the order of work is in logical sequence.

Accuracy in weighing or measuring is necessary to success in cooking: the experienced cook who can apparently guess the right amounts of ingredients probably has an accurate eye and is in reality most exact in her 'guessed' measurements. *Weighing* is more accurate than measuring provided that reliable scales are used; these may be of the spring-balance type or of the separate weight type and in either case they should bear a Government stamp and should weigh from ½ oz. to at least 2 lb.

To use a spring-balance check that the pointer is at 0 when the pan is empty (this can usually be adjusted by a screw); wait till the pointer is steady at the required weight. Never keep anything on the pan, as this will strain the spring.

To use scales and weights, the contents of the pan and the weight must balance evenly; neither side should go down with a bump.

Measuring. Most British recipes are expressed in weights, so that if scales are not used a correct measurement must be found to correspond to each weighed ingredient.

EQUIPMENT FOR MEASURING

Government-stamped measures each holding from 1 pint to ⅛ pint (not graduated).

British Standard Institute plastic measuring cups in sets of

$$1 \text{ cup} = \tfrac{1}{2} \text{ pint}; \tfrac{1}{2} \text{ cup} = \tfrac{1}{4} \text{ pint};$$
$$\tfrac{1}{3} \text{ cup} = \tfrac{1}{6} \text{ pint}; \tfrac{1}{4} \text{ cup} = \tfrac{1}{8} \text{ pint}.$$

Graduated measure-jugs, metal, glass or plastic, graduated in fractions of 1 pint and in liquid ounces. One make also shows the corresponding weights of different foods.

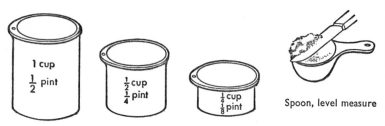

Fig. 1. BRITISH STANDARD MEASURES

Measuring spoons. Dining-room table- and teaspoons vary in size, but the British Standards Institute standard teaspoon and an average tablespoon measure as follows:

> 1 tablespoon = $\frac{1}{32}$ pint or $\frac{1}{16}$ cup.
> 2 level tablespoons measure 1 oz. flour.
> 4 B.S.I. teaspoons = 1 tablespoon.

Table for Use of B.S.I. Cups and Average Tablespoons

Food	*Weight of Cup*	*No. of Level Spoons to 1 oz.*	
Flour, cornflour and other starch powders	5 oz.	2 tablespoons	
Fresh breadcrumbs	3 ,,	4 ,,	
Grated cheese	4 ,,	3 ,,	
Oatmeal	7 ,,	2 ,,	
Oats, rolled	4 ,,	3 ,,	
Rice	9 ,,	2 ,,	(scant measure)
Sugar, granulated	8 ,,	2 ,,	
Sultanas, seedless raisins, currants	6 ,,	2 ,,	
Syrup and treacle	14 ,,	1 ,,	(approximately)

Note. All spoons are levelled, all cups loosely filled, not packed down. If a recipe states a rounded spoon this equals 2 level spoons.

Table of British Weights and Measures

Liquid Measure		Avoirdupois	
1 drop	= 1 minim	16 drams	= 1 oz.
16 minims	= 1 drachm	16 oz.	= 1 lb.
8 drachms	= 1 liquid oz.	14 lb.	= 1 stone
20 oz.	= 1 pint	3½ lb.	= 1 quartern (¼ stone)
2 pints	= 1 quart		
4 quarts	= 1 gallon		

Weight	Equivalent Metric Weights and Measures	Liquid	
1 oz.	= 28½ grams (roughly 30 grams)	1 litre	= 35 oz. = 1¾ pt.
3½ oz.	= 100 grams	½ litre	= good ¾ pint
1 lb. 1½ oz.	= ½ kilogram, i.e. 500 grams	1 decilitre	= about 4 oz.
2 lb. 3 oz.	= 1 kilogram		

American Measuring Cups

American cup = 8 fluid oz.
1 American cup flour = 4½ oz. avoirdupois
1 „ „ sugar = 7 oz. „
1 „ „ fat = 7 oz. „

Handy Measures and Weights

Packeted fats need not be weighed, but can be divided accurately into 1-oz. or ½-oz. blocks.

approximately
{
1 breakfast cup = ½ pint
1 teacup, small = ¼ „
1 wineglass, small = ⅛ „
3 halfpennies = ½ oz.
3 pennies = 1 „
}

Temperatures

British culinary and oven thermometers are graded on *Fahrenheit* scale:

boiling-point of water 212°
freezing-point 32°

Most Continental and scientific thermometers are graded on *Centigrade* scale:

boiling-point of water $100°$

freezing-point $0°$

To convert ° *Centigrade* to ° *Fahrenheit*, multiply by $\frac{9}{5}$, then add 32.
To convert ° *Fahrenheit* to ° *Centigrade*, subtract 32 then multiply by $\frac{5}{9}$.
See p. 62.

Oven Temperatures, Regulo Numbers and Foods cooked at each

Description	Temperature in °F	Gas No.	Foods cooked at each
Very slow or cool	Under 250	$\frac{1}{4}$ to $\frac{1}{2}$	Meringues, drying rusks, raspings
Slow	250–300	$\frac{1}{2}$–1	Stewing, rice puddings, rich fruit cakes after 1 hour
'Very moderate' or Moderately slow	300–325	1–2	Custard Stewing, rich fruit cake (1st hour), drying biscuits
Moderate	325–360	3–5	Creamed cakes, biscuits, gingerbread, fish, soufflés, shortbread
Moderately hot	375–400	6–7	All pastries, roasting meat; rock cakes
Hot	425–450	8–9	Rich yeast mixtures, Swiss roll, Yorkshire pudding
Very hot	450–500	9	Bread, scones

Notes

1. There is a slight variation in the Gas No. settings of different makes of gas cooker.

2. Electric cookers do not always use the Fahrenheit thermometer scale.

3. The size of oven, and the amount of food baked in it at any one time, may make apparent alteration to the gas setting or temperature. The bigger the load the slightly higher the temperature needed as the cold food reduces the heat of the oven.

THE MAIN METHODS OF COOKING

BAKING

Cooking in an oven by heat radiated from the hot metal lining of the oven and by convection currents set up in the hot air.

The hot air in the oven rises and therefore the top shelf is the hottest; middle and lower shelves may be 5 to 10 degrees cooler than the top shelf. Steam given off by the food in the oven keeps it from getting too dry.

The oven is often used for moist methods of cooking such as stewing in a casserole or poaching, but food so cooked is not really baked in the usual sense of the word. Baked food has a crisp brown surface when cooked, as in pastry, cakes or baked meat. See 'Roasting'.

BOILING

Cooking in water at boiling-point, i.e. 212° F. The water should barely cover the food, and usually the pan should just fit the food, so that very little water will cover it and flavour therefore will not be lost, e.g. meat, green vegetables. In practice the water should generally not actually boil, but *simmer*—that is, bubbles should rise slowly at one side of the pan.

Simmering temperature is about 190° Fahrenheit.

True boiling gives rise to rapid bubbling and to rapid evaporation of water as steam and is used for:

> jam-making to concentrate sugar and pectin;
> cooking starchy foods such as rice or macaroni—the quick bubbling lifts the grain off the bottom of the pan and prevents sticking;
> reducing the volume of liquids, such as syrups.

BRAISING

Cooking meat, poultry, fish or vegetables on a bed of fried root vegetables, called a 'mirepoix', and with enough stock or water barely to cover the mirepoix. It is a combination of stewing, steaming and pot roasting; the food being braised is basted at intervals with the hot liquid; it is kept covered with greased paper or foil and a weighted lid: meat is

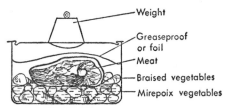

Fig. 2. BRAISING MEAT AND VEGETABLES

browned, either in hot fat before the moist cooking or under a hot grill afterwards. All the liquid from the braising pan is used with the dish; it may be reduced to a thin glaze or thickened with starch and should be brown and very savoury. The mirepoix vegetables are usually slightly over-cooked and a little discoloured but are well flavoured—they may be served, in a separate dish, with the braised food or used to make a vegetable purée soup.

Braising may be used to make tough cuts of meat tender or to make a deliciously savoury dish of reasonably tender meat. See p. 258.

BROILING

Another name for grilling, not often used nowadays except in the U.S.A.
Sometimes used to denote cooking in a hot, greased frying-pan. A 'broiler'
is a young chicken so tender that it may be cooked by grilling or frying.

FRYING

Cooking in hot fat in a frying-pan: there are two kinds of frying—shallow
frying in a wide, shallow pan and deep frying in a deep fat bath or strong
saucepan. Shallow frying may be termed dry-frying when the only fat
used is that which runs from the food, e.g. bacon or sausages, otherwise the fat should either just grease the pan as for pancakes or come
half-way up the food to be fried. Frying is sometimes used as a preliminary to a moist method of cooking such as stewing or braising.

Some Rules for Shallow Frying

1. Food to be fried should not be more than one inch thick.
2. There should be enough fat in the pan to come half-way up the
   food, except for dry frying or frying pancakes.
3. The food to be fried must be coated with a starchy substance that
   will form a crisp coating and prevent moisture escaping into the
   fat, exceptions: meat and some vegetables.
4. The fat must be at the correct temperature for the food to be fried
   (see p. 125): if the fat is too cool the food will absorb it and will be
   greasy; if the fat is too hot the outside of the food will be overcooked and the inside will be undercooked.
5. The food must be lowered gently into the hot fat to prevent
   splashing.
6. One piece of food should be lowered into the fat at a time and the
   fat allowed to heat up again after each addition.
7. The frying-pan should never be filled with food but space should
   be allowed for turning the pieces, for checking the rate of cooking
   and for lifting them out.
8. Most foods, except meat, should be drained on absorbent paper
   after being fried, and all should be served at once and very hot.

Deep frying requires from 2 to 4 lb. fat or 2 to 3 pints of oil for a medium-
sized pan but this fat can be used many times if correctly strained and
stored, see rules below. The equipment for deep frying includes a strong
pan with no seam or rivet holes to allow leakage of fat and with a flat
base so that it cannot be tilted or tipped over, a wire draining basket to

fit the pan and if possible a lid (Fig. 3). This equipment may be bought as a set or a suitable saucepan can be fitted with a wire basket. A curved draining spoon or wire 'spider-lifter' is necessary as a flat tool lets the food slip back into the fat with a splash. Lastly the most important item is a thermometer, as the temperature of the fat is the only safe test to find the correct heat for frying and to prevent fat reaching smoking or decomposition temperature, see p. 124.

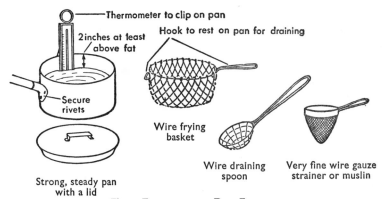

Fig. 3. Equipment for Deep Frying

Some Rules for Deep Frying

1. To avoid any risk of fire the pan must be little more than ⅔ full so that it will not spill over even when it bubbles during frying.
2. For the same reason a naked flame must not lick up the side of the pan.
3. Fat must be watched while it is being heated and all the time that frying is in progress, this is best done by checking the thermometer reading.
4. Boiling water, whether in kettle or saucepan, must not be near enough to the frying-pan for any drops to splash into the hot fat as this will cause the fat to spurt and possibly burn the cook.
5. All food must be coated in batter or egg and crumbs unless it is itself starchy, e.g. raw potato chips or doughnuts. A flour coating is not sufficient for deep frying.
6. After use the fat should be warmed gently till all bubbling stops, this is to ensure that no water is left in it which would hasten its decomposition. It should then be strained through a wire strainer fine enough to hold back even small crumbs of food as these not only get charred during frying but also cause the fat to decompose,

in time. The fat should be stored in a covered light-proof container, for solid fats this may be the fat-pan but for oils a metal can or an earthenware jar is safer. See also pp. 125, 235 and 260.

GRILLING

Cooking by radiant heat, nowadays from a metal fret heated by a gas flame or an open electric element, formerly over a glowing coal, wood or charcoal fire.

A gas grill consists of a metal fret heated by one or by two long gas-burners: an electric grill consists of an open, coiled element arranged in parallel lines between fireclay ribs. The grill is made red hot, the food is placed on a grid standing in a grill-pan. Food to be cooked by grilling should not be much over one inch in thickness.

Foods suitable for grilling include very tender cuts of meat such as fillet and rump steak; chops and cutlets of lamb, mutton and pork; liver and kidney; bacon and sausages; wings and breast of chicken, some fish and mushrooms and tomatoes.

Grilling may be used to brown the tops of dishes finished 'au gratin'.

One modern type of electric grill cooks by 'dark' or infra-red heat: this is a very quick method but the apparatus is costly. See pp. 262–264.

POACHING

Cooking below simmering point, with water only half covering the food, in a shallow pan, the food being basted with the hot liquid from time to time. Poaching is used for foods that require only low temperatures or that require gentle handling, e.g. fish and eggs.

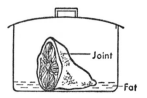

Fig. 4. POT-ROASTING

POT-ROASTING

Cooking meat in a little hot fat in a strong, covered saucepan on top of the cooker; it is useful where no oven is available, as in camp or caravan. The meat must be basted occasionally and turned over in the hot fat and once the meat is brown it must be cooked very gently or it will be dry (Fig. 4). See p. 255.

PRESSURE COOKING

Cooking in a pressure pan or pressure cooker, which is a strong pan, usually steel or aluminium, with a lid which locks into place and is made airtight by a rubber 'gasket' fitted between the edges of lid and pan.

If the pan were entirely airtight it would burst when heated, because air and steam inside it must expand; therefore a pressure pan has:

1. A control valve in the lid which allows a little steam to escape.
2. A safety valve which will open automatically if the pressure inside becomes too great. This valve is either a little rubber button which will jump out under high pressure or a spot of soft metal that will melt at a high temperature.

The control valve may be combined with a pressure gauge, usually a needle which rises to a definite height for each of three different pressures, or it may be controlled by three weights which each represent a different pressure: 5 lb., 10 lb. and 15 lb.

How a pressure cooker works

At ordinary atmospheric pressure water boils at 212° F.; at high altitudes (over 1,000 feet) where pressure is lower, water boils at lower temperatures, but if the pressure can be increased by preventing the escape of steam the boiling-point of water can be raised:

Atmospheric pressure
= 15 lb. per square inch.   Water boils at   212° F.
If pressure is increased by:
        5 lb. per square inch   „   „   „   about 225° F.
     10 lb. „   „   „   „   „   „   „ 235° F.
     15 lb. „   „   „   „   „   „   „ 250° F.
        Some pressure cookers work at only one pressure of 15 lb.

To use a pressure cooker

A leaflet of instructions is issued with every cooker and this should be kept and followed; the important points are:

1. Use the correct amount of water, usually between ½ pint and 2 pints and usually half the amount in a normal recipe.
2. Lock the lid in position and open the control valve. Always make sure that the steam outlet is clean and not clogged with food.
3. Exhaust the air by bringing the water to boiling-point and letting steam escape through the open valve for 1 to 2 minutes. Air in the pan will prevent the correct rise of temperature.

4. Close the valve and wait until the needle, or a steady hissing, indicates that the right pressure is reached, then time the cooking exactly.
5. The time taken to cook food is from $\frac{1}{4}$ to $\frac{1}{3}$ of the normal time.
6. Cool the pan by (*a*) leaving it for 10 minutes to cool at room temperature; or (*b*) running cold water over it (avoiding the valve) for 2–3 minutes.
7. Test the valve with a fork to see if it still hisses and NEVER open the lid until the valve is quite silent. Superheated steam produces a very bad scald.

ROASTING

Strictly speaking, this is cooking by radiant heat in front of, or over, a very fierce, glowing source of heat, the food being rotated on a spit. Nowadays the term is used of the cooking of meat or potatoes in an oven.

A modern return to true roasting is the electrically heated 'rotisserie' or the revolving spit fitted to some grills and in some ovens. See pp. 251–255.

STEAMING

Cooking in the steam from boiling water. The equipment used must be arranged so that no water touches the food but so that steam can circulate freely round or under it. Steamers are available that fit over a saucepan of boiling water and allow the steam to enter through perforations in the base. Three-tiered steamers have an inner tube with an outlet to pass steam into each of the two upper tiers and a cap that must be kept on the top of the tube. Another method is to put the food in a covered basin set in boiling water to reach half-way up the basin and a third is to put a plate on a pan of boiling water covering the food on it with the saucepan lid.

In all methods of steaming the lid must fit well so that steam does not escape and a kettle must be kept boiling, ready to replenish the water as it boils away.

Steaming is suitable for suet or cake-mixture puddings and for fish, tomatoes and potatoes. It is not a suitable method for cooking meat as the temperature is too high for moist cooking, there is no liquid to soften the connective tissue, and juices are lost into the water.

STEWING

Cooking in a small, measured amount of liquid which is allowed to simmer only and which is always served with the cooked food. It is useful for tough foods, such as tough cuts of meat, which need softening, and also for soft foods such as fruit which easily break up in cooking. Stewing may be preceded by frying for tender meat, or by 'fat-steaming' for vegetables. Stewing is most easily carried out over a long period by using a casserole or other covered vessel in an oven set at Gas No. ½ to 1 or 250-300° F.

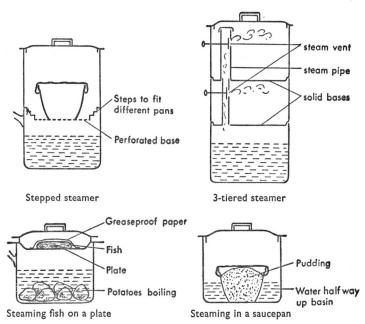

Stepped steamer   3-tiered steamer

Steaming fish on a plate   Steaming in a saucepan

Fig. 5. STEAMING

SOME COOKERY PROCESSES AND TERMS

Aerating: Mixing air into flour by passing it through a sieve or by lifting it and letting it fall through the fingers.

Barbecue: An open-air meal at which meat is roasted or grilled over an open fire.

Barding: Covering with fat bacon before cooking, usually done for poultry and game.

Basting: Pouring liquid from a spoon over food during cooking, usually hot fat during roasting.

Batter: Literally 'to beat', the name given to mixtures of flour with enough liquid to give a cream-like consistency which may contain other ingredients, such as eggs, fat and sugar. The mixtures may be the uncooked form of pancakes, fritters, dropped scones and sometimes of creamed cakes.

Beating: Mixing, and mixing in of air to any semi-liquid mixture. The spoon is held so that it cuts into the mixture and at the same time introduces air. The movement is one of lifting the liquid over the spoon.

Blanching: Literally 'whitening'; covering the food to be blanched with cold water, which is brought just to a boil and then strained off. Used to whiten rice, to cleanse some offal and to remove skins from almonds.

Blending: Mixing smoothly, usually of a starchy powder with an equal volume of cold liquid, prior to mixing it with boiling liquid.

Bouquet garni: A bunch of fresh herbs, usually containing a sprig each of thyme and marjoram; parsley stalks, one leaf of sage sometimes adding a bay leaf and a strip of lemon rind, which are tied together (for easy removal) and used to flavour soups and stewed or boiled meat.

Breadcrumbs—to make: To make fresh breadcrumbs, a wire sieve really produces the fine, even crumbs needed for most purposes, but as this is an old-fashioned piece of equipment, the modern way is to use very stale bread and grate it. For stuffing or bread sauce and other moist bread mixtures, a thick slice of bread, with crust completely removed, may be soaked in the liquid needed for mixing and, when soft, mashed smooth with a fork or potato-masher.

Buck-Rarebit: A poached egg served on Welsh Rarebit.

Clarifying: Clearing: if used of syrup—straining through muslin. To clarify dripping cover it with water in a deep saucepan, add 2 teaspoonfuls salt to each pint water and boil the whole for 2 or 3 minutes: strain and leave till cold and hard, then lift the cake of fat off the liquid, scrape off the sediment and dry the fat by gentle warming until all bubbling stops.

Caramel: A syrup made of 1 lb. sugar to 1 pint water (or golden syrup with no water) boiled till it turns gold-brown: used for flavouring sweet sauces and custard or for lining a mould for steamed caramel custard. Sometimes used as a decoration for fancy cakes.

Chopping: Cutting into very small pieces as of parsley or onion. To chop parsley, wash or scald it and dry it well in a cloth; hold the parsley in a tight bunch and keeping the point of a sharp knife on the chopping board work the blade up and down to cut first very thin shreds, then across the shreds and finally through and through the pile of pieces. To chop suet, shred it first on a coarse grater, sprinkle it with flour from the mixture and then chop it: it will almost crumble to fine pieces. To chop onion, peel the onion leaving the root on, to hold the 'leaves' together, cut in half, put each half face down and cut it into very narrow strips from near the root to the stalk end, leaving the root uncut; then slice across the strips so that they are cut into tiny squares (Fig. 6).

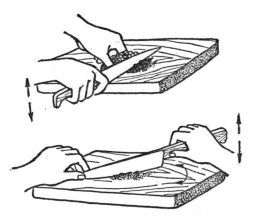

Shred into thin strips, keep point of knife down, move handle and blade up and down, work right to left across board

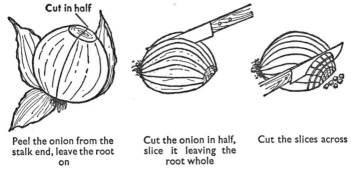

Cut in half

Peel the onion from the stalk end, leave the root on

Cut the onion in half, slice it leaving the root whole

Cut the slices across

Fig. 6. CHOPPING

Coating: Covering with a thin layer of a semi-liquid, such as batter or sauce or beaten egg with breadcrumbs. Coating sauce and coating batter should coat the back of a spoon and just find their own level in the pan or bowl.

Creaming: Beating fat or fat and sugar until it is creamy in both texture and colour, showing that a great many tiny bubbles of air have been enclosed. The fat must be soft but not oily before beginning or much energy is wasted in softening it. One of the methods by which fat (and air) is mixed into a cake mixture.

Croûtes: Neatly cut fingers, rounds or squares of fried bread as a base for some soft mixture.

Croûtons: Small dice or neatly cut pieces of fried or toasted bread, eaten as an accompaniment to soup or as a garnish to a dish with a sauce.

Curd: The solid part of sour milk or junket or a creamy preserve made from lemon or orange, eggs, butter and sugar.

Dice: Small cubes usually of vegetables or meat. To cut dice cut slices, then strips, then cut the strips across into cubes (Fig. 7).

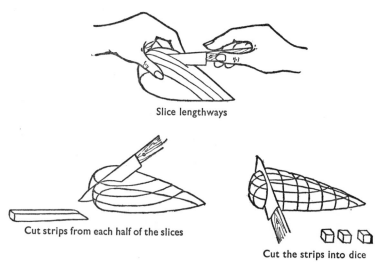

Slice lengthways

Cut strips from each half of the slices

Cut the strips into dice

Fig. 7. CUTTING DICE

Dough: A stiff mixture of flour and liquid, usually 1 lb. flour to ½ pint milk or water as used in bread and scones.

Dredging: Sprinkling lightly with a powder, using a perforated dredger. Used of flour, caster sugar, pepper and salt.

Dripping: The fat that runs from a roast joint and therefore has the flavour of the meat and probably some meat essence. Also used of rendered or melted meat fat that has not been roasted.

To Farce: To stuff—the same word as the 'force' of forcemeat.

Fillet: A slice of meat with no bone, e.g. fillet steak cut from undercut of sirloin, or fillet of veal cut across the leg muscle.

A fillet of fish is the flesh neatly lifted off the bone with a sharp knife, chiefly of flat fish such as plaice and sole, but also of cod and haddock.

Flan: In England is used to denote an open pastry tart filled with neatly arranged fruit or vegetables, the sort of thing that would be called 'tourte' or 'tarte' in France where flan denotes a custard tart.

Forcemeat: Stuffing usually for meat or vegetables: there are many different recipes, the most common in British cooking being 'veal forcemeat'. Originally 'farce' from the French—see above.

Fruit Cheese: A stiff paste or clouded jelly made by boiling sieved fruit with sugar as for jam.

Garnish: A decoration, usually of a savoury dish; it must be edible and is usually brightly coloured, e.g. parsley, lemon, hard-boiled egg, or bacon-rolls (Fig. 8).

Gelatine: Modern gelatine is sold in fine granular form which is easy to dissolve by stirring it into cold water and at once heating the water without boiling. Produced in meat cookery by simmering meat and bones in water when connective tissue—collagen—is converted to gelatine. It is extracted from clean, degreased bone, gristle, skin and feet of young animals by prolonged boiling, subsequent purifying and drying. It is used for setting sweet and savoury jellies and many cold sweets made with milk, eggs, fruit and cream. Neither form has much food value.

Girdle: An iron plate about ¼-inch thick on which scones and several types of girdle cake are baked. Originally hung over an open fire probably of peat; traditionally in Scotland, and in Ireland where it is called a 'griddle'.

One modern substitute is an electric solid hot-plate.

Glaze: A thin, shiny coating which may be of beaten whole egg, egg-white, milk, sugar and water or stiff jelly.

Gratiné or *au gratin:* This in French is derived from 'gratter', to scratch, and means a rough, crumbly surface browned under a grill or in a hot oven: it does not necessarily contain cheese although it may do so.

Gravy: The juice from meat, usually roast, which may or may not be thickened but is usually seasoned.

Thick gravy, served with pork   1 oz. flour to 1 pint liquid.
or stuffed joints.

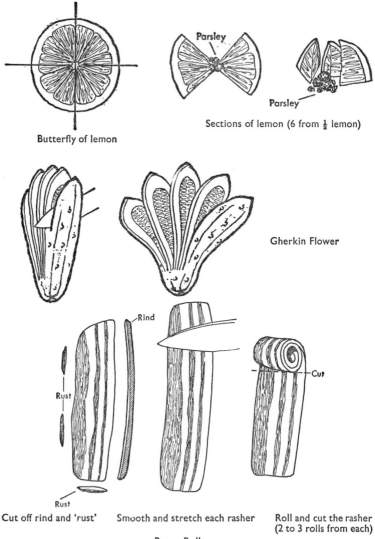

Butterfly of lemon

Parsley

Parsley

Sections of lemon (6 from ½ lemon)

Gherkin Flower

Rind

Rust

Rust

Cut off rind and 'rust'   Smooth and stretch each rasher   Roll and cut the rasher (2 to 3 rolls from each)

Cut

Bacon Rolls

Thread rolls on a skewer

Fig. 8. SOME GARNISHES

Thin gravy, served with most roast joints.   Just enough flour to thicken.

Clear gravy, served with poultry and game.   No thickening.

Goulash or *Gulyas:* A stew of beef, veal or chicken containing tomato, paprika pepper, onions, sour cream and sometimes potatoes.

Haggis: A Scottish national dish consisting of minced sheep's offal, mixed with oatmeal and seasoning and cooked in the sheep's stomach bag.

Hors d'œuvre: Small portions of cold, savoury foods served to stimulate the appetite before a dinner or lunch. There are hundreds of different kinds, popular ingredients being highly seasoned vegetables, fish, ham, other meat, and fruits.

Hors d'œuvre, meaning 'outside the main work', is always singular although it may contain many items.

Irish Moss or *Carragheen Moss:* A seaweed found on the coasts of Ireland and used for making a vegetarian substitute for gelatine.

Jugged: Cooked in a 'jug' or earthenware casserole, chiefly used nowadays of a rich stew of hare.

Junket or '*Curds*': Milk clotted by rennet which contains rennin, an enzyme from the calf's stomach. Not to be confused with sour milk curd.

Kedgeree: An Indian dish of dry, boiled rice mixed with flaked cooked fish and flavoured with curry. Usually made with smoked haddock in Britain.

Kebabs: Small pieces of assorted food threaded on a skewer and grilled or fried; one skewerful forms one serving: for example, squares of raw lean lamb, small tomatoes, onion, mushrooms and liver. Originated in Turkey, now served in E. Europe.

Kneading: To work together by hand, used in making scones, pastry, shortbread and yeast mixtures: for scones light kneading with fingertips; for pastry firm, gentle kneading with fingertips; for bread heavy prolonged kneading and rubbing with the 'heel' of the hand where palm joins wrist.

Kromeskis: Balls of minced meat, wrapped in bacon, coated with batter and fried.

Larding: Threading strips of fat bacon, with a special needle, into the surface of meat before grilling, roasting or braising.

Macedoine: A mixture of neatly cut vegetables, e.g. carrot, turnip, green peas; also used of a fruit salad cut small and sometimes set in jelly.

Maître d'Hôtel: This may be used of butter, sauce or garnish and always means lemon and chopped parsley, these supposedly being the only ingredients that the maître d'hôtel (the manager) can find when the chef is off duty.

Marinade: Originally the brine used to pickle fish before cooking; now used of any liquid used to flavour or soften meat or fish before cooking, e.g. olive oil, lemon juice or vinegar with seasoning and herbs, used for veal.

Meringue: Egg-white whipped stiff, mixed with caster sugar and dried till crisp in a slow oven.

Parkin: A flat, gingerbread cake containing oatmeal, from Scotland and the north of England.

Petits Fours: Very small fancy cakes; if 'sec' they are made of marzipan in fancy shapes and baked, or they are tiny rich biscuits, decorated, or tiny macaroons or glacé fruits or meringues with sweet fillings; they are always decorative and may be iced.

Piping: Forcing icing, cream or butter out of a special bag through a fine pipe to decorate a cake, also to shape mashed potato or some cake mixtures and meringues. The bag is called a forcing bag, or, if large, a Savoy bag, and may be cotton, nylon or plastic. The pipes are made in small sizes for icing and butter or in larger ones for potato, cake mixtures and meringues. For cream and icing the bag may be made of paper.

Pizza: An Italian flat yeast cake with a savoury topping, usually put on it before baking.

Purée: A smooth pulp made by pressing vegetables, fruit and, rarely, meat through a sieve.

Also used as the name of a group of soups made with sieved ingredients.

Quince: A hard fruit like a pear, golden-yellow when ripe, which may be used to flavour apple or to make quince 'cheese' or jelly.

Ragoût: A savoury meat stew; the French word means to 'give back the flavour', meaning that the meat is fried to develop flavour and has other flavours added.

Raspings: Dried, sieved breadcrumbs used for egg and crumb coating: to make raspings, dry stale scraps or crust of bread in a slow oven, crush them and sift them. Store them in an airtight tin.

Rechauffé: French for reheated.

Reducing: In cookery this means boiling a liquid to thicken it by driving off water.

Rennet: An extract from the calf's stomach containing the enzyme rennin; used to make junket. Rennet is also used in cheese-making.

Rissoles: Actually minced meat, wrapped in pastry, shaped as half-moons and fried; now generally used of cakes of minced meat coated with egg and crumbs and fried.

Rusks: Fingers or slices of bread slowly dried in an oven till crisp. Suffolk or Norfolk rusks are rich scones, split while hot, and dried till crisp in a slow oven.

Sandwich: Two thin slices of bread with a sweet or savoury filling; modern sandwiches may be made with hot toast or of 3 or more layers of bread. Also used of cakes—Victoria Sandwich and Sponge Sandwich.

Sauerkraut: German pickled cabbage, pickled in the acid produced by its own fermentation.

Sauter: French for 'to jump', it means to shake (or cause to jump) pieces of food in fat at frying temperature. Sauté potatoes have been half-boiled and then tossed in hot fat to brown them. Not to be confused with 'faire suer' to cause to sweat, see below.

Scald: To bring milk just to boiling-point, also to cover with boiling water, as for skinning tomatoes.

Scone: A plain, but very light, cake originating from the town of Scone in Scotland. Originally cooked on a girdle but now more often baked. Scones must be eaten freshly baked or else toasted.

Score: To slash with a sharp knife just through the surface; used on fish for grilling, on some meat, vegetables and pastry.

Shred: To slice so thinly that the slices curl, or to cut in very fine strips or shreds, or to form strips by using a coarse grater.

Simnel cake: A rich fruit cake sometimes made with yeast and always having a layer of marzipan in the middle and another for the top. Eaten traditionally on 'Mothering Sunday' in mid-Lent.

Singe: To pass a flame over (a chicken, etc.) to burn off the fine hairs left after plucking: a gas taper or a wooden spill give the least smoke.

Soufflé: French for 'blown up'; denotes a very light mixture raised only by egg and baked, steamed, or set with jelly; soufflés may be sweet or savoury, hot or cold.

Sousing: To soak and cook in a pickle of vinegar, spices and salt, used chiefly for herrings or mackerel.

Soy sauce: A Chinese savoury sauce made from fermented soya beans.

Soya bean: See pulses in Chapter 7.

Sweat: To cook very gently in melted fat until the food (usually vegetables) 'sweats' or exudes juice: a preliminary of stewing and soup-making. Not to be confused with sauter, see above. Sweating is also called 'fat-steaming'.

Stock: The liquid made by simmering bones, skin and scraps of meat in water to produce a meat-flavoured broth; used for soups and sauces.

Syrup: A concentrated solution of sugar in water. To make a sugar-syrup the sugar and water must be warmed slowly so that the water does not boil until all sugar has dissolved; the syrup must not at any time be stirred or shaken as any disturbance will recrystallize the sugar into hard insoluble grains. A syrup may be 'stroked' by drawing the bowl of a wooden spoon slowly across the bottom of the pan to hasten the solution of sugar.

Golden syrup is a by-product in the refining of sugar.

Maple syrup is extracted from the sugar-maple of North America.

Truss: To tie a bird into a compact shape with string before cooking it whole.

Welsh Rarebit or *rabbit:* A savoury made of cheese toasted on buttered toast: the cheese is either warmed first, partially to melt it, or grated and softened with liquid fat or milk to make it possible to spread it evenly.

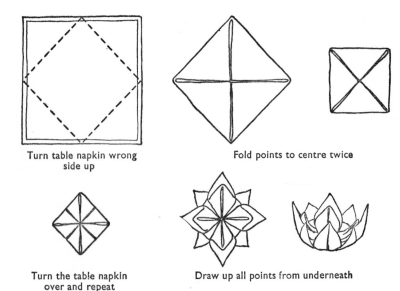

Turn table napkin wrong side up

Fold points to centre twice

Turn the table napkin over and repeat

Draw up all points from underneath

Fig. 9. A WATER-LILY FOLD FOR A TABLE NAPKIN

Water-lily Fold: Of a table napkin, to fold it corners to centre three times to make a cup shape in which rolls, scones, soufflés and other foods may be kept hot (Fig. 9).

Whip: The same as whisk but usually implying hand operating an egg-beater or fork; used of cream which is never whisked.

Whisk: To beat in air very rapidly with a lifting movement: (*a*) by hand using an egg-beater or egg-whisk or two forks as a slow substitute. The best egg-whisk has a long length of fine, coiled wire—as the finer the wire and the closer the coil the more quickly can air be beaten in: use a wide bowl; (*b*) by rotary egg-beater with a handle to turn the geared blades; (*c*) by electric beater which is very quick and can be adjusted to different speeds: is also expensive.

When whisking egg-whites the best temperature is about 70° F. When whisking eggs and sugar for sponge cakes the temperature should be a little higher, about 80° F., so that the bowl and sugar should be warmed, or, for hand tools, the whisking should be done over hot water.

Zest: The oil which gives the flavour to orange and lemon peel. To use the zest the peel is taken off so thinly that it is yellow both sides with no pith, or grated just to scrape off the shiny yellow part of the rind. The white pith being very bitter gives no zest to food.

FLAVOURING AND SEASONING

The term 'seasoning' is used only of savoury foods; 'flavouring' may be used of both savoury and sweet things and both words denote a most important part of skill in cookery.

Since one of the main reasons for cooking food is to make it taste nicer, the good cook spends as much care in flavouring foods as in any other cookery process and the first step towards good flavouring is the tasting of every mixture made. To keep to the rules for kitchen hygiene, a basin or beaker of boiling water, constantly renewed, should be at hand to rinse the tasting-teaspoon each time it is used.

The flavour of food is improved in many ways; sometimes it is only necessary to develop the natural flavours already in the food, as by frying onions or meat; sometimes flavours are improved by mixing different food flavours as by adding vegetables to meat in a stew or by mixing fruits or vegetables in a salad, but just as often foods that lack flavour themselves must have some flavouring added.

There are a great number of ingredients that may be added to food with the main purpose of improving flavour and all need a certain amount of restraint and caution on the cook's part; they should blend with the flavours of the main ingredients of a dish, and, as many of them are highly concentrated, they should always be used sparingly and never allowed to overpower other milder flavours. As a general rule natural flavours are pleasanter than synthetic essences, and there are many of them to choose from. Some flavourings contain one or more nutrients, others are used in such small amounts that their food value is negligible.

Some flavourings that are also foods
(see chapter on Food Values)

Vegetables, such as onions, celery, tomatoes and mushrooms.

Sugar

Fruits, such as oranges and lemons. It is important to notice that lemon juice can develop many natural flavours of other fruits and of vegetables, fish and meat.

Common salt, which, in very small amounts, can improve the flavour of almost all cereal dishes as well as its general use as a seasoning. Salt may be impregnated with vegetable juice as in *Celery salt* and *Onion salt* which are used by vegetarians as seasonings.

Yeast extracts, which give a subtle 'meaty' flavour to many dishes, such as soups, vegetarian foods and sauces.

Some meat extracts, which have a very high vitamin content.

Cheese, which can make any cereal, pulse, vegetable or fish dish most savoury.

Butter, margarine and olive oil, which, although not used primarily for flavour, yet bring out natural flavours from foods as well as adding their own rather subtle tastes.

Flavourings that supply little or no nutrient include spices, herbs, vinegar and essences.

SPICES

Spices are mostly dried fruits or seeds of tropical plants, grown originally in the Far East; they have been imported to Britain for hundreds of years, many of them probably by the Romans, and, until comparatively recent times, were greatly valued for their use in preserving meat before cold storage was invented. They all have very strong flavours and scents.

Some of the most generally used are listed below:

Spice	Origin	Use
Allspice berry	This is also called 'pimento' and 'Jamaica pepper' and is the dried berry of a West Indian shrub, called allspice because it is supposed to taste like a mixture of cinnamon, clove and nutmeg. Not to be confused with 'mixed spice', which really is a mixture of the three sweet spices above, with a little ginger.	Smooth, round and reddish-brown; whole or ground it is used mlainy in savoury dishes, such as potted beef or galantine.
Caraway seeds	The seeds of a feathery plant grown in Europe, which can be grown in Britain.	In Great Britain chiefly used in seed cakes; in European cookery used in soups, pickles, rye bread and cheese.
Cinnamon	The bark of a species of laurel grown in Ceylon, Java and India; a light tan in colour; the paper-thin bark is rolled as stick cinnamon or powdered.	Very fragrant and sweet; is used in cakes and sweet dishes, in potpourri and in sweet pickles, also in medicines.
Cloves	The name comes from 'clou', French for a nail, which a clove resembles in shape. They are the dried, unopened flower buds of a species of myrtle originally grown in the Moluccas Islands, and now chiefly grown in Zanzibar.	Very strong in flavour and aroma and can destroy other flavours. Traditionally used in cooked apple dishes—one clove will flavour over 1 lb. of apples. Also used in pickling and in savoury soups and in medicines. Supposed to relieve toothache.
Curry-powder	This is a mixture of as many as twenty-six different spices always hot to taste and usually yellowish in colour. The spices may include cardamoms, cassia, chillies, cinnamon, cloves, coriander, cumin, ginger, mustard, mace, fenugreek, pepper, poppy seed, turmeric, saffron.	There are many different recipes for curry-powder from different parts of India and the Fas East; used for currier and for adding to other savoury dishes.
Dill seeds	Rather like caraway seeds in appearance and flavour, and similar in growth. The leaves of dill are also used as a herb.	Used in pickling, particularly pickled cucumber.
Ginger	The dried root of a plant (*Zingiber officianalis*) grown in the East and West Indies; the root is used whole or ground; the root and stem are imported as sweet preserves in syrup or crystallized.	Used in cakes, sweet dishes and sweet-making, also in pickling. It has a sweet, hot flavour.

B

Spice	Origin	Use
Mace	The dried fibrous network which grows round the nutmeg. It is golden in colour and has a flavour like nutmeg but milder and less sweet.	Used whole in savoury sauces and soups, powdered in savoury meat dishes and in pickling.
Mustard	The dried seed of a plant, of two varieties which can be grown in Britain, common mustard and white mustard. French mustard is mixed with other spices, salt, vinegar and oil.	One of the most used condiments; used with beef and pork. In cooking it is used in cheese and other savoury dishes.
Nutmeg	The seed of the fleshy fruit of a tree grown originally in the Moluccas Islands, now also in Java, Sumatra and the West Indies.	Used mainly in sweet dishes; may also be added to potato and tomato dishes. Should be used sparingly.
Pepper	The dried berry of a shrub grown in Malabar and India, *Piper nigrum*.	
Whole pepper or: Black peppercorns	The whole berries with the skins on.	Used in soups, etc., that are strained.
White peppercorns	The whole berries with the skins removed.	Have a milder flavour than black peppercorns.
Ground black or white pepper	The peppercorns are milled with or without the skin.	One of the most generally used seasonings or condiments.
Cayenne pepper	Ground dried chillies or small red capsicums originally grown in Cayenne, in French Guiana, but now also in Mediterranean countries.	Very hot in flavour, must be used sparingly; dull red in colour. Used in cheese dishes and savouries.
Chillies	Red chillies are also imported fresh and dried whole.	Used in pickling and if fresh may be added sparingly to stews, etc.
Paprika pepper	Also called 'Krone pepper'; it is ground from a sweeter type of capsicum than cayenne.	It is mild in flavour and very bright scarlet-red. Used in Central European cookery.
Poppy seeds	Tiny, greyish black seeds of the poppy; although from the same plant as opium, they do not themselves contain opium.	Used in Jewish and continental cookery; now in Britain used on some rolls and as a filling in sweet pastries.
Saffron	The dried stamen of a species of autumn crocus. It is supposed to have been brought to Britain by the Romans. It was at one time cultivated in Essex and Cambridge.	Chiefly used in Cornish cake-making and as a culinary colouring as it is a rich, bright yellow. It has a mild flavour.

Spice	Origin	Use
Turmeric	The dried root of a plant similar to ginger. It is a deep yellow and is not as hot in flavour as ginger.	One of the ingredients of many curry powders, it is used in piccalilli and to colour savoury rice dishes.
Vanilla	The dried pods of a tropical orchid which grows in Mexico, Brazil and West Indies.	The sweetest of all spices with a delicious flavour and aroma. Used to flavour custards, ices and many sweet dishes. The pod may be infused in milk or made into Vanilla Sugar.
Vanilla Sugar	Vanilla pod stored, whole or crushed, in a jar of sugar gives a delicate flavour to the sugar which can be used for sweet dishes.	
Lemon or Orange Sugar	Grated lemon or orange rind can also be stored with sugar which it flavours for use in sweet dishes.	

HERBS

Herbs are green plants that can be used fresh or dried as flavourings; all those in general use can be grown in Britain. Herbs have been used from the earliest times for medicines, perfumes and in cookery.

Some of the herbs in general use are listed here:

Herb	Description	Uses
Basil	A sweet aromatic leaf of two kinds of plant, bush basil, which is a small short-stemmed plant, and sweet basil which is taller and has longer pointed leaves.	Basil has a spicy flavour, is used in sweet mixed herbs, and as a subtle flavour in soups, sauces, fish and other savoury dishes and stuffings.
Bay leaves	The leaves of a species of laurel shrub or tree, easily dried.	Bay leaves are used in savoury and sweet dishes, meat stews and soups and in milk puddings.
Borage	A tall annual plant with hairy leaves and blue flowers.	The leaves give a delicate flavour to salads and fruit drinks. The flowers are a pretty decoration in fruit salad.

Herb	Description	Uses
Chervil	A soft-leafed, delicate-looking plant with decorative, finely cut leaves; it has a mild flavour. It is an annual, and is a type of parsley.	May be used both as an ingredient and a decoration of salads and a decoration for cold savoury dishes.
Chives	A bulb with fine, grass-like leaves and a mauve shaggy flower. It is a member of the onion family, and its leaves have a delicate onion-like flavour.	Used in salads in place of onion or garlic, or in vegetable soups, omelets and with cream cheese.
Fennel	A tall perennial with feathery leaves and a mild flavour.	Used as a garnish for fish and in sauce, generally with salmon or other fish.
Garlic	A bulb related to the onion. The dried bulb is divided into sections known as cloves. The flavour and smell are both strong, penetrating and lingering.	Very little garlic will be enough to flavour salads (often the bowl is rubbed with a clove of garlic), soups and savoury stews. A garlic press to squeeze out the juice is useful.
Horseradish	The thick, white root of a perennial which has long leaves, rather like dock leaves in shape. It spreads very rapidly and is therefore often grown in a brick-lined pit.	The root grated is used mixed with cream or white sauce as horseradish sauce to be eaten with roast beef. Also used in a few savoury stuffings.
Marjoram	Sweet marjoram is an annual, pot marjoram a perennial, rather smaller than the sweet variety. Both have a pleasant savoury flavour.	Used in sweet mixed herbs, bouquet garni and in salad, soups and stuffings.
Mint	The second most popular herb in Britain; it is a perennial of free growth. Two kinds in general use are apple-mint, with rounded hairy leaves and mild flavour, and spearmint, with a pointed leaf and a stronger flavour.	Used mainly in mint sauce to eat with lamb and to flavour new potatoes and peas. Mint sauce can be bottled and stored, and mint added to gooseberry or apple jelly makes a preserve to replace mint sauce.
Parsley	The best-known herb, used for the decorative effect of its deep green, curly leaf as well as for its flavour; it is a biennial, grown slowly by seed.	The leaf is used as a garnish either whole or chopped, and chopped in sauces, soups and stuffings. The stem has more flavour than the leaf.
Rosemary	A small shrub with small, thick narrow leaves of a greyish-green colour; it has a pretty blue flower.	The flavour is pungent and must be used sparingly; it is traditionally used with roast mutton and may be added to soups, stews and salads.

Herb	Description	Uses
Sage	A shrub-like perennial with grey-green, oval, slightly hairy leaves and a mauve flower.	The flavour is very strong and overpowers other flavours: it is traditionally used (often to excess) in stuffing for pork, goose and duck.
Savory	There are two kinds, an annual, summer savory and a perennial winter savory; both kinds have narrow leaves and a spicy, savoury taste.	Specially used with broad beans, but also in soups, salads and stuffings and in mixed herbs.
Tarragon	A perennial plant with narrow, deep green leaves with a mild flavour reminiscent of aniseed.	It is a delicious addition to mixed and tomato salads, to fish dishes and to sauces for use with fish.
Thyme	Two kinds of thyme, black or common thyme and lemon thyme. Both have small shiny leaves, are most aromatic and have a pleasant spicy flavour and are perennials.	One of the most popular herbs, used in mixed herbs, in soups, omelets, salads and force-meats.

To dry herbs. All herbs for drying should be freshly gathered from the plants before they flower and neither in rainy nor hot, sunny weather. Small-leaved herbs such as thyme should be washed, lightly shaken dry, tied in bunches, which should be loosely tied in muslin and hung in a warm place for a few days. Bay leaves may also be treated in this way. Large-leaved herbs should be dipped into boiling water for 30 seconds, lightly shaken, then dried in an oven at 110° to 130° F. for an hour or on the rack over a cooker for several hours.

Parsley may be dried in sprigs under a moderately hot grill or for 1 minute in an oven at 400° F. or treated as for large leaves.

All leaves should be crisp when dry and may be stored whole or, except bay leaves, crushed and stored in labelled tins or screw-topped jars. The quicker the drying (without scorching) the better the flavour, and preservation of flavour and green colour is greater by the boiling-water treatment.

Herbs should not be dried in sunlight as this removes colour and flavour.

Herb Vinegars may be made simply by quarter-filling a vinegar bottle with the herb leaves, freshly picked, and filling up with hot vinegar. The bottle is corked and kept for about a month, then the vinegar is decanted, corked, labelled and stored to use in salad dressings. Tarragon vinegar and chillie vinegar (using fresh chillie pods) are both made in this way.

ESSENCES

Essences should, strictly speaking, be volatile, flavouring oils dissolved and preserved in alcohol; for example, vanilla and lemon essences. The only essence that is really made from the original plant nowadays is probably peppermint, because this herb is comparatively cheap.

Most essences nowadays are synthetic, 'vanilla essence' usually being made from *Vanillin*, a crystalline by-product of coal tar. Other 'fruit' essences such as banana, lemon and pineapple are equally synthetic and usually less successful (see vanilla sugar, etc., p. 27).

Mono Sodium Glutamate is not an essence but deserves a note as a flavouring synthesized from a food source; it has a penetrating flavour reminiscent of mushroom and chicken: it is harmless, has a little food value and is largely used in soup powders and bouillon cubes: it is also marketed under a brand name as a flavouring for savoury dishes.

2

PLANNING AND EQUIPPING
A KITCHEN

PLANNING

The name kitchen comes from the Old English 'cycene'—'to cook' because it has always been mainly the place in which cooking is done, but it is often also a centre for other family activities. Different families use the kitchen in different ways, perhaps as a kitchen dining-room or solely as a domestic workshop and only they should decide which is best for them. The pleasantest kitchen is probably one where the mother can have some contact with her family, can have room for younger children to play at helping her while she cooks, washes up, washes or irons and where older members of the family can talk to her, help her or learn from her while she is busy.

Whatever its other uses, planning of the work-room part of the kitchen can save the worker much time and fatigue. Although the shape and size, the position of doors and windows and of some fixed equipment cannot usually be altered, the arrangement of lights, working surfaces, movable equipment and store-cupboards can often be changed to make work simpler.

ARRANGEMENT OF EQUIPMENT

The larger pieces of equipment for cooking should be arranged reasonably close to each other and in the right order for food to be moved onward through the various stages of its preparation, with the cook wasting no energy in walking back and forth. These stages take the food from larder, refrigerator or vegetable-rack to the sink for washing them on to a work surface for preparation, requiring various utensils and dry stores, thence, in a suitable cooking-vessel, to the cooker and finally to a work surface for dishing and so to the dinner-table. If cooking is to be done quickly and efficiently the tools for each stage should be stored at the appropriate work-place: the equipment for scrubbing vegetables, and for washing and drying food and dishes should be stored by the sink; the tools and utensils for food preparation should be in drawers

and cupboards below the work-surface, with dry stores within easy
reach, preferably in a wall cupboard at eye-level above this surface and
saucepans and oven-ware should be close to the cooker.

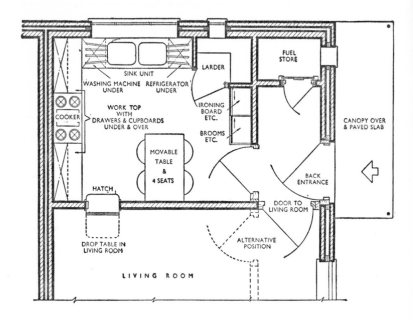

Fig. 10. A WELL-PLANNED KITCHEN

(Based on design by Maywen Godby, by permission of The Council of Scientific Management in the Home.)

To fit the equipment together in this way it may be grouped on two
walls to form an L or on three walls to form a U; if the kitchen is unfortunately also a passage from house to back-garden the sink, cooker
work-bench and, if possible, cupboards should all be on one wall or
two adjacent walls.

LIGHTING

A good light is needed for all work in the kitchen. As the sink is usually
fitted under or near the window it is well-lit by day and if the work-

surface and the cooker are placed near the sink they will also get adequate daylight. For artificial lighting separate points are usually needed for sink and cooker or work-bench: one central light is quite inadequate as in almost every position in the kitchen it throws the worker's shadow on to her work.

VENTILATION

The window should have separate top and bottom opening so that the kitchen can be cooled quickly or in cold weather rising warm air and steam can escape without a draught. If there is no chimney-flue there must be a ventilator as well as a window: an extractor fan is a useful addition but rather expensive to instal.

WALL AND FLOOR SURFACES

All surfaces in the kitchen should be easy to clean and in colours that make it bright and pleasant.

The walls should be finished in pale colours which do not absorb light: some suitable surfaces are gloss or enamel paint, emulsion paint, tiles or plastic sheet all of which can be washed. The ceiling should have a matt surface paint as this reduces condensation.

Woodwork can also be finished in pale colours in gloss or enamel paint; or natural wood may have a 'seal' or a hard varnish.

The perfect floor-covering for a kitchen has apparently not yet been discovered: it should be resilient so that it is not tiring to stand on, it should deaden sound, withstand heat, grease, frequent cleaning and pressure from heavy equipment and it should not be slippery even when wet or greasy.

Some surfaces that are resilient and reasonably easy to clean are:

1. Heavy quality linoleum; if treated with a seal it is easy to keep clean but it must have a level surface under it for long wear.
2. Various types of thermoplastic floorings, sheeting or tiles; these must not be made too wet when washed and only polishes recommended by the makers may be used on them: never use polishes containing turpentine.
3. Rubber: this is not as resistant to grease and heat as some coverings but is resilient.
4. Quarry tiles look attractive and are easy to clean but are rather hard and are slippery when greasy, or wet; they are rather expensive.

KITCHEN EQUIPMENT

SINKS

Modern sinks may be made of glazed fireclay with a porcelain finish, pressed steel with a vitreous enamel finish, stainless steel or other stainless metal alloy or a hard plastic. Stainless steel or metal alloy sinks are probably the most durable, provided that the metal is thick enough to be rigid; the quietest in use are plastic sinks but this material is not always suitable for hard wear, and both stainless metal and plastic are expensive.

One advantage of stainless metal, enamelled steel and plastic sinks is that draining surfaces, and often splash-backs, are moulded in one with the sink so that they have no crevices in which water and dirt can collect. A porcelain sink has draining-boards of wood or enamelled steel which must overhang the sink slightly and which are grooved under this overhanging edge to prevent water creeping underneath. This overhanging edge forms a dirt-trap that is difficult to clean unless the draining-boards are removable.

A sink may have one draining-board or two according to the space available, or a useful arrangement of one flat surface for stacking dishes and one grooved board for draining them: it is a matter of choice whether the drainer should be on the left- or right-hand side.

There should be a waterproof splash-back behind the sink which should have no crack which would allow water to run down between sink and wall.

The taps should be set at least 12 inches from the bottom of the sink so that tall jugs or buckets can be filled easily. Modern taps are always stainless and they should have no ridges or grooves to collect dirt: some useful modern designs have one outlet for hot and cold water which can be mixed to the required heat.

If cupboards are fitted below the sink there must be three inches of toe space below them.

All sinks have a 'trap' in the form of an S-bend in the waste pipe which should be kept full of clean water to seal off the smell of dirty water from the kitchen. The trap has a nut or a removable cap at its lowest point which can be taken off if the pipe gets blocked.

Keeping the Sink Clean

1. Use enough detergent to emulsify the grease in all washing-up and use the hot lather from washing-up to degrease the sink itself. Soapless detergents leave no scum with hard water.

2. Rinse the sink after use to leave the trap full of clean water.
3. Hard water film and slight stains can usually be removed with a little detergent on a cloth.
4. Never pour grease into the sink and always wipe greasy pans with paper before washing them or boil them with water and detergent.
5. Use as little scouring powder as possible—stainless metal sinks need none, only detergent, and enamelled, porcelain and plastic sinks need a very little only when they are stained. Scouring powders gradually roughen the surface, which then becomes more difficult to clean.
6. Avoid scratching the sink or denting or chipping it by careless handling of heavy pans, bowls and buckets. Plastic bowls and buckets are light to lift and do not damage the sink.
7. Enamel, metal and plastic draining-boards are easily washed, but wooden ones must be scrubbed occasionally unless they are finished with a waterproof sealer.
8. Once a week pour hot water and soda down the waste pipe to clean it, then refill the trap with clean, cold water.
9. Never let solid particles slip down the waste pipe, avoiding specially match-sticks and bristles from stiff brushes as these quickly block the pipe.

KITCHEN FURNITURE

Furniture for the kitchen workshop must include a rigid surface—usually the top of a cupboard, for working on; cupboards, drawers and shelves to house all the necessary dry stores and utensils and a stool or chair high enough for the cook to sit on for some of her work.

The Height of Working Surfaces

If cooking is to be done without unnecessary fatigue it is important that work-surfaces should be of a comfortable height for the worker: when standing easily, with elbows very slightly bent, she should be able to put her hand flat on the surface without either hunching or drooping her shoulders. This height will of course vary with the height of the worker and the length of her arms and may be between 31 inches and 38 inches from the ground. Manufacturers have tended to standardize this height at 36 inches, but fortunately it is now realized that a range of heights is necessary.

The Height of the Sink

As most washing-up is done with the hands holding dishes and mop half-way down the sink the correct height is tested by letting the arms hang loosely, a little forward, then, with elbows very slightly bent, the finger-tips should just touch the bottom of the sink. With a sink of the average depth of 8 inches this usually means that the draining-board is a little higher than the comfortable work-top; this is quite satisfactory as the setting down of washed dishes involves little muscular effort.

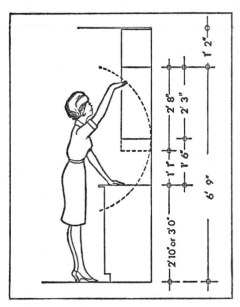

Fig. 11. THE CORRECT HEIGHTS FOR KITCHEN CUPBOARDS AND WORK SURFACES; 'ARC OF REACHABILITY'

The Height of Wall Cupboards

Store cupboards above the work surface should be easily reached without straining or tip-toeing and should leave about 15 inches clear above the work-surface. The lowest shelf should be well below eye-level and the upper ones should if possible have a false back so that they are narrower than the lower ones. All shelves should be rather narrow as it is difficult to find jars and tins when they are stored one behind the other.

Store cupboards above arm's length are usually termed 'dead storage', meaning that they are suitable only for reserve or rarely used utensils. To reach such cupboards a stool or chair that can be folded back to form a step-ladder is useful.

Height of Stool or Chair

When the worker is seated she should be the same height as when standing, so that with a kneehole space she can sit to do some jobs such as chopping or slicing foods.

CONVENIENT STORAGE OF EQUIPMENT

The best rule for storing utensils is to house them near the point where they will be used and there are many devices to make this possible, such as:

1. Drawers below the work-top to hold kitchen linen and small equipment, one drawer being divided for knives, spoons and other hand tools.
2. Racks or hooks fitted on a wall or inside a cupboard door to hold such tools as egg-beater, fish slice and strainer.
3. Shelf or rack to hold saucepans and their lids near the cooker.
4. Towel rail or hooks for dish cloth, tea towel and hand towel near the sink.
5. Cupboards below the work-top to house basins, oven-ware, etc.; these mean a certain amount of bending, but that is good exercise.

COOKERS

Choosing a Cooker

The choice of a cooker will partly depend on the fuel available: in a town this may be gas or electricity, which are both clean and easy to use or solid fuel which, although not so labour-saving, will heat water, warm the kitchen and dry clothes in addition to cooking. In country districts, if town gas or electricity are not available, an alternative to solid fuel is 'bottled' gas which is supplied in cylinders to be connected to cookers very little different in use from other gas cookers.

Some other points to consider in the choice of a cooker are:

1. The amount of money to be spent.
2. The size of oven and amount of hot-plate space.
3. The amount of space for warming plates and dishes.
4. Whether saucepans will balance safely on the hot-plate.

5. Whether it is easy to see food in the oven or under the grill.
6. Whether taps and switches are in an accessible place and out of reach of small children and whether the oven door fastens easily and securely.
7. Whether the cooker is easy to clean.
8. The durability of the enamel or other finishes on the surfaces.

All modern cookers are designed with reasonably simple, easily cleaned lines, are finished mainly with vitreous enamel and are lagged to keep the oven hot and the kitchen cool.

Modern Gas Cookers

Gas cookers are heated by a mixture of gas and air which gives a flame with a greenish-blue inner cone and a blue outer flame. The gas passes into the open tube of the burner through a small jet or injector and at the same time air is drawn in through an air 'port'. The mixture is adjusted on a new cooker, but if it should be altered by accident it can be readjusted by turning a screw or moving a shutter. If the flame is short and 'hard' the air must be reduced; if the flame is long, 'flabby' and yellow more air must be let in. When gas 'lights back' it ignites as pure gas, without air, at the injector.

A governor is fitted to every cooker to keep the supply and pressure of the gas to the cooker constant even though it may vary in the main supply pipe.

The burners. On a family-size cooker there are usually four burners, two large and two small, and a deep enamelled tray to catch spilt liquid. The burners may be of the ring type with open flame ports or they may have a solid centre which shields the ports from spilt food and over them is a series of bars to support saucepans. The burners are usually either enamelled steel or aluminium alloy and the pan supports are enamelled or stainless steel. One burner may be thermostatic.

The grill consists of one or two long, straight burners which are directed on to a metal fret which quickly gets red hot: the grill may be on the underside of the hot-plate, at 'eye'-level (actually well below the eyes) shielded by a canopy to prevent fat splashing in the cook's face, or at a new level half-way between the hot-plate and eye-level.

Lighting the top burners on modern cookers is automatic, on older cookers it may be done by a 'gas match' which ignites a tiny gas jet with a flint striker, or a 'gas pistol' which ignites it with an electrically heated filament.

Modern gas taps all turn on anti-clockwise; whatever their shape a horizontal position or a horizontal bar denotes 'off' and most have safety springs which require pressure to turn them on. Most modern taps are plastic so that they do not get too hot.

Oven. Gas ovens are now usually heated by a single back burner though at least one model has two side burners, so arranged that the direction of the flame sends currents of hot air to every part of the oven which is thus heated fairly uniformly, the top shelf being 10° F. hotter than the middle of the oven and the base plate 20° to 30° F. cooler than the middle. Modern ovens are wide enough to hold two dishes side by side. The enamelled sides of the oven are grooved to take the shelves; the roof lining of some ovens can be removed for cleaning; the door sometimes has a glass inner lining and it may open from right to left or it may have a 'drop down' opening.

Flue. The by-products of combustion of gas, which are carbon-dioxide and water vapour, together with the steam from cooking, are allowed to escape from the back of the oven up a tube which discharges in front of the back splash-plate, often just below the plate rack. In older cookers this flue discharged on to the wall behind the cooker and made it very dirty.

Thermostat. All modern gas ovens are thermostatically controlled, usually by a metal rod which as it expands with the heat of the oven closes a valve and reduces the flow of gas. A more modern type of thermostat has a bulb containing liquid fitted in the oven; the liquid expands on heating and through a flexible tube exerts the pressure necessary to control the flow of gas. The thermostat-head sets the required heat by a series of numbers (Fig. 12).

Using a Gas Cooker

Lighting the oven. The oven may be lit through a 'flash tube' running below the base plate, opening at the front and connecting with the back burner so that a flame held at the front end will flash back and light the back burner when the tap is turned on. Another device, used on all modern ovens, is a flash tube from the pilot light under the hot-plate which ignites a secondary pilot in the oven when the oven tap is turned on. This oven pilot, by heating a strip of metal, opens a valve which allows gas to enter the burner and ignite at the pilot flame. With this type of ignition there is a short pause before the oven burner ignites, but there is no danger of gas escaping into the oven as only heat from the pilot can turn it on.

The Hot-plate

1. The tip of the flame, being the hottest part, must be kept underneath any saucepan—never allowed to lick up the sides.

2. Asbestos stove mats, very large wash-boilers and buckets, when used on the hot-plate, all tend to concentrate heat downwards on to the enamel of the hot-plate which will then often splinter and chip off.

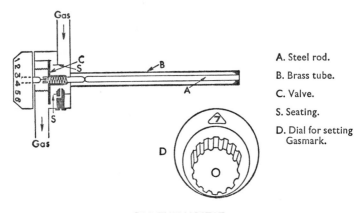

A. Steel rod.

B. Brass tube.

C. Valve.

S. Seating.

D. Dial for setting Gasmark.

GAS THERMOSTAT

The brass tube B in the diagram encloses a rod A, made of special steel, to which is attached a valve C.

The valve C regulates the amount of gas flowing to the burner.

When gas is burning, the brass tube becomes heated and as it expands it carries with it the inner rod A, which expands very little, and brings the valve head C closer to its seating S, thus reducing the flow of gas. If the air in the oven or the water in the heater cools down, the brass tube becomes less hot, contracts a little and moves the valve C slightly away from its seating and so allows more gas to pass to the burner until once again the proper temperature is reached.

(*By permission of the Gas Council*)

Fig. 12. GAS THERMOSTAT

The Oven

1. The oven should be set at the required number when it is lit; it should reach the corresponding heat within ten minutes.

2. The baking tray supplied with the cooker is the right size to allow free circulation of hot air round the oven and if other trays and tins are used they must not be larger or they will trap the heat, become overheated underneath and burn the food cooked on them.

3. It is more economical to cook several dishes in the oven than to use separate burners on the hot-plate: the oven burner, when full on,

uses less gas than a large burner full on on the hot-plate, and, as it is thermostatically controlled, it maintains the oven at a fairly high temperature with as little gas as a small burner turned low.

4. Most stewing may very well be done in the oven in casseroles as the rate of cooking can be controlled exactly. The base-plate of the oven is suitable for slow cooking of stews even though the middle of the oven is moderately hot.

5. Many dishes are satisfactorily cooked starting in a cold oven; examples are short pastry, some cakes, all casserole dishes and roast meat, which is actually more tender by this method (see p. 91).

Examples of whole meals cooked in an oven are given on p. 45'.

Modern Electric Cookers

Electric cookers are heated by elements: these are coils of wire made from a metal alloy which resists the passage of electric current and becomes red hot because of this resistance. The coils are packed closely into grooves in a hard cement which is heat resistant and the whole element is embedded in a hot-plate or in the oven, under cover, from whence it radiates and conducts heat and sets up convection currents of hot air. There are no by-products of combustion.

Hot-plates. There are three main types of hot-plate, with slight differences in some modern cookers:

1. *Solid hot-plates*, in which the element is enclosed under a disc of iron alloy. The heat passes into this solid plate and is conducted to the underside of the saucepan, which must have a flat, machined base. Modern solid plates, made of new types of alloy and of cement, are designed to heat more quickly (Fig. 13).

2. *Radiant plates*, in which the element is packed in a spiral tube of iron alloy which radiates heat, glows red and also conducts heat to the base of the saucepan, which may be of any type; the tubes are flattened on top to increase conduction. These coiled plates have drip-trays below them (Fig. 13) and one hot-plate may be thermostatically controlled.

3. *Thermostatically controlled hot-plates.* The 'loading' or hourly consumption of electric current varies from 1,500 watts for a standard solid plate to 3,000 watts for some very modern types.

Grills and Grill-boilers

Most grills are also hot-plates and are similar to the solid hot-plates but are open below so that most of the heat is radiated downwards. The hot-plate above is not as efficient as an ordinary hot-plate, but can be used for top cooking while the grill is in use. Some cookers have a single-purpose grill below the hob, at eye-level or even in the top of the oven.

On modern cookers the hot-plates can all be unplugged for cleaning by lifting them free of their sockets and radiant plates are also hinged so that the drip tray below can be lifted out to clean up spilt food. The hob is either hinged, so that it can be tilted up to clean below it, or it can be lifted right off.

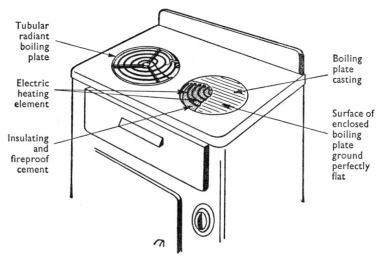

Tubular radiant boiling plate

Electric heating element

Insulating and fireproof cement

Boiling plate casting

Surface of enclosed boiling plate ground perfectly flat

Tubular-Radiant and Solid or Enclosed Boiling Plates

Tubular-radiant type

Section of tube showing surface flattened for increased conductivity

(*By permission of the Electrical Development Association*)

Fig. 13. ELECTRIC BOILING PLATES

Heat Control

Hot-plates may have three-heat or multiple-heat switches or variable heat control.

Three-heat Switches. The element is in two parts; at High the two

sections are at full heat, at Medium one part is at full heat and at Low
the two sections give quarter heat.

Multi-heat Switches. These have up to six different heat settings. The
element has several sections with different loadings; at Full all are at full
heat and at lower settings different groupings or separate elements are
at full heat.

Variable Heat Control. The switch has a numbered dial—each number
representing an amount of heat which is maintained by the flow of current: the current is automatically switched on and off for different lengths
of time according to the dial setting.

Electric Ovens

An electric oven is heated by elements fixed behind the lining of the oven
or sheathed in metal and plugged into place; they are usually arranged in
the sides, but occasionally in the top or bottom. A few cookers have a
grill in the top of the oven which can be used to heat the oven extra
quickly. Modern ovens are designed to reach 400° F. in about 12 minutes
and have loadings usually between 2,600 and 3,600 watts. The heat should
be almost equal throughout the oven, the top shelf being a little hotter
than the middle one and occasionally, with a bottom element, the bottom
shelf is also hotter than the middle.

As there are no by-products of combustion there is only a very small
ventilation outlet to allow steam to escape.

Modern electric ovens are all thermostatically controlled on a temperature scale which, unfortunately, at present varies slightly between
different makes of cooker.

The lining of the oven can usually be lifted out for cleaning. Some
cookers have an inner glass door, a light that is switched on in the oven
as the door is opened and can be fitted either with doors that open from
right to left or that drop down.

Separate Ovens and Hot-plates

Both gas and electric cookers can now be supplied as two separate
units—a hot-plate, and an oven which can be fitted at eye-level.

Using an Electric Cooker

Many rules that were necessary when using older electric cookers are no
longer important: an electric cooker of modern design can be used in
very much the same way as a gas cooker.

It is more economical to boil water in an electric kettle with an internal element than on a hot-plate.

Saucepans with flat, machined bases must be used on solid hot-plates and are advisable on radiant plates to ensure maximum conduction in addition to radiation.

A hot-plate should be entirely covered by the saucepan to avoid waste of heat.

It is wasteful to use the grill-boiler for top cooking unless the grill is also used, if it is used for top-heat alone the deflector plate provided must be in place to deflect radiant heat from the grill upwards to prevent waste of heat. This plate must be kept clean and shining.

The grill-boiler, with switch at low, makes an excellent girdle for cooking pancakes and scones.

Time-controlled Ovens

A time-controlled oven is a modern development of a gas or electric cooker to help the cook who must spend part of the day away from home and return too late to cook a meal. In her absence the oven will be lit at a pre-arranged time and thermostat setting; it will cook the food for a set time and then switch off.

The automatic timing device consists of an electric clock or a clock-work device which can be set to control the required delay before cooking shall begin, and either is connected to mechanical controls of the electric or gas supply to the oven and, on some electric cookers, to the hot-plate also.

There are several different makes of dial, but most have *the clock* which must first be set at the right time and also *two* or sometimes *three knobs*, one to indicate the time at which cooking is either to start or finish, one to indicate the duration of cooking and one to switch the cooker to automatic time control. Little windows in the clock face show the required time-settings, and all that remains to be done is to turn the oven thermostat to the required heat-setting. Detailed instructions, issued with every cooker, must be followed to get the sequence of operations right.

Planning Meals for Automatic Timing

1. All the dishes must need about the same time and temperature for cooking.
2. To prevent overcooking, dishes needing less than the set time should be covered with a lid or foil.

3. Foods needing the highest temperature are baked on the top shelf and, usually, those needing the lowest at the bottom of the oven.
4. All foods should be quite cold when put into the oven or micro-organisms may develop before cooking begins.
5. Meat should not be left for more than an hour before cooking in any but cold weather.
6. Suitable dishes are those which can be cooked successfully from a cold start; these include short pastry, plain and creamed cakes, all stewed foods, milk puddings, root vegetables, dried and fresh fruit, poached or baked fish and roast meat.
7. Some foods need special preparation: potatoes and other root vegetables should be brushed or tossed with melted fat and cooked with little liquid. White vegetables and apples may be rubbed with cut lemon to avoid discoloration.
8. Potatoes, onions and apples can be baked in their skins.

Examples of Suitable Meals for Time-controlled Cooking

Food	Cooking utensil	Position
1. Roast $\frac{1}{2}$ shoulder lamb (2 lb.) Roast potatoes in fat	Roasting tin	Top shelf
Sliced turnips with margarine and $\frac{1}{8}$ pint water	Oven-ware casserole, greased paper under lid	Bottom shelf
Fruit pie	Foil to cover the crust	Middle shelf

Thermostat setting: 400°-425° F. or Gas No. 7.
Timing: $\frac{1}{4}$ hour to heat + 1 hour cooking = $1\frac{1}{4}$ hours.

Food	Cooking utensil	Position
2. Fricassee of veal	Oven-ware casserole	Middle or bottom shelf
Stewed celery	„ „ „	Bottom shelf
Potatoes in jackets	Open shelf	Top or middle shelf
Apple charlotte	Pie dish	Top shelf

Thermostat setting: 325°-330° F. or Gas No. 2 or 3
Timing: $\frac{1}{4}$ hour to heat oven + $1\frac{1}{2}$ hours to cook = $1\frac{3}{4}$ hours.

The veal dish would have thickening added to the sauce after removal from the oven.

Foods that are not successful from a cold start include:

(a) those needing a high temperature such as yeast mixtures, flaky and puff pastries, scones;

(b) those into which air is whisked, such as whisked sponge cakes, meringue;

(c) those needing very short cooking time such as green vegetables.

Solid-fuel Cookers

A modern solid-fuel cooker is very different from its predecessor the coal range although it retains whatever good points that black, labour-making monster may have possessed. It keeps the kitchen warm, it heats water, dries clothes and burns rubbish as well as cooking by top or oven heat from the one fire. Modern solid-fuel cookers are designed to burn any type of coal, coke, manufactured fuel or even wood; they have most exact draught control; they are semi-insulated to keep the heat in the cooker and the kitchen cool; they are easy to clean, refuel and de-ash and they are designed to look attractive.

Three types of cooker are: *free standing*; *combination-grate* with an oven, hot-plate and openable fire for a kitchen living-room, and *back-to-back* cooker with one fire heating cooker and sitting-room grate. All can have a water boiler fitted, all have some cover to the hot-plate to prevent loss of heat, can be riddled without opening the fire-door and have an enclosed ash-box. The rate of burning can usually be regulated by a spinner on the door of the ash-box or a damper at hob-level and most cookers have an oven-thermometer or a heat-indicator. There may be a second oven which is often only suitable for very slow cooking or warming plates.

Using a Solid-fuel Cooker

Fuel. A smokeless fuel such as gas coke, hard coke, anthracite, steam coal or manufactured fuels should be used to reduce cleaning of flues and kitchen as well as to lessen the smoke-pollution of the atmosphere.

The fire should be freed of ash by riddling it and it should then be refuelled well before the time when cooking will begin. As each addition of fuel reduces the heat for a short time, any extra fuel needed during cooking must be added a little at a time.

The air inlet should be adjusted to maintain the required heat.

The hot-plate should be kept covered when not in use as heat lost through it cools the oven; a hinged 'bolster' cover is fitted on some cookers.

As heat cannot be regulated quickly, cooking should be planned so that dishes requiring a high temperature are baked first, followed by those needing moderate or low heat. The oven can often be used for stewing when baking is finished.

The heat in the oven and on the top-plate corresponds—a hot oven means a hot top-plate.

Remove ash when the ash-box is over half-full and clean the flues weekly if house coal is used, once a fortnight for smokeless fuels.

Heat-storage Cookers

Heat-storage cookers are most efficient solid-fuel cookers. The name is applied to only two makes of cooker which have been specially designed to economize fuel. They are expensive to buy because the design includes most exact draught control, very heavy construction and most efficient lagging to conserve as much heat as possible.

These cookers burn continuously, using smokeless fuels of a size recommended by their manufacturers. They are designed to use only 2 to 3 tons of fuel a year when cooking for four to six persons.

(One model is adaptable to different kinds of fuel, but for clean air and to save cleaning of flues smokeless fuel is recommended.)

Heat-storage cookers can all be fitted with a boiler for domestic hot water.

Using a Heat-storage Cooker

The fire should be riddled, the ashes removed and the cooker should be refuelled at regular intervals, usually twice in 24 hours.

The heat regulator should be used well ahead of cooking time and varied as little as possible: it is usually turned to low at night and turned up a little in the morning.

The two ovens have a difference in temperature of about 100° to 125° F., depending on the model and this difference should be used in preferance to altering the regulator unnecessarily.

The covers of the hot-plate, usually two or three in number, must be shut down except when the plate is in use.

More cooking should be done in the oven than on top, to include stewing, soup-making, steaming and baking in hot fat instead of frying.

Any pan used on the hot-plates should have a heavy, flat machined, base.

Refrigerators

Every refrigerator, whatever its make or design, is in effect a cabinet with thick, well-lagged walls and a lagged door which closes tightly to insulate the inside, which is cold, from the warmer air outside. Inside the cabinet an 'evaporator' surrounds a smaller compartment used for ice-making. The evaporator absorbs heat from the storage compartment and from any food in it and in doing so sets up convection currents in the

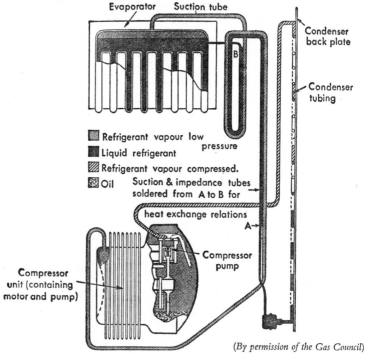

Evaporator   Suction tube

Condenser back plate

B

Condenser tubing

▨ Refrigerant vapour low pressure
■ Liquid refrigerant
▨ Refrigerant vapour compressed.
▨ Oil   Suction & impedance tubes soldered from A to B for heat exchange relations
A→

Compressor pump

Compressor unit (containing motor and pump)

(By permission of the Gas Council)

Fig. 14. MECHANISM DIAGRAM—MOTOR COMPRESSOR-TYPE REFRIGERATOR

air enclosed in the cabinet and also draws moisture out of the food: this moisture condenses and then forms hoar frost on the outside of the evaporator.

In order to extract heat from food, a refrigerator makes use of the principle that a liquid on changing to a vapour uses up the latent heat of its surroundings. Refrigerators effect this change from liquid to vapour in one of two ways: by compression or by absorption.

Compression Method

This type of refrigerator has an electric motor, which drives a pump to compress the gaseous refrigerant, and a fan to cool it: the compressed, cooled refrigerant turns to a very cold liquid which is next released from pressure and passes into the evaporator where it absorbs heat from the cabinet and so evaporates. The vapour (gaseous refrigerant) is drawn into the compressor to repeat the cycle of operations.

Absorption Method

This type of refrigerator is operated by heat which may be provided by gas, electricity or liquid fuel such as paraffin. It is a little more complicated in operation, but, briefly, the heat is used to 'boil' a solution of ammonia in water, to vaporize the ammonia and drive it off,

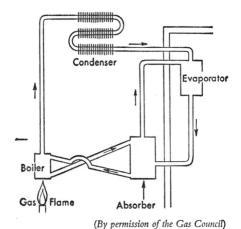

(By permission of the Gas Council)

Fig. 15. ABSORPTION-TYPE REFRIGERATOR

under pressure, from the solution. The vapour is next air-cooled and condensed to liquid ammonia which passes into the evaporator where it mixes with hydrogen. The liquid ammonia now absorbs heat from the cabinet and vaporizes; then the mixed gases pass on to the absorber where the ammonia is once more absorbed into the water, the hydrogen passes back to the evaporator and the cycle of operations begins again.

The absorption type uses rather more fuel than the compressor type but is convenient when electric current is not available.

Temperature in a Refrigerator

A refrigerator is designed to store food at temperatures between 40° F. and 50° F., that is, at temperatures in which bacteria cannot multiply but in which food will not deteriorate through frost. A thermostat controls the operation of the compressor or the absorber by switching off the electric current or reducing the flow of gas when the air in the cabinet reaches the temperature set by a regulating dial, and conversely by switching or turning on again when the temperature rises.

Using a Refrigerator

1. Open the door as seldom and for as short a time as possible to keep the cold air in the cabinet and to exclude warm air from outside.
2. Arrange food so that air can circulate round it so that convection currents can be set up to draw heat from the food and pass it up to the evaporator.
3. Keep all food covered to prevent it from becoming dried as heat is extracted from it and to prevent smells and flavours from mingling in the air currents. Cover with plastic bags or basin covers, aluminium foil, greaseproof paper or the lids of containers. If food is left uncovered the moisture which evaporates from it produces an extra amount of frost which reduces the efficiency of the refrigerator.
4. Never put warm food into the refrigerator as this will overwork the evaporator, produce too much moisture and warm other foods.
5. Arrange foods in the refrigerator in the position which gives them the most suitable temperature, as follows:

Position	Relative coldness	Food
Inside evaporator	Freezing	Ice cubes, ice-cream for 6 hours Jellies to be set in ½ hour Frozen foods for up to 2 days (see p. 52)
Drip tray below evaporator	Very cold	Fish wrapped or covered with ice cubes
Shelf below evaporator	Very cold	Milk (a space in the shelf above fits the bottles) Jellies and cold sweets, sausages Cooked meats
Middle	Cold	Cooked foods, sausages, meat
Bottom, rack in door shelf beside evaporator	Least cold	Meat, salads, cheese, fats, eggs, bottles of drink to be kept just cold Soft fruits, fruit salad, cut citrus fruits

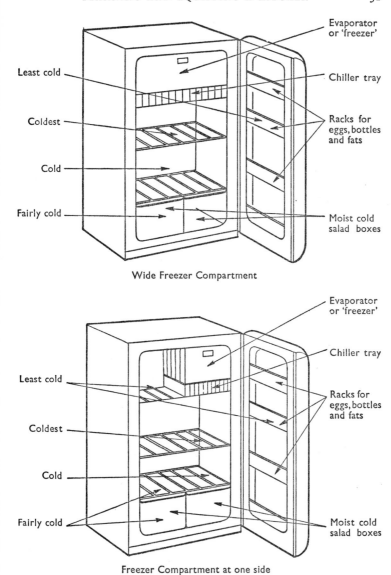

Wide Freezer Compartment

Freezer Compartment at one side

(By permission of the Electrical Development Association)

Fig. 16. ZONES OF COLD IN TWO DESIGNS OF REFRIGERATOR

Foods that should not be stored in refrigerator:

>   root vegetables, onions;
>   apples;
>   bananas;
>   pineapple and melon except after cutting them up and then only
>   long enough to chill them;
>   strong-smelling cheeses.

Eggs need not be stored in a refrigerator but if they are, they should be upright, in a rack, and they should be taken out and allowed to reach room temperature before use.

Most modern refrigerators have a special compartment with a star-rating indicating the length of time for which frozen foods may safely be stored.

Cleaning a Refrigerator

Keep the cabinet clean by wiping up at once any food that is spilt, by wiping the outside of milk bottles and making sure that all containers are clean.

Whenever ice has formed to a thickness of $\frac{1}{8}$ inch on the evaporator the refrigerator must be defrosted:

1. Switch 'Off' or turn the indicator to 'Defrost' and remove the contents.
2. Leave the drip tray in place under the evaporator, fill one ice tray with hot water and put it in the evaporator.
3. Remove the shelves, wash, rinse and dry them.
4. Leave the door of the cabinet ajar.
5. In about $\frac{1}{2}$ hour, when all the ice should have slipped off, wash all the inside surfaces with a clean cloth wrung out in warm water containing an unscented detergent or 1 tablespoon bicarbonate soda in each gallon.
6. Rinse and dry the cabinet, replace shelves, refill ice-trays, close the door and turn to the normal setting.
7. After about $\frac{1}{4}$ hour replace the contents.

Some modern refrigerators do not need defrosting as the frost is automatically removed.

SMALL EQUIPMENT

The right tool for the job is as important in cooking as in any craft and, as there is a very wide variety available, choice requires some thought.

Each cook will have her own preference for particular tools and the number, kind and size of these will also depend on the amount and the kind of cooking and on the money that can be afforded.

Some Necessary Small Equipment

Item	Some points to consider
Saucepans	They should balance both in the hand and on the cooker.

The handles should be comfortable to grasp, should be securely fixed and insulated to prevent them getting too hot.

Large and heavy pans should have a handle each side.

Lids should fit well.

A milk saucepan usually has no lid, but it should have a pouring-lip on each side or a flat pouring-rim all round.

Rounded edges are easier to clean than right-angled ones.

Thick metal, particularly on the base, spreads the heat more evenly and is less likely to get dented or buckled than thin metal.

Flat, machined bases are necessary for all solid hot-plates on electric and solid fuel cookers.

At least one pan with short, heat-proof handles is useful for cooking in the oven.

Metals used for Saucepans

Aluminium. This is really an alloy of aluminium, a soft metal, with one or more harder metals such as iron. It is very light and durable. It is usually given a 'mirror' finish outside which looks bright and resists dirt. The insides of aluminium pans turn black when alkaline foods and hard water are heated in them; this black deposit is not harmful and need not be removed.

Aluminium is easily scratched and therefore metal spoons should not be used for stirring, as the scratched surface soon becomes pitted through the chemical action of various foods. Reasonably thick aluminium pans are long-wearing and an economical choice.

Stainless Steel. This is steel alloyed with a very little of a softer stainless metal. It is very hard and durable, it resists dirt and stains but is expensive.

Item   *Some points to consider*

The pans are thin because of the cost of the metal and therefore often have copper or aluminium welded over the base which serves to spread the heat more evenly.

Vitreous Enamel on pressed steel. These pans are heavy but easy to clean; they are durable except to heavy blows; they are rather expensive, but their colours and finish make them suitable for oven-to-table use.

Soft Enamel. These pans are inexpensive, less durable than the vitreous enamelled kind, but are light and suitable for foods which do not readily stick or burn. The very cheap ones are not really economical in use as they chip easily.

Copper. Very tough and durable, a very good conductor of heat, but expensive and needs frequent cleaning to remove tarnish. Except for sugar-boiling, copper pans should be tin-lined.

Frying-pans   These may be of any of the metals above and also of cast iron or pressed steel which are both efficient in use and do not rust if lightly greased. Tinned frying-pans are not desirable because the tin lining melts.

Vitreous enamelled frying-pans may have a dimpled inner surface to prevent food sticking.

The thicker the frying-pan the better.

The omelette pan usually has rounded inner edges and should be very smooth inside.

Kettle   This may be of any of the metals suggested for saucepans and also of tinned iron which is not very economical because, although cheap, it rusts at the joins.

A wide base (often 'finned' for a gas cooker) economizes fuel; a machined flat base is necessary for a solid-fuel cooker.

An electric kettle is the most economical kind to use with an electric cooker and provides a quick way of boiling water with any type of cooker.

Steamer   Usually aluminium and with a stepped base to fit different saucepans (Fig. 5).

Casseroles   These may be made of:

Oven-glass. This is a specially tough glass which contains

Item	Some points to consider
	boron to make it heat-proof and which expands very little when heated and therefore does not readily crack with quick changes of temperature. There are several makes of oven-glass and the newest development is to make it *flame-proof*. 'Oven-glass' may not be used on any hot-plate or flame, 'flame-proof' glass may.
	Heat-proof Earthenware. This is only suited to cooking in the oven and may not be used on a gas burner or solid hot-plate.
	Flame-proof Earthenware and Porcelain. This may be used either in the oven or, as its name suggests, over a moderate gas burner or solid hot-plate.
	These four types of cooker-to-table ware save time in dishing and washing-up and can look most attractive on the dining-table.
	Vitreous enamelled casseroles are heavier than glass or earthenware but are more durable and they are of course flame proof. They are expensive.
Knives	These should be well balanced.
	The handles should fit the hand comfortably and should be riveted to the shank of the blade.
	The sizes should be suited to the strength of the cook's hand and to the work they are to do—short blades for peeling vegetables and fruit, longer blades for slicing, chopping and cutting meat and fish.
	Stainless steel needs no cleaning and can nowadays be sharpened in the same way as ordinary steel.
	Ordinary steel is sometimes considered to have a better cutting edge than stainless steel but it must be cleaned frequently.
Sawknife	This is useful for slicing such things as tomatoes.
Breadsaw	Useful for slicing other foods as well as bread.
Palette knife	Flexible, stainless and with a comfortable handle, this is a very useful tool for lifting, mixing, spreading and for scraping out bowls.
Scissors	Chromium plated or stainless steel (which is expensive) are suitable because they will not rust. Scissors with saw-edged blades are useful for cutting many food-stuffs and can be sharpened by the makers when necessary.

Item	Some points to consider
Vegetable parer	This should be stainless and some are now made to be used by both the left- and right-handed cook.
Steel or knife sharpener	This is often shared by kitchen and dining-room, but it is essential for keeping kitchen knives sharp.
Spoons	Table and teaspoons of stainless or plated metal or plastic are needed for measuring, stirring and tasting foods; teaspoons used for measuring should be of British standard size.
	A larger spoon is often found useful for basting.
	A perforated draining spoon is useful but not essential.
Wooden spoons	The wood should be fine grained, hard and smooth. Several sizes are needed and useful shapes include round bowl, square-ended blade and a bowl rounded at one side and right-angled at the other.
Fork	Stainless metal is best and three or four prongs are needed for mashing and beating small quantities of food.
Fish slice	Aluminium, stainless steel or chromium plate are suitable; if the blade is long it should be flexible, if rigid it should be short. A modern fish slice is made as a pair of tongs, which makes the turning of food easy during frying or grilling.
Grater	This should be stainless metal and with grating edges that retain their sharpness: it should have fine, medium and coarse sections and should be rigid and steady in use. Cylindrical and box-shaped graters are efficient.
Mincer	This should have a strong clamp to fix it to a table edge, or widely straddled legs and rubber feet: it should have two or three discs with different-sized holes.
Sieve	Sieves may have wooden or metal frames and tinned steel, stainless metal or nylon mesh: nylon is useful— prevents discoloration of fruit and acid or white vegetables: stainless metal serves the same purposes, but is more expensive.
	A bowl-shaped wire strainer is equally efficient for sieving and does double duty for straining.
Colander	Colanders are usually of aluminium. They are useful for straining heavy foods such as vegetables and are easiest to lift if they have two handles.

Item	*Some points to consider*
Pastry-board	A plastic work surface often serves for rolling pastry; if a board is needed, plastic or very fine-grained wood are suitable, or, better still, is a slab of marble from a discarded table top.
Chopping-board	The pastry board should not be scored by chopping, so a chopping-board of hardwood is useful.
Rolling-pin	Fine-grained hardwood, or more modern porcelain or fire-proof glass are suitable, wood being cheaper and more durable. A long rolling-pin is best as it leaves room for the hands beyond the edges of the pastry.
Pastry or coating brush	Soft nylon or hair fixed into wood or twisted wire are durable and useful for brushing flour, for coating and glazing food.
Egg-whisk and Rotary beater	A whisk with a coiled edge is inexpensive and efficient, giving a greater volume when whisking egg-whites than a rotary beater.
	A rotary beater should be stainless, working on ball-bearings, geared so that one turn of the handle makes several revolutions of the blades, comfortable to grasp and of strong construction.
Bowls and Basins	Several sizes are generally needed. Plastic bowls are useful for washing food, but are easily scored by spoons and beaters. Oven glass is pleasant to use and often less expensive than earthenware. A wide mixing bowl is comfortable for hand whisks and general stirring, but a deep shape is needed for use with a rotary beater.
	Several sizes of pudding basin have many uses in cooking.
Oven tins	There are many sizes and shapes to choose from; those of strong tinned steel or fairly heavy gauge aluminium are more durable than thin, cheap ones.
Roasting tin	One of these is provided with any new cooker. Corners should be rounded for easy cleaning.
Baking tray	One is provided with a new cooker; two or three may be needed; they must fit the oven shelf with room to spare all round; rigid metal is essential.
Cake tins	Several sizes are usually needed in deep round or trough shapes and shallow round for sandwich cakes.
	Cake tins with loose bottoms or ring shaped are popular.

c

Item	Some points to consider
Bun tins	Sheets of 6, 9, or 12 patty tins are made in several shapes: large, deep ones are useful for individual Yorkshire puddings.
Yorkshire tins	These are useful for some cakes as well as for their main purpose.
Cutters	Different sizes of round and other shapes, made of tinned steel or plastic are useful.
Can opener	The easiest to use are those with a cogwheel operated by a winding handle or lever action and a small steel cutting blade.
Scales and Measures	See Chapter 1.
Sundry 'gadgets'	There are countless hand-operated mechanical tools for chopping, grating, milling, sieving and carrying out other processes; choice of these depends on the money available, storage space in the kitchen and personal preference.

Electric Labour-saving Apparatus

This mainly consists of food mixers with many attachments for whisking, beating, mincing, grating, extracting juice, 'liquidizing' and milling foods. They vary in size from the large expensive models with many extra attachments to small ones that can be held in the hand and which carry out a few processes only.

The points to consider are:

How much money can you afford and are there any more important items needed, such as a refrigerator or a new cooker?

How often do you do the work for which the machine is designed and how long does it take?

How long will it take to assemble and dismantle the machine and how long to clean it?

How much space does the machine take up, how strong is it and how long is it likely to last?

Kitchen cloths	
Hand towels	Should be absorbent and easily washed; for this reason small ones are preferable to roller towels.
Tea towels	May be made of linen which is durable and leaves no lint on dishes after drying; cotton, which is cheaper but

Item	Some points to consider
	usually less absorbent unless it is in the form of terry-towelling or honeycomb weave, both of which are popular because they need no finish when laundered.
Dish-cloths	Soft cotton mesh or knitted cotton are easy to rinse and wash because of their open mesh.
	Cellular synthetic sponge cloths or mops absorb dirt less easily than ordinary fabric and can easily be rinsed and boiled.
Paper 'cloths' for food	Cloths for wiping and drying foodstuffs such as meat or fish are nowadays usually replaced by tough, absorbent paper which is hygienic as it can be destroyed after use.

Keeping Kitchen Equipment Clean

Washing-up: As soon as they have been used all basins and tools should be scraped to remove traces of food and washed at once or soaked.

Wash in hot water with just enough detergent to make a lather.

Rinse in scalding hot water and drain; dry only glass and metal hand tools, using a clean cloth.

Saucepans of all kinds: Scrape out all food, fill with water, hot if possible, and soak them.

Remove any food that has hardened, with a nylon scouring pad or a stiff brush.

Wash as above, removing stains with fine steel wool or scouring paste or powder, rinse and dry with a clean dish-cloth; do not replace lid until the pan is aired.

Aluminium: Soda, or scouring agents containing soda, roughen and pit the surface of aluminium; wire saucepan brushes score the surface, which then becomes pitted by the action of some foods.

Fine steel wool is the best abrasive to use. Black coating inside may be removed by boiling with lemon or apple rinds.

Copper: To remove tarnish use a fine scouring powder at every washing and for a bright shine use metal polish only on the outside.

Frying-pan: Drain out all fat, wipe the pan with soft paper to remove grease. Fill the pan with hot water and detergent or soda and boil this, or soak the pan, then treat as saucepans.

Omelet pan: Wipe the pan free of all food and grease and polish it well with clean soft kitchen paper. Wash it only occasionally. If food sticks to it, rub it hard with dry salt then polish with paper. Washing spoils the surface and allows the omelet to stick.

Tins: Wash, rinse and dry with a clean dish-cloth, then leave in a warm place to dry completely to prevent rusting.

Cake tins: Treat like omelet pans, omitting the salt treatment and washing only occasionally.

Roasting tins: Treat as frying-pans; dry in a warm place.

Wooden utensils: Scrape off all flour or food scraps.

Scrub with warm water and hard soap, or with a nylon scouring pad and scouring paste or powder and rinse extra well.

Rinse, dry first with a clean dish-cloth and then in a draught.

Kitchen cloths: Wash tea towels and hand towels every day and dry, if possible out of doors.

Boil the dish-cloth or mop every day with detergent in the water and tea towels and hand towels once a week.

Plastics in the Kitchen

Some of the plastics used are:

Melamine: this is very hard, tough and almost unbreakable, used for table-ware, storage jars, and work surfaces, e.g. 'Formica' and 'Wareite'; it is unharmed by boiling water but blistered by hot saucepans and hot fat.

Nylon: this is very tough, slightly flexible, used for sieves and gear-wheels of mechanical mixers and beaters; it is unharmed by boiling water.

Perspex: this is very tough and rigid and almost unbreakable, used for sinks and waste-pipes and refrigerator dishes; it is unharmed by boiling water but is distorted by hot utensils and hot fat.

Polythene or 'Alkathene' is tough and flexible, used for bowls, buckets, colanders and many other utensils; it withstands very hot but not boiling water.

Care of Plastics

Never put hot utensils on them.
Never put them in an oven or on a hot stove.
Never cut or chop food on them.
Never beat or whisk with metal tools in plastic bowls.
Never use them for hot fat.

Cleaning Plastics

Wipe with a cloth wrung out of hot water when they are slightly dirty; wash them with hot water and detergent or soap when they are sticky or really dirty. Avoid abrasives, bleaches and grease solvents. Never boil plastic utensils.

3

FOOD HYGIENE

To civilized people, food that is prepared and served in dirty conditions is disgusting and not fit to eat, and, since one of the aims of cooking is to make food enjoyable this is a sufficient reason why a cook should work in a clean kitchen, should herself be clean and should keep absolutely clean everything she uses and the food she cooks. It is, however, important to realize that visible dirt is only dangerous because it probably harbours bacteria which are themselves invisible and that, in fact, food which appears to be quite clean may really be so dangerously contaminated with bacteria as to cause food poisoning.

If bacterial contamination of food cannot be detected how can it be prevented? Fortunately the nature and behaviour of bacteria have been studied for many years and are now well known to bacteriologists who have formulated certain rules for keeping food free from infection.

Bacteria are minute, one-celled, living organisms which are everywhere around us, in the air, in water and soil, in dust and, more important still, in our own bodies and in the food we cook and eat. They are by no means all harmful; many are, indeed, necessary to food production as they speed the natural decay of organic matter, turning it into valuable manure for plant crops; while others, together with yeasts and moulds, which are similar micro-organisms, are made use of in the manufactuer of foodstuffs such as butter and cheese and in the fermentation of beers and wines. The dangerous bacteria, which may contaminate food, are of several different kinds. Each type produces slightly different symptoms of disease but the general effects are similar; they include violent vomiting and diarrhoea, sometimes fever, headache, cramp and great weakness: the attack may last for a few hours only or for several days and it may even be fatal.

Bacteria in food cause disease in two ways; either by invading the human body directly in large numbers, multiplying in the body and giving rise to the illness; or by producing in the food certain poisons or *toxins* which cause similar symptoms. In either case, to have any ill-effect the bacteria must be present in large numbers in the food when it is eaten; the food is then said to be the *vehicle* of infection. The vehicle, however, is only the means of conveying to the consumer bacteria which have been put into it from some *reservoir* of infection which is always animal. The most usual reservoirs of infection are the human bowel, nose and throat, in all of which large numbers of disease-causing bacteria may be carried, even though the owner of these organs, that is the *host*, may not be suffering from any disease. Human beings who handle

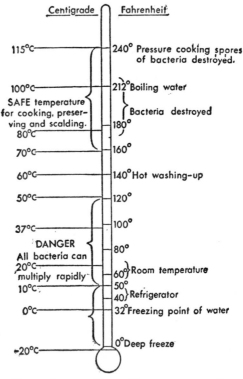

Fig. 17. SAFE AND UNSAFE TEMPERATURES FOR FOOD

food with hands unwashed after going to the lavatory, or blowing the nose, or licking the fingers, or who cough and sneeze over food, may, by these disgusting habits, infect food with such bacteria. Flies, which feed on animal excreta and thereafter walk on food and vomit and excrete on it, are another source of infection while, less frequently, mice, rats, cockroaches and domestic animals may affect food in similar ways.

The food which has become the *vehicle of infection* does not carry a dangerous load until the bacteria have had time to multiply, which they

How Food-Poisoning is carried

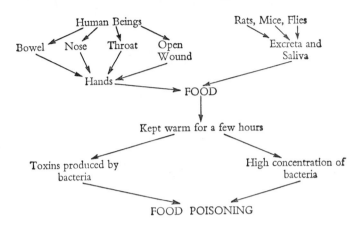

Some Forms of Bacterial Food Poisoning

Bacteria or Toxins	Usual reservoir	Incubation time	Usual symptoms
Salmonella	Bowels of humans and animals	12 to 24 hours	Fever, headache, aching limbs, vomiting, diarrhoea
Staphylo-coccal toxins	Nose and throat of humans, septic cuts and sores	2 to 6 hours	Acute vomiting then diarrhoea, pain, cramp, fainting and collapse
Various micro-organisms: streptococci, paracolon bacilli, clostridium Welchii	Various; often meat stored warm and with-out air	8 to 22 hours	Abdominal pain and diarrhoea of short duration
Bacillus Botulinus	Very rare	24 to 72 hours	Fatigue, headache and paralysis. Often fatal

do very rapidly, each cell splitting into two about every 20 minutes so that within 6 hours one micro-organism may have produced several hundred thousand. Some bacteria, as well as splitting into two produce spores which can lie dormant in a cold, dry state for months or years, ready to grow into bacteria and to multiply rapidly as soon as they find suitable conditions. The conditions that favour the multiplication of bacteria and the germination of spores are warmth, moisture, and, for some 'aerobic' bacteria, air; for other 'anaerobic' bacteria, lack of air. The foods which are the most usual vehicles of bacteria are meat, milk, lightly-cooked, sweet milky dishes, synthetic cream, ducks' eggs, and more rarely, tinned foods, fish, raw vegetables and salads. Foods that rarely carry infection are those containing a high proportion of sugar, such as jam, or of vinegar and spices, such as pickles; dried and powdered foods, fats, dry, baked foods such as bread and biscuits and all foods that are eaten at once after having been thoroughly cooked.

Food-borne bacteria can be destroyed by heat and rendered inactive and unable to multiply by cold. They multiply most rapidly at temperatures near to those of the human body, that is from 97° to 100° Fahrenheit: at temperatures slightly above or slightly below this range they can still multiply but more slowly. At 145° Fahrenheit they begin to die: the higher the temperature the more quickly do they die. At temperatures below 50° Fahrenheit, although they are not killed, they cannot multiply and are therefore harmless until they are allowed to get warm and lively.

Rules of Food Hygiene

To make certain that food is free from bacterial contamination and therefore safe to eat:

1. It must not be touched by hands that have been in contact with any likely reservoir of infection.
2. It must be protected from flies, mice or rats or domestic animals.
3. It must be stored, prepared and cooked in clean vessels and touched only with clean tools.
4. It should be cooked while fresh and at a temperature of over 165° F. (Although oven temperatures are usually far higher than this, heat penetrates food slowly and a really well-cooked joint for example will only reach about 180° F. in the middle.)
5. Cooked foods should be eaten while hot or cooled quickly to below 50° F. and eaten cold.
6. Cold, cooked food should be stored at a temperature below

50° F.: a good place to store it is a refrigerator which keeps the correct temperature and protects food from flies.

7. Cooked food should not be stored for more than three days even at this temperature: for longer storage the modern method of deep-freezing is advisable.

Personal Cleanliness of the Cook

1. The hands must be washed with soap and hot water just before handling food and always after going to the lavatory or using a handkerchief.
2. The hands must be well-kept with short, clean nails, unbroken cuticle and with no chaps or cracks.
3. The cook must never lick her fingers nor finger her mouth, nose, ears, hair nor in fact any part of her person.
4. Any cut or sore place on the hands must be covered with water-proof-plaster dressing.
5. No one should cook or prepare food when suffering from or recovering from a bad cold or from diarrhoea or sickness.
6. Food should be handled as little as possible, and cooked food not at all—it should be lifted and served with suitable, clean tools.

Cleanliness of the Kitchen

1. There must be nothing in the kitchen to attract flies, mice or beetles, therefore spilt food must at once be cleaned up, crumbs swept up and all food scraps removed after every meal.
2. All cookery utensils must be kept perfectly clean; they must be washed and scoured according to their kind and scalded after use, then drained dry or dried with a perfectly clean cloth.
3. All cloths used in the kitchen must be washed daily with soap or soapless detergent and boiled at least twice a week; if possible they should be dried out of doors. Dirty cloths are dangerous vehicles of infection.
4. All work surfaces in the kitchen must be washed every day; the floor swept, if necessary, several times a day, and washed at least once a week or whenever food is spilt on it.

Disposing of Kitchen Waste

Food scraps must not be left about to attract flies and mice or rats, therefore a water-tight dustbin with a tight-fitting lid should be used and this should be kept out of doors, away from kitchen or larder windows. It is a good plan to raise the dustbin off the ground on bricks, the bottom is less likely to rust and the ground below and around it may more easily be swept.

In hot weather, unless dustbins are emptied daily by the local authority, food waste should be wrapped in dry paper so that it is less likely to attract flies; better still it should be burnt.

Disinfectant powder sprinkled in the dustbin also discourages flies.

Occasionally the dustbin should be scraped and scrubbed inside with soda water and drained dry.

A refuse bin in the kitchen must be covered, and emptied, washed and drained daily.

STORAGE OF FOOD AT HOME

Perishable foods that are dust-laden or mouldy or beginning to 'go bad' or decompose are obviously not fit to eat, and, what is worse, they probably also harbour harmful bacteria. Conditions of storage that keep foods safe from bacterial infection will also keep them palatable.

Perishable food, that is: meat, fish, milk, fruit and vegetables and cooked dishes made of these foods, should be stored for the shortest possible time and should, if possible, be bought on the day they are needed and in the amount needed for that day or the next. When this is not possible they must be kept cool, at temperatures below 50° Fahrenheit; the easiest way to do this is to use a refrigerator, but other ways may be devised to keep food cool for a short time. For much of the year, in Great Britain, a larder or food cupboard with ventilation on the north of the house or an airy cellar will have a suitable temperature. For cooling in very hot weather use can be made of the fact that the evaporation of water uses up heat from the surrounding air. Porous, ventilated, earthenware covers and containers, soaked in water, or clean cloths dipped in water will provide sufficient coolness to keep milk fresh or fats firm for a few hours (Fig. 18); neither method is suitable for storing fats for long as the water vapour hastens the decomposition of fats.

Milk should be kept in the bottle with the cap on.

Do not keep untreated or unpasteurized milk for more than 24 hours in a larder or two days in a refrigerator.

Do not pour milk back into the bottle from a milk jug.

Do not mix milk of different deliveries unless it is to be cooked at once.

Boiled milk should not be kept any longer than fresh milk.

Wash, scald and drain all milk jugs and measures, never dry them with a cloth as this may harbour bacteria.

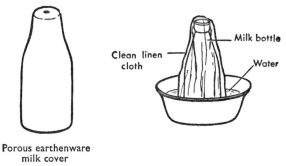

Clean linen cloth

Milk bottle

Water

Porous earthenware milk cover

Fig. 18. KEEPING MILK COOL

Meat must have air round it as, with too little air, anaerobic bacteria can multiply on it and begin to decompose it.

Hang meat when possible or stand it on the grid from a roasting tin or grill pan.

Store it for not more than 2 days in an airy, cool larder protected from dust and flies by a metal gauze window or a fly-proof dish cover (Fig. 19).

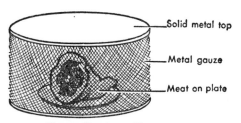

Solid metal top

Metal gauze

Meat on plate

Fig. 19. FLY-PROOF MEAT-COVER

In a refrigerator meat can be loosely covered with greaseproof paper or polythene to prevent drying, and should not be kept for more than 3 days.

Cooked meat should not be stored for more than 2 days.

Fish: Fresh fish must be cooked within 24 hours after buying it, and is much better cooked immediately. If it must be stored loosen the greaseproof wrapping paper and keep it near the open window, protected from flies.

In a refrigerator store fish for not more than 24 hours in the chilling tray directly under the evaporator.

Smoked fish should be hung in the larder with air circulating.

Green Vegetables and Salad Plants must be dry or they will rot if stored for more than an hour or two.

They should be used as soon as possible after being cut from the garden or bought very fresh.

If they must be stored for a few hours, wrap them loosely in newspaper or put them in a covered pan or bowl to prevent them withering through loss of moisture to the air round them.

In a refrigerator store them in a plastic or enamelled box with a lid or in a basin with a plate as cover.

As they are valueless when stale, do not store them for more than 2 days, or 3 in a refrigerator.

Root Vegetables soon shrivel once they are out of the ground: store them only two or three days indoors. For longer storage keep them in dry soil or sand in a shed or out of doors.

Polythene bags keep them from shrivelling for a few days but they must have a little ventilation or they will rot.

Bread: Do not try to store bread beyond the stage when it is pleasant to eat; when stale, toast it or use it in cooking.

Store it in a ventilated bin or tin or crock.

Remove all crumbs from the container every few days and every week or fortnight, wash, dry and air it.

Frozen Foods once they leave the deep-freeze container can only be kept a few hours in the main cabinet of a refrigerator, for 2 days in the evaporator of a small refrigerator and must be used as soon as they thaw if there is no refrigerator. Most modern refrigerators have a compartment specially designed for storing frozen food graded as one-star, two-star or three-star, to indicate safe storage time.

To use frozen food thaw meat, fish and fruit at room temperature but vegetables should be plunged while frozen into boiling water for cooking.

Dried Foods: Once these are soaked or mixed with water they are just as likely to become vehicles of infection as are fresh foods.

Dried Eggs and Milk: Mix only the amount required and use it all at once.

Dried Vegetables: Soak the amount required and cook them as soon as they have softened sufficiently.

CARE OF A LARDER

A larder or food cupboard must be on the cool, north or north-east side of the building and must have free circulation of air inside. There should be no ventilator from kitchen into larder, the door of the larder should fit closely and there must be no hot-water pipes running through the larder.

The window must be kept open and screened with metal-gauze.

The shelves are easiest to keep clean if made of slate, but wood covered with hard plastic is a good modern alternative.

Lower shelves should be kept for perishable foods, higher ones that are not easily reached, for longer term storage.

Store as little as possible on the floor so that it can easily be cleaned.

Hot food must not be put into the larder as it will make the atmosphere warm and moist.

Keep the larder absolutely clean; wipe up any spilt food at once, wash lower shelves and floor every week.

Never store food once it begins to get stale or mouldy.

Every few weeks remove all perishable foods and remove dust from ceiling, light, all shelves and ledges and floor.

For the Refrigerator, see Fig. 16.

STORING GROCERIES

Most groceries, being dry, do not become infected with bacteria and many will keep in good condition for months in a dry, cool, store-cupboard. However, some dry goods do deteriorate in various ways when stored, therefore, unless shops are a long way from the home, there is no advantage in storing most groceries for longer than a month.

Useful Rules for storing Groceries

1. Keep groceries in a cupboard in the kitchen, easily reached from the work surface.
2. Store only the amount that is convenient for the household shopping routine.
3. Use screw-top jars, or tins or plastic containers rather than paper packets. Even if transparent containers are used label all white powders and any stores not easy to identify.
4. When refilling containers, occasionally empty, wash, dry and refill with new stock using up the old, which should not be put back in the container.
5. Wash the shelves once a month.

The following table is a guide to the length of time for which storage is safe and to the kinds and causes of deterioration of some groceries.

Food	Approximate shelf life	Cause of deterioration	Kind of deterioration
Baking powder. Bicarbonate of Soda	2 to 6 months / 1 to 2 months	Absorption of moisture	Loss of carbon-dioxide and therefore of raising power
Canned foods	6 months to 1 year, unless perfectly dry then up to 2 years	Rusting and therefore perforation of tin	Bacterial contamination inevitably
Cocoa	6 months to 1 year	Loss of volatile oils	Spoilage and loss of flavour
Coffee (ground)	1 to 2 weeks	Loss of volatile oils unless 'vacuum packed'	Loss of aroma and flavour
Dried fruits	2 to 3 months	Drying. Faulty hygiene during drying and warehouse storage	Drying and hardening. Maggots appear
Cereals, e.g. wholemeal, oatmeal, semolina.	1 month	Small amount of fat in the grain goes rancid.	Bitter or rancid flavour. Maggots appear
Flour (white)	1 to 2 months	Faulty hygiene during milling or storage	Maggots and later moths or tiny beetles appear, hatched from eggs laid in the cereal
Pure starch, e.g. tapioca, sago, cornflour	6 months	As above but as there is no fat, flavours are not spoilt	
Preserves	Note: any fault in making or processing will cause deterioration of some kind, see chapter on Preserves		
Chutney	2 to 3 years	Evaporation of moisture	Shrinkage, crystallization of sugar

Food	Approximate shelf life	Cause of deterioration	Kind of deterioration
Jams	2 to 3 years years	(a) Evaporation (b) Damp storage	(a) Shrinkage, crystalliza- tion of sugar (b) Moulds form or yeasts cause fermentation
Pickles	Variable, up to 1 year	Damp storage. Slight chemical changes varying with the ingredients. Evaporation	Moulds form. Flavour and colour slowly deteriorate Pickled ingredients not cov- ered by liquid decompose in the usual way
Salt (block)	Indefinite if dry. 1 to 2 weeks, damp	Absorption of water from atmosphere	Salt becomes damp then dissolves
Salt (table)	Indefinite if dry. 1 to 2 weeks, damp	Very slow absorption of water from atmosphere as table salt contains a drying powder	As block salt but much slower
Spices	Several years	If not in airtight con- tainers, loss of volatile oils	Very slow loss of flavour
Sugar	2 to 3 months	Moisture absorbed	Caking, later dissolving of surface sugar
Syrup and Treacle	6 months to 1 year	Evaporation	Crystallization of some sugar
Vinegar	1 to 2 months	'Mother of Vinegar' is grown and forms a sediment, this is a fungoid plant which gives rise to the fermenta- tion necessary to the manufacture of vinegar, harmless but unsightly	

4

NUTRITIVE VALUE OF FOODS

All living things need food to keep them alive. This is because the state of being alive is one of continual change in which the millions of cells that make up the living plant or animal wear out and must be renewed, and because, if life is to continue, new plants and animals must be produced and must grow to maturity. To maintain this change and growth all living organisms need food from which they can get the material to make new cells; in addition, living animals need food as fuel to give them the energy they need to enable them to move about and to keep their bodies warm.

Plants, with the help of sunshine, can use the elements in the air, water and soil and make from them suitable foods for themselves; animals, although they need the same elements, can only use them as food after they have been changed by plants into plant structure. Animals must therefore have as food plant-products or the flesh, milk or eggs of other animals which have fed on plants. Human beings are like other animals in taking their food from these two groups, but, whereas most animals select their food by instinct, human beings choose theirs freely, at will. They often choose unwisely, because modern civilization makes available such a bewilderingly wide range of different foodstuffs, some in their natural state, others ready-prepared and often ready-cooked, that only with sound knowledge of food values and of the human body's needs of food, can unerringly wise choice be made.

The detailed study of the composition of foodstuffs, of the amount of different foods needed by human beings and of the ways in which the human body uses these foods is included in the science of Human Nutrition which is a fascinating subject but one of great complexity to which this chapter can only attempt a brief introduction.

Food may be defined as anything which, when eaten or drunk, can be absorbed by the body to be used as fuel to produce energy, or as building material to provide for growth, repair and reproduction, or as protective material to keep it healthy by regulating the use of both fuel and building foods. To rank as a food any foodstuff must contain one or more of certain substances known as nutrients.

The Nutrients and their uses in the Body

1. *Proteins* provide building material for repair of worn body tissues and for growth; if eaten in excess of the body's needs for building and repair they may be used as fuel foods; this also happens if proteins are eaten without fuel foods at any meal.
2. *Carbohydrates* supply energy; if eaten in excess of the body's needs they may be converted to body fat.
3. *Fats* supply energy; if eaten in excess of the body's needs they may be stored as body fat.
4. *Mineral Substances* regulate many of the body's activities and provide extra building material.
5. *Vitamins* regulate the body's activities and ensure the proper use of other nutrients.

Both mineral substances and vitamins are sometimes known as 'Protective Foods' because with a shortage of any one of them the body may have poor resistance to certain diseases and because a total lack of any one of them would cause a deficiency disease. In addition to the nutrients, the body needs oxygen from the air, which is not classed as a food, and water, which forms a large part of all foodstuffs. In addition to the water taken in food, 1½ pints at least should be drunk in some form of liquid every day.

PROTEINS

The name protein comes from a Greek word meaning 'first' showing that proteins are the most important of the nutrients. In fact every living thing contains protein: the flesh of all animals is largely composed of protein while all plant structures contain a little and the seeds of all plants contain useful amounts.

Proteins are of many kinds, being made up of a large number of different *amino-acids* which are grouped together in various ways. There are many amino-acids, of which eight are absolutely necessary to adult human beings and ten to growing children. Most animal proteins contain all the eight and some of them the ten essential amino-acids. Proteins from vegetable sources contain as a rule only one or two of the essential amino-acids. By using only different vegetable foods in the diet it is possible to include all the essential amino-acids but it is unlikely that they will be in the best proportions for human food. The most satisfactory way for human beings to get the right mixture of amino-acids in their diet is by using a variety of vegetable proteins which are usually relatively cheap, with animal proteins which are usually more expensive.

Animal Protein	*Vegetable Protein*
Lean meat of all kinds.	Pulses, i.e. peas, beans, lentils, ground-
Poultry and game.	nuts and soya beans.
Fish of all kinds.	Cereals, i.e. wheat, oats, barley and
Eggs.	rye.
Cheese.	Nuts of all kinds.
Milk.	All vegetables in their natural state
	contain proteins but often in too small
	an amount to be considered as pro-
	tein foods.

Food-scientists describe animal proteins as being of '*high biological value*'.

CARBOHYDRATES

Carbohydrates supply the largest proportion of energy to the body: in British diet usually about ⅔ of the total food. Carbohydrates are all, with one exception, of vegetable origin and are of three kinds, sugars, starch and cellulose.

Sugars: these are all more or less sweet to taste, are all easily soluble in water and all form crystals in a saturated solution. They are in two classes, simple sugars or monosaccharides and complex sugars or di-saccharides.

Two important simple sugars are:

1. *Glucose* which occurs in the blood of all animals and in the juices of fruits and plants. It can be made from starch either by plants or by chemical treatment. It is useful to the body in the digestion of fats.

2. *Fructose* which occurs in the juices of fruits and plants and in honey and is the sweetest of all sugars.

The principal complex sugars are:

3. *Sucrose*, which is the sugar known in everyday use as cane or beet sugar. It is made up of the two simple sugars, glucose and fructose.

4. *Lactose*, which is the sugar occurring in the milk of all animals, is made up of two simple sugars, glucose and galactose and is only slightly sweet to taste.

5. *Maltose*, which is made from starch by the germination of grain, is made up of two glucose sugars.

Sugars of all kinds, because they are easily dissolved, are the most quickly absorbed of all the nutrients.

Starch is the form in which plants store most of their food; they manufacture sugar in their leaves whence it flows in the plant juice to be converted into starch for storage as minute granules in seeds, stems, roots and tubers. Each type of plant has characteristically shaped granules which can be recognized under a microscope. Starch is insoluble in water, and, when raw, is indigestible; when cooked in water the granules swell and burst and the starch then forms a smooth, thick mixture with the water. When starch is heated it may be changed to *dextrin* which is soluble in water and which is used commercially as the gum on postage-stamps and some adhesive labels. The light golden colour of the crusts of bread, cakes and pastry and of toast shows that some starch has been turned to dextrin.

Carbohydrate Foods

Containing Starch	*Containing Sugar*
All cereals, e.g. wheat, oats, barley, maize and millet and all manufactured forms of these cereals, i.e. bread, cakes, biscuits, pastry, cornflour, macaroni, custard powder. Tapioca and sago. Potatoes.	Cane and beet sugar and all sweets and confectionery made with sugar. Treacle and golden syrup. Honey. Fruits, both fresh and dried. Jam. Some vegetables, e.g. beetroot, parsnips, green peas.

Glycogen is the one animal form of starch: it is stored in the liver and is present in the muscles of all animals while they are alive. When starch is digested it is converted to sugar and then changed again, for storage, to glycogen—much as plants change sugar to starch.

Cellulose, which is insoluble in water and which cannot be digested by human beings, forms the fibrous structure of vegetables and their seeds. It is useful in adding bulk to the diet and in aiding the passage of waste material through the bowel: because of this function it is sometimes called roughage. Many animals can digest cellulose, and even straw can be treated chemically to convert it to suitable food for cattle.

Pectin which is a complex carbohydrate has no food value but is important because of its property of forming a jelly with fruit-juice and sugar in the making of jam.

FATS

Fats are of animal and vegetable origin as both animals and plants can convert carbohydrates to fat which they store. As food, fats are highly concentrated sources of energy. It is characteristic of fats that they are insoluble in water, that they will not mix with water and that they can only be dissolved in grease-solvents such as petrol and ether, which have no place in human food.

Oils only differ from fats in that they melt at a comparatively low temperature: even solid fats become liquid at high temperatures. Fats and oils, at really high temperatures have a 'flash point' at which they ignite spontaneously if they are open to the air.

Fats are all made up of several different *fatty acids* combined with *glycerol*. The particular fatty acids in any fat give it its characteristic flavour and its solid or liquid state. There are many fatty acids; some that occur in the commonest fats are:

> Stearic acid and Palmitic acid give hardness to many fats, e.g. beef and mutton fats.
> Butyric acid gives the characteristic flavour to butter.
> Oleic acid makes fats soft or liquid, but is found in small quantities in many hard fats.
> Caprylic acid gives the characteristic flavour to goat's milk and is also present in many other fats.

Animal Sources of Fats

Beef and mutton fat, suet and dripping.
Pork and bacon fat.
Lard.
Herrings, mackerel, sardines, Salmon.
Eggs.
Milk, cream.
Butter, cheese.

Vegetable Sources of Fats or Oils

Frying oils; ground-nut, sunflower, cotton-seed, and maize oils.
Olive oil.
Nuts.
Margarine (which may contain animal fat).
Prepared nut fats.

All fats that are suitable as foods can be made into soap when heated with an alkali such as washing soda or caustic soda; the fatty acids combine with the alkali leaving the glycerol free. A similar saponification occurs in the digestion of fats and it is worth noting that mineral oils which do not form soap are useless as food.

MINERAL ELEMENTS

The body, in addition to protein and fat, contains many mineral substances which must therefore be present in food. These minerals have three main uses in the body; they form the main fabric of bones and teeth; they are contained in all body cells of which muscles, vital organs and blood corpuscles are made and they maintain the correct composition of all body fluids such as blood, lymph and perspiration.

The most important mineral elements are:

Calcium, magnesium and phosphorus for bones and teeth.
Iron, phosphorus, potassium and sulphur for body cells.
Sodium, chlorine, potassium for body fluids.

There are many other minerals needed in minute amounts for different special purposes; some of these are copper, fluorine, iodine.

A well-mixed diet, with hard water to drink, usually ensures a sufficient supply of most of these minerals. Some minerals, however, need special mention.

Iron, which is an essential ingredient of haemoglobin, the colouring matter of the red corpuscles of blood, is lost very slowly but continuously by the body in normal digestion and bowel action, and also more rapidly whenever bleeding occurs. Haemoglobin and therefore iron is responsible for carrying oxygen to every part of the body and, if enough iron is not included in food, anaemia will result.

Foods with a Good Proportion of Iron

Liver and kidney.
Beef, especially corned beef.
Eggs.
Mutton.
Pulses.
Dried fruits, e.g. raisins.
Bread, especially wholemeal.
Green vegetables, especially watercress.

Although many foods provide useful amounts of iron, in its organic form it is often not readily absorbed by human beings: drinking-water in some parts of the country, and iron and steel cooking vessels and knives, contribute small quantities in a mineral form which is readily absorbed.

Calcium and Phosphorous form the greater part of the structure of bones and teeth and are therefore most important in the diet; especially that of growing children and of expectant and nursing mothers. Calcium is also essential to the normal working of muscles and to the clotting of blood; phosphorous is necessary for the body to make proper use of the energy supplied by nutrients.

Some Foods supplying Calcium

Cheese and milk.
Bread (particularly white).
Fish, particularly herrings, and tinned fish of which the bones can be eaten.
Eggs.
Many vegetables, particularly watercress, cabbage, carrots and turnips.
Meat.
Potatoes.

Some Foods supplying Phosphorous

Cheese and milk.
Meat and fish.
Liver and kidney.
Eggs.
Bread (particularly white bread).
Many vegetables contain a little phosphorous.

When the above two lists are compared it will be noticed that several foods provide both calcium and phosphorous, most common foods containing more phosphorous than calcium. This is important as the human body needs an exact ratio of calcium to phosphorous; one part of calcium to one and a half of phosophorous for adults and slightly more calcium than phosphorous for growing children. Vitamin D in the diet helps to correct a wrong ratio.

Sodium, which, as sodium chloride or common salt, is present in all body fluids and is lost continuously in sweat and urine, is another extremely important mineral element. Fortunately it is present in almost all foods and is also added during cooking and at table so that it is unlikely that any diet will contain too little. It is interesting to note that in hot weather more salt is needed by the body as more is lost in sweat.

Potassium is used by the body in a similar way to sodium but is more important in muscle and blood cells than in the body fluids. It is lost in urine but not in sweat. It is essential in the diet but it occurs in so many foods that it is only likely to be lacking in a diet composed mainly of refined starch.

VITAMINS

It is only during this century that the importance of vitamins in the diet has been realized and that vitamins have been identified and analysed. Indirectly, however, it was known as early as Elizabeth I's reign that a lack of certain foods might cause disease, notably that seamen on long voyages suffered from scurvy when their supplies of fresh fruit and vegetables ran out and that they were cured surprisingly quickly once they reached land and could once more eat fresh fruit and greenstuff. Nowadays it is recognized that their diet on board ship lacked Vitamin C.

Gradually it was discovered that as well as the nutrients in food there were some unidentified substances which were essential to health and which were given the name 'Vitamins' from the Latin word meaning life: they were also called, at first, 'Accessory Food Factors'. The name Vitamins has been kept but knowledge of their composition and their value in dietary is now most detailed and exact: they have been identified as complex chemical substances and have mostly been given chemical names in addition to the letters by which they were originally known. Only minute amounts of all the different vitamins are needed to maintain health: reckoned in milligrams ($\frac{1}{1000}$ gram) or even micrograms ($\frac{1}{1,000,000}$ gram).

Vitamin A

Vitamin A is necessary to the growth of children, it makes eyes readily adaptable to light and protects from disease the skin and the moist surfaces of eyes, nose, throat and bronchial tubes. Vitamin A is fat-soluble and occurs mainly in certain animal fats, in the fatty part of some animal foods and in orange, red and dark green vegetables: it is not destroyed by normal cooking.

Animal Foods supplying Vitamin A	*Vegetable Foods supplying Vitamin A*
Cod and halibut liver oil.	Red and orange-coloured fruit and vegetables:
Liver.	
Butter and Margarine.	tomatoes,
Cheese.	carrots,
Egg.	oranges,
Oily fish, fresh, smoked or canned.	apricots
Kidney.	Dark green vegetables:
Most meats.	spinach,
Milk.	cabbage (outer leaves).
	watercress.

The animal and vegetable forms of Vitamin A differ in that the animal form is the real vitamin and the vegetable form is an orange-coloured substance called *carotene* which is converted to Vitamin A in the body during digestion. To obtain the same amount of Vitamin A the body needs three times as much carotene as of the animal form of the vitamin.

Vitamin D

Vitamin D is necessary for the formation of bones and teeth, and children who lack this vitamin in their diet suffer from rickets, a disease which causes malformation of bones. Vitamin D, calcium and phosphorous work together in the formation of bones and teeth and all of the three must be present if this work is to be well done.

Vitamin D is produced by the action of sunlight on certain animal substances, including human skin, so that in sunny climates less of the animal sources of the vitamin are needed in the diet. Vitamin D, like Vitamin A, is fat soluble, and is found mainly in the fatty parts of animal foods: it is not destroyed by normal cooking.

Foods supplying Vitamin D

Cod and halibut liver oil.
Oily fish.
Margarine (to which it must be added commercially).
Butter ⎫
Eggs ⎬ especially in these foodstuffs when they are produced in sunny
Milk ⎭   weather.

A substance in certain foods which is converted to Vitamin D by sunlight is called *ergosterol*. Ergosterol is irradiated by the ultra-violet light in sunlight and is then called *irradiated ergosterol* or *calciferol*. *Sterol* in human skin can also be irradiated by the ultra-violet rays in sunlight.

Vitamins E and K

Two other fat-soluble vitamins, E found in milk, wheat-germ and green vegetables and K found in many green vegetables, are usually in good supply in a reasonably mixed diet.

Vitamin B

Vitamin B, which is water soluble is really a group of at least eleven different substances which are not all found in the same foods. The B group of vitamins are destroyed by prolonged cooking, by drying and by alkalies such as washing-soda.

Three important parts of this group are:

Vitamin B_1 or thiamine.
Vitamin B_2 or riboflavine.
Nicotinic acid or niacine.

B_1, *thiamine*, has the power of releasing energy from carbohydrates and proteins. The need for B_1 is in direct proportion to the total energy provided by these nutrients. Insufficient Vitamin B_1 in the diet causes a check in the growth of children and depression and irritability in adults; a serious lack of this vitamin, very rare in Europe nowadays; causes a disease called *beri-beri*.

B_2, *riboflavine*, like Vitamin B_1 helps the body to make use of the energy supplied by carbohydrates.

Insufficient Vitamin B_2 in the diet causes a check in the growth of children, and, in old and young, cracks and soreness at the corners of the mouth, sore tongue and sometimes mistiness of the eyes.

Nicotinic acid is a third aid to the use by the body of the energy supplied by carbohydrates.

Insufficient nicotinic acid causes a check in the growth of children, and rough, redness of skin exposed to light, sore tongue, diarrhoea and in extreme cases the disease *pellagra*.

Some Foods supplying the B Group of Vitamins

B_1, *thiamine*	B_2, *riboflavine*	*Nicotinic acid*
Yeast	Yeast	Meat Extract
Bacon	Liver	Yeast
Oatmeal	Meat extract	Liver and Kidney
Wholemeal	Cheese	Beef
Green peas	Eggs	Bacon
Mutton	Beef	Wholemeal
White flour	Wholemeal	Fish
Potatoes	Milk	Potatoes
	Potatoes	

Many other foods have small amounts of one, two or all of these three vitamins.

Other parts of the B group also help in maintaining the health of the skin, in promoting the growth of children and in preventing anaemia.

Vitamin C, Ascorbic Acid

Vitamin C or ascorbic acid is water-soluble and is the vitamin most easily lost in the preparation of meals as it is destroyed by exposure to air; by solution in cooking-water and by any but very brief cooking. It is also the vitamin most often lacking in the diet as it occurs mainly in fruit and fresh vegetables which are often scarce and dear.

Insufficient Vitamin C causes a check in the growth of children, leaves gums and mouth unprotected against infection, retards the healing of wounds, causes undue tiredness and in extreme cases causes the disease *scurvy*.

Some Foods supplying Vitamin C

Blackcurrants.
Gooseberries and other summer fruits.
Oranges, lemons and grapefruit.
Brussels sprouts.
Cauliflower, cabbage, curly kale, sprouting broccoli, spinach.
Watercress.
New potatoes (the content gets steadily less as potatoes get older).
Lettuce, tomatoes.
Carrots, onions and turnips.

THE AMOUNT OF FOOD NEEDED

The total amount of food needed by the body in a day is in proportion to the amount of energy expended by the body. This energy is measured as units of heat called Calories (with a capital C); a Calorie being the amount of heat required to raise the temperature of 1,000 grams of water through 1 degree Centigrade.

The number of Calories expended by any individual each day, and therefore needed in the daily food, varies with size and surface-area, with the amount of muscular exertion, with age and sex and also with the climate.

The effect of size and build. Even when completely at rest the human body uses energy to keep the heart beating, the blood circulating, the lungs breathing and to maintain a normal temperature in spite of a constant loss of heat through the skin. This use of energy, which is called *basal metabolism*, is obviously greater in a large body than in a smaller one and the loss of heat, in particular, is greater from the surface of a large body or from a long thin one than from a small or a short, plump one.

The effect of muscular activity. In addition to basal metabolism energy is used by a healthy person, at a moderate rate, for such everyday activities as sitting, standing, dressing, eating and moving about and at a greatly increased rate for more strenuous exercise such as going up stairs, walking, running, doing light or heavy muscular work and playing active games.

The effect of age and sex. Growing children and young people, because they are increasing in size and weight and because they are usually more active than adults, use more energy in proportion to their weight, than do adults. Old people, being less active, use less energy than do adults in the prime of life. Women and girls usually expend less energy than do men and boys even doing similar work.

The effect of climate. As more heat is lost by the body in cold weather than in hot, so more energy is used up in replacing bodily heat in a cold climate.

Some Average Daily Calorie Requirements

A man weighing 10 stone: when asleep uses 65 to 70 Calories per hr.

when sitting up uses	100	,,	,, ,,
when taking light exercise uses	170	,,	,, ,,
when taking strenuous exercise uses	250 to 300	,,	,, ,,

during 24 hours he needs: for basal metabolism 1,700 Calories.

doing sedentary work 2,500 ,,

doing active work 3,500 ,,

doing heavy muscular work 3,700 to 4,000 Calories.

A woman weighing $8\frac{1}{2}$ to 9 stone needs $\frac{8}{10}$ to $\frac{9}{10}$ of the food needed by the man.

She needs during 24 hours: for basal metabolism 1,400 Calories.

doing sedentary work 2,100 ,,

doing active work 3,000 ,,

A boy of 15 years, if normally active

needs during 24 hours 3,150-4,000 Calories.

,,	,,	,,	18	,,	,,	,,	,,	,,	3,400-4,000	,,
,,	girl	,,	15	,,	,,	,,	,,	,,	2,750-4,000	,,
,,	,,	,,	18	,,	,,	,,	,,	,,	2,500-3,750	,,
,,	child	,,	12	,,	,,	,,	,,	,,	2,450	,,
,,	,,	,,	3	,,	,,	,,	,,	,,	1,300	,,

It is important to note that a boy and a girl in their late teens may need far more Calories than a man and a woman respectively, even if their activities are similar.

These figures are for comparison only as they are meaningless unless the fuel value of foods is also known.

The main nutrients when absorbed by the body provide energy as follows:

1 gramme *protein* yields 4 Calories or 1 oz. *protein* yields 116 Calories.
1 gramme *carbohydrate* yields 4 Calories or 1 oz. *carbohydrate* yields 116 Calories.
1 gramme *fat* yields 9 Calories or 1 oz. *fat* yields 263 Calories.

Foods mostly contain a mixture of nutrients together with water and some unusable waste material: the Calorie yield of a few representative foods are:

1 oz. *bread* contains about 2·5 gm. protein, 0·2 gm. fat, 15 gm. carbohydrate and yields 73 Calories.
1 oz. *lean beef* contains about 5 gm. protein, 4·5 gm. fat and yields 60 Calories.
1 oz. *Cheddar cheese* contains about 7 gm. protein, 10 gm. fat and yields 117 Calories.
1 oz. *butter* contains about 25·5 gm. fat and yields 211 Calories.
1 oz. *jam* contains about 17·5 gm. carbohydrate and yields 71 Calories.
1 oz. *potato* contains about 0·6 gm. protein, 4·6 gm. carbohydrate and yields 21 Calories.

It will be seen from these few figures that there are many ways of making up the necessary daily total of Calories; what is most important is that this total shall include a good proportion of body-building foods and of fats. One authority suggests that, of the total Calories, 14% for children and 11% for adults, should be derived from protein and that for all diets 25% should be derived from fats. In other words, in a diet yielding 2,500 Calories, for an adult, protein should supply $2,500 \times \frac{11}{100} = 275$ Calories and fat should supply $2,500 \times \frac{1}{4} = 625$ Calories which would mean a daily allowance of about 70 grammes of protein and of 69 grammes of fat. Remembering that at least half the protein should be from animal sources, the day's allowance of protein might be made up as follows:

4 oz. fish or 4 oz. lean meat, providing	17 gm.	
1 pint milk	,,	18 gm.
1 oz. cheese or 1 egg	,,	7 gm.

42 gm yielding 168 Calories

this total leaves 28 grammes of protein yielding 107 Calories to be taken from vegetable sources, for example:

8 oz. bread,	providing	20 gm.
1 ,, flour	,,	3·4 gm.
6 ,, potatoes	,,	3·6 ,,
¾ ,, plain biscuits	,,	2·0 ,,

29 gm. yielding 116 Calories.

It will, by now, be obvious that to compile a diet that contains the correct total of Calories and also the correct amount of all the nutrients for any particular case, calls for exact knowledge and elaborate calculations: while such calculations are necessary when diets are planned for large numbers of people, for example in schools or hospitals, they are not possible in domestic catering. A useful short cut to the planning of of a good mixed diet, sometimes called a 'balanced' diet, is:

1. Make sure of a good supply of building or protein foods.
2. Make sure that all the protective foods are included.
3. Let appetite decide how much of the energy foods are still required.

5

PROTEIN FOODS

MEAT

Meat is the name used for the flesh of animals and birds and for some of their internal organs or 'offal'. In Britain the chief sources of meat are:

Animals: The ox or bullock giving beef (occasionally the cow giving 'cowbeef').

,,	calf	giving	veal
,,	sheep	,,	mutton
,,	lamb	,,	lamb
,,	pig	,,	pork, and when salted and smoked, ham and bacon

        ,, rabbit (becoming scarce nowadays, but new methods of rearing rabbits like 'broiler' chickens may increase the supply).

Poultry: chicken, duck, goose and turkey.

Game: that is any animal or bird protected by game laws and shot for sport, including among many others partridge, pheasant and hare.

FOOD VALUE OF MEAT

Meat is a good and popular source of first-class protein; it is also rich in fat; it is a good source of two vitamins of the B group, riboflavine and nicotinic acid; it contains a little of another member of this group, thiamine, and a fair amount of iron (which is not all available) and phosphorus. Thiamine is, moreover, in good supply in pork and in moderately good supply in heart, while Vitamin A is richly supplied by liver and moderately by kidney. Meat is not a good source of calcium and, except for liver, is lacking in Vitamin C. Meat contains from 60 to 75% water and widely varying percentages of fat.

EXPERIMENTS WITH MEAT TO DISCOVER HOW COOKING AFFECTS ITS TENDERNESS AND FLAVOUR

Cut $\frac{1}{4}$ lb. stewing beef into four equal pieces; at the same time notice the size of each piece and examine the appearance of the meat. Label four small saucepans 1 to 4.

1. Put one piece of meat into $\frac{1}{4}$ pt. cold water.
2.   ,,   ,,   ,,   ,,   ,,   ,, $\frac{1}{4}$ pt. cold water and add $\frac{1}{2}$ teaspoonful lemon juice.
3.   ,,   ,,   ,,   ,,   ,,   ,, $\frac{1}{4}$ pt. fast-boiling water.
4.   ,,   ,,   ,,   ,,   ,,   ,,   1 level teaspoonful dripping heated to haze point, and fry the meat on all sides very quickly, then add $\frac{1}{4}$ pint boiling water.

Now bring 1 and 2 very slowly to simmering point, being most careful not to let them boil; put lids on all four pans and keep them all simmering very gently for $1\frac{1}{2}$ hours at least: this may be done most easily in a slow oven. Notice carefully every change that occurs up to the time when the lids are put on. After $1\frac{1}{2}$ hours, turn the contents of each pan into a separate glass basin. Notice the colour of the meat and of the liquids; test the meat for tenderness; notice if it is still the same size, and taste meat and gravy in each sample. (The flavour of gravies will be dilute as in such small amounts the proportion of water is high.)

Results

Examination of the raw meat will have shown that it is bright red in colour; possibly 'marbled' with a very little fat; that it is fibrous or 'stringy' and very likely has some thin skin or gristle amongst the fibres.

The results of cooking will have shown a change in colour of the meat from red to greyish-brown and of the water to a pale brown with flakes of brownish curd. The four samples will probably show little variation in the colour of the liquids.

The piece of meat that was first fried will have a brown colour on the outside (it probably smelt most savoury during the frying) and its flavour may be better than that of the other three, but both this piece and the one put into boiling water will have shrunk more and will be found to be tougher than the two put into cold water. The most tender of the four will be the piece cooked with acid. These results serve to show the complex nature of meat and the problems it presents to the cook.

THE STRUCTURE OF MEAT

Lean meat is the muscle of the animal and is made up of many little bundles of very fine fibres. The bundles can be seen with the naked eye but a microscope is needed to see the fibres (Fig. 20). The fibres are really tiny tubes filled with water containing, in solution, *extractives*, which give the meat flavour, *mineral salts* and the *proteins*, albumin, globulin and myosin. A white, transparent connective tissue called *collagen* ties the fibres into bundles, ties the bundles together to form the muscle and wraps the muscle in a thin sheath which thickens at the tapering end of the muscle to tie it to the bone. The walls of the little tubular fibres are made of a second kind of connective tissue called *elastin* which may also be seen in other parts of the animal as yellow tendons.

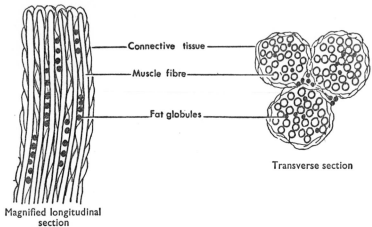

Connective tissue

Muscle fibre

Fat globules

Transverse section

Magnified longitudinal
section

Fig. 20. STRUCTURE OF MEAT-MUSCLE BUNDLES

A certain amount of fat is packed as little globules amongst the fibres, the amount varying in different kinds of meat, there being very little in the flesh of chicken, veal and rabbit, more in beef and mutton and a great deal in pork.

TENDERNESS

The length and thickness of the fibres and the amount of connective tissue determine the tenderness or toughness of meat. The flesh of an old animal is tough and so is any muscle that has been worked very hard because, in both cases, the fibres are long and thick and there is a large amount of connective tissue: conversely the flesh of a young animal or a little-used muscle is tender because the fibres are short and fine and there is less connective tissue. For example, shin of beef is always tough, but loin from the same ox may be very tender, and breast of chicken is very tender but a leg of the same bird may be tough.

Toughness is reduced in all meat by hanging, or conditioning it, after slaughter. When an animal is first killed the myosin (a soluble protein) clots and becomes insoluble; this causes stiffening of the flesh known as 'rigor mortis' and at this stage the meat is very tough. After a few days the rigor passes off because lactic acid is produced in the fibres and this, together with enzymes in the meat, softens the meat and not only makes it tender but also improves its flavour.

FLAVOUR

Mineral salts and extractives give meat its characteristic flavour and the lactic acid, produced not only after death but also in hard-worked muscles, further improves the flavour. The flavour of meat from a mature animal is better than that from a young one and, as might be expected, a well-fed animal produces meat with a finer flavour than does a poorly fed one. A certain amount of fat, both on the outside of the cut and dispersed amongst the fibres further improves the flavour of meat and in addition helps to keep it from drying during cooking.

COOKING MEAT

Meat is cooked to make it appetizing, to destroy bacteria, and always in the hope of making it tender. During cooking several changes take place in meat.

The fat melts when it is heated and, in roasting or grilling, it is useful in preventing the meat from becoming dry in the strong radiant heat: in boiling, it floats to the top of the fluid and is usually skimmed off: in stewing, lean meat is used and the little fat is easily incorporated in the gravy. The soluble proteins coagulate at the comparatively low temperatures of 145° to 150° F. and the meat therefore becomes firmer. At the same temperatures the elastin of the muscle fibres contracts, squeezing juices out of the meat, making it still firmer and causing a certain amount of shrinkage. In the dry heat of an oven, or under a grill, or in hot fat during frying, this shrinkage is rapid, but as the juices are squeezed out they form a most savoury, brown sticky coating on the surface of the meat. This sticky, brown compound of extractives, mineral salts and fat gives added flavour to the meat and accounts for the popularity of roast, grilled and fried meat. Any juices that later run out of the meat are used in gravy and served with the meat. Meat overcooked by dry heat becomes dry and hard as the proteins are 'denatured'.

When meat is cooked in water, as in stewing and boiling, the shrinkage is a little less than in dry cooking and any escaping juices flow into the water and are either served as part of the stew or in a sauce or soup in the case of boiled meat. Modern research has shown that if meat is put into cold water and brought slowly to simmering point not only is there less shrinkage and no greater loss of juices into the water than if boiling water were used, but the meat will also be more tender. When simmered in water the connective tissue, collagen, is gradually changed to gelatin which dissolves and allows the fibres to fall apart making the meat tender. The conversion of collagen to gelatin is more rapid when acid is added to the water.

To make Meat Tender

The surest way to make meat tender is to cook it by a method suited to its quality and to carry out the cooking carefully. Dry methods of cooking, baking, frying and grilling are suitable only for the best quality, tender meat: for tough meat the moist methods of cooking, stewing, boiling and braising must be used.

Meat, however, is not always as tender as it should be and there are several ways of treating it before cooking to increasing tenderness:

1. Beating the meat with a rolling-pin or a steak-hammer to crush the fibres and so reduce the stringiness.
2. Painting the meat with lemon juice or vinegar before cooking, or adding these acids or tomatoes to the cooking liquid. By both these methods the acid converts some of the connective tissue, collagen, to gelatin.
3. Painting or rubbing the surface of the meat with an extract of the fruit, leaves or sap of the papaw, a South American fruit rather like a melon. This extract contains an enzyme, 'papain', which acts in the same way as certain enzymes of the human digestive tract, partially digesting the meat and so softening even the elastin of the muscle fibres. This extract can be bought in liquid or granular form.

Methods of Cooking Meat

Roasting or Baking is suitable for prime or second-quality cuts of meat weighing at least 1½ lb. and having a fair proportion of fat. Strictly speaking, roasting is cooking by rotating the meat in front of a fierce source of glowing heat—a method which is again popular now that mechanically-operated spits are fitted to some gas and electric cookers. Modern 'roasting' is, however, usually baking. There are several methods of roasting meat which vary the temperature at which cooking is begun and continued:

By the *searing method* a high temperature at the beginning of cooking changes the extractives to the highly savoury, brown, sticky substance known as osmazome and also gives a crisp brown finish to outside fat, but, at the same time, the sudden, strong heat shrinks the meat considerably and does not make it tender. *Roasting at a low temperature* for the whole time of cooking makes the meat tender but does not develop the flavour and results in a high loss of juice. *For maximum tenderness* the meat should be heated gradually so that the inevitable shrinkage occurs slowly and the meat is not toughened: this is done either by beginning the roasting in a cold oven or by slow roasting throughout. *For maximum flavour* the meat may be seared in strong heat at the beginning of cooking but this is only suitable for very tender meat.

For a good flavour combined with tenderness the meat should be put into a cold oven, set at the moderately high temperature of 400° F., and cooked for the whole time at this temperature, except for large joints for which the heat is reduced after one and a half hours. *For accuracy in estimating* the correct time for roasting, a *meat thermometer* may be inserted in the meat which is put into a cold oven set at 400° F., cooking then continues until the thermometer registers an inside temperature suitable for the kind of meat—from 140° to 180° F.

Adding dripping to the meat before roasting is only necessary for a very lean cut: a good roasting joint should have enough fat to prevent it becoming dry. Basting is also, nowadays, considered unnecessary for the same reason, and both the addition of dripping and basting are both deplored by the manufacturers of electric cookers because the dripping inevitably gets overheated and smells unpleasant with the minimum ventilation of the oven and opening the door at intervals in order to baste the meat causes too much heat to be lost.

During baking the meat may be covered with the lid of a double roasting tin or with aluminium foil: this may result in the loss of more juice into the tin, but it keeps the oven clean: 20 minutes must be added to the cooking time.

Boiling is suitable for second-quality cuts of meat weighing at least 1 lb., for tough fowls, some cuts of bacon and for ham. Beef and pork are usually salted by the butcher if they are to be boiled. The meat should be put into cold water (only just enough to cover it), brought slowly to simmering-point, and simmered gently for a length of time calculated on the weight of the meat. Actual boiling, or putting the meat at first into boiling water, causes undue shrinkage and loss of extractives into the water, and also toughens the meat. Fat may be skimmed off the liquid at the end of cooking, but no brown scum should be removed as this contains the extractives. The liquid should always be saved for soup or gravy.

Frying is only suitable for really tender meat, which should not be much over 1 inch thick. It is put into dripping at hazing-heat, browned rapidly on each side and then cooked slowly until done, the length of time depending on the thickness of the cut. This quick, short cooking produces a very good flavour but does nothing to make meat tender.

Grilling, like frying, is suitable only for really tender meat of not over 1 inch in thickness: it is turned rapidly under a red-hot grill, is usually extremely savoury but is not made more tender by this method.

Stewing is the most suitable method of cooking any tough meat: there are two types of stew:

1. *Cold-water Stew.* The meat, which may be beef, mutton, veal or rabbit, is cut in convenient pieces, covered with not more than $\frac{1}{2}$ pint water to each pound, brought very slowly to simmering-point and simmered for from $1\frac{1}{2}$ hours for moderately tough meat to $3\frac{1}{2}$ hours for the very tough cuts. This is most conveniently done in a slow oven. The flavour of the gravy is very good by this method and can still further be improved by the vegetables and herbs that are usually added; the meat itself is moreover made tender by the gradual heating and long cooking in water.

2. *Brown or Fried Stew.* This method is not suitable for very tough meat but may be used for the better stewing-cuts. The meat is first fried in hazing-hot fat for a few seconds on each side until it is brown, and then cooked in the prescribed amount of water. The flavour of the meat itself is improved by this method, but the fibres are inevitably shrunk and toughened and unless the meat is reasonably tender to begin with no amount of moist cooking later will make it really soft.

Soup-making

Soups contain very little of the food value of meat unless pieces of meat are served in them.

Bone-broth or Bone-stock is made by simmering chopped bones in water for several hours: the resulting liquid forms a jelly when cold. This jelly, which used to be considered highly nourishing, in fact contains only a small percentage of gelatin and a negligible amount of calcium. Its chief value is that it draws this small amount of gelatin, together with a little flavour, from scraps of meat and bones which would otherwise be thrown away. If stock or broth is made with raw meat it will have a good flavour derived from the extractives of the meat, but the value of the liquid will be no greater than that of bone-broth as, though extractives stimulate appetite and digestion, they have no food value. Only the solid meat, if served in the broth, will contain protein.

Internal Organs

The internal organs most used as food are the following:

Liver and Kidney. These contain no muscle fibre and no connective tissue but are cellular in structure and are easily made dry and solid by cooking. They are best lightly fried or grilled or gently stewed and should not be overcooked.

Heart, being muscular, is very like lean meat though rather dense in structure. It is best cooked by stewing or pot roasting.

Tongue is very like heart in structure but is not so dense and has a higher proportion of fat. Ox tongue is often salted and is boiled: sheep's tongues are stewed or boiled.

Tripe is the lining of the three stomachs of the ox; when sold it has been thoroughly cleaned and partially cooked by the tripe-dresser or butcher. It has a large proportion of collagen and little flavour: it is therefore best cooked by stewing with well-flavoured additions such as onion. It is a good source of calcium.

Sweetbreads are of two kinds—'stomach' which is the pancreas (a digestive organ) and 'throat' which is the thymus gland. They are cellular tissue, are very easily digested and are valuable in the diet of convalescents. They are best stewed.

Brains contain a high proportion of fatty substance and little protein; they are not very valuable as food. They are best served as sauce with the cooked head, or they may be coated and fried or poached and served on toast.

Blood has little food value as it is over 80% water and most of the iron which it contains is not absorbed. It is used in black puddings.

COST OF MEAT

Meat is an expensive source of first-class protein and the more tender the cut the more costly it is. Cheaper cuts of meat may not always be very tough but may contain a high proportion of waste; for example, breast and shoulder of mutton are not expensive, but they may have a very large amount of fat and bone, while shin of beef, which is cheap because it is tough, has very little waste.

Rules for Buying Meat

1. Choose a cut of meat that is suitable for the method by which it is to be cooked, or suit the method to the quality.

2. Even if expensive meat can be afforded, it is unfair to the butcher to expect prime cuts every time—there is a larger proportion of second quality cuts on every animal.

3. A good butcher does not sell meat that is not fresh, but to make certain:

> Notice the colour—deep red for beef, pinkish-red for mutton, pale pink for pork and pinkish-beige for veal, and with no dark or discoloured patches.
> Notice that the fat is firm and not oily.
> Notice that there is not much juice running from the meat.
> Notice that it smells fresh—an unpleasant smell is always an indication of stale meat that will taste unpleasant even though it may be safe to eat.

4. Unless it can be stored in a refrigerator, buy meat only one day at most before it is to be cooked. The butcher's store is the best place for the meat to hang till it is tender.

5. Remember to ask the butcher to chop bones or to divide chops or cutlets for you, as his knives are sharper and his skill greater than yours. He will usually also bone joints if asked at a suitable time.

KEEPING MEAT

Raw meat may contain, along with many harmless bacteria, some stray micro-organisms that could cause disease. In addition, during handling and cutting up it may acquire other bacteria; as it is also a good medium for the growth of bacteria it must be cooked while it is in a fresh condition. It must not be stored at home for more than two days even in cold weather or not more than three days in a refrigerator. During storage air must be allowed to circulate all round the meat (see chapter on Food Hygiene).

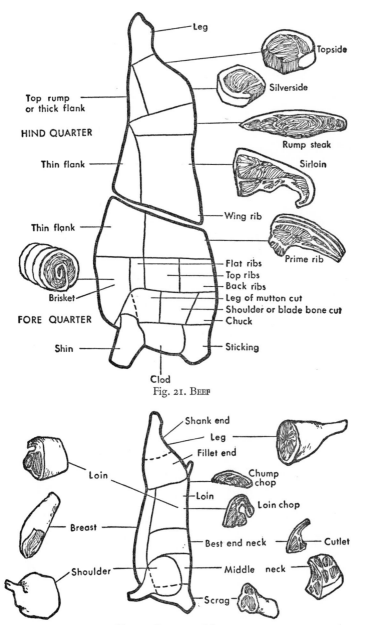

Leg

Topside

Silverside

Top rump or thick flank

HIND QUARTER

Rump steak

Thin flank

Sirloin

Wing rib

Thin flank

Prime rib

Brisket

Flat ribs
Top ribs
Back ribs
Leg of mutton cut
Shoulder or blade bone cut
Chuck

FORE QUARTER

Shin

Sticking

Clod

Fig. 21. BEEF

Shank end
Leg
Fillet end

Loin

Chump chop

Loin

Loin chop

Breast

Best end neck

Cutlet

Shoulder

Middle neck

Scrag

FIG. 22. LAMB AND MUTTON

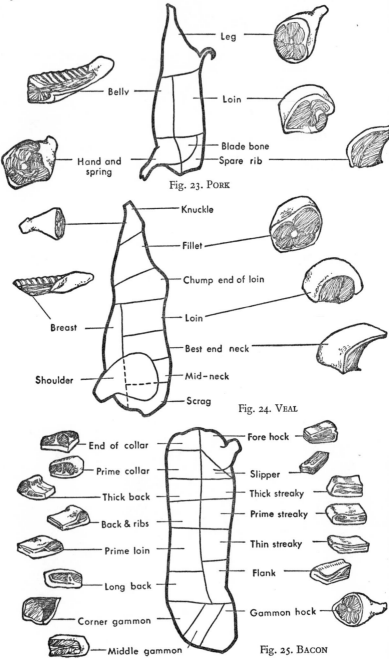

Leg
Belly
Loin
Blade bone
Spare rib
Hand and spring

Fig. 23. PORK

Knuckle
Fillet
Chump end of loin
Loin
Best end neck
Breast
Shoulder
Mid-neck
Scrag

Fig. 24. VEAL

End of collar
Prime collar
Thick back
Back & ribs
Prime loin
Long back
Corner gammon
Middle gammon

Fore hock
Slipper
Thick streaky
Prime streaky
Thin streaky
Flank
Gammon hock

Fig. 25. BACON

Table to show Suitable Methods of Cooking Different Cuts of Meat

Method	Beef	Mutton, Lamb and Veal	Pork	Bacon
Baking or 'Roasting'	Sirloin Wing rib Prime or Fore ribs Topside Middle ribs Top rump Brisket	Loin Shoulder Best end neck Leg Breast (boned, stuffed) Saddle, i.e. 2 loins undivided	Loin (any part) Leg Blade Hand	Hock or gammon if first wrapped in a flour and water 'pastry'
Pot Roast	Heart and small joints	Heart and small joints		
Boiling	Salted: Silverside Top Rump Brisket Flank Tongue (salt or fresh)	Leg Middle neck	Salted: Leg Hand Belly Head (salt or fresh) Tongue (salt or fresh)	Hock Gammon Long loin Collar Streaky
Frying	Fillet steak Rump steak	Cutlets (from best end neck) Chops: loin— from best end loin or chump from chump end loin Liver Kidney	Loin chops Spare rib chops Fillet Kidney Liver 'Pigs Fry' Sausages	Back rashers Loin „ Gammon „ Streaky „ Collar „
Grilling	Fillet steak Rump steak Sirloin steak or 'Porterhouse' steak	Chops Cutlets Liver Kidney	Loin chops Spare rib chop Kidney Liver Sausages	Gammon rashers Any bacon rashers
Braising	Topside Top rump Brisket Flank	Loin Neck Breast	Not usual but no known reason why this method should not be used	
Stewing	Buttock steak Top rump Flank Chuck steak Skirt Clod and sticking Oxtail Leg and shin Liver Kidney Heart	Mid-neck Scrag neck Breast Tongue Liver Kidney (Best end neck for very special stewed dishes)	Not usually stewed except in Chinese cookery Pickled, streaky pork may be added to stewed rabbit	Added to stewed rabbit or veal it adds flavour; usually streaky

GELATINE

Gelatine, which is the setting agent in most jellies other than preserves, is derived from the connective tissue, collagen, by boiling or stewing. It is prepared commercially from bones and the skins and hooves of young animals. The grease and other impurities are removed and the resulting gelatine solution is concentrated and dried. It is sold nowadays as powdered gelatine or in a less concentrated form as 'packet jellies' to which synthetic colouring and flavouring are added.

NUTRITIVE VALUE OF GELATINE

Gelatine, although from an animal source, is a protein food in a limited sense. It contains only two of the ten essential amino-acids with slight traces of others. Its value as a food is still further reduced because very little of it is eaten, $\frac{1}{4}$ oz. to $\frac{3}{4}$ oz. being sufficient to set a pint of jelly, providing three to four helpings.

USES OF GELATINE

In cooking, gelatine provides a pleasant way of serving other foods such as fruit juice or milk and gives an attractive texture to many cold dishes.

Isinglass, the gelatin derived from fish, is little used nowadays except for the clearing of wines.

RULES FOR USING GELATINE

1. Use the envelopes of gelatine provided by some makers or measure it: 4 level B.S.I. teaspoons to $\frac{1}{2}$ oz.
2. Add gelatine to cold or warm, not boiling, water or fruit juice and stir it while heating it. Use a bright metal spoon so that undissolved granules can be seen.
3. Never boil a gelatine solution as this makes it too concentrated and gives it the taste of glue, and may reduce its setting power.
4. If gelatine is to thicken a milky mixture it must be dissolved in $\frac{1}{4}$ pint of warm water to each 1 oz. and this solution must be added at once, while hot, to the rest of the ingredients. If it is allowed to cool first it forms 'ropes' in the mixture which it does not set.

5. Solution is easy, if the liquid is put into a small basin standing in a pan of boiling water and the gelatine measured into the basin and at once stirred.

6. A gelatine mixture should be poured into its mould when cold and beginning to thicken.

7. Allow an hour in a cold part of a refrigerator or up to 12 hours in a cool larder to set a jelly.

FISH

Fish is a name used to include sea fish, freshwater fish and shellfish. *Sea fish* can be classified according to their way of life; as '*demersal*' if they live at the bottom of the sea, or as '*pelagic*' if they swim freely near the surface. Demersal fish are caught in nets dragged along the sea bed by boats known as *trawlers*, and pelagic fish, which usually swim in shoals, are caught in nets hung vertically from the surface of the sea by boats known as *drifters*. *Shellfish* are of two main kinds; *crustacea* which have legs and a partially jointed shell and include crabs, crayfish, lobsters, prawns and shrimps; and *molluscs* which have a hard outer shell and no legs; these may be *bivalves*, which have a shell in two hinged parts such as oysters, mussels and scallops, or they may have a *shell like a snail*, such as cockles and winkles. Shellfish have no backbone.

Freshwater fish are mostly caught for sport, and, with the exception of eels, salmon and trout, do not often appear in fish shops. It is interesting that eels, sea-trout and salmon spend part of their lives in fresh water and part in the sea.

FOOD VALUE OF FISH

Fish is a valuable and popular source of first-class protein and although, on the whole, it contains rather less protein than meat, it is also a useful source of calcium, phosphorus and nicotinic acid; while sea fish, in addition, has traces of iodine, which prevents goitre, and fluorine which preserves teeth. Certain fish also contain some fat and these provide Vitamin A and are the most important source of Vitamin D of any natural food.

KINDS OF FISH

According to their food value fish are classified as:

Fat or oily fish	*Lean or white fish*	*Fish containing a little fat*
	Round Fish	*Round Fish*
Eel	Cod	Gurnet
Herring and	Haddock	Hake
Bloater	Ling	Mullet
Kipper	Pollack	Rock-fish or Cat-fish
and Red herring	Saithe or Coley	or Dogfish
Mackerel	Whiting	Trout
Pilchard		
Salmon	*Flat Fish*	*Flat Fish*
Sardines	Dab	Bream
Sprats	Dover Sole	Brill
Whitebait, i.e. young	Flounder	Halibut
herrings	John Dory	
	Lemon Sole	
	Megrim	
	Plaice	
	Skate	
	Turbot	
	Witch	

Shellfish as a group contain little fat.

Fish roes provide protein, fat, Vitamin A, nicotinic acid and ribo-flavine.

Smoked fish. To preserve it some fish is salted and smoked.

The fish most usually smoked are haddock, herring, eels, cod's roe, sprats and, in the luxury class, trout and salmon.

Smoked, or 'finnan' haddock (after the Scottish fishing village where it was first smoked) is smoked whole or in fillets.

Herring, when split, salted and smoked for one day become *kippers*, salted whole and smoked for one day, *bloaters*, and when more strongly salted and smoked for several days, *red herring*.

The food value of smoked fish is more concentrated than that of fresh fish as it loses moisture in the curing.

Canned fish. The fish most usually canned are salmon, sardines, herrings and pilchards and as all these are oily fish they are good sources of Vitamins D and A; their protein content is a little higher than that of fresh fish as water is lost in cooking before canning. In addition they contain a little fat: if the juices are all used they provide a useful amount

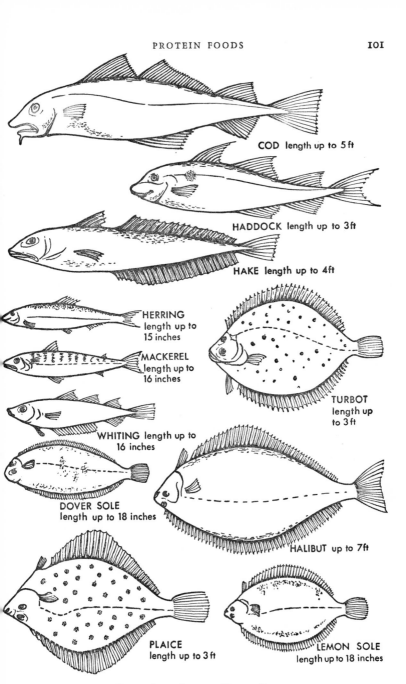

Fig. 26. SOME COMMON BRITISH FISH

of nicotinic acid and if the bones are eaten they are a good source of calcium.

Frozen fish. Modern quick-freezing of fish is usually carried out at − 5° F. immediately after it leaves the nets. Fish so treated is perfectly cleaned, filleted and often in better condition than fresh fish that has had a long journey from the coast.

STRUCTURE OF FISH

The flesh of fish, like meat, is composed of muscle fibres which vary in length and thickness in different fish, being long and coarse in lobster; fairly long and coarse in cod; very fine and short in herring and whiting. On the whole the fibres in fish are shorter and finer than those of meat and moreover are packed together in flakes with little connective tissue. Any connective tissue occurs only between the flakes and the fat is dispersed among the fibres.

FLAVOUR

The characteristic flavour of fish is due, as in meat, to mineral salts and extractives, but the extractives in fish are not as rich in flavour, even after cooking, as are those of meat. The flavour of fish deteriorates quickly and for this reason fish must be eaten fresh. To this end, deep-sea fish is usually cleaned and frozen on board ship so that it keeps fresh during the return to port.

COOKING FISH

Effects

Fish behaves like meat during cooking, that is, the liquid proteins coagulate at temperatures of from 140° to 160° F. and at 160° F. the juices begin to be squeezed out. Fish has such a small amount of connective tissue that it never needs long, moist cooking and in fact most fish can be cooked in a very short time. If overcooked, the flakes fall apart, the juices run out and the fibres become dry and tough.

Methods

The aims in cooking fish are to conserve and to add to its natural flavour; to prevent the flakes from falling apart, and, in the case of white fish, to add extra fat either during cooking or in a sauce.

Frying is a most popular method of cooking fish and one that fulfils the aims set out above. The fish is coated with egg and crumbs or batter and fried in shallow or deep fat: the coating keeps in the juice of the fish and itself becomes crisp and savoury during cooking Some fat is inevitably absorbed by the coating. Filleted flat fish may be coated with dry flour and herring with oatmeal before frying in shallow fat.

Grilling is another method of cooking to conserve the flavour of fish. It is suitable for whole flat fish, herrings or mackerel and cutlets not more than 1 inch thick. The flesh of whole fish is scored with a sharp knife, the outer surfaces are painted with liquid fat and dredged lightly with flour. The grill should be moderately hot and the fish turned only once to keep it from breaking.

Baking. An alternative to frying, and one that is just as savoury, is baking coated fish in hot fat: this may have extra flavours added in a savoury stuffing.

Moist Methods of Cooking. Fish should not be boiled, as much flavour is lost and the flakes easily separate. The only exceptions are herrings and mackerel, which, if boiled in strongly salted water when very fresh, are delicious and do not lose flavour if the salt solution is really strong.

Poaching. To poach fish it is cooked in very little liquid to which salt, lemon juice or vinegar, onion and herbs may be added for flavour. The liquid is allowed to simmer gently and is from time to time basted over the fish. The cooking may be done in a slow oven and the liquid may be used in a sauce.

Steaming. A perforated steamer is not suitable unless the fish is wrapped in aluminium foil or parchment, as juices are lost into the water below. To steam fish it is put on a greased plate, covered, and cooked over boiling water.

Fish Stock. The skin, heads and bones of filleted fish may be simmered, after washing, to give a well-flavoured liquid with which to make a sauce. Only enough liquid for immediate use should be added as fish stock does not keep its flavour and the stock should be cooked for 20 minutes only or it becomes bitter.

THE COST OF FISH

Prices of fish vary widely for several reasons. The size of the catch (which is largely affected by the weather in the fishing grounds) varies and a glut of fish lowers the price while a poor catch raises it.

Fish of particularly good flavour and texture, such as salmon, halibut, turbot and Dover sole, are always expensive, and saithe, whiting and (because of its less attractive appearance) rock-fish are comparatively cheap. The real value of fish will also depend on the amount of inedible waste in head, bones, fins and internal organs; for example, whiting has a high proportion of waste and therefore even if it is inexpensive it may not be any better value than more expensive filleted cod in which there is no waste.

The best value of any fish is usually the herring because, although it has a fair amount of waste, the price is low and the food value very high.

Rules for buying Fish

Buy fish on the day that it is to be cooked: if this is not possible, frozen or smoked fish are both a good choice.

To make sure that fish is fresh notice:

1. That the smell is not unpleasant.
2. That the eyes of whole fish are bright, moist and not sunken.
3. That the scales of whole fish are plentiful, shining and moist.
4. That the flesh is firm and moist.

EGGS

The term 'eggs' is used for eggs of the domestic fowl: the eggs of ducks and geese, of which comparatively few are eaten, are always named as such. Eggs are probably the most useful of all foodstuffs in cookery, as not only are they popular cooked as themselves in various ways, but they also have many important uses, such as making sponge cakes and batters light, thickening custards and increasing the food value of any dish to which they are added.

FOOD VALUE OF EGGS

As an egg is intended as the food for the embryo chick until it is ready to leave its shell, it is easy to realize that it must contain all the nutrients necessary to build bone and muscle and to supply the baby chick with energy. The egg consists of the shell, made of inedible calcium carbonate and lined with a tough white membrane; the white which is thin near the shell and thicker round the yolk; and the yolk which is enclosed in a thin membrane, and suspended in the white by means of string-like membranes called *chalazae* (Fig. 27).

The yolk contains two *proteins*, vitellin and livetin, containing all the essential amino-acids and therefore making egg yolk the most valuable of all protein foods; a high proportion of *fat* in a finely emulsified and easily digested form and Vitamins A, D, B_1 (thiamine), B_2 (riboflavine), a little nicotinic acid and the *minerals* iron, calcium and phosphorus. *The white* contains a complex *protein* called albumin, a little riboflavine, some *minerals*, which include sulphur, and a high proportion of water. Neither yolk nor white contains carbohydrate.

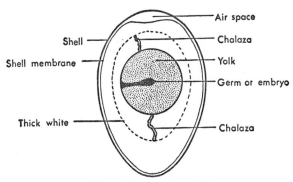

Fig. 27. DIAGRAM OF AN EGG

APPROXIMATE COMPOSITION OF EGG

	Yolk	White	*Whole egg without shell*
Protein	16%	13%	15%
Fat	32%	0·25%	10%
Minerals	1%	0·75%	1%
Water	51%	86%	74%

One egg, weighing two ounces, is roughly equivalent in protein and fat to the same weight of fairly fat meat and yields 90 Calories.

EXPERIMENTS WITH EGGS

Tests for Freshness

1. Dissolve 2 level tablespoonfuls of salt in a pint of water in a jam-jar or jug and into it lower an egg; notice whether it sinks and lies on its side, stands on end, or floats.
2. Break the egg carefully on to a saucer and notice every detail of its appearance including the inside of the shell.

3. Pour the white into a basin by holding an egg-cup or half eggshell over the yolk. Now beat the white till just liquid and divide it into two equal amounts—each in a basin.

4. Beat one half egg-white vigorously with an egg-whisk or rotary beater, notice any changes until nothing further happens, and from time to time try if it is possible to hold the basin upside down without losing any of the white.

5. Repeat 4 with half the yolk.

To find the Effect of Heat on Eggs

(For these three experiments test tubes and a Fahrenheit dairy thermometer are useful.)

6. Into a test tube put a teaspoonful of unwhisked egg white, stand the test tube on a thick pad of paper in a saucepan with an inch depth of cold water: hold the thermometer in the white and heat the water slowly. Note any changes and the temperatures at which they occur.

7. Repeat 6 with egg yolk. If no thermometer is available, stand both test tubes in the water and compare the rate of change in yolk and white and notice how much of these changes takes place before the water boils.

8. Mix the remaining yolk and unwhisked white with 2 tablespoonfuls of milk, pour the mixture into a small basin, stand this in the pan of water and with the thermometer in the egg-milk liquid, heat the water slowly. Note the temperature at which the little custard is just firm to the touch, then continue heating, allowing the water to boil for ten minutes and notice any further changes.

Results of Experiments

Tests for Freshness

1. If the egg lay on its side in the salt water it was really fresh, if it stood on end it was not very fresh, but if it floated it was very stale: this is because the shell, being porous, allows water to evaporate from the white, and air to enter between the shell and the lining membrane to form an air-pocket which acts as a float at the rounded end of the shell.

2. If the egg broken on to a saucer was fresh the yolk would stand up as a well-rounded dome, the white would be thick round the yolk

with only a narrow border of thin white outside this and the pocket of air in the blunt end of the shell would be very small. As the egg becomes stale, the membrane round the yolk gets weaker and the yolk will be flattened and will moreover be difficult to separate from the white without breaking: more of the white will be of the thinner consistency and in extreme staleness the egg will have an unpleasant smell.

The little white 'strings' or *chalazae* do not indicate freshness, but they are most important in keeping an egg fresh as they suspend the yolk in the centre of the egg where it is surrounded by the white if the egg is stored correctly with the rounded end uppermost. If the egg is stored on its side the *chalazae* get stretched and the yolk rests on the shell where air can reach it and cause it to decompose rapidly.

3. As was noted above, if the egg is fresh the yolk can be separated from the white without breaking.

4 and 5. The white of a reasonably fresh egg can be whisked to a very stiff, white foam because it can enclose a large amount of air as minute bubbles; this foam slowly liquefies when left to stand and cannot be re-whisked because, during whisking the egg cells are ruptured and therefore the liquefied, beaten egg-white is physically different from unbeaten white. The yolk of egg became paler in colour and a little thicker when whisked but would not form a foam.

Effects of Heat on Eggs

6 and 7. The white and yolk both coagulate on heating well below boiling-point of water, in fact at about about 150° Fahrenheit for white and 158° to 160° Fahrenheit for yolk. Above these temperatures both yolk and white became increasingly tough.

8. The little egg custard will set to a jelly-like consistency at a temperature below the boiling-point of water but higher than that needed to set the yolk by itself, about 170° F. This higher temperature of coagulation is due to the protection from heat afforded by the milk.

When the custard was heated beyond setting-point it developed many small holes and became rather tough because, although when it coagulates egg can hold the milk in a jelly-like 'set', as it is further toughened by heat it shrinks slightly, squeezing out the watery part of the milk and holding only the solids. In this state a custard is said to be 'curdled', but this must not be confused with the curdling of sour milk.

COOKING EGGS

The experiments showed two important properties of eggs, their *coagulation at low cooking temperatures* and their *ability to hold air*, which is slight in the case of yolk but considerable in the white.

The fact that egg proteins coagulate well below boiling-point is important when they are *cooked by themselves;* for boiling and poaching them the water should only simmer; for frying and scrambling them the fat should be just hot, not smoking, and in each case the egg is completely cooked in a few minutes.

Hard-boiled Eggs. A greenish-black film is often seen on the yolk of a hard-boiled egg due to hydrogen sulphide given off during boiling and combined with iron in the yolk to produce iron sulphide. To avoid this unsightly coloration the egg must not be overcooked, but put into boiling water, simmered steadily for 10 minutes and at once cooled in cold water. A fresh egg is less likely to produce the black film than a stale one.

The coagulation of egg is made use of in *thickening many liquid and semi-liquid foods* such as 'boiled', baked and steamed custards, milk puddings, some jellies, sauces and soups. In these dishes, except for baked and steamed custard, thickening is easier if the yolk alone is used as the white, coagulating at a lower temperature, tends to be overcooked before the yolk is completely thickened. Before adding egg to a dish any other ingredients, such as cereal in a milk pudding, should be completely cooked, the mixture should be cooled to well below boiling-point and the cooking of the egg must be done without allowing it to boil.

This thickening power of eggs is also used *to bind together* the loose particles of cooked food in such things as croquettes and fish cakes; in *coating food* before frying to give it a crisp, protective crust which keeps out the fat and keeps in the moisture; and in setting batters and cake mixtures.

In cake-making the ability of eggs to hold air is of the greatest importance: in *creamed mixtures* the egg is beaten into the creamed fat and sugar and if done thoroughly this adds to the lightness of the finished cake. In *whisked mixtures* the eggs are whisked with half their weight of sugar and so much air can be whisked into them that no other raising agent is needed. The especial power of holding air which egg whites possess is made use of in hot and cold soufflés, meringues and macaroons and many cold sweets set with gelatine. When whisking egg-whites the greatest volume of foam is produced at about 70° Fahrenheit, that is in egg-whites that have been in a warmish kitchen for at least an hour.

Eggs have still another useful property not shown in the experiments: the *yolk can hold fat in emulsion;* that is in tiny globules suspended in the semi-liquid yolk. This property is used to a certain degree in creaming cake mixtures, where the egg is beaten into the creamed fat and sugar; the stiffening of this mixture shows that the fat has formed an emulsion with the egg. A still better example is mayonnaise, in which one egg yolk can hold $\frac{1}{4}$ pint of olive oil in emulsion.

GRADING EGGS

Eggs for sale to the public are sent by the poultry farmer to a packing station of the British Egg Marketing Board where they are tested for quality, graded for size, stamped according to size and with the lion mark if they are of perfect quality and packed in cases of 30 dozen, or 3 'long hundreds' (a long hundred being 120); the case is also marked with the date in code.

Testing eggs for quality and freshness is done by *candling*. For this a lamp is used fitted with a shade with a round hole in it of about the circumference of an egg. The egg is held over the hole so that the light shines only through the egg, which is slowly revolved. By this test the white of a new-laid egg is transparent and unclouded; the air space is small and the yolk is seen as a pinkish circle with no dark spots. If the egg is not fresh the white is cloudy, the air space is larger, and the yolk shows red, while if the egg is really stale it appears quite opaque.

Eggs that are not new-laid but not stale or that have harmless blood spots or streaks are not given the lion mark but are stamped 'second' and are not graded by weight.

Grading for size is done by weight and the grades are:

'Large'   weighing not less than $2\frac{3}{16}$ oz.
'Standard'   ,,   ,,   ,,   ,, $1\frac{7}{8}$ oz. but less than $2\frac{3}{16}$ oz.
'Medium'   ,,   ,,   ,,   ,, $1\frac{5}{8}$ oz.   ,,   ,,   ,, $1\frac{7}{8}$ oz.
'Small'   ,,   ,,   ,,   ,, $1\frac{1}{2}$ oz.   ,,   ,,   ,, $1\frac{5}{8}$ oz.

STORING EGGS

A fertile egg begins to incubate at once at 60° F. and turns into a chick in 21 days if it is kept at blood heat. Fortunately there are few fertile eggs sold, but infertile eggs rapidly deteriorate and lose their food value at such temperatures. Eggs should therefore be stored in a cool place, preferably in a refrigerator, where, at a temperature of 45° F., they will remain fresh for as long as two months. It is, of course, rarely necessary to store eggs for so long, but cool storage is essential to keep eggs really fresh for even a few days.

They should be stored, blunt end uppermost, either in the egg box in which they are bought or in a rack, so that the yolk, which deteriorates more quickly, is kept surrounded by the white. As eggs absorb smells and strong flavours they must not be stored near strong-smelling food.

A broken egg or separate yolk must be covered with a little cold water, to prevent a skin forming, and also with a plastic cover or lid and of course stored in a cool place; egg-white is best stored in a screw-topped jar. Broken, separated or cracked eggs should be used as soon as possible as the yolk is a particularly good food for bacteria.

Preserving Eggs

Eggs may be preserved for several months in a solution of water-glass (sodium silicate) or by coating them with melted paraffin wax or a commercial preparation which is applied as a coating. Both these methods prevent the entry of air through the normally porous shell.

Commercially, eggs are preserved by canning them in bulk (with a preservative chemical), by drying them and in U.S.A. by deep-freezing them in plastic containers.

MILK

In this country 'milk' is taken to mean cows' milk although a certain amount of goats' milk is used. In some countries the milk of ewes and mares is used. As milk is the natural food for a young animal it obviously must contain all the nutrients needed to make the little animal grow and to give it energy. Milk is often called a 'perfect' food', but for human beings, although it is an excellent, complete food, in fact one of the most important foods, it is still not quite perfect because, although all the nutrients are there, they are not in exactly the right proportions and are diluted with too much water. An adult would need to drink a large volume of milk to obtain the nutrients necessary for one day if the diet consisted solely of milk.

FOOD VALUE OF MILK

Milk contains two main proteins, lactalbumin and caseinogen with a small amount of a third, lacto-globulin. The caseinogen is only slightly soluble in water and is kept in solution by the calcium salts in milk; lactalbumin is something like the albumin in egg-white and the three proteins together have the highest biological value of all protein foods; that is, they contain the best proportion of the ten essential amino-acids.

Milk contains fat which is easily digested because it is very finely emulsified, and carbohydrate in the form of a sugar called lactose which has no sweet taste and is not fermented by yeast. In sour milk the lactose has been changed by the action of certain bacteria to lactic acid. The mineral matter in milk includes plenty of calcium, potassium and phosphorus which make it a good food for bone and teeth-building; it also contains some magnesium but only very little iron.

Milk is a good source of Vitamin A and B_2 (riboflavine); it contains a moderate amount of B_1 (thiamine) and nicotinic acid but is deficient in Vitamin C and usually in Vitamin D except in very sunny weather when the cows can synthesize this vitamin from their food.

Average Composition of Milk

Protein	3	to	3·5%
Fat	3·5	,,	4·5%
Sugar	4	,,	5%
Minerals		,,	0·7%
Water	87	,,	88%

1 quart milk contains about the same amount of protein as 6 oz. meat or 3 small eggs.

$\frac{1}{3}$ pint (average glassful) of milk yields 102 Calories.

The exact composition varies widely between different breeds of cow (Channel Islands cows yield milk which may contain over 5% of fat), the length of time since the cow calved and the quality of the food she eats. Milk, as it is sold to the public, is usually a mixture of milk from different cows and even from different herds and so is of fairly uniform composition.

EXPERIMENTS WITH MILK

1. Leave $\frac{1}{4}$ pint of untreated or pasteurized milk and $\frac{1}{4}$ pint boiled milk in a warm place for 2-3 days. Compare the two results.
2. To $\frac{1}{4}$ pint fresh milk add $\frac{1}{4}$ teaspoonful of lemon juice or vinegar.
3. Warm $\frac{1}{4}$ pint fresh milk to blood heat, stir in $\frac{1}{4}$ teaspoonful of rennet and leave the milk undisturbed in a warm place for 20 minutes.
4. Repeat 3 using the milk at boiling-point.
5. Boil $\frac{1}{4}$ pint of milk, strain it through a fine strainer, scrape any sediment off the pan and dry the pan; repeat this 4 or 5 times with the same $\frac{1}{4}$ pint of milk.
6. Divide the much-boiled milk in two; to one part add 3 drops of

vinegar; cool the other half to blood heat, add to it 3 drops (about ⅛ teaspoon) rennet and leave it undisturbed for 20 minutes.

7. If time allows, heat ¼ pint milk in a double boiler for 2 hours.

Results of Experiments

1. Fresh milk if kept in a warm place for 2 to 3 days will clot and taste sour. For a further experiment the clot may be stirred vigorously and then strained through muslin; if the muslin is hung up, tied as a bag, until no more liquid drips from it a crumb of soft cheese can be made which, though very mild, will be quite palatable with a pinch of salt added. The boiled milk will be found to smell bad but not sour and will not have clotted: pasteurized milk will usually sour unless the pasteurizing has been prolonged.

2. The same clotting, with a different taste, can be produced by adding a little acid to milk. These results show that milk produces acid by the action of certain bacteria which work slowly at a warm temperature and that boiling which destroys these bacteria prevents the milk from going sour but does not prevent it putrefying. During pasteurization some of the lactic-acid-producing bacteria may be made inactive and pasteurized milk may not readily sour. Clotting takes place because the acid changes the calcium salt which kept the caseinogen in solution; the caseinogen then becomes insoluble casein which forms the solid curd.

3 and 4. When rennet is added to warm milk it forms junket, that is, a curd similar in texture to sour milk curd but with no acid taste. To form this curd, rennet, which is a digestive enzyme extracted from the calf's fourth stomach, partially digests the milk (just as in the human stomach) changing the soluble caseinogen to solid casein and combining it in this curd with the calcium. Rennet, being an enzyme, will only act at the temperature of the digestive tract, that is, at blood heat, and will therefore not form junket with boiling milk.

5, 6 and 7. When milk is boiled it forms a skin which can be removed, but is succeeded by another skin; at the same time a thin film of solid is deposited on the pan and at each subsequent boiling more skin and a little more deposit are formed. Boiling also changes the flavour of milk and, if prolonged for several hours, changes it still more and deepens its creamy colour to pale fawn: it may finally produce a broken type of curd. These results show that heat throws some of the protein out of solution: if tested in a laboratory the skin will be found to contain some fat and the deposit a trace of calcium. Milk that has been boiled, owing to the precipitation of some of the calcium and changes in the proteins, will not make a normal junket with rennet.

Effects of Heat on Milk

As has been found, boiling spoils the flavour and slightly reduces the food value of milk as well as forming an unpopular skin; so a wise rule is never to boil milk unless some other food such as cereal is to be cooked in it. For hot drinks and for serving with coffee remove the milk from the heat as soon as a thin skin forms and before it actually boils: if the milk is now whisked lightly this skin will completely disappear. It is well known that milk readily boils over; therefore it is wise either to watch it and to stir it as it comes to the boil for any cooking purpose or to use a double saucepan. Contrary to popular belief, if sugar is added to a starch and milk mixture such as cornflour sauce at the beginning of cooking it lessens the amount of sticking at the bottom of the pan and prevents burning of the bottom layer.

SAFE MILK

As well as being an excellent food, milk also provides an excellent breeding-ground for harmful bacteria, so that, unless it is produced and marketed in conditions of absolute cleanliness, it can become a most dangerous vehicle of infection. In the past, outbreaks of such diseases as typhoid and 'summer diarrhoea' of infants were probably caused by milk infected after it left the cow, while tuberculosis was frequently transmitted by milk infected by the cows themselves.

Nowadays there are very strict regulations governing the standard of hygiene that must be observed throughout all processes of dairying. To begin with, the cows are periodically tested with tuberculin to make sure that they are free from tuberculosis, and since the end of 1960 only milk from T.T. (tuberculin tested) herds has been retailed. The cows must be clean, their tails and hind-quarters groomed and their udders washed immediately before milking. The milkers must wash their hands and don clean overalls and caps before milking which is done in a scrupulously clean cowshed or 'milking parlour', by machinery, into covered pails. The milk is at once cooled and poured into 10-gallon churns ready for despatch to the bottling plant. All the machinery and utensils for milking are cleaned and either heat-sterilized or sterilized by chemicals after each milking.

At the creamery or bottling plant the milk is first tested for freshness by a 'sniffer', then a sample is tested in a laboratory for bacteria and for its content of butter-fat and other solids. Any milk that is not up to standard is rejected, the farmer being told of its defects and given advice on how to remedy them.

Next, the milk is again cooled to 40° F. and turned into cooled tanks ready for the bottling plant. Before being bottled it is *pasteurized* by one of two methods: either the *holder method* by which it is heated to 150° F. and kept at that temperature for ½ hour, or the *flash method* by which it is heated to 161° F. for 15 seconds; again cooled, to 50° F., and filled, by machinery, into cold, sterilized bottles and sealed with caps, coloured and printed according to its grade.

Some large dairy farms have their own bottling plant and bottle their cooled, T.T. milk without pasteurizing it, while some milk is sterilized at a bottling plant. The milk to be sterilized is first homogenized, that is processed, to break up the globules of fat to a finer emulsion which will prevent the cream from separating and rising in the bottle. Sterilization is by heat treatment under pressure and is carried out after the milk has been bottled and sealed. The degree of heat is higher than boiling-point and the milk therefore has a slightly cooked flavour, but it will keep fresh for seven days.

The grades of milk available to the public are:

1. Pasteurized.
2. Homogenized.
3. Sterilized, homogenized.
4. Channel Islands (untreated or pasteurized).
5. South Devon (untreated or pasteurized).
6. Untreated, farm-bottled.
7. Ultra heat treated (U.H.T.). This has been available since October 1965: it can be kept indefinitely. The milk is heated to 270° F. and packed in sterile conditions into containers.

MILK IN THE HOME

Although milk when bought is perfectly fresh, clean and sealed, it can still provide a good breeding-ground for harmful bacteria if these are allowed to enter it. Therefore to keep it safe it must be kept cool—not left in the sun on the doorstep; it should not be stored for much over 24 hours unless sterilized and it must never be left exposed to dust and flies.

Milk jugs must be washed clean, scalded and drained—not dried with a cloth; milk in the jug must be covered, preferably with a saucer or plastic cover, and never poured back into the bottle.

The best way to store milk is in the covered bottle in a refrigerator, or failing that standing in a bowl of cold water with a porous cover or damp linen cloth over the sealed bottle (see Fig. 18). Instant dried milk is available under several brand names; it may be fat-free or full cream and is compact to store and easy to mix for beverages or cooking but is not for babies.

Other Milk Products

Cream is a digestible, delicious but expensive source of fat. It is collected from milk at a temperature of 90° to 120° F. by a centrifugal separator which spins very rapidly, forcing the heavier liquid milk outwards and collecting the lighter fat at the centre.

> 12 pints of milk are required to produce 1 pint of double cream.
> Double cream contains 48% fat and 1 to 2% protein, 2 to 3% lactose.
> Single cream contains 18% fat.
> Cream for butter-making contains 35% to 40% fat.

After separating, the cream is pasteurized, bottled and sealed or made into butter; 'cultured cream' has been treated with a culture of certain bacilli to sour it slightly without solidifying it.

The skimmed milk remaining still contains protein, lactose and minerals and may be used for animal feeding; it may be sent to a factory to be condensed, or it may be dried or used by other industries, for example, in the manufacture of plastics, textiles, paints or glues.

Yoghurt is a semi-solid, creamy curd which does not readily separate into curds and whey although it has a pleasantly fresh, acid taste. It is made from milk treated with a 'starter' containing lactic acid and certain bacilli. It can be served plain with fruit or sweetened and flavoured or used in cooking; it makes an excellent foundation for salad cream.

Butter is included in the chapter on Fuel Foods.

'*Instant*' *dried milk*, both skimmed and full cream, is easily mixed to a liquid form for cooking and in beverages.

CHEESE

Cheese is really solidified milk from which much of the water has been removed, and as it takes a gallon of milk to make one pound of cheese it is obvious that cheese contains most of the nutrients of milk in a compact form. Some soluble components are lost in the whey, notably the lactose and any trace of Vitamin C, but this does not alter the fact that cheese is the most concentrated of all protein foods. As it is also comparatively cheap it is an important item of diet: 1 lb. cheese may cost only half as much as 1 lb. beef but may be equal in food value to 2 to 3 lb. lean beef.

There are many different kinds of cheese, but they can be roughly classified as:

Hard cheese from which the whey has been squeezed under pressure; examples are Cheddar, Cheshire and Dutch cheeses.

Soft cheese from which the whey has only been drained, without pressure; examples are Stilton, Danish Blue, Gorgonzola, Brie, Camembert and Demi Sel; these cheeses have a more open texture and keep for less time than do hard cheeses, which are often at their best after a year of 'ripening'.

Lean cheese made from skimmed milk; example, Dutch cheese.

Rich, 'fat' or whole-milk cheese made from whole milk; examples, Cheddar and Cheshire, or, with added cream; examples, Stilton and Double Gloucester.

Cream cheese, made from cream; such cheeses are always soft and do not keep for long.

Processed cheese. A hard cheese such as Gruyère or Cheddar, milled, mixed with milk to a soft consistency, pasteurized and usually wrapped in foil in portions.

Some well-known British cheeses are:

Caerphilly, a Welsh mild, fairly hard, white cheese.

Cheddar	
Cheshire	
Derbyshire	
Gloucester	all English hard cheeses, each with its own character-
Lancashire	istic flavour, colour and texture.
Leicester	
Wensleydale	

Stilton, English, soft, 'fat' cheese.

A few well-known foreign cheeses are:

Camembert, a French soft cheese.

Danish Blue, a soft cheese.

Edam and Gouda, Dutch hard, lean cheeses.

Gorgonzola, an Italian soft cheese.

Gruyère, a Swiss hard cheese.

Parmesan, an Italian very hard cheese from goats' milk.

Roquefort, a French cheese from sheeps' milk.

Each of these cheeses is named after the district in which it was first made and there are very great differences amongst them of flavour, texture and colour. The characteristics of any kind of cheese depend on the kind of milk used, the degree of acidity, the particular kinds of harmless bacteria that are allowed to multiply in it and are developed by the various processes in the manufacture and by the length of time of ripening.

CHEESE–MAKING

Although there are so many different cheeses the methods of making them all follow the same pattern although the details differ. The milk is first clotted by allowing it to sour or by adding rennet, or both; this stage is usually speeded up by the addition of 'starter', which is a prepared culture of lactic-acid-forming bacteria together with certain other harmless bacteria which gave the particular flavour to each kind of cheese. When a curd has formed it is cut in pieces, heated, stirred, salted and drained; these operations vary in method, sequence and duration, but are all directed to producing a curd of the right texture and acidity. The drained curd is moulded, usually in a cloth-lined mould of the traditional size and shape for the kind of cheese. For a hard cheese the moulded curd is pressed mechanically for a definite time: for a soft cheese no pressure is applied and such cheeses therefore have a more open texture which may allow certain moulds to enter and produce characteristic veining and coloration as in Stilton. The final stage is the ripening of the cheeses in a special room where the humidity and temperature are exactly controlled. The ripening may be for 10 days or up to 3 or 4 months and during this time the cheeses are turned at regular intervals.

Meanwhile the whey, which is $\frac{9}{10}$ of the original milk, will not be wasted: it may be used directly for feeding live-stock; it may have the fat separated for use in making whey-butter and it may be dried for use in animal feeding-stuffs.

FOOD VALUE AND COMPOSITION OF CHEESE

The exact composition of cheeses varies widely, but a fair average for hard, whole-milk cheese is 30% protein, 30% fat and 30% water.

The protein is of a biological value only slightly lower than that of milk, only a little liquid protein having escaped in the whey, and the fat contains some free fatty acids which add to the flavour of the cheese. Cheese is also a rich source of calcium and phosphorus and a good source of Vitamins B₂ (riboflavin) and A. It contains no carbohydrate as the soluble lactose is lost in the whey.

One ounce of cheese yields an average of 120 Calories and contains as much protein as 3 ounces of lean meat.

An interesting point is that the proteins of cheese and of white bread supplement each other, so that the traditional meal of bread and cheese is an excellent one if eaten with salad to supply its lack of Vitamin C.

DIGESTIBILITY OF CHEESE

Cheese is often considered indigestible because of the high proportion of fat which forms a waterproof coating over the protein and so keeps the digestive juices from acting on the casein; the digestion of protein normally begins in the stomach whereas fat is not broken down until it leaves the stomach. Two additional reasons for difficulty in digesting cheese are the fact that it is often eaten at the end of a full meal and that it is a food that needs thorough chewing because of its compact texture.

To make cheese digestible it should always be eaten with a starchy food, as part of a meal, not an 'extra', and it should be chewed thoroughly, or it may be grated before adding it to a salad or a starchy food.

EXPERIMENTS WITH CHEESE

To make a sample of soft cheese see chapter on Milk (Experiment 1).

1. Cut a thin slice of hard cheese and in a small fry-pan or saucepan warm it, gently at first and then more strongly until no further change is noticed. Watch carefully everything that happens and prod or stir the cheese frequently.
2. Grate a teaspoonful of hard cheese and to half of it add a small ½ teaspoonful of fresh breadcrumbs. Have ready two small pieces of dry toast: on one pile the grated cheese alone, and on the other the grated cheese and crumbs. Grill both pieces under a moderately hot grill.

Results

1. The cheese will have melted, the fat will have run out of it and the solid mass left will be tough and stringy at first. As heating is increased

and prolonged the fat will smell acrid and the solid protein mass will get harder still.

2. The cheese in each case will melt, the fat as it runs from the cheese will soak into the toast. It should be easier to get a brown, crisp surface on the mixture of crumbs and cheese than on the cheese alone.

The reasons for these results are that the high proportion of fat in cheese is easily separated from the protein: if the cheese is warmed gently it can be melted without giving up all its fat, but if heating is strong or prolonged the fat, instead of giving a savoury taste and smell, will be rancid to taste and will have an acrid smell due to decomposition of the fat, while the protein, without its protective coating of fat, will become very tough and hard. These unpleasant results are avoided if cheese is heated for a short time only and mixed with a starchy food.

RULES FOR COOKING CHEESE

The aim is to increase the savoury flavour of cheese and often to use it to improve more insipid foods.

1. Grate the cheese finely—hard, dry cheese is the easiest to grate.
2. Before cooking cheese, mix it with starchy ingredients.
3. Have all other ingredients cooked and hot before adding the cheese.
4. Heat the cheese for the shortest time needed to brown it using a moderately hot grill or a hot oven.
5. Mix half its volume of breadcrumbs with grated cheese that is to form a coating of an 'au gratin' dish; this increases crispness and absorbs fat.
6. Never keep a cheese dish hot for more than a few minutes.

6

FUEL FOODS

FATS

A great number of fats and oils are now available for cooking: many of them were unheard of fifty years ago or less. Margarine was in fact invented in France during the Franco-Prussian war, but was not widely used until the 1914-18 war. What may be called the 'traditional' fats were mostly from animal sources; butter, dripping, lard and suet with olive oil as the only vegetable oil in general use. The list is very much longer now because, during this century, the production of vegetable oils has been enormously developed as have the techniques of manufacturing these oils into solid fats to make them easy to use in many processes of cooking. Roughly speaking, the manufacturing processes consist in hydrogenating the oils to harden them and blending them in various ways to give pleasant flavours and textures. Some vegetable oils are sold in the liquid form, mainly for frying, but some brands are recommended by the manufacturers for use in other cooking, such as cakes and pastries.

THE FATS USED IN COOKING

Butter is made by churning cream until the butter-fat is thrown out of emulsion when it is pressed to squeeze out the water, and often salted. If the cream is 'ripe' or slightly soured the butter is termed 'lactic'; if the cream is fresh it is termed sweet butter. Lactic butter is usually salted, sweet butter is sometimes sold unsalted. Butter is rather expensive, but gives a delicious flavour in cooking.

Margarine costs only about half to two-thirds the price of butter, which it is meant to resemble. Originally made from meat-fats and milk and named after the Greek word 'margaron', a pearl, because of its pearly appearance, it is now made from partially hardened oils together with milk, cultures of certain harmless bacteria from milk and lactic acid. These three latter substances are added to give the desired flavour of butter. Some of the oils that may be used are coconut, cotton-seed, ground-nut, palm, palm-kernel, soya-bean and sunflower oils and sometimes whale oil. By law, margarine must contain Vitamins A and D in definite proportions and palm oil is used to supply these vitamins and also to give a yellow colour.

Cooking Fats. There are several brands of these on the market, with prices about equal to those of margarine. They are made from the same partially hardened oils as margarine, but with no attempt at imitating butter and with no colouring or vitamins added. Some of them are described as 'ready creamed' as they contain a certain amount of air-in-fat foam and possibly an emulsifying substance.

Lard. The vegetable cooking fats must not be confused with lard, although both are white. Lard is fat from the pig, the best qualities being leaf and bladder lard, which are firm in texture; the second quality being bulk lard, which is softer and greasy. All lard has a characteristic flavour.

Dripping. Strictly speaking this is the fat which drips from a roast joint, in which case it will have a good, savoury flavour from the meat essences, but the name is also given to any meat fat that has been melted at a moderate temperature and strained to free it from skin; such dripping has no meat essence, but all dripping has a characteristic taste according to the meat that it came from.

Suet. This is the hard fat packed round internal organs, chiefly the kidneys of ox and sheep; it it interspersed with varying amounts of connective tissue as thin membrane. Beef suet is a little less hard than mutton suet and its flavour is usually preferred.

Shredded Suet. This is made by melting solid suet, to free it of tissue, forcing it through small, round holes and solidifying it in tiny cylindrical shreds which are coated with rice starch to keep them separate. Shredded suets costs about twice as much as butcher's suet.

Oils

Frying Oils and Cooking Oils. Several brands of these oils are now on the market, some of them are only intended for frying, others for many cookery processes. They are prepared from one or more of the vegetable oils listed under margarine. They are mostly dearer than cooking fats.

Olive Oil. This is the best known of the vegetable oils: it is very expensive, but is valued for its flavour and is used more for salad dressing than for cooking, in this country.

Salad Oil. This is not olive oil: it is very much cheaper but has not the characteristic flavour of olive oil. It is a single vegetable oil or a blend of several chosen for a delicate flavour.

E

CHIEF USES OF FATS IN COOKING

1. Frying.
2. Basting meat, etc.: use dripping or any fat suitable for frying.
3. Greasing cooking vessels: use fat free from water and solids and with a pleasant flavour, e.g. cooking fat, lard, frying-oil.
4. Shortening pastry, biscuits and cakes (discussed later in this chapter).
5. Including air in cakes and pastry and improving flavour, texture and keeping quality: use margarine, cooking fat, butter.
5. Improving flavour, texture and fuel-food value of soups, sauces, salad dressings, various starchy mixtures and cooked vegetables: use fats with a pleasant flavour such as margarine or butter.

EXPERIMENTS WITH FATS

Fats for Frying

I. *To find out if there is water or solids other than fat* present in butter, margarine, cooking fat and lard. (Oils being transparent do not need to be tested and dripping is such a variable fat that different samples would give quite different results).

> (a) Put ½ ounce of each fat into a separate test tube and warm it gently over a low flame or stand it in a pan of boiling water until all the fat is just melted, then leave the tubes to cool. If there are two distinct layers let the fat harden completely and then lift it off the bottom layer. Taste both layers.
>
> (b) Heat ½ ounce of each fat in a separate small pan or test tube more strongly than in (a) and notice all the changes in each fat.

II. *To find the smoking temperature of fats.* A thermometer registering over 450° F. is necessary for accurate results in these tests; a dark, dull surfaced background makes it easier to see the smoke. For a secondary check of smoking-heat have a 1-inch cube of stale, white bread for each fat to be sampled. Carry out the test with margarine, lard, cooking fat, a frying oil and as many others as are available or not too expensive. If dripping is used it should be clarified and dry.

In a small pan put the thermometer and enough of the fat to be tested to cover the bulb. Heat the fat steadily over moderate heat until blue smoke begins to rise; notice the temperature and any other changes in the fat. Keeping the temperature steady drop in a cube of bread and time it in seconds until it is golden on *one* side. Taste the result. Make one chart showing the smoking temperature of each fat, and another showing the time it takes bread to brown at different temperatures.

Questions: 1. Do all fats and oils smoke at the same temperature?
2. Did bread brown in the same number of seconds in each sample of smoking-hot fat?
3. Is the smoking-point a reliable test for the correct temperature for frying?
4. Is there any disadvantage in using fat when it is smoking?
5. Which of the fats tested would be suitable for frying?

Results

I. (a) and (b). From melting the samples of fat it will have been found that cooking fat and lard contain no water and no other solids than fat and that when heated more strongly although there may be a few small bubbles there is no spurting. Neither of these fats tastes of salt.

The sample of butter when melted showed two distinct layers, the lower one being a milky liquid tasting very salt; when heated more strongly the butter bubbled, formed a scum, then a brown deposit which finally turned black. The sample of margarine behaved in much the same way as butter but probably spurted more and formed even more deposit.

The explanation of these results is that lard and white cooking fats are pure fat with no water, salt or non-fat solids, whereas butter and margarine both contain water and salt which cause the bubbling and spurting, also non-fat solid, probably casein of milk, which forms the deposit and becomes discoloured.

II. The exact temperature of smoking-point in fats is difficult to check, but it will be clear that different fats reach this point at widely different temperatures, also that the smoke smells unpleasant and may make the eyes smart. It will also be clear that bread fried at smoking-point browns in different numbers of seconds in different fats. It should also be clear that all fats are not equally good for frying: that those with water, salt and non-fat solids are unsuitable and that smoking-point is not an indication of correct heat for frying as not only does it vary with different fats, but it is accompanied by a disagreeable smell and imparts an equally unpleasant taste to the fried bread.

The explanation of these results is that for every fat there is a temperature at which it begins to decompose, freeing some of its fatty acid and changing some of the glycerol (see page 76) to a substance called *acrolein* which accounts for the acrid, blue smoke which makes the eyes smart and is, furthermore, highly indigestible. It will have been noted that the fats containing salt, water and solids smoked at low temperatures: this illustrates the fact that any impurity of this kind lowers the temperature of decomposition.

The chart of smoking temperatures and frying times should approximate to the following:

Fat	Smoking temperature, °F.	Browning of bread in seconds
Cooking fat	440–450	5
Lard, leaf or bladder	400–420	10–15
„ bulk	380–390	18–20
Margarine	270–290	(3–5 minutes)
Frying oil, mainly cotton-seed, maize or sunflower oil	450	5
Frying oil, mainly ground-nut oil	300	(2–3 minutes)
Olive oil	345–350	35–40

Dripping, not being a manufactured fat, has not been included in this chart because its decomposition temperature will vary widely according to the amount of heat to which it has been subjected and to the amount of water and other impurities in it. Perfectly clarified and dried dripping is usually equivalent to bulk lard for frying.

From this list the best *fats to select for frying* are, in order:

1. Cooking fats and frying oils containing no ground-nut oil.
2. Good quality lard.
3. Bulk lard and clarified, dried dripping.

Fats to avoid for frying are:

Margarine and ground-nut oil.
Olive oil and butter are used for low-temperature frying in some special dishes, but they are neither suitable nor cheap enough for ordinary use.

Suitable Fats for frying:

1. Contain no water, salt or non-fat solids.
2. Are tasteless or pleasantly flavoured even at high temperatures.
3. Should not begin to decompose until they reach a temperature higher than any needed to fry food.

Correct Temperatures for Frying

Food	Temperature	Browning of dry bread in seconds
Raw, starchy foods, e.g. potatoes, doughnuts	320°-340° F.	(1-1½ minutes) 60-90
Fish coated in batter	340° F.	(1 minute) 60
Fish coated in egg and crumbs or flour	360° F.	30
Reheated foods	380° F.	20

Fats for Shortening

Experiments to test the shortening power of fats

1. Control. Make a dough with 1 oz. plain flour and 3 teaspoonfuls cold water; with a little flour, press or roll it to ⅛-inch thick.
2. With each of the fats: butter, margarine, lard, cooking fat and a frying oil make a pastry using

1 oz. flour ⎫ mixed together till like fine crumbs with a
½ oz. fat   ⎭   4-prong fork,

adding 1¼ teaspoonfuls cold water to bind the whole; as in 1 press or roll to ⅛-inch thick: label each piece.

Now, in an oven pre-heated to 380° F. or Gas No. 6, bake No. 1 and all five pastries on the top shelf for 10 minutes. Test them all by breaking them in half and by crumbling a piece between finger and thumb. Taste each pastry.

Results

Control No. 1 will be found difficult to mix and when baked will be blistered, tough, hard and will not crumble.

The pastry results will be something of this order:

Butter:	crisp, fairly short	very good flavour.
Margarine:	crisp, less short	good flavour.
Lard:	soft, very short	lacking flavour.
Cooking fat:	crisp, very short	,, ,,
Frying oil:	very soft, very short	,, ,,

From this it may be concluded that all these fats are suitable for pastry (although oil is not often used in this country), but that for shortness, lard, oil, cooking fat are best and for flavour butter and margarine are pleasanter. In practice, butter is only used for rather special dishes as it is expensive and for general use half margarine and half lard or cooking fat give flavour and shortness.

The explanation of the shortening power of fat is that when it is rubbed into flour it coats small groups of flour particles with a waterproof layer (fat and water being unable to mix) leaving a little loose flour uncoated and able to absorb the water. Now, to go back to control No. 1, water and flour make an elastic dough which is hard and tough when baked. In the pastry only a little of the flour can make this elastic mixture, which forms a kind of meshwork between the fat-flour groups, and so the baked pastry is only slightly hardened—only enough to give it crispness.

The different shortening power of the different fats can be explained by the fact that some are more easily wrapped around the groups of flour particles than are others; this is called 'the plasticity theory'. (There is a more complicated chemical explanation which may be left to students of food chemistry.)

Fats for Creaming

In making richer cakes, fat is creamed with sugar to make a foam of air in fat and the more plastic fats are on the whole best for this purpose. As the flavour of the cake is important, a fat with a pleasant flavour, or no flavour is preferred. The choice then is narrowed to butter, margarine and cooking fat, lard being omitted on account of its flavour and because, although a plastic fat, it is actually difficult to cream.

> Butter is used for special cakes for its extra good flavour: it creams only moderately well.
> Margarine is the most generally used fat for creaming.
> Cooking fats are very easy to cream, but the cake will require extra flavouring.

The presence of a little water as in margarine or a little foam as in some cooking fats speeds the creaming and seems to give a lighter result. Creaming is most easily carried out when the fat is soft without being oily, that is, at temperatures of about 70° F., so that in practice, in cold weather or after storage in a refrigerator, the fat should be creamed in a warmed bowl or even with warmed sugar.

Melting the Fat for a Cake Mixture

The simplest and quickest way of adding fat to a mixture is by melting it, together with any sugar and usually syrup and treacle, and stirring it warm into the sieved, dry ingredients. By this method the fat does not enclose any air in the mixture, which is raised by a high proportion of added raising agent, as bicarbonate of soda. Almost any fat except suet is suitable for this method; dripping is in fact often used as ginger and other spices are added to the most usual cake of this type which is ginger-bread.

SUET IN COOKING

Suet is such a hard fat that it cannot be added to a mixture by any of the three methods above but must be chopped finely before mixing with the dry ingredients. Suet added in this way cannot add extra air to the mixture nor can it, until it is melted, shorten the mixture. As it takes over an hour to melt the suet completely in quite a small pudding, the mixture is made as a soft dough with a high proportion of baking powder and is cooked by steaming for $1\frac{1}{2}$ hours at least—for a really short suet pastry 2 to $2\frac{1}{2}$ hours are better.

Suet pastry is occasionally baked, but the result is, of course, tough and hard.

The food value of fats is of course mainly that of a fuel, fats yielding from 200 to 263 Calories per ounce.

As fats are absorbed slowly by the body the energy they give is more lasting than that produced by carbohydrates.

Butter and margarine are, in addition, good sources of Vitamin A, margarine also being a good source of Vitamin D, whereas butter only gives a good supply of Vitamin D when made from milk produced in sunny weather.

Butter contains a little calcium.

CARBOHYDRATES

CEREALS

The word cereal comes from Ceres, the Romans' name for the Greek goddess of tillage and harvest and is used to denote seed-grains of culti-vated grasses. The kind of grain used as food varies in different parts of the world, but in temperate or dry, sub-tropical climates wheat is the largest crop and in moist, hot climates, rice takes its place. In addition, in soils or climates of Europe where wheat does not thrive, **oats**, **barley** and **rye** are grown and in warmer, moister climates **maize** is an important grain. In the English-speaking countries **wheat** is the most important of the cereals.

The word 'cereal' is now often used as a general name for the many varieties of ready-cooked, flaked, 'shredded' or puffed breakfast foods which are made mainly from wheat, maize (or 'corn' in U.S.A.) and oats with various additions of malt, wheat-germ, and sugar.

Wheat

The importance of wheat, in cooking, lies in its ability to form an elastic dough which can be raised by air or carbon dioxide to form light, spongy bread and cakes.

The Composition of Wheat varies between different species. Of wheats used in Britain, Canadian wheat is harder and has a higher proportion of protein than British wheat and as a rule a mixture of the two is milled into flour.

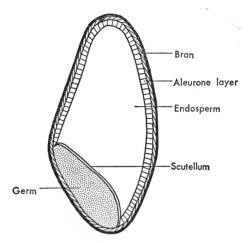

Fig. 28. DIAGRAM OF A GRAIN OF WHEAT

Percentage Composition of Wheat:

Water	Protein	Fat	Carbohydrate	Cellulose
13	9 to 14	2 to $2\frac{1}{2}$	68 to 64	5 to $1\frac{1}{2}$

Wheat also contains a good proportion of calcium and iron and a high proportion of phosphorous. It is an important source of Vitamin B_1 and contains nicotinic acid, some riboflavine and yields from 96 to 100

Calories per ounce. These nutrients are not evenly distributed throughout the grain which is made up of:

the *endosperm:*   85% of the grain, the main store of carbohydrate
and protein

,, *aleurone* layer: the outer layer of the endosperm, containing a high
proportion of protein

,, *germ:* $1\frac{1}{2}$% of the grain, containing the young plant, a high
proportion of protein, most of the fat and much
of the Vitamin B complex

,, *scutellum:*   a very thin layer between germ and endosperm
containing thiamine

,, *bran:*   13% of the grain; the fibrous covering with a high
proportion of cellulose, but also rich in calcium,
iron and phosphorous

Wheat is a hard grain that is difficult to cook and eat whole and it has
therefore, for thousands of years, been ground into flour. Grinding was
originally done between grooved, flat, round stones and this method is
still in use to a limited extent today. Stone-ground flour may contain the
whole grain, 100% wholemeal, or varying amounts of bran may be
sieved or 'bolted' out of it to give 95% brown flour or an almost white,
80% to 85% flour.

The modern method of grinding or roller-milling consists in first
cleaning the grain of small seeds and dust by sieving it; of metal impurities
by means of a magnet and of mud by washing it. Next the clean, dry
grain is passed between spirally-grooved steel rollers which crack it, and
shear off the outer coating from the endosperm which is separated off
by elaborate sieving. The bran and aleurone layer are returned to the
spiral rollers to remove more of the white flour particles; these rolls are
called 'breaks' and the grain is subjected to four breaks in all. The crushed
endosperm is called semolina and at the final stage all the white flour is
passed between smooth rollers to reduce it to an even, fine powder.

The bran and germ separated from the flour are both collected for
further use.

The flour may be mixed in several ways:

1. all four breaks mixed are called 'straight run', contain 70% to 75%
of the grain and make a flour suitable for bread;
2. second and third break, called 'patents' or 'pastry whites', contain
less protein and more starch than straight run and form a really
white flour for biscuit making and confectionery;

3. the germ and some of the fine bran returned to the straight run give *'wholemeal' or wheatmeal flour* containing 100% to 92% of the grain;
4. the germ, sterilized and ground, may be added to straight run to give a special flour for germ-enriched bread.

The germ is used in other food manufacture such as in breakfast foods, and the bran for animal food.

Food Value of Wheat Flour

The bran and germ were originally removed to produce white flour as a luxury for the wealthy and so it remained for several centuries until, in the nineteenth century, it became cheaper with new methods of milling. Nowadays one reason for removing the germ is that the fat which it contains goes rancid and spoils the taste of the flour.

There are at present two different groups of opinion as to the relative merits of brown versus white flour for bread.

In favour of brown bread:

1. Wholemeal or brown bread contains more protein, fat, calcium, iron and phosphorus and more vitamins of the B complex than white bread.
2. Wholemeal and brown bread contains more roughage in the bran which promotes bowel action.
3. Wholemeal and brown bread are preferable in texture and flavour to white bread. This point is, of course, unanswerable.

In favour of white bread:

1. The proportion of protein is only slightly higher in wholemeal than in white flour and bread is not eaten chiefly as a protein food; the extra phosphorous in wholemeal is not an advantage (phosphorous is rarely, in any case, lacking in any diet) because it is in the form of phytates which prevent the body from absorbing the calcium; the iron is probably not absorbed and the B group of vitamins are available in other foods.
2. The roughage in wholemeal over-stimulates bowel action for many people and in any case lessens the amount of all the nutrients that can be absorbed.
3. Bran is better digested by animals which in turn produce food for man.

Fortunately both kinds of bread and flour are available so both sides can be satisfied and it is of interest that by law all flour must contain a minimum quantity of iron, B_1 and nicotinic acid equivalent to 80% extraction flour and that all but wholemeal must have calcium added.

To summarize the food value of wheat flour: it is eaten mainly as a fuel food because of its carbohydrate content and when made into bread yields from 66 to 73 Calories per ounce; it contains 9% to 13% vegetable proteins which supplement the proteins in some animal foods, notably cheese. The most important of the proteins are gliadin and glutenin which together form gluten and which do not occur in any useful amount in other cereals.

Flour in Cooking

Flour is sold for domestic use as:

Stone-ground:	usually 100% wholemeal but it may also be almost white.
Wholemeal:	100% extraction.
Wheatmeal:	80%–92% extraction, i.e. coarser bran particles removed.
Strong Plain:	for yeast cookery, puff and flaky pastry and batters.
Plain or Soft Plain:	for light cakes, short pastries and biscuits.
Self-raising:	soft flour with sufficient baking powder to raise scones and plain cakes.
Wholemeal or Wheatmeal *Self-raising:*	with baking powder as above.

It is interesting to note that yeast increases the Vitamin B content of flour, whereas bicarbonate of soda and baking-powder destroy some of this vitamin group.

Another important point is that English wheat is 'soft', having a rather low gluten content and producing what millers and bakers term 'weak' flour which does not alone make good bread, for which a 'strong' flour with some 'hard' Canadian wheat is required.

EXPERIMENTS WITH FLOUR

1. To test for the presence of starch, put one drop of iodine on a little of the flour; if there is any starch the iodine will stain it deep blue. Test any other cereals with iodine.

2. To test for gluten: (a) mix 1 ounce of strong plain flour to a dough with 3 teaspoonfuls of water (this should be quite difficult to mix). Rub

and knead and twist the little ball of dough for about 5 minutes, by which time it should be tough and rubbery. Put ½ pint cold water in a pudding basin and in it knead and squeeze the little ball of dough for another 5 minutes; test the water with iodine, throw it away and continue kneading in clean water until not much more starch can be washed out. For a complete result bake the little ball of dough in a moderately hot oven.

(b) Repeat this experiment if possible with soft plain and compare the resulting doughs.

3. Try mixing 1 ounce cornflour (fine oatmeal or patent barley, if they are available) with 3 teaspoonfuls of cold water.

Result of Experiments

2. (a) The strong plain flour should form an elastic dough which gets tougher the more it is kneaded and from which much of the starch can be removed by squeezing in cold water. When baked the dough should produce a light, hollow, very crisp 'bun' resembling a commercial starch-free roll.

(b) The soft plain flour should not make so firmly elastic a dough, nor should it be so easy to free it of starch without losing some of the dough, nor should the baked bun be as large as (a).

3. It is impossible to make cornflour into a dough, and very difficult with oatmeal and barley, which get sticky but not elastic.

The explanation of these results is that gluten only occurs in a useful amount in wheat flour and that soft plain has noticeably less than strong plain flour; that gluten has the property of absorbing water to make a tenacious, elastic mass that will expand when cooked to give a very crisp, crusty substance.

Choice of Flour for Different Purposes

For all *yeast cookery* a *strong flour*—household plain or wholemeal.

For *flaky and puff* pastries and batters—*strong flour*, i.e. household or plain.

For cakes both plain and rich and for short pastries and biscuits plain flour is suitable (it may have 1 ounce of cornflour added to every 7 ounces to give a lighter result).

Self-raising flour is only suitable for plain cakes and scones; for richer cakes it may have too much baking powder.

Wholemeal flour, if liked, can be used for most cakes, but does not make good pastry.

In addition to baking, flour is used for thickening sauces, soups and batters for coating and frying: it can easily absorb its own weight of fat and hold it in an emulsion in such mixtures as White Sauce.

Other Wheat Products

Pasta or Macaroni, Spaghetti and many other shapes of Italian paste are all made from a particular species of wheat, rich in gluten. The flour from this grain is made into a paste which is extruded or moulded into the required shapes and dried. Pasta are all cooked by boiling and used as accompaniments to or ingredients of savoury dishes. A milk pudding can be made with macaroni.

Semolina is produced in the first break of flour-milling. It is used in milk puddings, in cheese mixtures, for thickening soups and to give a crumbly texture to some biscuits.

Oats

In the past oats were the staple food of Scotland and they still figure largely in Scottish cookery, for example, porridge, oatcakes, parkin and the traditional haggis.

Oats are prepared as *rolled oats* by passing the whole grain through heated rollers or by milling to different degrees of fineness as *coarse, medium or fine oatmeal*: a still finer product, *oat flour*, has the bran removed.

Composition and Food Value

Oats contain slightly more protein than English wheat, much more fat and more calcium and iron and they also have a similar amount of bran and phytic acid to wholemeal flour with the same disadvantages of incomplete absorption of the nutrients. However, as oats are often eaten as porridge, which is served with plenty of milk, these deficiencies are made good by the protein and calcium in the milk.

Oats in Cooking

Because it contains so little gluten, oatmeal cannot be used in light, spongy cake mixtures, but it gives a very short texture to biscuits, either alone or mixed with flour; it is traditionally used with very little fat to make oatcakes and it is satisfactorily mixed by the melting method to make parkin. Porridge may be made with medium and coarse oatmeal as well as with the more usual rolled oats. Oatmeal very soon becomes bitter if it is stored too long, as the fat turns rancid, but rolled oats keep their flavour because the hot rollers partially cook them and preserve their flavour.

Rice

Rice has the highest proportion of starch and the lowest of protein, fat and minerals of any cereal. On the other hand, as it is usually polished to free it from bran it contains little roughage and is therefore almost completely absorbed during digestion. Polishing rice has been found inadvisable in parts of the world where rice is the staple diet, as the lack of Vitamin B$_1$, removed with the bran, causes the disease beri-beri. In a mixed diet this is not important as rice is usually eaten for its calorific value.

Rice in Cooking

Rice of two different types is available, the round-grain 'pudding rice' or *Carolina rice* which becomes soft and creamy with suitable cooking and the long, thin, hard *Patna rice* which is used where the grains are required to remain separate and dry.

Rice is used for milk puddings; in such savoury dishes as Italian 'risotto', Spanish 'paella' and Near-Eastern 'pilaff' or 'pilau'; and plain boiled as an accompaniment to curry and other savoury dishes.

Ground rice and the finer, more expensive, rice flour are used for milk puddings, for thickening soups and to give a crumbly texture to biscuits and 'sand' or rice cake.

Barley

Most of the barley grown in the British Isles is used for making malt or for animal food.

Barley contains less protein and less fat than wheat and because of its lack of gluten is no longer used in baking.

It is available as *pearl barley* which has been polished to remove the bran and is used in broths such as Scots Broth or milled as 'patent' barley or 'cream of barley', a fine flour which can be used to thicken soups.

Barley water may be made from pearl barley (taking several hours) or more quickly from patent barley; it has little food value but, if well flavoured with lemon juice, it is refreshing and is often given to invalids.

Maize

Maize, known as 'corn' in U.S.A., is little used for human food in Great Britain, but in parts of America, southern Europe and Africa it is an important article of diet. It contains a fair amount of protein of rather poor quality and a good proportion of fat, but as it contains no gluten it cannot be used for bread.

Cornflour is made from maize and is almost pure starch; it is useful for thickening sauces and soups and for milk puddings and is an ingredient of some custard powders.

As sweet corn, or corn-on-the-cob, unripe, juicy maize is a delicious vegetable, which must be cooked when very fresh, by boiling for not more than 20 minutes.

OTHER STARCHY FOODSTUFFS

Arrowroot, Sago and Tapioca are not cereals, but they are all used for their starch content.

Arrowroot is made from a West Indian root which is crushed, mixed with water and dried as a very fine powder. It is useful because it requires a very short time to cook; it is used to thicken sauces, but is a very costly form of starch; both arrowroot and cornflour are used to make a glaze for fruit flans and tartlets, arrowroot giving the clearer, if more expensive, result.

Sago is made from the pith of the sago palm from which the starch is washed, dried and granulated as round 'pearls'.

Tapioca is made from the root of the cassava plant from which a bitter, poisonous juice must first be washed. The starch is dried and granulated, like sago, into 'pearls' or finer 'seeds' or is crushed into rough flakes; in some parts of the world it is used as 'cassava' or 'manioc' flour. Both sago and tapioca are used in milk puddings and sometimes for thickening soups. They are not important fuel foods as so little, usually under $\frac{1}{2}$ ounce, would be eaten in a serving of milk pudding.

Potatoes

Although potatoes are really vegetables, they are an important carbohydrate food. Originally cultivated in Peru and Bolivia and brought to England in the sixteenth century by Sir Walter Raleigh, they did not become popular for nearly two centuries, but by the end of the eighteenth century they had become the staple food of the Irish peasantry. containing as they do a little protein with a moderate amount of starch,

Composition of Potato

If a potato is cut in half it can be seen that it has distinct layers; these layers are interesting because their composition varies a little as follows:

1. skin: more protein, more fat and more minerals than the main flesh;
2. thick fibrous layer under the skin: more protein and more minerals than the main flesh;
3. the main flesh: less protein, more carbohydrate, less mineral than the two outer layers; less fat than the skin.

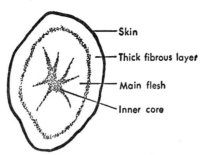

Fig. 29. SECTION THROUGH A POTATO

The whole potato contains about 81% water, very little protein, still less fat but an important supply of minerals, notably potassium, with a little calcium, and in addition it contains a useful amount of the B group of vitamins and may be a good source of Vitamin C.

Although potatoes are eaten chiefly for their fuel value, which is not very great (21 Calories per ounce, raw), the Vitamin C is important because potatoes are relatively cheap and are eaten regularly in many diets. The content of Vitamin C varies, however, during the year; when early and main crop potatoes are first dug it is high, so that 6 ounces of boiled new potatoes contain a day's ration, but on storage the Vitamin C is gradually lost, so that by December, the amount is quite small and by March, negligible.

Cooking Potatoes

Like all vegetable foods, potatoes absorb water during cooking; they also lose minerals and Vitamins B and C by solution in the cooking water when they are boiled without their skins. They should therefore be cooked in their skins, with enough boiling water barely to cover them if their maximum value is to be conserved. (See p. 142 for enzyme and Vitamin C.)

Other excellent ways of cooking potatoes are: *roasting in their skins, baking with hot fat* and *frying*, as by these methods no nutrients are lost by solution and a fair amount of fat is absorbed to raise the fuel value.

Mashing potatoes with milk and fat adds protein as well as fat and so improves the food value.

The loss of Vitamin C during cooking is not important if the diet is adequately supplied with this vitamin from other sources, but in a cheap diet it is most important.

SUGAR

Sugar is the most concentrated of the carbohydrate foods, yielding 112 Calories per ounce, and is eaten in large quantities in many modern diets. It is an easily and quickly absorbed fuel but has no other nutritive value and this fact causes some dietitians to suggest that we eat too much of it.

Sugar was probably used in Asia for many centuries before it was imported to Europe during the Middle Ages. Originally all sugar was made from sugar-cane, but nowadays, although it is grown in many hot countries other than in Asia, sugar-cane only provides some one-third of the sugar eaten in Great Britain, the larger proportion being made from sugar-beet. Cane sugar and beet sugar are chemically identical and there is no difference between them in any cookery process.

Sugar-cane is processed first by crushing, then by squeezing between heavy rollers and the juice so obtained is clarified with lime and heated, cleared of scum and concentrated by boiling. The crude sugar crystallizes and is sent to sugar refineries to be further purified, decolorised and again crystallized for granulated and caster sugar, moulded and cut for lump sugar or powdered for icing sugar.

Sugar-beet has been cultivated for over 100 years, but has only been used extensively in Great Britain during this century. The beet is harvested in the autumn and processed by pulping it, squeezing out the juice which is clarified, decolorised and crystallized into the same finished types as cane sugar.

The types of sugar are:

White, granulated, suitable for sweetening liquids, rubbed-in cake mixtures, preserving and sweet-making.

Caster, fine grained, suitable for creamed cake mixtures.

Brown, Barbados, fine grained and of dark, medium and light colour; it should be cane-sugar; the flavour of brown sugars is preferred by some.

'Pieces' or *'Foot'* sugar, very fine grain, light brown; may be beet or cane sugar: both Barbados and pieces may be used for any brown-coloured cakes.

Demerara, a coarse-grained, medium brown; should be cane; if beet usually called 'yellow crystals' or just 'brown sugar'.

Icing sugar is ground to a fine powder.

The brown sugars are purified but not decolorised.

Black treacle and *Golden syrup* are by-products of sugar manufacture; they both contain some invert sugar, which prevents their crystallization, and colouring matter and minerals, notably iron in black treacle.

Glucose can be bought in a white powder form chiefly for use in sick-room cookery, because it can supply energy without making food too sweet. It is also used as a syrup by confectioners for many processes in which it is necessary to retard crystallization.

Invert sugar (see p. 160).

Honey is a form of invert sugar, that is a mixture of glucose and fructose (see p. 160). It is prized for its flavour which is due to the perfume essence of the flowers from which it was collected. The more expensive types of honey are named according to their source, for example, heather or clover honey. Thick or cloudy honey occurs naturally, as a little crystallization takes place when honey is kept. Honey is too expensive to use in cooking in any but a few special dishes.

Sugar in Cookery

In cake making sugar not only sweetens but also gives a soft or 'silky' texture because it dissolves in the liquid used for mixing, or the liquid of the eggs, making a thick syrup. The less liquid, the softer the cake as a rule, partly on account of the thicker syrup formed.

In cakes made by creaming, the sugar, which should be caster, encloses air when creamed with the fat, so making the mixture lighter. The sugar syrup slightly *softens gluten* in cakes, short pastry, biscuits and yeast buns.

Sugar, when heated dry or dissolved, at first produces a syrup which gets gradually thicker, producing various degrees of hardness on cooling, and at 380° F. finally forms 'caramel', a brittle brown toffee, used for flavouring or for sweets. Dissolving sugar must be done carefully; the sugar and water should not be stirred or shaken, nor must it boil until all grains of sugar have disappeared, otherwise very small crystals form in the syrup which are very difficult to dissolve.

Treacle and Golden Syrup

Both of these are used in the making of gingerbread, in which a syrupy texture is characteristic: this texture is due to the invert sugar which does not crystallize and so does not give a crisp texture. A little of either added to any cake helps to keep it moist for the same reason.

There is a little acid in black treacle, but not enough to neutralize the proportion of bicarbonate of soda required to raise any gingerbread mixture.

7

FOODS MAINLY PROTECTIVE

VEGETABLES

Different parts of a great number of different, cultivated plants are used as vegetables; they may be classified as:

Part of the Plant	Examples	Season
Below ground:		
Bulbs	Leeks	Autumn to spring
	Onions	All year
Roots	Carrots, beetroot	All year, new in early summer
	Parsnips, swedes	Autumn to spring
	Salsify	Autumn to spring
	Turnips	Autumn to spring (new in summer)
	Radishes	Spring to autumn
Tubers	Potatoes	All year, new spring and summer
	Jerusalem artichokes	Autumn to spring
Above ground:		
Flowers	Broccoli and cauliflower	All year (one or other) but dear in winter and early spring
	Globe artichokes	Summer
Fruits and	Beans, broad and French	Summer
Seeds	Beans, runner	Late summer
	Peas	Summer
	Cucumber	Spring to autumn (mostly in greenhouses)
	Marrows	Summer and autumn
	Sweet corn	Summer
	Tomatoes (greenhouse)	Spring and summer
	Tomatoes (outdoor)	Late summer and early autumn
Leaves	Brussels sprouts	Autumn to spring
	Cabbage	All year
	Cabbage (savoy)	Autumn to spring
	Chicory	Autumn to spring
	Cress	All year (often greenhouse)
	Curly kale	Winter and early spring
	Endive	Summer
	Spinach	All year (different varieties)
	Spring greens	Early spring
	Sprouting broccoli	Early spring
	Watercress	All year; poor in early summer
Stems	Asparagus (with leaf bud)	Spring and summer
	Celery	Autumn and winter
	Seakale	Winter and spring

These seasons are average for vegetables grown out of doors or in cold greenhouses in the British Isles; seasons may be late or early according to the weather and many vegetables are nowadays grown in hot-houses or are imported from warmer countries and are in season all the year round.

Some edible fungi are eaten for their flavour; in this country mushrooms are the only popular fungus, but on the Continent several other kinds are used.

One seaweed, Welsh laver, is used as a vegetable locally.

Wild plants, for example, dandelion, 'Good King Henry' or wild spinach and nettles, are used by some people.

COMPOSITION OF VEGETABLES

With such an assortment of plant-forms the composition of vegetables naturally varies widely, but all are eaten for their vitamin and mineral content, for the roughage which they provide and not least for their succulence and flavour: they contain only small proportions of protein and carbohydrates, no fat and 90% to 95% water.

Protein in vegetables is represented chiefly in peas, broad beans and sprouts, which contain from 3% to 6%, and in cauliflower and leeks which contain about 2%; it is found in very small amounts in the rest.

Carbohydrate occurs as sugar or as starch or sometimes as a mixture of the two: as sugar it is found in beetroot, cabbage, carrots, onions, leeks and tomatoes; as starch, in potatoes and as a mixture, in parsnips, broad beans and peas, but in no vegetable is the calorific value high. Potatoes, broad beans and green peas provide 17 to 21% Calories per ounce, the rest much less.

Some carbohydrate occurs in the fibrous part of all vegetables as *cellulose*, which is not digested, but acts as roughage, the amount varying widely with the age and hardness of different kinds.

The real value of vegetables as food lies in their vitamins and minerals.

Vitamin C is richly supplied in curly kale, sprouts, turnip tops and sprouting broccoli; well supplied in cauliflower, cabbage, spinach and watercress and in a moderate amount in broad beans, leeks, radishes, spring onions and swedes. It is interesting to note that all these vegetables contain more than lettuces and tomatoes, the two most popular salad vegetables.

Vitamin A occurs in all dark green and orange-coloured vegetables as carotene, with turnip tops, carrots, curly kale, spinach, sprouting broccoli, watercress, cress, cabbage, tomatoes and lettuce at the top of the list and in that order.

Vitamin B group. Thiamine occurs in useful amounts in most vegetables, particularly green vegetables, peas and beans; *riboflavine* occurs in some, such as sprouting broccoli, lettuce and spinach, but *nicotinic acid* is in very small amounts except in potatoes.

Calcium occurs in most vegetables, the richest sources being watercress, kale, cabbage, root vegetables and celery, with fruits lowest in the list.

Iron is in good supply in most green vegetables, broad beans, peas and endive: in spinach the iron is made useless by oxalic acid which this vegetable contains.

COOKING VEGETABLES

Cooking makes many vegetables more palatable and more digestible, mainly by softening fibres and softening and rupturing starch cells, but some of the protective nutrients of each group, except Vitamin A, are lost during even the most careful cooking. The minerals and vitamins of the B group and C are all soluble in water and therefore easily washed or boiled out and these water-soluble vitamins are also destroyed by prolonged heating. Vitamin C may also be destroyed by the enzyme oxidase, which occurs naturally in vegetables and fruit, and which hastens the destruction of Vitamin C by oxidation when the cell walls become weakened as the plant wilts or when they are crushed or bruised. This oxidase can be destroyed by plunging the vegetable into boiling water which conserves the Vitamin C. In addition to the loss of protective nutrients, overcooking or bad cooking can render any green vegetable useless as food by ruining its flavour, colour and texture and so making it quite unpalatable.

Even with good cooking some Vitamin C is lost into cooking water and therefore vegetables may often be better eaten raw, as salad, provided that they are liked and can be digested. For example, children will often eat with delight such raw vegetables as grated carrot, shredded cabbage or sprigs of cauliflower although, when cooked, they may regard the same vegetables with loathing. Adults may have more difficulty in digesting raw vegetables and would therefore absorb more vitamin from them cooked.

Rules for Preparing and Cooking Green Vegetables

1. Use all vegetables as fresh as possible and gathered when young or just mature for maximum vitamin value and for the best flavour and succulence.

2. Soak the vegetables (to drown and float out any caterpillars or slugs) for not more than 10 minutes in cold water, to which salt has been added to slow up the solution of vitamins and minerals. *Note:* Green and black fly are more easily floated away from the vegetable if salt is omitted.

3. Rinse them thoroughly to remove all the above-mentioned additions.

4. Only discard fibrous or withered parts; dark outer leaves contain more Vitamin A. If necessary begin cooking stalks and outer leaves 3 to 5 minutes before the main part.

5. Shred or slice hard and large vegetables with a sharp knife (a blunt knife will crush cells and release oxidase) to shorten the time needed for cooking.

6. Cook them in not quite enough boiling water to cover them, putting them in about one-third at a time so that the water does not go off the boil.

7. Cook them, with a lid on the pan, for the shortest time needed to make them tender. Never keep them hot—serve them at once.

8. Test the cooked vegetables for tenderness with a sharp skewer to avoid breaking them.

9. Use the small amount of cooking water for gravy, soup or for a sauce, for example, with cauliflower.

Note: Soda, sometimes added to green vegetables to brighten their colour, destroys Vitamins B and C unless used in very small amounts.

For root vegetables the same rules apply, but cooking can be started by tossing the sliced vegetables in melted fat for 10 minutes over low heat, covered (this is 'sweating' or 'fat-steaming'), then adding the boiling water. Cooking in this way is immensely better for flavour and is quicker than the traditional boiling of whole vegetables.

Chopped Parsley. Though parsley is a herb rather than a vegetable, it can add a little Vitamin C and iron to the diet and adds flavour and colour to many root vegetables.

Dry it well in a cloth, use a sharp knife and chop it just before serving, to avoid loss of Vitamin C by solution, by crushing or oxidation. The oxidase may be destroyed by holding the bunch of parsley in boiling water for 2 seconds before chopping it; it must then be dried in a cloth before being chopped.

STORING VEGETABLES

Green vegetables, peas and beans and green salads should all be eaten as fresh as possible. If they must be stored for a day they should be dry, kept covered from the air and in the dark. This can be done by putting them in a covered box or basin in a refrigerator, or in a plastic bag or paper parcel in a cool, dark place.

Root vegetables are stored in bulk in clamps, that is, in long heaps covered with straw and then earth to exclude air, or in small quantities either left in the ground or covered with dry earth or ashes. Indoors they should not be kept for more than a few days, as for green vegetables, as if stored uncovered they lose moisture, become limp and then shrivel.

CANNED VEGETABLES

Vegetables are canned when they are in prime condition and their food value is in almost every respect equal to that of the same vegetables when fresh. They will have lost some Vitamin C, but possibly not more than by the usual procedure of gathering, marketing and cooking. It is important to remember, however, that 'processed' tinned peas have no Vitamin C at all.

FROZEN VEGETABLES

As with canned vegetables, the modern, quick-frozen vegetables are equal to the fresh varieties in food value, and are in fact often in better condition than those on sale in shops. The quick-freezing process conserves Vitamin C which is only diminished by the necessary cooking just as it is when fresh vegetables are cooked.

To cook frozen vegetables they should be plunged, while still solid with ice, into the minimum of boiling water and simmered for the shortest time needed to soften them.

Both canned and frozen vegetables usually cost more than the fresh varieties in their season, but the price covers the cost of preparation waste.

PREPARATION OF SALADS

Salads may be made of many different mixtures of raw and cooked vegetables with fruit and nuts, for example, 'summer salad' with lettuce, tomato, cucumber and spring onions; a salad of cooked new potatoes with green herbs, spring onion, radishes and watercress, or a 'Waldorf' salad with lettuce, grapefruit and walnuts.

Important points to remember

1. Raw salad vegetables must be very fresh and free from water.
2. If outer lettuce leaves, etc., are to be cut up this must be done with a sharp knife, which is better than the old-fashioned method of tearing as it does not crush or bruise the cells so much and so avoids unnecessary loss of Vitamin C.
3. Cutting of salad plants should be done at the last moment before serving.
4. Dressing improves the food value of a salad as the oil helps to convert carotene to Vitamin A during digestion, but dressing must be added at the last moment before serving, as it makes all green leaves limp in a very short time.
5. If salad must be prepared in advance the ingredients should not be cut up and the salad must be covered closely and kept cool.

PULSES

Pulses are dried seeds of leguminous plants; those most often used in Great Britain are:

Butter beans—white, flat, large.
Haricot beans—white, small.
Lentils—orange or Egyptian—small split, without skins.
Lentils—brown—round, flattish, with skins.
Peas—whole, with skins.
Peas—split, either green or yellow, without skins.
Peanuts or ground-nuts.
Soya beans—round, whitish, usually ground to a flour.

Pulses are sometimes served as a vegetable but, as they contain no Vitamin C or A, they do not take the place of fresh vegetables in the diet. They may be used as substitutes for animal protein foods because they are cheap and their proteins, although second class, can supplement those found in fish, meat and milk. They form an important source of protein in vegetarian diet.

A statement of their food values is misleading unless it is remembered that they are dried and must therefore be soaked, to replace the lost water, before they can be cooked. It is wiser to consider the food value of cooked pulses.

FOOD VALUE OF COOKED PULSES

All pulses contain protein, a rough average being under one-third of the amount in lean meat; they contain 18 to 20% carbohydrate; they are all good sources of calcium and iron and all contain some of the B group of vitamins, but no fat and no Vitamin A or C.

Soya beans need special mention because they contain protein in almost double the amount found in other pulses and of a higher quality; they contain a large amount of fat and their carbohydrate is in the form of dextrin and sugar. Soya beans are used commercially in many food products and can be bought in powder form for adding to milk, vegetarian and starchy foods and for thickening soups and stews.

Peanuts or ground-nuts although resembling nuts are really legumes and as they are not soaked but roasted their food value is different from the other pulses. They contain a good proportion of protein and a very high proportion of fat. Apart from being eaten roasted they are used as peanut butter.

COOKING PULSES

All pulses, except the small orange lentils, must be soaked before they can be cooked; if they have skins on them, soda should be added to the soaking water to soften the skin and to remove any bitter flavour: $\frac{1}{8}$ teaspoon washing soda or $\frac{1}{4}$ teaspoon bicarbonate of soda dissolved in a little boiling water and added to 1 pint cold water is enough to soften $\frac{1}{2}$ lb. pulse, and 8–12 hours should be allowed for soaking: rinse well.

Pulses are used in soups; as additions to meat dishes, e.g. haricot beans with meat stews and pease pudding or butter beans with boiled salt pork or bacon; and in many savoury vegetarian dishes such as lentil roasts. Except in soups, all pulses should be cooked in the minimum of water and should be well drained or dried before serving: because of their mealy, filling quality they are best served with a sauce and with some added flavour such as herbs.

NUTS

Nuts are not used a great deal in British cookery with the exception of almonds, chiefly in confectionery, and chestnuts in savoury dishes and sweets, but for vegetarians they provide a useful source of protein.

FOOD VALUE OF NUTS

Nuts vary widely in their food value, but they mostly contain a fair proportion of protein, a high proportion of fat, a little carbohydrate and a fair supply of iron and calcium. Almonds are very rich in calcium, chestnuts have far more carbohydrate than protein or fat, which are both low. Most nuts contain Vitamin C and thiamine.

FRUITS

Fruit is eaten for its delicious flavour and for its refreshing juiciness. The juice is, of course, largely water: fruits contain from 75% to 95% water and the refreshing quality is largely due to acids which all fruits contain.

FOOD VALUE OF FRUIT

The food value of fruits varies considerably, but in general they provide a little carbohydrate as sugars, negligible amounts of protein and fat and variable small amounts of minerals. Their chief value lies in their Vitamin C and Vitamin A content. They mostly contain a little thiamine but no nicotinic acid or riboflavine. In the order of vitamin content some everyday fruits are:

Vitamin C	*Vitamin A as carotene*
Blackcurrants	Apricots
strawberries	peaches
oranges ⎱ the rind also being	blackcurrants
lemons ⎰ rich in Vitamin C	oranges, particularly
redcurrants	tangerines
gooseberries	bananas
grape-fruit	some others contain a little
loganberries	
raspberries	
blackberries	
the rest contain a little.	

Rhubarb, which is not a true fruit, contains very little sugar, no Vitamin C or A and is eaten mainly for its flavour and colour.

Like vegetables, all fruits contain a little cellulose and are useful therefore for their laxative property.

COOKING FRUIT

Many fruits are delicious raw, when they are fully ripe, and, as some Vitamin C is unavoidably lost during cooking, it is as well to eat raw fruit when possible.

The rules for cooking fruit are similar to those for vegetables:

1. Wash gently and quickly, never soak them.
2. Avoid crushing fruit before cooking.
3. Stew for the minimum of time in the minimum of water, covered.
4. If fruit is wanted whole, sugar dissolved in the cooking water may prevent it breaking; the syrup or water should be boiling when the fruit is put in.
5. Serve all the juice with the fruit.

Fruit cooked in a pie is, of course, heated slowly, but air is excluded by the crust.

DRIED FRUIT

Dried fruits have lost most of their Vitamin C and B, but have concentrated amounts of sugar and minerals; they are valuable sources of calcium and iron.

CANNED FRUIT

Canned fruits usually have a large proportion of their Vitamin C conserved during the canning process which excludes air and applies heat for a short time only. They will also have been canned when just ripe and therefore with their maximum Vitamin C and sugar content.

FROZEN FRUIT

Frozen fruits are mostly those which have a short season and therefore a high price when fresh and are rather a luxury. They are equal in Vitamin C and sugar content to the fresh varieties.

8

MAKING FLOUR MIXTURES
LIGHT: I

EXPERIMENTS WITH RAISING AGENTS

1. Make a soft, elastic dough with flour and water, knead it lightly and roll it very thin, shaping it to a neat round. Bake this dough or 'damper' on a hot baking sheet in a hot oven until it is just crisp. Examine the result; eat a piece when just cold. If there are any air spaces in the damper how did they get there?

2. Measure $\frac{1}{4}$ pint of flour in a graduated pint measure; sift it on to a sheet of paper, carefully pour it back into the measure, gently shake it level and remeasure it. Repeat the sifting twice more then again measure it.

   If there is any difference in volume how do you account for it?

3. Tie a toy balloon over the neck of an empty bottle and stand the bottle in a saucepan with water to come half-way up it. Gradually bring the water to boiling-point, watch the balloon.

   What has happened inside the bottle and the balloon?

4. (a) Make a small quantity of Yorkshire pudding batter from the recipe on page 383 but add only half the given amount of milk or milk and water. Pour half of this batter into a cold, greased patty tin, put it into an oven then light the oven set at 320° F. or Gas No. 3 and bake it till brown. Heat a little fat in a second patty tin and when it begins to 'smoke' pour into it the other portion of batter and bake it at 420° F. or Regulo 8.

   (b) Make a small quantity of Yorkshire pudding batter using the correct recipe and bake it in two halves one in a cool oven—starting from cold, and one in a hot oven as in (a).

   Notice which batter has risen the most and which the least. Which are the two conditions that made the best one rise more than the others and what was the important raising agent?

5. (a) Into each of two test tubes put an equal small amount of bi-carbonate of soda,

   to (i) add cold water;

   to (ii) add an equal amount of boiling water;

when nothing further happens in either tube, heat (i) to boiling-point, then reboil (ii).

When activity stops again, test the remaining solutions with litmus paper.

(b) To the remaining solution in tubes (i) and (ii) add vinegar drop by drop until there is no more activity; test again with litmus paper.

Write down exactly what happened in the two tubes.

6.   Repeat experiments 5 (a) (i) and 5 (a) (ii) using tartaric acid and then cream of tartar in place of bicarbonate of soda. Notice any differences in behaviour between these two powders compared with each other and with bicarbonate of soda.

7.   Into each of two test tubes put an equal, small amount of bi-carbonate of soda, add to (i) an equal amount of tartaric acid; add to (ii) twice the amount of cream of tartar, to each add an equal amount of cold water, wait till any activity stops then gently warm each tube over a gas flame. Test the solutions with litmus paper.

Notice any difference in the speed of reaction between the two mixtures and the effect of warming the solutions.

8.   Repeat Experiment 7 using two different brands of baking powder instead of the mixtures of bicarbonate of soda and tar-taric acid or cream of tartar. Notice any similarity between the speed at which either baking powder reacts, with that of the mixtures (i) and (ii) in Experiment 7.

9. (a) Make a scone with 2 oz. flour, $\frac{1}{4}$ level teaspoonful of bicarbonate of soda and enough water to make a soft dough. Bake the scone in a hot oven, 450° F. or Gas No. 9 for seven minutes.

Examine the result, noticing smell, colour and taste.

(b) Make a similar scone, adding $\frac{1}{2}$ level teaspoonful of cream of tartar as well as the $\frac{1}{4}$ level teaspoonful of bicarbonate. Bake and examine the scone as before.

(c) Repeat (a) using $\frac{3}{4}$ level teaspoonful baking-powder instead of bicarbonate of soda.

Compare scones a, b, and c for smell, colour and taste and for texture.

10.   Set an oven at 450° F. or Gas No. 9; warm a baking sheet. Using one of the recipes on page 423 make a scone dough with $\frac{1}{4}$ lb. flour. Pat the dough into a round, flat cake, $\frac{3}{4}$-inch thick and cut it into 6 triangular scones. Bake 3 scones at once in the hot

oven for 7 minutes; leave the other 3 scones to stand for $\frac{1}{2}$ hour before baking them at the same temperature and for the same time.

Compare the two results. Did waiting spoil the second batch of scones?

RESULTS

1. It was found by Experiment 1 that flour and water mixed together make an elastic dough capable of being pulled and stretched. This special property of flour dough is due to the two proteins in wheat, gliadin and glutenin, which, together with water form a sticky, elastic substance known as *gluten* which binds the whole into a tenacious mass (see Chapter 6). When this dough is baked as a thin cake, a hard, tough kind of biscuit is produced which is similar to the unleavened bread of the Israelites, to the 'damper' of prospectors and pioneers in North America and the 'flap-jack' of Australian swagmen. This primitive kind of bread is replaced in civilized communities by many different kinds of well-risen bread and cakes.

2-10. Experiments 2 to 10 explore some of the ways in which unleavened bread or damper may be improved. There are three gases or mixtures of gases which, singly or together, can be made use of to make flour mixtures light or to 'raise' them; they are air, steam and carbon dioxide. Air is enclosed in a mixture by such mechanical means as sieving the flour or by beating or whisking the mixture; steam is given off by any moist mixture when it is cooked, while carbon dioxide is produced by the chemical action of ingredients which have been added with the special aim of raising the mixture.

These gases, as they get hot during cooking, expand (see Experiment 3) the gluten strands in the enclosing flour mixture stretch with the expanding gases and finally set the cooked mixture in its expanded shape. In this way a light, open textured loaf, cake or pudding is made.

MECHANICAL METHODS OF RAISING FLOUR MIXTURES; AIR AS THE RAISING AGENT

SIEVING

Flour can be aerated by sifting it repeatedly through the fingers or more quickly and efficiently by shaking it through a sieve. If the aerating process is repeated several times the flour can entrap still more air (Experiment 2).

Aeration is a useful preliminary to the mixing of any scone, pastry, cake or batter mixture.

CREAMING AND BEATING

In the creaming method of cake making some air is enclosed in the fat and sugar as they are creamed together; it is minute air bubbles, invisible to the naked eye, which make the mixture look pale in colour or 'creamy' and give it a slight sheen. When eggs are beaten into the creamed fat and sugar, still more air is enclosed, as both the yolk, to a slight degree, and the white of egg to a much greater degree, have the power of holding bubbles of air to form a foam. As egg proteins coagulate when heated, their power of holding air is of great value in cake making but, nevertheless, baking powder is added to all but the richest creamed cake mixtures to produce carbon dioxide as an additional raising agent.

When a Yorkshire pudding batter is beaten a little air is enclosed in it but as the mixture is fairly liquid and as it has only one egg in half a pint of liquid the amount of air that can be held by the raw batter is not very great and there is no advantage in continuing to beat it once it is smoothly mixed. Some recipes advise leaving batters to stand, before cooking, to soften the starch grains. As air is lighter than the batter any air incorporated with the flour, or during beating, tends to escape while the batter stands. Steam, rather than air, is the more important raising agent in this type of batter.

WHISKING

When the white and yolk of egg are beaten together they will enclose a certain amount of air but the foam produced soon rises to the top of the liquid and some of the enclosed air escapes. If egg yolk alone is whisked, little air can be enclosed; but egg white alone is easily whisked to a stiff foam which is more stable than that of the whole egg. The addition of about half its weight of sugar to an egg yolk or a whole egg before whisking produces a more stable foam than the egg alone, so that in making sponge cakes, caster sugar and eggs are whisked together and flour is lightly folded into the foam. Air is the only raising agent needed for this type of cake though the steam produced during baking increases the lightness. To fix the air in the mixture it should be baked immediately the flour has been folded in, the oven heat should be moderate so as to set the mixture but not to expand the air too rapidly.

PHYSICAL METHOD OF RAISING FLOUR MIXTURES; STEAM AS THE RAISING AGENT

Steam, which is produced when the water in any moist mixture reaches boiling-point during cooking, may be considered a by-product of the mixing and cooking of flour batters and doughs but, although no special process is needed to introduce it into flour mixtures, its importance as a raising agent should not be underestimated.

To make effective use of steam as a raising agent two conditions are essential, a high proportion of liquid in the mixture and a high baking temperature as in Yorkshire pudding. Given these two conditions, the water soon reaches boiling-point, gives off a good head of steam which forces its way up through the mixture and so stretches or raises it, while the heat of the oven sets the mixture of flour and egg in this stretched or risen shape.

The characteristic texture of any mixture raised mainly by steam is very open and rather uneven, having pockets of air left after the steam has escaped. Yorkshire pudding, flaky or rough puff pastry and choux pastry are all good examples of the raising power of steam; all are rather moist mixtures when raw, all are baked at temperatures of 400° Fahrenheit or over and all should have open textures.

CHEMICAL METHODS OF RAISING FLOUR MIXTURES; CARBON DIOXIDE AS THE RAISING AGENT

Carbon dioxide gas is produced in flour mixtures by the action of the inorganic chemical bicarbonate of soda, alone or with an acid. In home baking, the bicarbonate of soda is sometimes used alone, but more usually in the mixture sold as 'baking-powder' in which it is combined with an acid substance. By whichever means it is produced, carbon dioxide escapes through the crumb and crust of a mixture when it is cooked and is replaced by air.

BICARBONATE OF SODA

It has been found by Experiment 5 that bicarbonate of soda with boiling water effervesces leaving an alkaline solution and that when acid is added to this solution more effervescence occurs. Experiment 9 has shown that scones made with bicarbonate of soda, although they rise in the oven, have, when baked, an unpleasant taste and smell and a dark yellow colour, but that if an acid substance such as cream of tartar is added as well as bicarbonate of soda, the resulting scones have none of these unpleasant characteristics and are, moreover, better risen.

These results are explained by the fact that bicarbonate of soda in boiling water gives off half its content of carbon dioxide, leaving as residue carbonate of soda or washing soda which gives the scone mixture the disagreeable taste and smell and the dark yellow colour. The equation is $2NaHCO_3 \longrightarrow CO_2 + H_2O + Na_2CO_3$. This action of bicarbonate of soda is made use of in baking but only for mixtures to which are added dark-coloured and strongly flavoured ingredients, such as black treacle, syrup, ginger, spices or chocolate. In such foods as gingerbread, parkin and inexpensive chocolate cake the harsh flavour is disguised and the yellow colour is even an advantage as it deepens the brown colour of the other ingredients. Another advantage of using bicarbonate of soda is the weakening effect which it has on gluten, making the finished cake soft and crumbly.

One serious disadvantage, however, outweighs any minor advantages from the point of view of nutrition: this is that bicarbonate of soda destroys vitamins of the B group, thiamine and riboflavine, which are present in flour.

Experiments 5 and 7 show that, in order to free all the available carbon dioxide in bicarbonate of soda, an acid substance must be added to it. In some recipes, vinegar, sour milk, jam or marmalade supply acid but not always enough to counteract the undesirable effects of the soda. Cream of tartar and tartaric acid are the two acid substances most often mixed with bicarbonate of soda for home-baking because both leave a tasteless, colourless residue and may be used in sufficient amounts to liberate all the gas without altering the flavour. This is a neutralization reaction:

Bicarbonate of soda + acid $\longrightarrow$ tasteless salt + CO_2 + water

Experiments 6 and 7 showed that tartaric acid reacts quickly, and cream of tartar more slowly even when heated with bicarbonate of soda. In order that the cook may have time to mix and bake any flour mixtures before the carbon dioxide has all been given off, it is customary to use either cream of tartar, or a mixture of the two acid powders, with bicarbonate of soda.

BAKING POWDER

For convenience, a mixture of bicarbonate of soda with the correct proportion of an acid reacting powder, which might be cream of tartar, a mixture of cream of tartar and tartaric acid or nowadays almost always an acid phosphate of calcium or sodium, is made commercially and sold as 'baking-powder'. As these ingredients will react together if they become damp, a filler, usually a starch powder, is added to absorb moisture from the atmosphere and to keep the active ingredients separated. The filler also, by increasing the bulk, makes it easier to measure the powder accurately.

To release all its carbon dioxide, bicarbonate of soda needs an equal weight of tartaric acid or twice its own weight of cream of tartar, so that in order to make all baking-powders of uniform raising power one quarter of the powder should always be bicarbonate of soda and the amount of filler added should be varied to make up the total weight as follows:

Baking-powder Recipes

I. *Slow action*
25% bicarbonate of soda
50% cream of tartar
25% filler

___

100

II. *Medium action*
25% bicarbonate of soda
$12\frac{1}{2}$% tartaric acid
25% cream of tartar
$37\frac{1}{2}$% filler

___

100

According to the kind of acid reacting powder used, the mixture will give off carbon dioxide at different rates, but as the baking-powder is used in a comparatively large bulk of a moist flour mixture, which hinders the escape of gas, there is never any danger that all the raising action will take place, or any gas be wasted, before baking, at normal speed of work.

In the making of scones it has been found by Experiment 10, that scones left waiting for half an hour before being baked were rather lighter and more even in texture than those baked at once.

Baking-powder may be made at home from either of the two foregoing recipes but apart from being interesting as an experiment there is no advantage of either quality or price over the commercial brands. Commercially, calcium-acid-phosphate or sodium-acid-phosphate is generally used nowadays as the acid ingredient of baking-powder. In the past there has been a wide variation in the amount of carbon dioxide produced by different brands of commercial baking-powder but the manufacturers of several well-known brands have now agreed that their baking-powders shall all produce the same proportion of carbon dioxide. They have, furthermore, agreed to alter the recipes that they publish, to fit this new formula.

SELF RAISING FLOUR

'Self raising' flour is usually a weak flour (that is, one which produces a relatively low proportion of a soft gluten, which is suitable for cakes and biscuits), with an admixture of bicarbonate of soda and an acid phosphate. The raising power of these ingredients is usually equivalent to the addition of four level teaspoonfuls of baking-powder to each pound of flour, and is only suitable for scones and very plain cakes.

Proportions of Baking-powder to Use

Kind of mixture	Amount of baking-powder to 1 lb. flour
Girdle Scones	4 to 5 level teaspoonfuls
Oven ,,	4 to 5 ,, ,, ,,
Suet pastry	4 to 5 ,, ,, ,,
Plain cakes, rubbing-in method, 2 eggs	4 to 5 ,, ,, ,,
Cakes, half fat to flour, rubbing-in or creaming method, 4 eggs	4 ,, ,, ,,
Cakes, three-quarters fat to flour, 6 eggs	3 ,, ,, ,,
,, equal fat to flour, 8 eggs	2 ,, ,, ,,
,, Christmas, i.e. equal fat to flour, heavily fruited, 8-10 eggs	None
Whisked sponge cakes	None

Note: These proportions are based on experiments with modern baking-powder of the newly-agreed formula with a fairly high production of carbon dioxide—in the past some brands required different proportions.

BIOLOGICAL METHOD OF RAISING FLOUR MIXTURES; CARBON DIOXIDE AS THE RAISING AGENT

Carbon dioxide gas may also be produced in flour mixtures by the biological action known as fermentation, which is brought about by yeast combining with the sugar in flour in moist, slightly warm conditions.

9

MAKING FLOUR MIXTURES
LIGHT: II

EXPERIMENTS WITH YEAST

1. Consider very carefully the differences of texture and flavour between a scone and a bread roll and between a rock cake and a bath bun.
2. Examine a piece of baker's yeast for colour, smell, texture and taste; put a small piece aside and allow it to get dry.
3. Cut 1 oz. baker's yeast into 8 equal pieces; make $\frac{1}{4}$ pint water lukewarm or tepid by mixing $\frac{1}{3}$ boiling with $\frac{2}{3}$ cold; this is approximately blood-heat and can be tested with the little finger to which it should feel neither hot nor cold. Put 5 pieces of the yeast each in a small basin, tumbler or test tube and label them (a) to (e).

    (a) To this add 1 tablespoon lukewarm water
    (b) To this add 1 tablespoon lukewarm water and $\frac{1}{2}$ level teaspoon sugar.
    (c) To this add 1 tablespoon lukewarm water and 2 level teaspoons flour
    (d) To this add 1 tablespoon boiling water and $\frac{1}{2}$ level teaspoon sugar
    (e) To this add 1 tablespoon very cold water and $\frac{1}{2}$ level teaspoon sugar

    Keep (a) to (d) just warm for $\frac{1}{2}$ hour.
    Keep (e) cold for $\frac{1}{2}$ hour then warm for $\frac{1}{2}$ hour.
    Notice everything that happens to each sample during this time.
4. (a) Have 3 tablespoons flour slightly warm, and heat an oven to 450° F. or Regulo 9.
    Mix $\frac{1}{8}$ oz. piece of yeast with first a few drops of lukewarm water then with 1 tablespoon and with this liquid mix the warm flour to a dough.
    Cut the dough into 3 equal pieces and label them (i), (ii), (iii).
    (i) Bake this in the hot oven at once for 10 mins.
    (ii) Keep this very cold for 20 mins. then bake it.

    (*iii*) Keep this warm for ½ hour then bake it.

    (*b*) Repeat 4 (*a*) using very hot flour and boiling water.

    (*c*)   ,,   ,,   ,,   ,,   cold flour and very cold water.

5.   Make a soft dough with 2 level tablespoons of flour, 1 tablespoon cooked potato mashed, 1 level teaspoon sugar and tepid water; keep this dough in a warm place uncovered for two or three days, damping the top with tepid water as it dries.

RESULTS

It should be found from these experiments that bread and yeast buns have a softer, more elastic texture and a firmer crust than similar mixtures raised with baking-powder and that they have a characteristic flavour. Baker's yeast may best be described as putty-coloured, smooth-textured and moist; it will be found to have a fruity or beery smell and to hold together in one block when fresh but to become dry, crumbly, hard and darker in colour when stale.

Experiments 3 and 4 will have shown that, with warm water and either sugar or flour, yeast if kept warm will produce bubbles; if sufficient flour is used to make a dough this bubbling can make the dough rise. As well as warmth, water and sugar or flour it will have been noticed that yeast needed a little time to raise the dough—the dough baked at once being smaller and harder than the one which was kept warm before baking.

Throughout the experiments it will have been found that the yeast when made really hot or kept really cold did not produce bubbles; that the hot sample even when cooled to luke-warm did not bubble but that the cold sample when warmed began to produce bubbles.

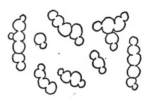

Fig. 30. Yeast Cells Budding

If Experiment 5 was successful the moist mixture, after two or three days, will have begun to bubble or to *ferment*, showing that 'wild' yeast had settled on it and was behaving in the same way as baker's yeast.

The explanation of these results is that yeast is really a minute plant of the fungus type; each plant being made of only one cell which measures about $\frac{1}{3,600}$ inch across. Tiny as this plant is, it can, like all plants, reproduce itself which it does by separating off a part of its one cell to form a bud, which grows into a full-size cell and in its turn buds: so that one cell can, in favourable conditions, produce a chain or colony of new cells (see Fig. 30). During this process of reproduction the yeast cells need sugar as food and this they split up releasing carbon dioxide gas and alcohol.

Yeast was probably discovered by accident by leaving a moist flour paste or a sweet fruit pulp in a warm place for some hours when it would collect wild yeast which is always present on the skins of fruit and the husks of grain, and which would multiply and cause fermentation. Yeast of this type was used for thousands of years. For bread-making a leaven was used which was a moist piece of dough kept from one batch of bread to the next and which would collect wild yeast in addition to the yeast already allowed to multiply in it. As well as for leavening bread, wild yeast was used for fermenting alcoholic liquors such as beer and the surplus yeast thus produced might also be used for bread-making. Up to about 100 years ago brewer's yeast was commonly used for bread-making but its raising power was variable and it was so lively that it was not easy to use and impossible to store.

Nowadays the yeast used for bread-making is cultivated from molasses or from malted grain and is usually a by-product of distilling. It is washed and then compressed for easy storage and weighing. Fresh baker's yeast cannot be stored for more than a few days but it may also be bought in a dried 'live' form (not to be confused with dried 'autolysed' yeast, for medicinal use) which may be stored indefinitely.

THE ACTION OF YEAST IN BREAD-MAKING

In bread-making it is, of course, the carbon dioxide gas produced by yeast that is required to raise the dough—the alcohol is allowed to evaporate. The more air that can be supplied to the yeast, the more carbon dioxide and the less alcohol will it produce. The necessary conditions which allow the yeast to raise the bread satisfactorily are a temperature of between 76° and 82° Fahrenheit, a supply of water at this temperature, a small supply of sugar which is found in the flour itself and time, varying conversely with the proportion of yeast to flour.

The whole action of producing carbon dioxide from yeast and flour is complicated, but briefly stated, the flour contains 2% sugar and an enzyme, diastase, which changes some of the starch of the flour to a sugar, maltose; the yeast also contains three enzymes; maltase which changes maltose to glucose; sucrase, also called invertase, which changes sucrose to invert sugar, a compound of glucose and fructose and thirdly zymase, which splits up both glucose and invert sugar into carbon dioxide and alcohol (see Fig. 31).

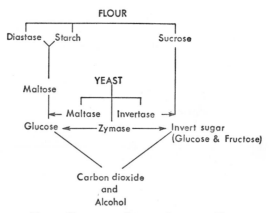

Fig. 31. DIAGRAM OF ENZYME ACTION OF YEAST

USE OF YEAST IN BREAD-MAKING

For bread-making at home the following rules are a guide:

1. Buy fresh baker's yeast which may be stored in a cool place, covered, for not more than three days.

2. Use strong flour, that is flour containing a high proportion of gluten of good quality. A simple test for the strength of flour is to clutch a handful of it tightly; when released it should hold together in a cake.

3. Have all ingredients warmed to 80° Fahrenheit, that is just tepid (water, $\frac{1}{3}$ boiling and $\frac{2}{3}$ cold will give the right temperature) and keep them at this temperature throughout the mixing. If yeast is made too warm the tiny plants weaken and then die, if flour is made too hot some of the enzyme diastase is destroyed.

4. Use $\frac{1}{4}$ oz. salt in each pound of flour (more retards the action of yeast) and aerate the flour and salt well to increase the proportion of carbon dioxide and lessen the proportion of alcohol produced;

yeast can respire both aerobically and anaerobically, but the more air the more carbon dioxide, the less air the more alcohol.

5. Use yeast for plain bread in the following proportions:

$\frac{1}{2}$ oz. yeast to 1 lb. flour.

1 ,,   ,,   ,, 3 ,,   ,,

$1\frac{1}{2}$,,   ,,   ,, 6 ,,   ,,

The reason for decreasing the proportion of yeast in the larger amount is that the larger bulk of flour provides the yeast with more sugar to start its action.

6. Mix the dough with about $\frac{1}{2}$ pint tepid water to each pound of flour, using a little water to liquefy the yeast. Sugar, given in some recipes, should not be used to 'cream' or 'liquefy' the yeast as it ruptures the yeast cells and weakens the action. The dough should be soft and pliable but not sticky and must be kneaded heavily for about 10 minutes so that yeast cells are distributed evenly all through the dough and so that the gluten of the flour is strengthened to give the loaves firm shapes and crisp crusts.

7. Keep shaped loaves in an airy place with a temperature of 80° Fahrenheit until they have doubled in size.

8. Bake at 450° Fahrenheit, a high temperature which will soon kill the yeast (so that the loaves do not rise too much) and which will expand the gas already produced and also harden the crust. The expansion of the loaves in the oven is known as 'oven spring'. During baking the carbon dioxide escapes through the dough and is replaced by air.

THE EFFECT ON YEAST OF ADDITIONAL INGREDIENTS

As well as bread, many kinds of buns, cakes and even pastry are made with yeast and these require such ingredients as sugar, fat and eggs which all have some effect on the action of yeast.

Sugar, in small quantities, hastens the production of carbon dioxide but in proportions of over 2 oz. to 1 lb. of flour it increasingly retards the action.

Fat in proportions of over 1 oz. to 1 lb. flour retards the action of yeast.

Eggs, although they contain fat which would slow up the production of carbon dioxide, have such a marked ability to hold air in a mixture that their inclusion helps to make a lighter yeast mixture.

It should be noted that excess salt, which would in any case make bread or cakes unpalatable, can retard the action of yeast but in bread the standard proportion of $\frac{1}{4}$ oz. to 1 lb. flour is essential to a good 'nutty' flavour.

In order to overcome the adverse effect of adding sugar, fat and milk, which contains fat, to a yeast mixture, one of the following variations on the standard method for making bread may be used.

1. Extra yeast may be used: 1 oz. or for very rich mixtures 2 oz. of yeast to each 1 lb. of flour.
2. Additional time may be allowed for rising: 2 hours or even over-night rising may be allowed.
3. The mixture may be prepared in two parts: a dough of flour, liquid, a little sugar and a high proportion of yeast is made and allowed to rise, then to the risen dough, extra ingredients as sugar, fat, dried fruit and eggs are added, and further rising or proving allowed.

Note on Dried Yeast

Dried 'live' or 'baker's' yeast may be used if fresh yeast is not available. It is sold in small envelopes or in tins and if sealed it may be kept in a cool place for several weeks. The instructions on the pack must be followed carefully. Half the weight of fresh yeast is used, the dried yeast is sprinkled on to the warm liquid and kept warm for 15 minutes before mixing into the dough.

10

PLANNING AND SERVING
MEALS

The whole of this book is really about meals because, of course, all food is cooked to be eaten as meals, but this chapter is to consider particularly how the good cook can reach her final aim of serving really good meals. A good meal is a pleasant occasion at which everyone enjoys the food, has the right kind of food at the right time for his or her special needs and eats it in a happy, peaceful atmosphere.

That sounds simple enough, but the production of such a meal calls for a certain amount of organization, as well as a knowledge of cooking. The organization is often not apparent, because an expert cook, who feeds her family well, has probably learnt, partly by experience and often partly by following custom or tradition, what food suits the different members; what different foods go well together; when and where to buy them; how much she can afford to spend on food and how much time to allow for getting the meal ready so that it is served on time and no one is hurried or anxious. To consider these points one at a time, the most important is the choice of food to suit the needs of different individuals. This topic has been discussed in Chapter 4 so that only a short résumé is needed here.

FOOD TO SUIT THE INDIVIDUAL

Although everyone needs a mixed or balanced diet, the total amount of food and the proportion of the main nutrients vary considerably with:

Age: All growing babies, children and adolescents need a relatively higher proportion of protein and protective foods than do adults. Adolescents may need more food than their parents. Old people, needing less food in proportion to their decreased activity may, like children, need relatively more protein and protective foods than carbohydrate foods.

Sex and Work: The more active the work the more Calories will the workers need from their food, but it has not been proved that the proportion of protein need increase as much as the energy food.

Women, as a rule—being smaller and doing less active work—need less total of food than men.

Climate: Common sense shows that in hot weather there is need for a little less of the energy foods which of course also supply heat and for more of the cooling, refreshing foods such as salad and fruit, the difference being more between the kinds of foods that are attractive than between amounts of nutrients required at different seasons. Perhaps custom also determines that certain food is eaten in winter and not in summer, for example, roast turkey and Christmas pudding.

THE BALANCED DIET

The balanced or mixed diet must be an everyday rule and in fact each meal should if possible contain some of all the nutrients. The reasons for this are that many of the protective foods cannot be stored in the body and therefore must be supplied daily and that protein foods, if eaten without carbohydrates, will be used by the body as fuel instead of for tissue building. Each meal should contain some protein, fat, minerals and vitamins and sufficient carbohydrate foods to 'fill up the corners' or to satisfy hunger.

There are two simple ways of checking the nutrients: by listing the foods important for supplying each nutrient and making up the diet from this list:

1. *Building foods, Animal*   *Vegetable*

Meat		Bread and other foods	
Bacon	serve at least	made from wheat	serve one or
Fish	two normal	flour	other at
Eggs	helpings	Whole cereals	each meal
Cheese	daily	Pulses	

Milk—at least 1 pint daily.

2. *Protective foods* (in addition to the above, which all contain minerals and vitamins)

Raw and cooked green vegetables
Raw or cooked root   „   At least two helpings daily for
Raw fruit, e.g. oranges or grape-fruit   Vitamin C and Vitamin A
Canned or cooked fruit

Butter or margarine: At most meals for Vitamins A and D.

Liver: At least once a week for Vitamins A, D, B and iron.

Oily fish, such as herrings: At least once a week for Vitamins A and D.

Sea fish: At least once a week for the body's iodine needs.

3. *Fat in addition to butter and margarine* for long-lasting energy.
4. *Lastly round off the meal with energy foods:*
   Bread, buns, biscuits, cakes, pastry, puddings, jam, marmalade, honey or syrup, ice-cream.

The second way to check the balance of a meal or the diet is to list the foods actually served and to tabulate them with the different nutrients, putting a tick against the food which is a good source of the nutrient or two ticks for a very rich source, thus:

Meal	Food	Protein	Fat	A	D	B	C	Iron	Calcium	Carbohydrate
						Vitamins				
Breakfast	Orange juice			✓			✓		✓	✓
	Bacon	✓	✓			✓		✓	✓	
	Bread and cereal	✓				✓		✓	✓	✓✓
	Butter or margarine		✓	✓	✓					
	Jam, marmalade						a little			✓
	Milk, ¼ pint	✓	✓	✓	a little	✓			✓	✓
Dinner	Beef	✓	✓	✓		✓		✓	✓	
	Yorkshire pudding	✓	✓	✓	✓			✓	✓	✓
	Potatoes, roast		✓			✓	?			✓
	Cabbage			✓			✓✓	✓	✓	
	Stewed gooseberries					✓	✓	✓	✓	✓
	Powder custard	✓	a little	✓	✓	✓			✓	✓
High tea, supper or lunch	Cheese	✓✓	✓✓	✓		✓			✓✓	
	Bread	✓				✓		✓	✓	✓✓
	Butter		✓	✓	✓				✓	
	Watercress			✓		✓	✓✓	✓	✓	
	Milk, ⅓ pint	✓	✓	✓	✓	✓			✓	✓
	Cake (with egg)	✓	✓	✓	✓	✓			✓	✓✓

From these examples of meals it is easy to check whether the nutrients are present, though not, of course, the amount of each. These meals would give a well-balanced diet for the day, while snacks might add extra protein probably in milk and would certainly add carbohydrate in the odd bun or biscuit.

Notice what a good balance the light tea or supper meal has. It is similar to the 'Oslo breakfast' which is so called because, in Oslo, undernourished school-children who arrive at school without any breakfast, have been given this type of meal every day before lessons with resulting great improvement in their health. The Oslo meal consists of wholemeal bread, butter, a glass of milk, cheese, green salad and an orange: this is an excellent, quickly prepared meal at any time.

Notice also that the traditional British roast beef dinner is a good one with all the nutrients represented, as they are in several other examples of *traditional dishes* such as Lancashire Hot-pot, Scotch Broth and Irish Stew.

ECONOMY OF FUEL

Careful planning of meals can reduce the consumption of electricity or gas for cooking: with solid fuel the economy is not so marked but the same rules will serve to reduce the rate of burning by conserving the heat in the cooker.

SOME SUGGESTIONS FOR ECONOMY OF FUEL

A meal may be cooked entirely by top heat by using a steamer: if the steamer has several tiers this is easy but with a little ingenuity a complete meal can be fitted into a saucepan with a steamer top; for example fish may be steamed over a pudding and vegetables can be cooked round the pudding or steamed round the fish.

Top heat can also be used economically if two or three saucepans are arranged over one hot-plate or gas-ring: semicircular and triangular pans are made for this purpose.

One cold course, cooked beforehand, may be served with a hot one, for example, a cold sweet after grilled meat or cold meat with salad before a steamed pudding.

A pressure cooker can save a great deal of fuel as only $\frac{1}{4}$ to $\frac{1}{3}$ normal cooking time is needed and the whole first course can be cooked at one time.

The oven may be used for entire meals which may be more varied than those cooked by top heat only. For meals cooked in the oven, dishes must be chosen which all need about the same temperature and which can all be fitted into the oven within the time required for the longest dish. The difference of several degrees in the temperature of the top and bottom of the oven should be made use of in fitting in several dishes. It is useful to note that some dishes normally simmered on top heat can quite well be cooked in the oven, for example, potatoes brought to boiling-point in very little water or milk may be simmered in the oven.

It should be realized that very little fuel is used in keeping a thermo-statically controlled oven at 300° to 350° F. for an hour or more.

Modern kitchen-ware designed for use in the oven includes oven-glass, heat-proof oven-ware and, most useful of all, vitreous enamelled steel casseroles and flame-proof porcelain and glass dishes which can be used both for top and oven heat.

The heat needed for cooking a meal in the oven can also be used for an extra dish such as stewed fruit or a cake and if, for example, pastry is baked, extra pies or tarts may be made for other meals.

Examples of Meals Cooked in an Oven

Dish	Oven setting	Time needed and position in oven	Additional notes
1. Stewed meat and casserole of root vegetables	300°-325° F. Gas No. 2-3	2-2½ hours for lamb or veal 2½-3 hours for mutton or beef: lower half of oven	Cold water or fried stew may be begun on top heat if time is short
Potatoes baked in skins	„ „ „	1¼ hours to 1½ hours: round other dishes	
Apple charlotte or		1½ hours: top shelf	If the pudding is put into the oven for the same
Eve's pudding or		1¼ hours: top shelf ¾ hour: top shelf	time as meat it must be covered to prevent
Any baked cake-pudding			overcooking
with stewed fruit		½ to ¾ hour: top shelf	
2. Roast Meat and potatoes	400° F. or Gas No. 6-7	Time according to weight of joint: top shelf	If Yorkshire pudding is included the pie must be baked early then the
Roast parsnips or casserole of carrots, leeks		Vegetables ¾ to 1 hour: bottom of oven	roast moved to lower shelf and the pudding
Fruit pie	„ „ „	35 to 45 mins.: middle of oven	baked on top
Yorkshire pudding	„ „ „	35 to 45 mins.: top shelf	
3. Baked stuffed fish	350°-360° F. or Gas No. 4-5	40-50 mins.: according to weight of fish: top shelf	Fish coated with egg and crumbs and cooked in hot fat
Baked tomatoes		20 mins.: tomatoes, middle	
Creamed potatoes in a casserole		40 mins.: potatoes, top	
Stewed fruit		30-40 mins.: bottom plate	
Baked custard or Bread and butter pudding		40-50 mins.: middle	
4. Meat pie (steak)	400° F. Gas No. 7	2-2½ hours (1½ hours if meat is partly pre-cooked): top	Brown the pie at the higher temperature for 20 mins. then reduce heat
Stewed celery	320° F. Gas No. 3	1 to 1½ hours: middle or bottom	to cook filling and other dishes
Creamed potatoes	„ „ „	40 mins.: middle	
Stuffed baked apples		Middle	

SERVING MEALS AT THE RIGHT TIME

The time for any meal must be fixed by the family's other activities of work, school, sports and other clubs and bedtime. Timing may be difficult because the fixed times are rarely the same for everyone in the household but the aim must be to have the main meal of the day at a time when most of the family have time to eat it. If this time is in the evening younger children may need their meal earlier, but this can be a meal taking little time to prepare without spoiling the balance of the nutrients. One point to remember is that food kept hot for more than a matter of minutes usually becomes less attractive, less digestible and loses practically all its Vitamin C, so that any individual meal that must be served much later than the main meal should have the meat carefully reheated or even cold and vegetables freshly cooked or served as salad.

When the time of the meal has been agreed, it is important that the cook should serve it on time so that nobody is anxious about being late and no one has to eat the food hurriedly. On the other hand, it is equally important that the family co-operate and come to the meal in time to do justice to the food which the cook has prepared skilfully and carefully.

In order to be punctual the cook must decide how much time she has available so that she can fit the preparation of the meal into her day's work and avoid elaborate dishes that could not be prepared in the time. An important rule is to begin the cooking in time and, if necessary, fit other jobs in later. For a beginner a timetable is a great help to show her the length of time needed for cooking each dish and to remind her of the time at which cooking must begin, always allowing time for laying the table, for collecting and heating serving dishes and plates as well as a few minutes for dishing:

MENU AND TIMETABLE FOR DINNER AT 1.0 P.M.

Stewed steak	2½ hours to cook;	put in oven by	10.15 a.m.
Apple charlotte	1½ ,, ,, ,,	,, ,, ,, ,,	11.30 a.m.
Boiled potatoes	20-30 mins. to cook:	,, ,, pan ,,	12.25 p.m.
Sprouts	10-15 ,, ,, ,,	,, ,, ,, ,,	12.40 to
			12.45 p.m.

The time needed for preparing each dish will vary with the skill and speed of the worker and on this will depend the amount of time to spare for other household jobs. It is obvious that the meat must be prepared first and its gentle simmering begun; next all root vegetables will be scrubbed and those for the stew peeled, sliced and added. As the apple charlotte must go into the oven one hour later this can be made next and the worker should have well over an hour to spare before peeling potatoes and washing sprouts.

In planning a meal it is also important to make sure that the suggested dishes can all be prepared with the equipment and in the cooking space available and that only one dish needs close attention at the last moment. For example, if the cooker has only two boiling rings or plates ingenuity will be needed to arrange top-heat for three or four dishes and if the meat course is to be grilled it is wiser to serve a grilled vegetable or a salad than to have a boiled green vegetable to dish at the same moment as the grill.

ENJOYMENT OF THE MEAL

The enjoyment of food is an aid to good digestion because the secretion of digestive juices is stimulated by pleasant sensations such as smelling and tasting appetising food and enjoying its attractive colour. The opposite is also true, that the digestive juices do not work so well if the food smells, tastes or looks unpleasant, or if it is actively disliked. Still worse, any unpleasant emotion of anger, worry or grief can cause indigestion. A calm, happy meal-time is, therefore, not only pleasant, but necessary if everyone is to derive the greatest benefit from the well-balanced meal. Any trouble taken to make meals attractive is well worth while.

Meals are made attractive in the first instance by good cooking and also by variety of flavour, texture and colour in the food and by gaiety and neatness in dishing and in laying the table.

Variety of flavours. The same foodstuff or sauce or decoration should not be used in any two dishes in a meal nor the same flavouring of any kind be used so often that it becomes monotonous.

Texture. It is not good dietetically, nor does it make an interesting meal, if several dishes are, for example, fried or made with pastry. Two stewed dishes in the same meal would probably be too much alike in texture: a better contrast of texture would be one dish with pastry and one soft, creamy-textured dish.

Colour. Contrasts in colour can make a meal look gay and inviting, for example, carrots on brown sauce or tomatoes with a white fish would be pleasanter than all brown or all white dishes.

Dishing. All dishes look more attractive if they are neatly arranged and if the dishes themselves are free of splashes and fingermarks.

Laying the table. If nothing necesssary is forgotten and if the china, glass and cutlery are all clean and shining and the cloth or table mats clean and crisp the appearance of the table can add to the enjoyment of the food and make a worthy setting for a well-chosen and well-cooked meal.

SHOPPING FOR FOOD

WHAT TO BUY

As well as knowledge of the different groups of foodstuffs that are needed for a balanced diet there are several other points to consider when shopping for food. For most households the question of expense is most important and wise shopping can keep down the cost without cutting down the food value. A budget is usually made to allot a reasonable proportion of the household income to each of the many items on which money must be spent for the family; the money allocated to food should be kept separate and never borrowed for other purposes because good food is needed every day. An account should be kept of all money spent.

When shopping for food, a shopping-list should be made and the money to be spent put in a separate purse—never mixed with personal pocket-money. The items on the list are usually grouped according to the shop, stall or department in which they will be bought: some of these groups will cost more than others but an understanding of the nutritive value of foods will make it possible to substitute cheaper foods for the dearest items in the group. The shopping-list can rarely be followed exactly: a quick change of mind may be necessary to buy what is best and cheapest on the day.

WHAT TO SPEND

The butcher's bill is usually a heavy one and, as first-class protein is extremely important in the diet, money should be saved by substituting cheaper cuts for the prime ones rather than buying a smaller amount. The butcher is often glad to help in the choice because there is far less of the prime quality meat on any animal than there is of the second quality. For example, brisket and top-side are cheaper than sirloin, and stewing meat is always cheaper than the tender cuts needed for frying. It should also be remembered that cheese is very much cheaper than meat and contains equally good proteins and that vegetable proteins can supplement those in meat.

The fishmonger's bill can also be reduced without loss of food-value. Cod fillet and rock-fish are much cheaper than plaice, sole or turbot for example, and herrings, usually the cheapest of all fish, have not only a good flavour but also a very high food value indeed.

The greengrocer's bill is another heavy one that may be reduced without any loss of balance in the diet: cabbage for example, is cheaper than sprouts or cauliflower but contains just as much Vitamin C and A. In this shop the most expensive items are perhaps more obviously luxuries than in any other.

The dairy bill should be comparatively heavy because milk, eggs and cheese are extremely good foods which, compared with meat and fish, are not dear. Butter is the item which allows of economy because its price varies but its food value does not; and margarine, at half to two-thirds the price, contains as much Vitamin A and rather more Vitamin D.

The grocer's and baker's bills may also allow a margin for saving, as bought cakes, biscuits, and tarts are much dearer than home-made varieties and are often of much less nutritive value, and many prepared and packeted foods and mixes are dearer than the same ingredients bought more simply. The food value of the more expensive groceries and confectionery is not usually worth the higher cost.

WHERE TO SHOP

Prices of perishable foods vary from one district to another but shopping far from home is only worth while if time can be spared for the journey and if the price of the fare is saved in the lower cost of the food. The choice of the kind of shop also needs some thought as each type has its good and bad points.

Supermarkets and Self-service Shops

Shopping for many items under the one roof saves time; many goods are sold at 'cut prices'; there is usually a wide variety to chose from but, unless the shopper is strong-minded she may be tempted to buy attractive but unnecessary things.

Shops Giving Personal Service

Many shoppers enjoy the personal contact with the salesman who will also often give sound advice but in a small shop the choice of food-stuffs may be more restricted and there may not be any cut-price offers.

Stalls and Street-markets

Fruit and vegetables are often sold cheaply by street vendors who do not have such heavy overhead costs as do shop-keepers. Their produce is usually fresh as they cannot as a rule store perishable goods and therefore stock only as much as they can sell in one day.

When to Shop

Shopping for groceries should only be necessary once a week or even once a fortnight if a list is kept in the kitchen of the items that need replacing. The aim is never to run out of any essential item nor to stock so much of it that it will get stale.

Shopping for perishable foods should be done daily unless there is a cool safe place for storing them—preferably a refrigerator in which they may be stored for two to three days. Fresh foods should, however, be bought early enough to allow time for the necessary preparation and cooking.

APPROXIMATE AMOUNTS OF FOOD TO BUY OR SERVE

Appetites and personal liking for different foods vary widely as do fashions and habits of eating and as these all affect the amount of food that will be eaten this list is only approximate. It is based on average tastes of adults with moderate appetites.

Raw foods	Amount per helping
Eggs	1 to 2
Meat, without bone or waste	4 oz.
,, with ,, ,, ,,	6 to 12 oz.
Fish, filleted	4 to 6 oz.
,, with bone and/or head	6 to 12 oz.
Cheese	1 to 2 oz.
Vegetables: Potatoes	4 to 12 oz.
Green vegetable	4 oz.
Root ,,	4 oz.
Spinach	$\frac{1}{2}$ lb.
Peas	$\frac{1}{2}$ lb.
Broad beans	$\frac{1}{2}$ to $\frac{3}{4}$ lb.

Raw foods		Amount per helping
Fruit:	Raw, fresh	$\frac{1}{4}$ to $\frac{1}{2}$ lb.
	for stewing	$\frac{1}{4}$ to $\frac{1}{3}$ lb.
Pasta or rice for savoury dishes		1 to 2 oz.
Pulses		1 to $1\frac{1}{2}$ oz. (before soaking)

Cooked dishes	
Sauces	$\frac{1}{6}$ pint
Gravy	,, ,,
Custard	$\frac{1}{8}$ to $\frac{1}{6}$ pint
Milk puddings	$\frac{1}{4}$ to $\frac{1}{3}$ pint milk
Pastry	1 to 2 oz. flour
Steamed or baked puddings	1 to $1\frac{1}{2}$ oz. flour

Beverages		
Milk for tea		$\frac{1}{8}$ to $\frac{1}{6}$ pint (to allow 2 cups)
,, ,, coffee		$\frac{1}{3}$ pint (,, ,, ,,)

Coffee: $1\frac{1}{2}$ to 2 level tablespoons in $\frac{1}{3}$ to $\frac{1}{2}$ pint water (to allow 2 cups)
Tea: Amount cannot be estimated for home consumption!

PLANNING MEALS FOR SMALL CHILDREN
(ONE TO FIVE YEARS OLD)

Meals for little children are not only important to them for building strong, healthy bodies but they can also form a valuable part of their education by teaching them to enjoy well-balanced meals and by helping them to acquire good food-habits and good table-manners. To achieve these aims meal-times should be enjoyable, which means that they should be calm and happy, with neither children nor grown-ups cross or worried and that the food served should taste good, look attractive and be reasonably easy for a child to eat.

To make food attractive to a child it should have some bright colours as of tomato, carrot, well cooked green vegetables or bright coloured fruit; it may be served in fancy individual shapes or moulds and it should be free of uneatable skins, bones, gristle and surplus fat. Helpings should be small enough for the child to eat willingly and, because small children have small appetites, it is wise to make sure that all the building and protective foods are eaten and that extra energy foods are only added after these.

Food should not be over-sweetened or over-flavoured in any way because children enjoy the natural flavour of food unless their palates are spoilt by too much added flavouring. To make food easy to eat the right tools should be provided for the child's age—a spoon and pusher and a plate with an upright edge for the very young and gradually more grown-up tools when the child wants to copy his elders. The food should be in pieces of a manageable size, particularly meat which should be cut into small, mouthful-sized pieces or minced, but food should not be too soft and pulpy.

SOME GUIDING RULES FOR SERVING MEALS TO
SMALL CHILDREN

1. Children should have some fresh air and exercise to get an appetite but they should have time to calm down, go to the W.C. and wash hands just before the meal.
2. Children should not be kept waiting for a meal because they soon get bored and may lose their appetites: for the same reason the meal should not be too long-drawn-out; 20-30 minutes is as long as good behaviour and interest can be expected.
3. Children should be allowed to feed themselves as far as they are able but help should be given as soon as they begin to get tired of this activity.
4. Food fads should be tactfully discouraged from the earliest age, partly by ignoring them, partly by setting a good adult example of appearing to enjoy all foods equally and never expressing dislike of a food in front of a child.
5. New foods may be introduced without comment together with well-known food: if the first attempt is unsuccessful coercion is probably useless but the same food should be offered again fairly soon until it is no longer strange.
6. No snacks should be given between meals except for milk mid-morning or possibly an apple or other fresh fruit. Sweets and ice-cream should be given as part of, or directly after, a meal and never as a bribe for eating less attractive food.
7. Every meal should include some crisp, hard food to exercise the jaws and so help teeth to grow straight and well spaced.

FOODS TO INCLUDE IN MEALS FOR SMALL CHILDREN

Food		Daily allowance
Building Foods	Milk	1 to 1½ pts. including that used in cooking
	Meat, liver, heart, bacon, ham, poultry Fish, including roes, herring, mackerel, tinned salmon or sardines drained of oil Cheese, eggs	At least 2 servings of 1 to 2 oz.
Vegetables and Fruit	Potatoes cooked in different ways	1 to 2 tablespoons
	Green or root vegetables	1 serving of 1 to 2 tablespoons
	Cooked or raw shredded salad	1 serving
	Orange juice, blackcurrant or rose-hip syrup	1 serving
	Raw or stewed fruit	1 serving, or at least every other day
Fats	Butter or margarine Suet or lard	1 to 1½ oz. including any used in cooking
Carbohydrates	Bread, toast, rusks, wholewheat or oat cereals, home-made cakes, biscuits, cake-puddings, suet puddings, plain pastry	
	Sugar, syrup, honey, jam	Not more than 2 oz. including that used in cooking
Cod-liver or halibut-liver oil	According to recommended dosage	

FOODS TO AVOID

Highly sweetened or flavoured foods and pickles

Tea and coffee

Bought cake with synthetic cream

Much fried food because unavoidably some fat is overheated and indigestible

Rich pastry

PLANNING MEALS

Each meal should be balanced, with all the nutrients represented.

Breakfast   Orange juice or blackcurrant or rose-hip syrup;
   whole-wheat or oat cereal or porridge with milk;
   1 to 2 tablespoons egg, fish or bacon;
   toast or rusks and butter;
   milk to drink.

Mid-morning   Milk to drink

Dinner   1 to 3 oz. meat, fish or egg
   or $\frac{1}{2}$ to $\frac{3}{4}$ oz. cheese
   1 to 2 tablespoons potato
   1 to 2   ,,   cooked or shredded raw vegetable or salad
   1 to 3   ,,   any milk pudding or 1 to 2 tablespoons cake or suet pudding
   1 to 2   ,,   stewed fruit if it goes well with the pudding

Something hard to bite should be included—rusk, raw vegetable or raw apple

Water to drink

Tea 1 to 2 tablespoons of egg, fish, bacon or ham $\left.\right\}$ these may be served as sandwiches
   or $\frac{1}{2}$ oz. cheese   using thin bread

   or 1 to 2 tablespoons milk pudding, junket or custard with fruit
   Bread and butter, toast, rusk or home-made cake or biscuit until appetite is satisfied
   Milk to drink

Supper (just before bed) Cup of milk

CARRIED OR PACKED MEALS

When planning a packed meal it is necessary to remember that, like any other meal it must be well balanced. As the easiest foods to pack are sandwiches, rolls, pastry and cakes or biscuits, these meals tend to contain rather too much carbohydrate and it is most important that a normal helping of protein food be included together with fat and some form of salad or fruit: it may also be necessary to pack something to drink.

In choosing the meal consider where it is to be eaten, how it is to be carried and by what means of transport and, of course, suit the food to the time of year or weather and to the person who is to eat it. The kind of food that is packed must also be suitable for the kind of meal, whether it is the lunch taken daily to work, to be carried on foot, in a train or bus, or on a bicycle, or whether it is a holiday picnic, perhaps to be carried by car.

The Meal Carried to Work

This meal must be easy to prepare in a hurry, compactly packed and easy to eat in the fingers, it need not always include a drink as, except for some outdoor workers, there are often facilities for buying or making a suitable drink at the place of work.

An office-worker does not need a bulky meal of high Calorie value so the starchy foods should be in small portions, but, because he or she may not get very hungry at work, variety in the daily lunch-pack will be welcome.

A manual or outdoor-worker, on the other hand, will probably be very hungry and will need a substantial meal with a high proportion of energy-giving foods and will not need to be tempted by a great deal of variety.

The Meal for a Coach or Train Journey

This meal should also be compactly packed and should be easy to unpack and eat; it should make as few crumbs as possible and leave no litter; if a drink is needed a vacuum flask is handy for either cold or hot liquids.

A Holiday Picnic

There may be more time to plan and prepare a more festive meal for a picnic and, if transport is by car, the packing need not be so restricted as for the other meals. Foods needing forks or spoons can be included and such things as canned foods, larger cakes or tarts and jellies are possible. For such a meal such items as forks, knives, spoons, can- or bottle-opener, salt, pepper and sugar in small containers, paper serviettes and a damp cloth for wiping sticky hands should be included and hot or cold drinks can be packed suitably, always remembering, however, that all litter, and especially cans and bottles, must be taken home or put into available litter-bins.

KINDS OF FOOD TO PACK

In general, choose food that will not get crushed or spilt in transit, and that can be eaten conveniently in the particular circumstances.

Protein Foods

These are generally made into sandwiches, pies, pasties or put into split rolls.

One or two points to remember

Sandwiches should have a filling as thick as either slice of bread; sliced loaves are most time-saving but need a really thick layer of filling.
Soft rolls are easier to eat with a filling than crisp ones.
Short pastry makes less crumbs on the whole, than the flaky kinds.
Fillings for sandwiches, rolls and pasties may include:
 all kinds of cooked or canned meats and cooked sausages; cheese, either sliced, or grated and made into a savoury paste; eggs, hard boiled and sliced or mashed with a moist, savoury ingredient such as chutney; or scrambled with savoury additions such as cheese; canned fish.
Protein foods that may be packed whole to be eaten in the fingers include cheese, hard-boiled eggs, cooked sausages, cutlets or joints of chicken, and, with these, buttered rolls, crisp-breads, plain biscuits or bread can be eaten.

Fat

This is usually plentifully supplied by the margarine or butter used in the sandwiches or the fat in pastry or cakes.

Protective Foods

These must be the vitamin-foods not included in the main foods, usually salad vegetables packed in airtight containers and kept whole and dry, or raw fruit which is easy to pack.

Carbohydrates

These are usually plentifully supplied by the bread or pastry of the main food, but to satisfy hunger, and for variety, biscuits, chocolate and cake are popular: cake is best packed as individual portions.

EQUIPMENT FOR PACKING A MEAL

Polythene bags keep food fresh and can be washed and used many times. Greaseproof or waxed paper keeps food fresh but cannot as a rule be used more than once.

Sandwich boxes can be bought but tin boxes, waxed boxes and cartons can make good substitutes.

Vacuum flasks are useful for either hot or cold drinks or in large sizes for other foods. There are also on the market special cool packs useful for keeping milk and meat fresh in hot weather and containers for keeping food hot.

A basket, case or box of suitable size for the particular means of transport may be bought ready fitted or good substitutes can easily be improvised.

PLANNING MEALS FOR THE SICK AND CONVALESCENT

In any illness, correct feeding, although not the cure, is an important part of the treatment and can help a great deal in hastening the patient's recovery. As far as diet is concerned, the illnesses normally treated at home can be divided into two groups, those for which an exact diet is prescribed by medical experts and those for which the doctor gives a more general order for a 'light diet', a 'liquid diet' or perhaps recommends certain foods and forbids others. In all cases the doctor's orders must be obeyed; for illnesses in the first group, which includes diabetes, gout and disorders of metabolism, of the circulation or of the digestive and excretory systems, there will be an exact plan to follow but in the second group, where less guidance is given, the amateur nurse will find a knowledge of nutrition and a sympathetic understanding of her patient's needs most valuable in interpreting orders and in planning from them the right diet for the particular patient.

LIGHT DIET

Anyone ill in bed uses less energy and therefore requires fewer Calories from food than in active health, but the need for protein to repair tissues is very little reduced, and the need for all the protective foods is greater than in health. A smaller total amount of food is therefore given but the balance is slightly different from a normal diet, the carbohydrates and fats being in a smaller, and the protective foods in a greater proportion.

Because the digestion is almost always impaired in illness, the food should be easily digestible and, because there is usually a loss of appetite, meals should be made as attractive as possible to the patient, carefully remembering any special likes and dislikes for food and omitting any foods that are known to disagree with the patient.

Foods included in a Light Diet

Protein foods
Eggs
Milk
White fish
Chicken
Rabbit
Sweetbread
Tripe
Tender veal and later lean beef
    and lamb

Fats
Milk and cream
Butter and margarine

Carbohydrate
Crisp plain biscuits
Crisp toast and day-old bread
Breakfast cereals
Cereals as milk puddings
Oatmeal
Light creamed or sponge cakes

Protective Foods
All fruits known to suit the patient, especially citrus fruits
Vegetable juices
Tomatoes, spinach, cauliflower
Root vegetables that normally agree
Salad if this normally agrees
These are in addition to protective foods in lists above

Foods to be omitted until health is normal
Oily fish
Salt and smoked fish
Fat meat (mutton and pork)
Fats with no vitamin content
Fried foods
Pastry and rich biscuits
New bread
Suet puddings
Pulses
Cheese
Any vegetables and fruits that are known to disagree
Coffee and strong tea
Strong condiments, pickles or bottled sauces

Some dishes suitable for a Light Diet

Breakfast   Lightly cooked egg (scrambled, poached or boiled)
Porridge made with milk
Whole-wheat or oat cereal with milk
Orange, grapefruit or blackcurrant or rose-hip syrup

Main meals, first course
Fish steamed or poached with a good egg or parsley sauce
Stewed veal, sweetbread or tripe with milk in the sauce
Stewed or grilled chicken
Liver, grilled or in a hot-pot, all these with potatoes and a suitable
vegetable

Pudding course
Milk puddings, egg custard, junket
Light cake mixtures steamed or baked
Stewed or tinned fruit with cream, milk pudding or dairy ice-cream
Jellies made with fresh fruit juice, milk or milk and eggs
Simple trifle

Tea and mid-morning lunch
Milk to drink or milky tea
Plain biscuits
Bread and butter
Light cakes
Honey or jam
Extra fruit or fresh fruit drinks, if liked, between meals

To Make Meals Attractive

1. The first point in making meals acceptable to the patient is to make them easy to manage: the tray should be a tray-table or very light in weight and it should not be overloaded. The food itself should be easy to eat: bones should be removed, meat should be free from skin, gristle and fat, and should be in mouthful-sized pieces or minced.

2. To make the meal attractive the tray should be carefully laid; unless it has a pleasant surface it should be covered with a fresh tray-cloth; the food should be served in individual dishes of the prettiest china and glass available and hot food should be covered to retain the heat. The food itself should of course taste very good and also look tempting, being neatly dished with some contrast of colours and bright-coloured garnishes such as tomato, carrot, parsley and on sweet dishes cherries or slices of orange.

3. Small helpings are better than large ones which may discourage a patient with little appetite; the patient may be encouraged to ask for a little more as appetite returns. The food should in any case include as much food value as possible in little bulk by adding eggs to puddings and jellies and by using as much milk as possible.

4. Although the patient's known likes and dislikes must be regarded it is not wise to let him or her know what the next meal will be as the element of pleasant surprise should make the meal more appetizing and a meal that is known beforehand may not come up to over-optimistic expectations.

5. Food that is left at one meal should never be served at a later meal but in the interest of hygiene should be thrown away.

6. Flowers should not be put on the tray as the vase can so easily be upset, and this might distress the patient: they are better put on a table in full view of the patient.

Diet in Fever

In a fever the diet is usually all liquid or semi-liquid because the patient is always very thirsty and because the liquid food is easier to digest and to take by a patient lying flat in bed.

Not many years ago it was customary to starve a fever but this treatment has now been found to be most unwise because in fever the body uses up food and produces energy at a greatly increased rate due to the toxins produced by the bacteria which caused the disease. If the patient is not given sufficient Calories in food then the body's own protein and fat will be used up to supply them and the sick person will lose much weight and become unnecessarily weak. An average of 2,000 to 3,000 Calories should be given to an adult fever patient, depending on size and build and these Calories should include the normal 70 grammes protein. To include this number of Calories together with the protein in a liquid diet poses a problem which can only be solved by planning the diet carefully.

The foods that should be included to produce the right balance of nutrients are:

Proteins from milk and eggs.
Fats from milk, eggs and cream.
Carbohydrates from cereals used to thicken the milk; oatmeal, semolina, patent barley and rice flour (cornflour, arrowroot, sago and tapioca

are best omitted as they contain negligible amounts of vitamins and minerals), sugar, glucose or lactose used to sweeten milk mixtures and fruit juices.

Protective foods: Vitamins A, D and B complex, with calcium and iron are fairly represented in the foods listed above; Vitamin C is supplied by fresh fruit and fresh fruit juices, particularly oranges, lemons, grapefruit and blackcurrant and rose-hip syrups, and these fruits also add carotene, Vitamin B complex, calcium and iron in useful amounts.

The necessary Calories may be supplied in the following way:

Food	Grammes protein	Calories
3 pts. milk	54	1,020
2 eggs	14	180
4 oz. sugar or glucose		432
2 oz. cereal	6	200
8 oz. fresh fruit		160
Total	74	1,992

This diet is a little high in protein and is 8 Calories short; as few patients would drink more than 3 pints of milk a day the extra Calories might be added by giving cream mixed in with the milky cereal, or by increasing the fruit and sugar. Glucose being less sweet than 'ordinary' sugar and lactose being not at all sweet either of these may be added to foods without making them unpalatable.

The high proportion of milk makes the diet monotonous so that it is important to vary the flavour of the milk mixtures as much as possible by using cocoa, very weak coffee essence, fruit syrups or even a savoury flavouring such as Bovril or Marmite and to vary the texture by thickening the milk for some feeds, serving it unthickened or as junket for others.

Two-hourly feeds are necessary if the patient is to be persuaded to take this amount of liquid food during the day, and at night an extra feed or a sweetened fruit drink may be given if the patient wakes.

This kind of diet is only necessary during a fever and should be changed gradually to a light diet as soon as the patient's temperature falls and, as convalescence progresses, the light diet should gradually change to the normal diet.

A note may be needed about two foods which used to be considered

most valuable for invalids, namely *beef tea* and *jelly*. In both of these the
food value is extremely low, probably less than 2% of nutrients. The
value of beef tea lies in its property of stimulating the flow of digestive
juices and so increasing appetite, it is therefore useful in the diet of convalescence but not in a liquid diet. Jelly also has a slight property of
increasing the flow of digestive juices but its chief value probably lies
in its attractive appearance and texture which make it a pleasant way of
serving fruit and milk and egg mixtures.

PLANNING MEALS FOR VEGETARIANS

Vegetarians may be 'strict' and eat no animal products whatever or they
may be 'lactovegetarians' or 'V.E.M.' which means that they add milk,
cheese and eggs to a vegetable diet. They may be vegetarians for a variety
of reasons; perhaps they are fond of animals and cannot bear to have
them slaughtered for food; they may consider meat to be coarsening;
they may think that meat has a bad effect on their health or their religion
may not allow the taking of any life.

Strict vegetarians, of course, need a balanced diet as much as anyone
else but the foods from which they can obtain the necessary nutrients
are limited as will be seen in the table below:

Sources of Nutrients for Strict Vegetarians

Protein	Fat	Carbohydrate	Vitamins	Minerals
Nuts, pulses, cereals, with very small amounts in many vegetables	Nuts, 'nut butters', 'nut creams', 'nut suet'; vegetable oils; prepared vegetable fats, vegetarian margarine	All carbohydrates are of vegetable origin	C always from fruit or vegetables. B group adequate in a wide mixture of vegetables, dried fruits, cereals, yeast and yeast extract. A as carotene in orange-red and dark green fruits and vegetables. D, margarine the only source.	Calcium adequate from a wide mixture of vegetables, fruits, cereals, nuts and pulses. Iron obtained as above, and from black treacle. Phosphorous and potassium are probably adequate.

The proteins are naturally all 'second class' but, by using a wide variety
of the available protein-foods, a mixture of amino-acids can be made,
containing the eight to ten essential ones and equal in food-value to
animal protein. Unfortunately protein is only found in comparatively

small proportions in vegetable foods so that large amounts of carbo-hydrate, cellulose and water must be eaten to reach the recommended daily average of 70 grammes of protein. A strict vegetarian diet is there-fore bulky and is made still more bulky by cooking because most vegetable products absorb water and swell during cooking in contrast to animal products which mostly lose moisture and shrink.

Practically the only source of Vitamin D available is vegetarian mar-garine, made from vegetable ingredients only, with Vitamins A and D added; strict vegetarians therefore have a real need for sunbathing so that ultra-violet rays can irradiate the sterol in the skin to produce Vitamin D (see p. 80). Vegetarian infants and children also need some form of calciferol or artificial Vitamin D to grow strong bones and teeth.

A possible shortage of calcium and of iron are usually avoided because a vegetarian diet will contain a fairly high proportion of dried fruits and pulses, both sources of these minerals, and of nuts which are rich in calcium.

A lactovegetarian diet is good and well balanced as the excellent protein foods, eggs, cheese and milk are included and as all these foods also supply calcium, while iron is supplied by eggs.

COOKING FOR VEGETARIANS

Cooking meals for strict vegetarians calls for some ingenuity. In the first instance the main protein dishes must often be made up from milled nuts, cooked pulses or cereals; then the texture of these mixtures must be varied and they must be carefully seasoned and flavoured if monotony is to be avoided.

Varying the Texture. To vary the texture of the protein dishes the various mixtures may be coated with egg and crumbs and baked or fried to give them a crisp crust; pulses may be added to vegetable stews and nuts can be served raw in salads. These dishes can also be served with moist vege-tables or crisp, juicy salads for contrast and different textures can be provided in the pudding course.

Varying the Flavour. There is a wide variety of flavours in the vegetables and salad plants which vegetarians generally use more plentifully than do meat-eaters but the main protein foods tend to be insipid and need added savoury flavourings; some of these are: onions, herbs, yeast and vegetable extracts, celery, some spices, prepared seasoning such as garlic, celery-or-onion-salt, and monosodium glutamate.

G

SHOPPING FOR VEGETARIANS

Vegetarians are catered for in special shops, often called 'Health Food Stores', where they can buy prepared protein foods such as packets of rissole mixtures and tinned vegetarian 'sausages', 'galantine' and 'luncheon meat' as well as many confections of dried fruit and nuts, nut 'butter', nut 'cream', vegetable cooking-fats and oils and many other ingredients of a varied and balanced vegetarian diet.

PRESERVING FRUIT AND VEGETABLES AT HOME

Fruit and vegetables, in the natural cycle of life, grow, mature then decay and return to the soil which they enrich so that other plants may grow; if they are to be preserved for use out of their normal season this cycle must be broken, for a time, by preventing decay. Decay is caused by enzymes in the fruit and vegetables and further hastened by yeasts and moulds and, in the case of vegetables, by bacteria as well which settle on them from outside. To preserve foods the enzymes must be destroyed; all micro-organisms must either be destroyed or at least rendered inactive; the flavour, colour and nutritive value of the foods must be retained as far as possible and the preserves must finally be stored in such a way that micro-organisms cannot re-invade them.

METHODS BY WHICH FOODS MAY BE PRESERVED

DRYING

When food is dry it no longer provides suitable conditions for the growth of micro-organisms. By modern methods, drying or dehydration is begun at a temperature high enough to destroy enzymes so that some at least of the Vitamin C is retained by this method. Commercially, dehydration is used to preserve fruits such as prunes and raisins, pulses and shredded root and green vegetables but in the home it is only practical for herbs or for an occasional glut of such fruits as apples, pears and plums.

HEAT TREATMENT

Sufficient heat must be applied to destroy micro-organisms without cooking the food to be preserved and the food must be sealed in an airtight can before heating or in a bottle which is made airtight immediately after heating.

Bottling

This is a convenient and popular method of preserving fruit by heat-treatment at home.

Canning

This method, although easy, is not practical for most homes as it requires an expensive can-sealing machine and cans which are normally only used once.

Fruit can be preserved safely by heating it to from 165° to 190° F. because all fruits contain some acid which prevents the growth of bacteria and reduces their resistance to heat so that, if by some rare chance bacteria should be present on the fruit, they will be destroyed at these comparatively low temperatures which are, furthermore, sufficient to destroy enzymes and to render moulds and yeasts inactive.

Vegetables, however, are both more likely to collect bacteria from the soil and, because they contain no acid, less able to resist their growth: they must therefore be preserved either in an acid solution as in pickling or by heat-treatment to a temperature high enough to kill bacteria and the spores of bacteria which can resist boiling for up to half an hour. A high enough temperature can only be reached by using a pressure cooker which at 10 lb. pressure raises the temperature to 240° F.

DEEP FREEZING

Most foods freeze at 32° F., or just below, but, although most micro-organisms are dormant at this temperature, some are not, and these can cause spoilage at temperatures as low as 15° F. Furthermore, at 32° F. to 15° F., large ice crystals form in food and spoil its texture when it is thawed. To preserve food by freezing very low temperatures are needed; in home 'deep-freezing' these are from 0° F. to − 10° F. and in commercial 'quick-freezing' they are as low as − 20° F. at first, followed by storage at 0° F.

The important thing to remember about freezing is that the micro-organisms are ready to come to active life again as soon as the food is thawed, and frozen food must therefore be used as soon as it thaws—never re-frozen.

Deep freezing at home requires a deep-freezing cabinet or a refrigerator with a deep-freezing compartment, not to be confused with the storage space for frozen foods. The equipment for deep-freezing is expensive, but it is a simple and effective way of preserving almost any food, cooked or raw, and space for deep-freezing can be hired in some places.

CHEMICAL METHODS

Most of the substances used for chemical preserving are not usually thought of as chemicals as they are edible: they are salt, sugar and vinegar.

Salting

Salt, used as a brine or dry, also prevents the growth of destructive micro-organisms though certain harmless ones can survive in it.

Jam-making, using Sugar

Sugar in a solution of 40% to 50% can prevent spoilage by most micro-organisms but certain yeasts and moulds can remain active in such a solution so that jam must contain 65% sugar if it is to keep well.

Pickling

Both salt and vinegar are used in pickling fruit and vegetables, the salt as a preliminary treatment which may last for 24 hours only or for several weeks, and the vinegar as the liquid in which the fruit and vegetables are immersed for storage.

Vinegar for pickling should contain 5% acetic acid which prevents the development of harmful micro-organisms.

In practice two or more methods of preservation are often combined as, for example, in deep-freezing salt may be added to vegetables and sugar to fruit, in bottling and canning sugar-syrup is often added to fruit, which is later heated, and salt, sugar and vinegar are used in pickling often with heating as well.

One chemical, which is not a foodstuff is, however, permissible because it is harmless, this is *sulphur dioxide* which is used commercially to keep the colour in dehydrated foods and some canned foods, it may be bought in tablet form for use at home. It has several disadvantages as it alters or bleaches some colours and it has a strong flavour which must be removed by boiling the preserve before it can be eaten: this boiling removes some of the Vitamin C.

JAM-MAKING

Jam should keep in good condition for well over a year: there is rarely any point in keeping it for more than a year because the same fruit will come into season again and because most jam, however well made, loses some of its colour and flavour and dries out a little when it is stored for two or more years. The colour of well-made jam should be clear and bright, it should have the full flavour of the fruit and it should set without being stiff: in a few jams such as strawberry or cherry the set is less important than colour and flavour.

The keeping quality of jam depends mainly on the proportion of sugar ('chemical' preservative), on the right amount of boiling (heat treatment), and on the exclusion of air and moisture in covering and storing it.

SETTING JAM

The setting of jam depends on a gum-like substance called *pectin*, which is in fruit, and which, with the right proportion of *acid* and *sugar*, will form a 'gel'. The pectin in ripe fruit is soluble and can be set free from the cell-walls of the fruit by crushing or by stewing for a short time; in under-ripe fruit it is in an insoluble form called *pectose* which can be freed from the fruit and converted to pectin by stewing with acid but in over-ripe fruit it has changed to *pectic acid* and has quite lost its setting-power so that over-ripe fruit is useless for jam-making. Of the three ingredients needed to form a gel, sugar is the only one that can be added in a known quantity: acid and pectin are contained in varying amounts in different kinds of fruit and in fruits of different degrees of ripeness and are diluted in fruit grown in very wet weather. *Acid* is needed in jam-making not only to change pectose to pectin and to help the pectin to form a gel but also to improve the flavour and colour of jam and to prevent crystals of sugar forming in it during storage.

Fruits that contain plenty of pectin and acid are:
Cooking and crab-apples;
Black and red currants;
Green gooseberries;
Damsons;
these all contain so much pectin that water is added to prevent the jam being too stiff.

Fruits that contain an adequate amount of pectin and acid are:
Apricots;

Blackberries (picked early in a dry season);
Plums;
Raspberries and loganberries;

water is only added to the harder kinds of fruit in this group to soften them and to free the pectin and will all be boiled away before sugar is added.

Fruits that contain little pectin and little acid are:

Blackberries (gathered late in the season);
Cherries;
Pears;
Most strawberries;

no water is added to these fruits but acid may be added; they may be mixed with other fruit or fruit juice rich in acid and pectin such as apples, red currants and gooseberries, or commercially prepared pectin may be added.

Adding Acid

To each 2 lb. fruit add 1-2 tablespoonfuls lemon juice or $\frac{1}{2}$-1 level teaspoonful tartaric acid; the acid is added to the fruit before cooking is begun.

Mixing Fruits

A fruit with a little pectin, mixed with one rich in pectin, is often improved in flavour as well as in setting quality; examples are:

Cherry or strawberry with red-currant juice;
Cherry or strawberry with gooseberry juice;
Blackberry and apple;
Pear and apple.

The amount of sugar is calculated on the total quantity of mixed fruits: if one fruit is harder it is cooked for a little while before adding the softer fruit.

Commercially Prepared Pectin

Pectin can be bought in liquid or powder form and always with suitable recipes enclosed: it is useful for making jam from fruits listed above as deficient in pectin but is unnecessary with fruits that will normally make a well-set jam.

Choice of Fruit and Sugar

Fruit for jam must be perfectly sound and, if possible, picked in dry weather so that moulds and yeasts will not have begun to develop on it. If fruit is bought for making jam it should be cheap enough to produce jam at a lower cost than the commercial kind.

Fruit should be just ripe, or a mixture of ripe and under-ripe for the reasons given above.

Cane and beet sugar are chemically identical and are therefore equally good for jam-making: as granulated sugar (usually made from sugar-beet) is the cheaper it is the best kind to use.

The Amount of Sugar to Add

To fruits very rich in pectin add $1\frac{1}{4}$ to $1\frac{1}{2}$ lb. sugar to each 1 lb. fruit (water will have been added up to $\frac{3}{4}$ pt. per lb. for stewing).

To fruit with an adequate amount of pectin add 1 lb. sugar to each 1 lb. fruit.

To fruit poor in pectin add $\frac{3}{4}$ lb. sugar to each 1 lb. fruit. When the jam is boiled sufficiently for it to set and keep well it should contain 65% sugar, 5% of which will be the natural sugar in the fruit and 60% added sugar. As a weighed amount of sugar is added it is easy *to calculate how much jam can be made from any recipe.*

Added sugar=60%, that is $\frac{3}{5}$, of the finished jam. Therefore added sugar$\times\frac{5}{3}$=weight of finished jam.

For example jam made with 4 lb. fruit and 3 lb. sugar will produce $3\times\frac{5}{3}$ lb.$=5$ lb.

As the amount of sugar needed depends on the amount of pectin a test must be made with the softened fruit before sugar is added.

To Test for Pectin

When the fruit has been simmered to extract pectin and is quite soft put one teaspoonful of the juice, free of skin and pulp, into a tumbler and cool it for 2 to 3 minutes, then pour on to it 3 teaspoonfuls methylated spirit and again leave it for 1 minute. Now gently free the juice from the bottom of the tumbler and pour it into a second tumbler:

One firm clot of juice shows a high proportion of pectin; several smaller but firm clots show an adequate amount of pectin; thin, soft, broken clots show very little pectin (Fig. 32).

If the pectin seems inadequate the fruit must either be simmered a little longer to extract more pectin or, if it has already been simmering for over $\frac{3}{4}$ hour, more pectin must be added by using a fruit with plenty of pectin or commercial pectin extract.

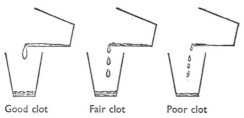

Good clot   Fair clot   Poor clot

Fig. 32. TESTING FOR PECTIN

EQUIPMENT FOR MAKING JAM

A preserving pan or a large saucepan is needed: it may be made of aluminium, stainless steel or heavy quality enamelled iron. If the cooker has a solid hot-plate the base of the pan must be ground flat and for all cookers a pan with a thick base distributes the heat more evenly than a thin one and therefore lessens the chance of burning the jam.

If enamelled iron is used it must not be chipped as, apart from the danger of chips of enamel in the jam, any exposed iron will discolour the jam and spoil its flavour.

Copper and brass preserving pans have been found by modern investigation to remove some of the Vitamin C from jam, furthermore, if the pan is carelessly washed any jam left in it will ferment and in the end produce acetic acid which, with copper, forms copper acetate or verdigris which is poisonous.

Where hard fruit needs long simmering to soften it this should be done in a saucepan with a lid, so that too much water does not evaporate.

Greasing the inside of the preserving pan with butter prevents the fruit sticking to the bottom and burning, the grease also reduces the scum.

A wooden spoon is needed with a handle so long that it cannot slip right into the jam or with a peg fitted into the handle to rest on the edge of the pan.

Jam-jars must not be chipped or cracked and should have old labels removed: they should be scrupulously clean.

Covers for jam-jars may be of cellophane or less often of parchment paper, all with rounds of waxed paper, and in sizes to fit the jars used —1 lb. or 2 lb.

Rubber rings are used to fix cellophane covers, string to tie parchment covers. Metal screw caps are not suitable for covering jam as they allow moulds to grow on the top of the jam.

A jug, jug-measure or large cup is needed for filling jars, and a saucer to be held beneath the jug to catch any drips is a help towards clean working.

Equipment for testing the pectin is methylated spirit and 2 tumblers.

Equipment for testing for setting-point is a thermometer, (efficient but not essential), a saucer chilled on ice if possible, or a clean, dry wooden spoon.

GENERAL METHOD FOR MAKING JAM

1. *Select suitable fruit*, sound, partly under-ripe and free of bruises.

2. *Wash the fruit* to remove dust and soil and drain it. Hard fruit may be stirred round in a bowl of cold water, soft fruit dipped quickly in and out of cold water in a colander, but very soft berries should be rolled gently about on a clean, damp cloth instead of washing.

3. *Prepare fruit* by removing any damaged parts, leaves, stalks, stones, and cores as necessary and by cutting large fruit in halves or apples and pears in quarters.

4. *Wash the jam-jars* using a detergent if they are really dirty, rinse them in very hot water and drain them, do not wipe them with a cloth. Dry and heat them by putting them open end upwards on several layers of paper (newspaper will do) on an oven tray in a very slow oven. This ensures that they are perfectly dry and hot enough to destroy moulds and yeasts and it prevents cracking when the hot jam is poured in.

5. *Grease the preserving pan* with butter to prevent fruit sticking to the pan and also to prevent scum forming as the butter later floats on the surface.

6. *Simmer the fruit gently* in the water or juice, if there is any in the recipe, until it is very soft and until its juice is flowing freely: for very hard fruit a lid on the pan prevents too much loss of moisture and hastens the softening of the fruit. The sugar will later harden all fruit skins, so that unless they are softened at this stage they will spoil the finished jam with their toughness. Soft fruit such as raspberries or strawberries will need 10 to 20 minutes simmering; fairly hard fruit such as apricots and some plums will need 30 to 35 minutes and very hard fruit, or fruit with tough skins such as blackcurrants will need 45 minutes and oranges even longer—up to 3 hours.

7. *Test the juice for pectin* and take the necessary steps to ensure an adequate amount.

8. *Warm the sugar* in a slow oven while the fruit is simmering, this makes it dissolve quickly and avoids cooling the panful of jam too much.

9. *Add the sugar* to the fruit, warm it steadily and stir it until all is dissolved.

10. *Boil the jam quickly*, stirring from time to time to prevent fruit from sticking and burning on the bottom of the pan and to prevent the formation of scum. The shorter the time taken to reach setting-point the better will the colour and flavour be as the acid in fruit, with the sugar, produce a slow darkening of the colours and a gradual change in flavours.

11. *Test the jam* for setting-point when it makes a faint knocking noise as it boils and when the bubbles begin to break more slowly. First remove the pan from the heat.

The tests for setting are:

(i) *The wrinkle test:* put half a teaspoonful of jam on a cold saucer, cool it quickly then push it with a fingernail across the saucer: if it forms wrinkles while still tepid the jam should set.

(ii) *The flake test:* dip a clean, dry wooden spoon into the jam, twirl it horizontally above the pan to cool the spoonful of jam then allow the jam to run off the spoon; if broad flakes form and break off short the jam is ready: if it still trickles in an unbroken stream it needs more boiling.

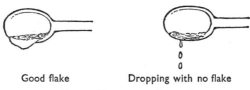

Good flake   Dropping with no flake
Fig. 33. TESTING THE SET OF JAM

(iii) *Temperature:* while still boiling the temperature of the jam should reach 220° F. when it is ready. This temperature will only be reached if the sugar has been concentrated to a 65% solution. The thermometer should be kept ready in a small saucepan of boiling water so that the new reading in the jam can be taken quickly; so that the accuracy of the thermometer can be checked on the boiling-point of water (212° F.) and so that the thermometer if put back in the water afterwards will be easy to wash.

It is a good idea to use two tests as a double check on setting-point.

12. *Filling the jars:* stir the jam steadily, off the heat, to break up the scum. The scum is simply air entrapped by the stickiness of the jam as bubbles rise, and if these bubbles can be broken before they set there will be no scum to remove. If the scum has dried and set it must be removed as it spoils the appearance of the jam.

Arrange the baking tray of jam-jars alongside the pan of jam and quickly scoop up the hot jam with the jug or cup, scrape jam off the side of the jug on the edge of the pan and pour the jam cleanly into a jar placed alongside the pan. Slide the filled jar along the tray and bring another one into position under the rim of the pan: in this way the edges of the jars and table top do not get sticky; alternatively, without moving the jars take the jug of hot jam to each jar and catch the drips in a saucer (Fig. 34).

Fig. 34A. FILLING JARS WITH JAM

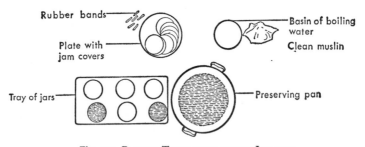

Fig. 34B. PLAN OF TABLE WHEN FILLING JAM-JARS

Jars should be filled to $\frac{1}{8}$ inch from the top, they will then really hold a pound of jam; the jam will in any case shrink as it cools and waxed discs are made to fit the top of the jar, not the narrower neck.

Never hold a jar while filling it as the jam is so hot that it will scald the hands badly if it is spilt on them.

13. *Covering the jars:* at once slip a waxed disc on to the top of each full jar and with the back of teaspoon press any bubbles gently out to the edges. Wipe the rims of all jars with a cloth wrung tightly out of very

hot water. Damp each cellophane cover on the upper side, making sure that the underside is dry and stretch it very tightly over the hot jar: fix it with a rubber band. When the cover is cold it should be concave.

Parchment paper covers are dipped in water, blotted dry in a clean cloth and tied on with string.

Lastly wipe the outside of all jars with a cloth wrung out of hot water to remove any sticky patches and, when cool, label jars neatly with the name of the jam and the date.

RECIPES FOR JAM

In each of the following recipes 3 lb. sugar is added and the yield should therefore be 5 lb. jam.

The general method should be followed as well as the particular points to be noted for each jam.

Recipes with 3 lb. Sugar

Apple Ginger

3 lb. apples

1 pint water, rind of 2 lemons or oranges

4 tablespoons lemon juice or 1 level teaspoon tartaric acid

2-3 level teaspoons ground ginger

3 lb. sugar

Special points

Peel, quarter, core and cut up the apples. Tie the cores and peels in clean muslin.

Grate the lemon or orange rind.

Add the bag of peel and cores, the lemon juice and ginger to the fruit when it is simmered in the water.

Remove the bag and squeeze its juice into the pan before adding sugar.

Add the sugar cold to deepen the colour.

Apricot, Greengage or Plum

3 lb. fruit

½ to 1 pint water (½ pint if ripe, 1 pint if very hard or under-ripe)

3 tablespoons lemon juice *or* 1½ level teaspoons tartaric acid ⎫ with apricots

3 lb. sugar

Halve and stone the fruit.

Crack some of the stones, blanch the kernels and add them with the sugar.

Stew the fruit with a cover on the pan.

Dried Apricot

1 lb. dried apricots
3 pints water
3 tablespoons lemon
  juice
1 oz. almonds
3 lb. sugar

Soak the washed apricots for 24 hours in the
  water in which the fruit will later be simmered.
Add the lemon juice when fruit has begun to
  soften. Total simmering-time may be as
  long as $\frac{3}{4}$ hour.
Blanch almonds and add them with sugar.

Blackberry and Apple

2 lb. blackberries
1 lb. green apples or
  crab apples (weighed
  after peeling and
  coring)
or equal quantities of
  the fruits
$\frac{1}{2}$ pint water
If either blackberries
  or apples are ripe add
  2 tablespoons lemon
  juice *or* $\frac{1}{2}$ level teaspoon tartaric acid
3 lb. sugar

Tie the peels and cores in muslin.
Stew the apples in the water till almost soft,
  then add blackberries and continue simmering, with lemon juice if necessary, until
  both fruits are quite soft.
If the jam is to be seedless, rub the softened
  fruit through a nylon sieve, weigh the pulp
  and juice and allow 1 lb. sugar to each 1 lb.
  fruit if a good pectin clot was found.

Blackcurrant

2 lb. blackcurrants
1$\frac{1}{2}$ pints water
3 lb. sugar

Keep a lid on the pan and have at least 3 inches
  depth of fruit and water or the mixture will
  lose too much moisture before the skins are
  soft.
Make sure that skins are *very soft*.

Green Gooseberry

2$\frac{1}{2}$ lb. gooseberries
1 pint water
3 lb. sugar

Cut large gooseberries in halves to free some
  juice more quickly: see notes for blackcurrants.
The green colour of this jam depends on the
  kind of gooseberry but is ensured if a copper
  pan is used.

Raspberry or Loganberry

3 lb. fruit   3 lb. sugar
(For home-grown dry
   raspberries, 3¾ lb.
   sugar, if pectin test
   gives a good clot
   Yield = $3\frac{3}{4} \times \frac{5}{3}$ =
   6¼ lb.)

Warm the fruit gently till the juice begins
   to flow and stir constantly until the fruit is
   quite soft.

For fruit rich in pectin, boil the jam for 3
   minutes only, after adding higher proportion of sugar.

For good pectin clot boil for about 10
   minutes after adding 3 lb. sugar.

Strawberry

3½ lb. strawberries
4 tablespoons lemon
   juice or 1 level tea-
   spoon tartaric acid
or
3 lb. strawberries
½ pint raw red-currant
   juice
3 lb. sugar

Cut large fruit in halves, warm gently till
   juice flows and stir constantly during simmering.

If red-currant juice is required put the washed
   currants (¾ to 1 lb.) in a very strong linen
   cloth and twist the ends in opposite directions, hard and continuously till only a dry
   mass of stalks, pips and skin remains.

Strawberry jam often needs a little skimming
   at the end of cooking and must be cooled
   till a skin begins to form before being
   bottled, otherwise the fruit will rise in the
   jars.

Special Jams with little Setting Quality

Rhubarb

3 lb. rhubarb
6 tablespoons lemon
   juice
rind of 2 lemons or
   oranges
or
2-3 level teaspoons
   ground ginger
3 lb. sugar

Cut the rhubarb in short lengths, put it in
   a basin in layers with the lemon juice and
   sugar; leave it for 24 hours. Grate the rinds
   and add them.

Add the ginger and boil quickly, stirring all
   the time till a jam-like consistency is
   reached. Test with a thermometer. This jam
   does not form a gel.

Vegetable Marrow

3 lb. marrow weighed without peel or seeds	Choose a ripe marrow with yellow flesh at the end of the season, peel it thickly.
4 tablespoons lemon juice, rind 2 lemons	Cut marrow in ½-inch cubes and put it in layers with sugar in a bowl; leave it for
1 oz. root ginger	24 hours.
3 lb. sugar	

Wash the root ginger and bruise it by putting it between two clean sheets of paper and hammering it, or banging it with a heavy weight.

Tie ginger and lemon rinds in muslin and add them to the marrow.

Simmer the marrow, sugar and lemon juice (with a bag of ginger or peel), *very gently* until all the marrow is quite clear; then boil till the juice is syrupy and test with a thermometer.

JELLY-MAKING

The rules for making and testing jam all apply to the making of jelly, but the amount of sugar must be calculated on the yield of strained juice from the fruit.

EQUIPMENT FOR JELLY-MAKING

This is the same as for jam with the addition of a woollen or felt jelly-bag or a strong linen cloth for straining the juice. A jelly-bag may have a wooden hoop at the top and be made to hang from a suitable hook; a felt jelly-bag and a jelly cloth are both hung from the four legs of an upturned stool or chair; the bag should have foor loops of tape to hang it by, the cloth should be tied on firmly with tape.

METHOD FOR MAKING JELLY

Choose and prepare the fruit as for jam, but skins, cores or stones need not be removed. Simmer the fruit in the water or sometimes only in its own juice until it is very soft. Mash it to a pulp with a wooden spoon. Scald the jelly-bag by dipping it in boiling water and draining it, then fix it in position with a large bowl below.

Pour the pulped fruit and juice into the jelly-bag and leave it until it stops dripping in 2 to 3 hours, or it may be left overnight.

Fruit rich in pectin may be removed from the bag after an hour, thinned again to a soft pulp with water, simmered for another ½ hour and this pulp also strained.

The juice, or the mixture of juices, is tested for pectin and then measured.

For juice giving a very good pectin clot allow 1¼ lb. sugar to each pint.

For juice giving a good pectin clot allow 1 lb. sugar to each pint.

For juice giving an adequate pectin clot allow ¾ lb. sugar to each pint.

For most jellies have the juice boiling and warm the sugar before adding it, but for a deeper colour in apple or gooseberry jelly add cold sugar to cold juice. Dissolve the sugar and boil and test the jelly for setting-point just as for jam.

All scum must be removed as it spoils the look of the clear jelly and the hot jars must be filled quickly before a skin can form on the jelly. The jars of jelly must not be tilted before the jelly has cooled and set.

RECIPES FOR JELLY

Hard fruits rich in pectin such as blackcurrants, gooseberries, green cooking or crab-apples

To 2 lb. fruit   water to cover

Fruits with a good supply of pectin such as red currants, damsons

To 2 lb. fruit   water to cover

(For both these groups a second extract can usually be made.)

Soft fruits with adequate supply of pectin such as raspberries, loganberries, blackberries, bilberries

To 2 lb. fruit   water to cover

Apple jelly may be flavoured as for apple ginger jam.

Mint jelly may be made by adding chopped mint to gooseberry jelly or lemon-flavoured apple jelly one minute before it is removed from the heat for bottling and after any scum has been removed.

Quinces are so rich in pectin and so hard that 3 pints of water at least may be added to 2 lb. fruit.

MARMALADE-MAKING

The name 'marmalade' comes from the Portuguese 'marmelada', a preserve made from quinces, but it now generally means a preserve made from citrus fruits, that is, from oranges, lemons, grapefruit or limes.

The same rules apply to marmalade-making as to jam-making but, as the citrus fruits contain a very high proportion of pectose in the pith and pips, they need long simmering in a large amount of water to extract the pectin. Citrus fruits, with the exception of lemons and limes, contain a fair amount of acid but not enough to form a gel with their very high proportion of pectin; they therefore all need some lemons or some tartaric acid in recipes for marmalade.

Bitter oranges are popular for marmalade as they give the sharp, slightly bitter tang that is usually liked for breakfast. Bitter oranges come from Seville or Malaga in Spain, from Italy or South Africa; Seville oranges are usually considered the best and may be recognized by their dark orange, deeply pitted skins and by the stalks which are often still attached to them.

It is specially important that the skins of citrus fruits should be soft before sugar is added to marmalade otherwise the sugar hardens them to an uneatable toughness.

METHODS FOR MAKING MARMALADE

I. Quick Method

1. Scrub the fruit and simmer it in a covered pan in the measured water until the skins are *very soft* in about 2 hours. This may be done in a slow oven once the liquid is simmering. Measure the water and reduce it or make it up to half its original volume.

2. Quarter the fruit, remove the pips.

3. Remove and cut up the fruit-pulp and add it to the liquid.

4. Slice the peel very thinly, and mix all the fruit, peel and liquid.

5. Bring the whole to simmering point, stirring it well, and test for pectin.

6. Add warmed sugar, stir till dissolved then boil the marmalade rapidly till setting-point is reached in about 10 minutes; test it as for jam.

7. Cool the marmalade slightly before filling the jars so that the peel will not rise.

II. Using a Marmalade Cutter

1. Halve the scrubbed fruit, squeeze out the juice and tie the pips in muslin.
2. Slice the peels in the cutter.
3. Put juice, peel, bag of pips and measured water into a large basin, cover it and soak it overnight, or put it all into the preserving pan and simmer it at once.
4. Simmer all until the peel is *very soft* and the volume reduced by one-third.
5. Test for pectin, remove bag of pips and finish the marmalade as for Method I.

III. Using a Pressure Cooker

1. Put the whole fruit (or halved grape-fruit) in *half the usual amount of water* in the pressure cooker without the rack.
2. Put on the lid with the valve open or without weights, bring the contents slowly to boiling-point, close the valve or put on weights and bring it to 10 lb. pressure.
3. Cook for 20 minutes at 10 lb. pressure, then cool at room temperature for 10 minutes.
4. Measure the liquid which should not have reduced at all. Continue as for Method I.

Note. For clear marmalade, by any method, remove as much of the pith as possible and stew it, tied in muslin, with the pips until the sugar is added. Grapefruit and sweet orange pith often remains cloudy in the marmalade and is often removed and treated in this way.

GENERAL RECIPE FOR MARMALADE

Yield slightly over 10 lb.

3 lb. fruit
6 pints water   } reduced by $\frac{1}{3}$ after simmering
6 lb. sugar

Variations of Fruit

Bitter Marmalade

3 lb. bitter oranges and 4 tablespoons lemon juice
or 2½ lb. bitter oranges and ½ lb. lemons

Grapefruit

     2½ lb. grapefruit, ½ lb. lemons
   or 3 lb. grapefruit, 2 level teaspoons tartaric acid

Three Fruit

    Roughly ¾ lb. sweet oranges, ¾ lb. lemons
    1½ lb. grapefruit.

BOTTLING FRUIT

Successful bottling depends on good quality fruit, accurate heat-treatment and secure, vacuum-sealing of the bottles. The seal is made by fitting a rubber ring under the cover of the bottle which is screwed or clipped tight while still very hot: as the contents of the bottle cool they shrink and, as no air can enter, a partial vacuum is produced.

EQUIPMENT FOR BOTTLING

Vacuum Bottles of two types are sold in sizes to hold from 1 lb. to 4 lb.

Screw Band

This type of bottle has a glass or lacquered metal lid, a flat rubber ring and a metal band to screw on to the neck of the bottle. The lids and screw bands may be used year after year. If the metal bands are greased before storage they will not rust.

Clip Top

This type has a lacquered metal cap, a thick rubber ring which fits a groove either in the neck of the jar or the rim of the cap, and a spring clip to grip the cap tightly to the bottle. Metal caps often get damaged as the bottles are opened and should generally be used only once.

Covers for Jam-jars

Several kinds of lacquered metal caps are sold to fit on to 1 lb. and 2 lb. jam-jars: they may be fitted with flat rubber rings and spring clips or the caps may have a depression all round filled with synthetic skin. This latter type may have no clips and must be treated according to the directions sold with them.

Rubber Rings

These must be bought in sizes and of the right shape to fit the kind of jars used. They should be used only once and should not be stored for longer than 2 years as rubber perishes.

Equipment for Heat-treatment of Bottles

A heat-controlled oven is a simple and satisfactory means of heating bottles though unsuitable for very tall shapes which would be overheated at the top. The bottles should be arranged, with a 2-inch space between them, on a shelf placed so that the middle of a bottle is half-way down the oven: if the bottles stand in a tin with $\frac{1}{2}$-inch depth of water the oven and the bottom of the bottles will not get sticky if any juice should overflow.

A water-bath, which may be a very deep saucepan or fish-kettle for short bottles, or a clothes-boiler, must hold a depth of water to cover the bottles completely and must be fitted with a false bottom of perforated metal, wooden slats or thick, clean paper or cloth.

A 'sterilizer', that is a ready-made water-bath with a thermometer fitted through the lid, may be bought if much bottling is done at home; being large enough to hold the tallest bottles, it is an unduly large piece of equipment to store if it is to be used only occasionally.

Preparation of equipment

As for jam-making all the equipment must be perfectly clean before use.

Bottles and glass lids should be washed, rinsed in very hot water and drained but are only heated for special cases; they should not be dried.

Rubber rings should be soaked before use.

Metal caps should be washed and scalded.

All bottles and glass lids must be examined to make sure that they have no cracks or chips.

Choice of Fruit for Bottling

Fruit for bottling is chosen as for jam-making, see p. 192, but freshness is even more important because in bottling less sugar is used and lower temperatures are reached. All fruit for bottling, except gooseberries, should be fully ripe so that it has the best possible flavour and colour but should be quite firm as the necessary heat-treatment will reduce over-ripe fruit to pulp.

Fruit for bottling is prepared as for jam-making with the addition of special treatment for certain kinds as in the list which follows.

Some Fruits suitable for Bottling

Apples. As sound apples may be stored satisfactorily without any preservation process, usually only windfalls or apples damaged by birds or by bruising are bottled. To prevent discoloration they are put into salt water (2 oz. to 1 gallon cold water) directly after peeling, coring and removing any damaged part; a plate floated on top keeps them under the water. They must be rinsed in cold water before the next process.

To save space in storage it is practical to stew apples to a pulp with only enough water to prevent them sticking, adding grated lemon rind for flavour if liked and from 3 to 4 oz. sugar to 1 lb. apples.

The boiling pulp is packed into hot bottles, covered at once and processed in boiling water for 5 minutes only, or in the oven at 300° F. for 20 minutes.

Apricots and large plums should be halved and stoned to take less room in bottles and because the stones, if left in the fruit, tend to give it a rather strong flavour as of almonds. Some stones may be cracked and the kernels added to the bottle.

Blackberries, raspberries, loganberries are best if picked with clean hands into a clean container and not washed. They keep their flavour best if packed with dry sugar, $\frac{1}{4}$ to $\frac{1}{2}$ lb. to each 1 lb. of fruit. When heated the fruit will shrink slightly. One bottle should be used to fill the others which must be covered again and reheated for 5 minutes.

Cherries, dark red varieties or morello cherries keep their colour best, they are often stoned and if this is done the juice should be collected and bottled with them.

Currants, both black and red and bilberries, keep their flavour and colour well.

Gooseberries should be 'topped and tailed' and a small slice taken off one end of each berry to allow syrup to penetrate the fruit to keep it from shrivelling and to sweeten it.

Pears. Dessert pears are prepared as for apples but are bottled in halves or quarters, the core is removed with a teaspoon. A strong syrup, $\frac{3}{4}$ lb. sugar to 1 pt. of water, should be used with $\frac{1}{4}$ level teaspoonful tartaric acid to each pint to keep them white. Cooking-pears should be stewed in syrup till almost soft before bottling.

Rhubarb, wiped with a damp cloth, cut in 2- to 3-inch lengths should be soaked in hot syrup overnight (¾ lb. sugar to 1 pt.): this sweetens and shrinks it. The syrup should be boiled down to its original volume and used for filling bottles.

Strawberries are not usually successful as they lose both colour and flavour and get very soft during heat-treatment. Small, dark red kinds may be treated like rhubarb.

Tomatoes. The most practical method of packing is a 'solid pack'. The tomatoes are plunged into boiling water for ½ minute, lifted out and put into cold water, they are then easy to skin. The tomatoes are cut in

Times and Temperatures for Three Methods of Bottlings

	Oven	*Water-bath*	*Sterilizer with thermometer*
Method	Heat oven to 300° F. or Regulo 1 to 2 for ¼ hour. Stand bottles in ½ inch water in a tin. Heat bottles for times shown below: for 4 lb. fruit the shorter time; for 10 to 12 lb. fruit the longer time	Heat water (to cover bottles) from blood heat to slow simmering in ½ hour. Maintain slow simmering for the times shown below	Heat cold water (to cover bottles) to temperature shown below in 1½ hours. Maintain this temperature for times shown below
Syrup	Boiling syrup to within ½ inch from top of bottle	Hot syrup to over-flowing	Cold syrup to over-flowing
Time and/or temperature for soft berries and currants	45 to 60 minutes	5 minutes	165° F. for 10 minutes
Gooseberries, small stone fruit, rhubarb	50 to 70 minutes	10 minutes	180° F. for 15 minutes
Apricots and large plums, halved	60 to 80 minutes	20 minutes	180° F. for 20 minutes
Pears	70 to 90 minutes	40 minutes	190° F. for 30 minutes
Tomatoes	80 to 100 minutes	50 minutes	190° F. for 40 minutes

quarters and packed very tightly with 1 level teaspoon salt and 1 level teaspoon sugar to each 1 lb. sprinkled in amongst the fruit: by the time the bottle is full there will be enough juice to cover the tomatoes.

Bottling in Syrup

All fruits develop more acid and lose their colour and flavour if they are bottled in water: a syrup of 8 oz. sugar to each pint water is sufficient to prevent this loss except in special cases such as strawberries and pears; more sugar may be used for a sweeter result.

To make the syrup bring the cold water and sugar slowly to boiling-point, if there is any grey scum, strain the syrup through clean muslin; use it hot or cold according to the method of heating bottles.

The amount of syrup needed depends on the tightness of the pack, a 2-lb. bottle rarely needs more than ½ pint.

Packing the Bottles

The fruit is packed into cool, rinsed bottles, small soft fruit such as currants and raspberries can be shaken down in the bottle, putting in one-third of the bottleful at a time. Small, hard fruit such as gooseberries can be shaken and packed into position with the handle of a wooden spoon. It is often found easier to add a little syrup with each layer of small fruit to expel air bubbles. Large fruit must be arranged carefully, fitting them in to waste as little space as possible.

All packing must be as tight as is possible without bruising the fruit and the fruit should be pressed firmly under the shoulder of the jar.

Filling Bottles with Syrup

Put the bottles on a tray, wipe the necks clean of pips or scraps of fruit, and, if the rubber rings are fitted on the jars, put them on or have the rubbers fitted into the caps. Fill the bottles with syrup almost to the top, then give each a quick twist or bump it gently on a folded cloth to expel air bubbles. The syrup is added cold or hot according to the method of heat-treatment and the bottles filled to overflowing for water-baths; to within ½ inch of the top for oven-method.

When all bubbles are expelled put on the lids, screw on the bands, giving the screw band a half turn back again to allow for expansion during heating, or fix the cap and clip in place (the clip allows for expansion).

After heating for the correct time, as shown in the chart on page 207, the bottles are removed, the screw bands tightened and clips checked to see that they are in position. Next day remove clips and screw bands and *Test the Seal* by lifting the bottle by its glass lid or metal cap only. If any caps come off, a new rubber must be fitted and the bottles re-heated for half the original time.

PICKLES AND CHUTNEY

Pickling is a 'chemical' method of preserving in which vegetables and fruits are stored completely covered with spiced vinegar to which sugar is sometimes added.

The vinegar should contain 5% acetic acid to be sufficiently acid to prevent the development of micro-organisms. Brown, malt vinegar gives a good flavour; white, malt vinegar gives a poorer flavour but keeps the colour pale and spices improve the flavour and possibly also the preservative action.

Vegetables are usually treated first with salt to extract some of the water and to prevent the growth of some bacteria; the salt may be used dry or as a strong solution or 'brine'.

Fruit is usually cooked gently in the spiced vinegar with added sugar.

Vegetables and fruit for pickling must be perfectly fresh and sound as for all preserving.

The only equipment needed is a supply of screw-topped jars with waxed cardboard discs to prevent the vinegar coming in contact with the metal, or wide-necked bottles with fitting corks which may be coated with melted paraffin-wax.

Recipe for Brine

$\frac{1}{4}$ lb. salt to each quart cold water

Recipe for Spiced Vinegar

to 1 quart vinegar:

$\frac{1}{4}$ oz. blade mace	$\frac{1}{4}$ oz. allspice berries
$\frac{1}{4}$ oz. stick cinnamon	$\frac{1}{4}$ oz. peppercorns
$\frac{1}{4}$ oz. cloves	$\frac{1}{2}$ oz. bruised root ginger

Put the vinegar in a double saucepan or a deep earthenware basin over a pan of water, cover it with a lid or plate. Boil the water and then keep it just hot over low heat for 2 hours. Strain the vinegar through a nylon strainer or muslin and bottle it for future use.

Cold Method. The spices may be added to cold vinegar, bottled and stored for two months before use.

GENERAL METHOD OF PICKLING

Wash any soil off vegetables, prepare them in the usual way, removing outer leaves of cabbage and any damaged parts and cutting large vegetables into suitably sized cubes or slices.

Put the prepared vegetables in an earthenware bowl and cover them

Recipes for Vinegar Pickles

Vegetable	Method of preparation	Salt	Spiced vinegar and additions
Beetroot	Cook (see page 329) till just tender, cut in $\frac{1}{2}$- to $\frac{3}{4}$-inch dice	None	Cold, white or brown about $\frac{1}{2}$ pint to each 1 lb.
Cabbage, red	Trim, quarter, shred finely	Dry	,, ,, ,, ,,
Cauliflower	Divide into small sprigs, stalk into $\frac{1}{2}$-inch dice	Brine	,, ,, ,, ,,
Mixed pickle, e.g. equal quantities	Cauliflower as above, Cucumber, diced, peeled if liked French or runner beans, $\frac{1}{2}$-inch lengths Green tomatoes, quartered Marrow, peeled, $\frac{1}{2}$-inch dice Onions, small for pickling, whole	Dry or Brine	,, ,, ,, ,,
Onions, small for pickling	Skin after brining	Brine	,, ,, ,, ,, or hot for soft result or quick use

Notes. (1) A few small red and green chillies and bay leaves add flavour and colour to light-coloured pickles.
(2) If a slightly sweet pickle is preferred, 2 to 4 oz. sugar may be dissolved in 1 pint spiced vinegar.

Piccalilli	Mixed vegetables as above, prepared as above, after brining stew in spiced vinegar till half cooked and unbroken, pack into hot dry jars	Brine	Add to 1 pint spiced vinegar: 2-3 oz. white sugar $\frac{1}{4}$ oz. turmeric powder $\frac{1}{4}$,, dry mustard $\frac{1}{4}$,, ground ginger $\frac{1}{2}$,, cornflour. Blend the powders with vinegar and cook as for cornflour sauce. Use hot

with brine and float a china plate on top to keep them under liquid or pack them in layers with salt, finishing with a covering of salt. Leave them for 12 to 48 hours then drain the brined vegetables or rinse and drain the dry-salted ones. Drain thoroughly or vinegar will be diluted.

Pack drained vegetables loosely but neatly into clean, dry, cold jars, only to within an inch of the top. Fill the jars with the spiced vinegar (cold for a crisp result, hot for a soft one) to ½ inch above the vegetables, screw on the caps and label.

Store most pickles for 2 or 3 months before using them. Cabbage may be eaten 2 weeks after pickling and gets less crisp on longer storage.

Sweet Fruit Pickles. Basic Recipe

4 lb. fruit:	1 pint spiced vinegar
damsons	
or morello cherries	2 lb. sugar
or stewing pears	
or 2 lb. crab-apples	

1. Dissolve the sugar in the spiced vinegar. Wash the fruit, warm jars.
2. Peel, quarter and core pears, leave small fruit whole but pierce them to prevent shrinkage. Leave crab-apples whole and pierce them.
3. Stew the fruit in the vinegar syrup, very gently till tender, pears may need as long as 2 hours, apples up to 1 hour and small fruit as little as ¼ hour.
4. Half fill hot, dry jars with drained fruit.
5. Boil the vinegar-syrup until it is reduced to half.
6. Pour hot syrup over fruit in hot jars, tap out air bubbles and screw down caps.

CHUTNEY

Chutney is the name given to a hot, sweet pickle or condiment originating in India where it usually contained mangoes and chillies. It is now widely varied but always includes fruit, sweet and hot spices, vinegar and sugar and is usually of the consistency of jam although it does not jell.

Very roughly the proportions are:

2 lb. fresh fruit	½ to 1 lb. onion
½ to 1 lb. dried fruit	½ to 1 lb. sugar
1 pint vinegar which may be spiced	
a variety of spices, including some hot ones	
salt to taste	

The sweet, savoury, hot and sour flavourings may vary widely.

The fruits may be any of which there is a glut, such as apples, blackberries, gooseberries, marrow, plums, rhubarb and tomatoes, either green or ripe.

The fruit and onions are chopped or minced and stewed in their own juice till soft then cooked with all other ingredients until the right jam-like consistency is reached. For long storage the chutney should be more liquid than for quick use.

The saucepan should be aluminium or stainless steel or an earthenware casserole may be used in an oven. Copper, brass and enamel are all acted upon by the strong acid and may spoil the flavour of the chutney; an enamel surface will be roughened, and copper and brass may produce verdigris (see p. 193).

Recipe for a Typical Chutney

Apple and/or Green Tomato Chutney

1½ lb. cooking-apples or green tomatoes
or ¾ lb.   „   „   ¾ lb. „   „

¾ lb. sultanas or seedless raisins

6 oz. onions or shallots
2 level teaspoons salt

1 level teaspoon mixed spice
1 or 2 level teaspoons ground ginger
½ level teaspoon cayenne pepper
½ lb. brown sugar
1 pint brown malt vinegar

Note: spiced vinegar may be used and mixed spice omitted.
Yield 4 lb.

1. Wash apples and tomatoes, peel, quarter and core apples, peel onions.
2. Put tomatoes, onions or shallots and raisins through a mincer or chop them with a stainless knife. Leave apples in quarters and sultanas whole.
3. Stew these fruits and vegetables with salt, spices and pepper in a covered pan till pulped.
4. Add sugar and vinegar and simmer without a lid for 2 hours or until the consistency is like jam.

   Warning. Chutney readily sticks to the pan and burns, the cooking must therefore be gentle and the chutney must be stirred frequently with a wooden spoon. The first cooking may well be done in a slow oven.
5. Fill dry, hot jars and screw on caps or fit corks (which should be painted with melted paraffin-wax or tied down with parchment) or cellophane jam covers. Jam covers alone are not sufficient covering as they allow the chutney to evaporate and shrink.

SALTING BEANS

French and runner beans are the only vegetables that are suitable for salting, and this is a worth-while method only if there is a glut which can be picked fresh, young, and tender, as salting inevitably toughens the beans which are much better eaten fresh.

Allow ⅓ lb. salt to each 1 lb. beans

Prepare the beans as for cooking. Pack them in layers of salt in an earthenware jar or crock, finishing with a layer of salt ½-inch deep and pressing each layer firmly down. After 3 or 4 days the beans will have shrunk and liquid brine will have formed. The brine must on no account be drained off as it serves to exclude air but the jar must be filled to the top with beans and salt as before.

Cork the jar firmly or seal on the lid of the crock with an adhesive tape and store it in a cool dry place.

To use the beans they must be rinsed in 3 or 4 changes of water and soaked for 1 hour in tepid water before cooking for rather longer than fresh beans.

For drying of Herbs, see page 29.

DEEP FREEZING

Deep freezing, also called quick freezing, is a method of preservation which is becoming increasingly popular, particularly in country areas. Where fruits, vegetables, poultry and game are readily available cheaply and in prime condition this method of preservation is excellent. It is extremely simple to carry out and the avoidance of waste in times of glut, the convenience of having a reserve of food and the enjoyment of eating out-of-season foods more than justify the cost of the special freezer cabinet.

These cabinets are of two shapes, chest-deep models with top opening lids and upright models with side-opening doors, just like a domestic refrigerator. The former take up more floor space but the top can be used as a working table and the heavy weight of a fully loaded cabinet is spread over the floor. The cabinet consists of two steel cases one inside the other with a 3½-inch space between them which is packed with fibre-glass and cork for insulation. Also in this cavity, up against the inner lining of the freezer, are coils through which there constantly flows the refrigerant, keeping the inner temperature of the cabinet at 0° F.

A few domestic refrigerators incorporate a small deep-freeze compartment, insulated from the rest of the refrigerator and with its own cooling unit so that defrosting the ordinary refrigerator does not affect the temperature of the deep-freeze compartment. (This type must not be confused with the domestic refrigerator with a larger-than-usual frozen food compartment in which purchased packets of frozen foods may be stored for several weeks.)

WHAT FOODS CAN BE DEEP FROZEN

1. Most fruits are excellent, with the exception of bananas, and can be frozen plain, in sugar, in syrup or as a purée. Bananas *may* be stored in purée form.
2. Vegetables, when very fresh and young, deep freeze well. They must be scalded in boiling water before freezing to retain colour, flavour and nutrients. Salad plants and new potatoes are not successful.
3. Meat, poultry and fish must be of first-class quality, clean and suitably trimmed before freezing.
4. Made-up mixtures can be most successfully deep frozen and the cook can save considerable time by cooking in bulk and storing her produce in the deep-freeze cabinet for another meal.

Examples are:

> Pastry, raw or cooked but preferably raw
> Yeast mixtures risen or un-risen
> Cakes, raw or cooked
> Soups
> Sauces
> Fried fish, fish-cakes
> Made-up filled sandwiches

Storage life in the deep-freeze cabinet

Whatever is deep frozen will not keep for years. Zero temperature slows the action of changes in food but does not altogether stop them and flavour and edibility is lost if foods are stored for too long a period.

Examples are:

Beef	10-12 months
Fruit in sugar	10-12 months
Cooked cakes	3- 4 months
Uncooked cakes	1- 2 months

GENERAL RULES FOR DEEP FREEZING

Full instructions for deep freezing are supplied in a booklet issued with the freezing cabinet. The following are general instructions only.

1. Freeze only best-quality foods, e.g. fruits ripe and just ready for eating; young vegetables; English meat; chickens straight from the poultry farm.

2. Freeze as soon as possible after gathering for fruit and vegetables. Hang beef 7-10 days after slaughter, 24-48 hours for pork.

3. Always use moisture- vapour-proof packaging materials in which to put the food before putting it in the deep freeze, in order to preserve texture and flavour. These include tubs made of waxed card, waxed cartons, rigid or soft plastic boxes with tight-fitting lids or polythene bags or sheets secured by wire ties or special waterproof sealing tape.

4. Pack in suitable quantities as food should never be re-frozen.

5. Label and date the food.

6. Cool food thoroughly before putting it into the freezer cabinet.

7. Place packages in the freezer in such a way that they touch either the sides or bottom of the cabinet and thus freeze quickly. There must be an air-space round each packet. When fully frozen, usually next day, stack the packets to give room for later additions.

8. In many cases thaw frozen foods before cooking or serving; exceptions are, vegetables and meat pies.

Part Two

RECIPES

12

SOUPS, BROTHS, VEGETABLE PURÉES

SOUPS

Food Value of Soup

Soup, being a more or less dilute form of food, can only have body-building or energy value in proportion to the amount of solids it contains: in a helping of a thick soup there may be as much as $\frac{1}{4}$ lb. vegetable or $\frac{1}{4}$ lb. meat or $\frac{3}{4}$ oz. pulse but in thin soups these foods may be in negligible amounts. In general the value of soups in the diet lies in the excellence of their flavour, usually partly due to meat extractives, and to the fact that they are generally served hot.

Well-flavoured hot soups can produce a feeling of well-being which may help to remove fatigue; they hasten the flow of gastric juices and so aid digestion and by their good flavour they stimulate the appetite.

Amount of soup to serve: If the soup is the first of three courses or more, $\frac{1}{4}$ pint is usually enough; if it is a main course $\frac{1}{2}$ pint at least will be needed and the soup must be a semi-solid one.

Classification of Soups

Soups may be classified according to their main ingredients as *Meat, Vegetable* or *Pulse soups* or as

1. *Clear Soups and Broths.*
2. *Thick Soups* which may be either: *Purées* or *Thickened Soups.*
3. *Mixed and national soups* such as Cock-a-Leekie of Scotland, French Pot au Feu and Italian Minestrone.

Clear Soups are really well-flavoured stock with added garnishes.
Broths contain meat and vegetables usually cut in tiny pieces; they may contain such starchy ingredients as rice, pearl barley or spaghetti but they should not be cloudy or thickened: example, Scots Broth.
Purées. The main ingredient of a purée is sieved and held in suspension in the soup by an additional starch thickening: example, Celery soup.

Thickened soups. These contain little or no solid ingredients but are thickened with some starchy food or egg-yolk: example, White Vegetable soup.

Cream soups. Both purées and thickened soups may be called cream soups if they have fresh cream added.

The liquid in soup may be stock, water in which meat, vegetables or cereals have cooked, water or milk. *Stock* is made by simmering bones and meat scraps for several hours in water to extract all possible flavour from them, it has very little food value but may greatly improve the flavour of soup. It is a common error to suppose that jellied stock is of high food value; at best it contains a small proportion of gelatine, a very little mineral matter and meat extractives but almost no calcium.

Substitutes for Stock. Instead of making stock, dissolve stock cubes in boiling water or add meat extract such as Bovril, or yeast extract such as Marmite, or add a meat bone to the liquid and simmer it with the other ingredients of a soup.

If soup is made regularly, or in large amounts, raw bones may be bought to make stock but it is usually an economical way of extracting the last vestige of flavour and gelatine from bones and meat scraps that would otherwise be thrown away.

Recipe for Stock

> raw or cooked bones, skin and gristle of meat, bacon or poultry
> *or* poultry giblets,
> cold water, salt,
> onion, carrot, celery (optional)

Rules for Making Stock

1. Use only fresh ingredients.
2. Have large bones sawn by the butcher, into convenient pieces and wash them.
3. Remove the fat and cut up any scraps of meat.
4. Put all the meat-scraps and bones in a saucepan, cover them with cold water, add 1 teaspoon salt to each quart and bring the water slowly to simmering-point.
5. Simmer the stock for 2 to 3 hours, add the raw vegetables and simmer for a further 2 or 1 hour.

6. Strain the stock and remove the vegetables.

7. Cool the stock as quickly as possible and store it in a cold place, preferably a refrigerator.

8. Do not store the stock for more than a few hours in hot weather if there is no refrigerator, or more than 3 days in a refrigerator, as stock is one of the best-known mediums for the growth of bacteria.

9. The fat should not be removed from stock until just before use: the fat may be clarified for use as dripping (see p. 14).

If the stock is to be used at once, while hot, skim off the fat and then draw absorbent paper over the surface to remove the last traces.

10. The bones may be boiled again for stock but little more meat-flavour can be extracted. Experts in nutrition and hygiene deplore the Victorian economy of keeping a stock-pot always simmering in the kitchen, as, if fresh ingredients are added to stale ones and the stock is cooled each night in a warm kitchen, it is for several hours in the warm state that renders it a potent source of bacterial contamination.

Make stock, cool it and use it within the shortest time possible.

BROTHS

Scots Broth   *6-8 helpings*

Cooking time   3 hours

1½ oz. pearl barley	1 medium carrot
1 lb. scrag neck of mutton	1 small turnip
1 quart water	1 leek
1 level teaspoon salt, pepper	1 level tablespoon chopped parsley

1. Blanch the barley (see p. 14) wash and joint the meat and remove any fat.

2. Bring meat, barley, salt and water very slowly to simmering point and simmer for 1 hour.

3. Prepare the vegetables and cut them into ¼-inch dice, Fig. 7; add them to the broth and simmer the whole for another 2 hours.

4. Lift out the meat, remove it from the bones and cut it into ¼-inch dice.

5. Skim the fat off the broth, taste and season it. Put the meat back, add the chopped parsley and bring the broth to the boil again before serving.

Other Broths made in the same way:

Chicken Broth   6-8 *helpings*

Cooking time   3 hours

>   1 carcase and giblets of chicken
>   *or* 3 sets of giblets and necks

1 quart water	1½ oz. rice
salt, pepper	1 onion or leek
1 blade mace	1 stick celery
1 bay leaf	1 level tablespoon chopped parsley

Method as for Scots Broth, but add washed rice with the vegetables. There may be little meat to add except on neck, this may be diced with the liver and the flesh of the gizzard.

Beef Broth

Cooking time   4 hours

Recipe as for Scots Broth, substituting ¾ lb. shin beef for the mutton. Method as for Scots Broth but simmer the beef and barley 2 hours before adding vegetables.

VEGETABLE PURÉES

General Recipe

Cooking time   ½-2 hours

1 lb. vegetable	½ oz. margarine or dripping
1 onion ⎱ for all	1 pint stock or water and stock cube
1 stick celery ⎰ purées	bunch of mixed herbs
1 carrot for brown purées	salt and pepper

Thickening: ⎧ ¼ pint milk
⎨ ½ oz. flour or cornflour or rice flour or barley flour
⎩ or fine tapioca to each pint of sieved purée.

General Method: 1. Prepare the vegetables and slice them thinly.
2. Melt the fat and add to it the vegetables, put a lid on the saucepan and shake it frequently over gentle heat for 10 minutes. This is called 'sweating' or 'fat-steaming'; it coats the vegetables with the fat and draws out their juices and flavour.

3. Boil the stock or water and add it to the vegetables with the herbs.
4. Simmer the soup for ½ to 2 hours until the vegetables are quite soft.
5. Turn the soup on to a sieve or into a bowl-strainer over a bowl, return the liquid to the saucepan.
6. Rub the vegetables through the sieve with a wooden spoon, vegetable presser or wooden roller, clearing the underside with a metal spoon (Fig. 35).

Wooden spoon and sieve   Soup roller and bowl strainer

Fig. 35. SIEVING SOUP OR SAUCE

7. Mix liquid and purée and measure them.
8. Blend the required amount of starchy thickening with milk, add it to the soup, bring it to the boil and stir till the starch is cooked.
9. Taste and season before serving; serve tiny dice of toast or fried bread with purées.

Examples

Vegetable	*Additions or variations*
Artichokes, Jerusalem	Add 1-2 teaspoons lemon juice to 1 pint. Omit celery. Use a nylon sieve.
Broad bean	Use pods and well-grown beans. Omit celery.
Carrot	Add nutmeg, sugar and lemon juice to taste.
Cauliflower	Remove green leaves but not stalks, add a little nutmeg, if liked. Cook for under ½ hour.
Celery	Use outer sticks and a few leaves. Use a nylon sieve.

Vegetable	*Additions or variations*
Leek	Add a little nutmeg.
Onion	If liked the onions may be browned in dripping.
Parsnip	Add a little nutmeg.
Pea, green	Use pods and well-grown peas. Add mint, sugar, lemon juice, Omit celery. Cook under $\frac{1}{2}$ hour. Use a nylon sieve.
Potato	Cut potato in thick slices. Add nutmeg.

Optional ⎰ Add $\frac{1}{2}$ bunch watercress, or 1 tablespoon parsley
⎱ chopped, a minute before serving.

No extra starch thickening is needed.

Tomato Soup

Cooking time $1\frac{1}{4}$ hour

> 1 lb. tomatoes, fresh or canned small onion
> 1 pint stock, juice from the can or small carrot
>   water and chicken stock cube salt and pepper
> 1 oz. bacon scraps, rinds or a a little nutmeg
>   bacon bone sugar and lemon juice to
> $\frac{1}{2}$ oz. margarine taste
>   bunch of mixed herbs

Thickening: $\frac{1}{2}$ oz. tapioca or $\frac{1}{2}$ oz. cornflour with 2 tablespoons water, to each pint of purée.

1. Method, as for other purées but fry the bacon for a few minutes, then fat-steam the onion and carrot in bacon-fat and margarine before adding the tomatoes.
2. Cook raw tomatoes in the fat for a few minutes then add the liquid, simmer the soup 1 hour.
3. Rub it through a nylon sieve.
4. If tapioca is used for thickening sprinkle it into the hot soup and cook it till quite soft in 10 to 15 minutes.

Note. Except when outdoor, home-grown tomatoes are at their cheapest a better flavoured and more economical soup is made from canned tomatoes than fresh ones.

Lentil, Dried Pea, Split Pea, Haricot or Butter-Bean Soup

Cooking time   1½ to 3 hours

3 oz. pulse	1 onion
1 pint stock or water	1 small turnip
2 oz. margarine or dripping	1 stick celery
bunch of mixed herbs	1 carrot (for lentil soup only)
a few bacon rinds or a bacon bone	1 medium potato, 3-4 oz.
	salt and pepper

no additional thickening is needed

1. Wash the pulse.
2. Soak pulses with skins, i.e. dried peas and beans, in ½ pint boiling water overnight and pulses with no skins, i.e. lentils and split peas in cold water and use this water in the soup. If soaking is omitted cooking-time must be longer.
3. Cook the soup as for any other purée, but allow 1½ to 2 hours for lentil soup and 2 to 3 hours for other pulses.

MEAT PURÉES

Unless a vegetable mill or an electric food-blender is available, making a meat purée is laborious; for a fairly quick and quite satisfactory result the meat may be minced or cut into tiny dice after cooking.

General Recipe

Cooking time   1-4 hours

½ lb. meat	1 stick celery
1 pint water	1 or 2 mushrooms, if available
or 2 pints stock	bunch of herbs
1 onion	1 teaspoon vinegar *or* 1 tomato
1 carrot	salt and pepper
1 small turnip	½ oz. flour to each pint sieved soup

General Method: 1. Wipe or wash the meat and cut it into thin strips.
2. Soak the meat 20 to 30 minutes in the cold stock or water.
3. Prepare the vegetables and slice them thinly.
4. Melt the dripping and in it gently fry the vegetables till they are golden brown.

5. Add the stock or water with the meat and 1 level teaspoon salt, the vinegar or tomato and herbs.

6. Bring all to simmering-point and simmer the soup gently till the meat is really tender.

7. Strain the soup through a wire sieve or strainer and remove the meat.

8. Sieve the vegetables and mince the meat or pass it through a vegetable mill or an electric blender, return all purée to the liquid.

9. The minced meat may be worked through the sieve or whisked into the soup.

10. Blend the flour with a little cold stock or water, stir it into the soup, bring it to the boil stirring the while.

11. Season to taste and serve.

Examples

Kind of Meat	Special notes
Ox kidney	Wash and skin kidney, remove core. Cook 1 to 1½ hours.
Ox liver	Wash and skin the liver and remove large blood vessels. Cook ¾ to 1 hour.
Rabbit	Use head (split), helmet, flaps and odd pieces to make up the weight. Blanch the rabbit pieces (see p. 14). When cooked remove all bones. Cook for 1½ to 2 hours.
Shin of Beef	Simmer 3 to 4 hours. Do not attempt to sieve the meat.
Veal	Use leg of veal, add lemon juice and rind while cooking. Simmer 2 to 2½ hours.

THICKENED SOUPS

Cream of Barley or Rice Soup

Cooking time   10–15 minutes

1 pint stock or stock substitute with a good flavour
½ oz. patent barley or rice flour
¼ pint milk   ½ oz. margarine
        ½ level teaspoon meat or yeast extract
Salt and pepper to taste   Optional 2 tablespoons cream

1. Boil the stock.

2. Blend the cereal with the cold milk, stir into this some of the boiling stock and return it to the saucepan.

3. Add the margarine and salt and meat extract to taste.

4. Simmer and stir the soup till the cereal has thickened it in about 10 minutes. If cream is used add it at boiling-point just before serving.

5. Taste and season the soup and serve it at once.

White Vegetable Soup

Cooking time   20-25 minutes

> ½ pint tiny dice or shreds of vegetables in season, e.g.:
>   carrot, turnip, leek, celery

½ oz. margarine	bunch of herbs
1 pint stock	½ oz. flour
¼ pint milk	salt, pepper, lemon juice to taste
1 teaspoon chopped parsley	Optional, 2 tablespoons cream

1. Prepare the vegetables and cut them into ⅛-inch dice, or into fine shreds 1 inch long, or shred them on a coarse grater.

2. Melt the margarine and in it fat-steam the vegetables for 10 minutes.

3. Boil the stock and add it to the vegetables with the herbs and a little salt.

4. Simmer the soup gently till the vegetables are just soft in 5 to 10 minutes.

5. Blend the flour with the milk and stir this into the soup off the cooker. Stir the soup till it boils again.

6. Add lemon juice and seasoning to taste. Stir in the cream if used and the chopped parsley.

7. Serve the soup at once.

Quickly made Vegetable Soup. I

Cooking time   8-35 minutes

1 oz. margarine	salt and pepper
¼ to 1 lb. vegetables	meat or yeast extract ⎫
½ oz. flour	nutmeg ⎬ to taste
½ pint milk	lemon-juice ⎭
½ pint stock or water	

1. Prepare the vegetables and shred or chop them fine.
2. Melt the margarine and in it sweat the vegetables till quite tender.
3. Stir the flour into the margarine unless much juice has run from the vegetable, in which case blend the flour with cold milk.
4. Add the liquids and stir the soup till it boils and thickens.
5. Taste and season it.

Examples

Kind of vegetable	Amount of vegetable	Special method
Mushroom	¼ lb.	Sweat mushrooms 20 minutes very gently.
Onions	¾ lb.	Cut onions in thin rings and fry them gently till golden-brown in 20 minutes.
Watercress	½ lb. (2 bunches)	Discard coarse stalks, sweat watercress 3 minutes.
Spinach or Lettuce	½ lb.	Use coarse leaves only of lettuce. Discard stalks of spinach, sweat leaves for 5 to 10 minutes; lettuce may need 30 minutes subsequent cooking.

Quickly made Vegetable Soup. II

Cooking time   about 1 hour

> ½ to ¾ lb. mixed vegetables, e.g.
>
> carrot   leek
> celery   onion
> turnip   tomato
> ¾ oz. dripping   ½ pint stock or water
> bacon rinds or bone   bunch of herbs
> 1 slice toast from a small   salt and pepper to taste
>   brown loaf   chopped parsley
> ½ pint milk

1. Prepare the vegetables and shred them on a coarse grater; chop those that cannot be shredded. Scald and skin the tomato.
2. Melt the fat and in it gently fry the vegetables, except the tomato, until they are golden-brown.
3. Add the stock, herbs, tomato and toast.
4. Simmer the soup for ¾ to 1 hour until vegetables are soft.
5. Beat the soup smooth, stir in the milk and re-heat it.
6. Add the chopped parsley, taste and season and serve the soup.

Minestrone (simplified recipe)   *4 helpings*

Cooking time   1½ hours

2 oz. haricot beans	about ½ oz. lean bacon scraps
1½ pints water	1 tablespoon olive oil
1 onion	a bunch of herbs
1 small carrot	1 tomato
1 stick celery	1 oz. cut macaroni or fancy
½ small turnip	Italian paste
1 medium potato	¼ small cabbage
1 to 2 oz. grated cheese	pepper and salt

1. Soak the beans in ½ pint boiling water overnight and next day simmer them in this water for ½ hour.
2. Slice the onion and cut carrot, turnip, celery in very small dice; slice the potato ½-inch thick.
3. Fry the bacon and onion gently in the oil for 5 minutes.
4. Fat-steam the diced vegetables for 10 minutes. Scald and skin the tomato.
5. Add the half-cooked beans, the water, bunch of herbs, the tomato cut up, and a little salt and simmer the whole for 1 hour.
6. Add the macaroni, if this is used, and simmer this for 20-30 minutes.
7. Shred the cabbage and add it 20 minutes before dishing.

If small shapes of Italian paste are used these will only need 5 to 10 minutes to simmer.
8. Taste and season the soup.
9. Just before serving it stir in a little of the grated cheese and hand the rest with the soup.

Accompaniments to Soups

Broths and soups with any neatly-cut vegetable garnish usually need no accompaniment but bread, toast, rolls, crispbreads, water-biscuits or rusked bread or bread-sticks are often eaten with them.

Croûtons of bread: These are tiny squares of toast or stale bread either buttered, cut in dice and baked in a moderately hot oven or cut in dice and fried till golden. The dice should be about ⅛ to ¼ inch across, as they are eaten from the soup spoon.

Fingers or sippets of toast: Thin, crisp toast is cut into fingers about 2 inches long by 1 inch wide.

Small cheese toasts: Sippets of toast with grated cheese pressed on top and browned under a grill: these are good with onion or mixed vegetable soup.

Bread-sticks: Soft roll mixture shaped into very thin rolls, 6 or 7 inches long and barely finger-thick and baked till crisp.

Forcemeat balls: Very small balls of forcemeat coated and fried take some time to prepare but are a good accompaniment to a meat soup.

Grated cheese: Dry grated cheese may be handed with a mixed vegetable or onion soup.

Tinned and Packet Soups

There are on the market many brands of tinned soup, most of which may be bought 'condensed' or double strength. Condensed soups can be used undiluted as sauces or, with at least their own volume of liquid, as soups.

Packet soups vary in the time needed to prepare them, some must be cooked for as long as $\frac{1}{2}$ hour; they usually owe much of their flavour to mono-sodium-glutamate (see p. 30) and have little food-value.

All bought soups cost more than the same recipe made at home and although they may not have as high a food value they are popular because they are very well flavoured and are quickly served.

13

FISH

To Prepare Fish for Cooking

The fishmonger will usually prepare fish by gutting it, filleting it, removing the head or skinning it as required but if it must be done at home the methods are:

To clean whole fish (Fig. 36)

1. With the fish on a sheet of newspaper remove the scales: hold the fish by the tail and with the back of a knife scrape it from tail to head, rinsing the knife and fingers in cold water.

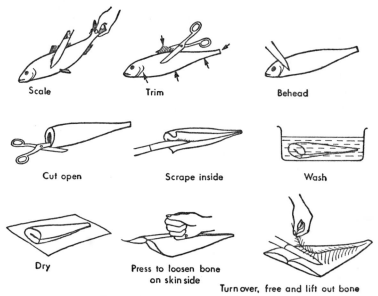

Scale   Trim   Behead

Cut open   Scrape inside   Wash

Dry   Press to loosen bone on skin side   Turn over, free and lift out bone

Fig. 36. CLEANING AND BONING HERRING

2. Cut off the fins with scissors and trim the tail.
3. If the head is to be left on (which is seldom necessary) remove the eyes by snipping with scissors all round the membrane covering them and

cutting through the muscle behind them: remove the gills by snipping with scissors at each end.

4. If the head is to be removed cut it off just below the gills.

5. Slit *round fish* from head to vent on the underside, slip out the entrails, sprinkle salt in the cavity and with a knife scrape out the black skin, blood and the silver swim-bladder.

Slit a *flat fish* just below the head on the dark skin to remove the entrails, clean the cavity as for round fish.

6. Wash the fish in cold water, wrap up the waste in the paper.

7. Dry the fish on absorbent kitchen paper or a clean cloth.

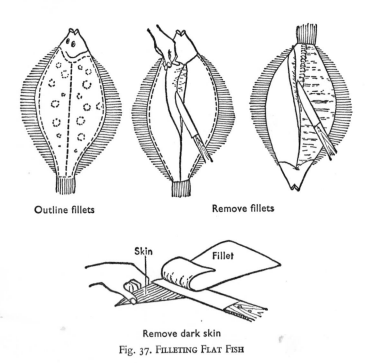

Outline fillets   Remove fillets

Skin   Fillet

Remove dark skin
Fig. 37. FILLETING FLAT FISH

To Skin Round Fish

Cut through the skin only, just below the head and above the tail. Slip the knife between skin and flesh to loosen the skin at head and tail. Dip the fingers in salt to get a good grip and slip the skin off from head to tail, easing it along the backbone.

To Fillet Flat Fish (Fig. 37)

1. Scale, wash and dry the fish and point its head away from you, white side up.
2. Outline the fillets with a sharp knife, under the head, round the side fins, then down the backbone.
3. Remove the fillet on the left with long strokes of the knife, keeping the blade on the bone and turning the flesh back with the left hand.
4. Turn the fish with head towards you and remove the other fillet from tail to head.
5. Remove fillets from the dark side in the same way.

To Skin Fillets (Fig. 37)

1. Only the dark skin of flat fish need be removed.
2. Put the fillet skin side down, tail towards you.
3. Dip the fingers of left hand in salt and hold the tail.
4. Slip a sharp knife between flesh and skin keeping it almost flat against the skin; with a sawing movement roll the flesh off the skin.

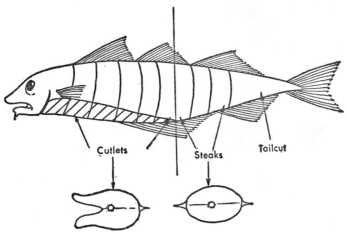

Fig. 38. CUTS OF LARGE ROUND FISH

To Clean Cut Fish

1. Remove any black skin and any blood near the bone with salt and a knife.
2. Wipe the fish with a damp cloth or damp kitchen paper.

The Cuts of Large Fish (see Fig. 38)

Middle-cut may weigh several pounds, it is cut from the middle of the fish and has a cavity from which the internal organs have been removed.

Cutlets are slices cut across the middle cut with a short section of backbone, cutlets of course have a cavity like middle-cut.

Tail-cut is the part of the fish below the cavity.

Steaks are slices cut across the thick end of tail cut and have no cavity.

Fillets: A fillet is the flesh from one side of the bone from head to tail, two fillets are cut from a round fish and four from a flat fish.

The Amount of Fish to serve

For each helping   4 to 6 oz. fish without bone
6 to 12 oz. fish with bone and head

Accompaniments for Fish

1. All fish may be served with sections of lemon to squeeze over it, these make a useful garnish with parsley.

2. Plain boiled potatoes or brown bread and butter may be served with most fish. Fried potatoes are popular with fried fish.

3. Almost all white fish, except when grilled, is improved in flavour and food-value if served with a sauce: $\frac{1}{2}$ pint to 4 to 6 helpings.

Suitable Sauces for Fish are: (pp. 346 to 347)

Anchovy	Curry	Parsley and lemon (Maître d'Hôtel)
Caper	Egg	Mustard (with herring and mackerel)
Cheese	Mushroom	Shrimp

(all of the above may be made with fish stock)
Tomato sauce is not made with fish stock.

To Make Fish Stock

This makes a well-flavoured foundation liquid for sauces to serve with fish.

The head, bones and skin of filleted fish; or cod or other fish-head
cold water	1 onion
1 teaspoon salt to each pint	1 stick celery
6 to 8 peppercorns	bunch of herbs
1 clove	1 bay leaf

1. Wash the fish trimmings and cut them up to fit the saucepan.
2. Add the amount of water needed for sauce and the other ingredients.
3. Bring all slowly to simmering-point and simmer it for 20 minutes.
4. Strain the stock and use it the same day as it will not keep.
5. Longer cooking or storing the stock for several hours both produce a bitter flavour.

To Test Fish to Find if it is Cooked

1. The flesh should be easy to separate from the bone and the flakes should part easily when tested with the tip of a knife or fork.
2. The flesh should look opaque, there should be no red blood round the bone and on white fish a milky curd may appear.

To Coat Fish for Baking and Frying

Coating with Flour

Suitable for whole fish with its skin on, before baking in fat or for any fish before frying it in shallow fat.
1. Clean, dry and season the fish.
2. Dredge it generously with flour, pat the flour firmly on to all surfaces then lightly shake off any that is loose.

Coating with Oatmeal or Rolled Oats

Suitable for herring and mackerel before frying.
1. Clean, dry, bone and season the fish.
2. Allow 1 rounded tablespoon of oats for each fish; put the oats on a plate or paper.
3. Press the fish on to the oats, turn over and press the other side, make sure that oats cover all surfaces. As the fish are lifted allow loose oats to fall off before they are put into the hot fat.

Coating with Egg and Dry Breadcrumbs (see Fig. 39)

1 egg   about ½ pint dry crumbs

Suitable for any fish before either frying or baking in fat.
1. Beat the egg and pour it into a plate, if many fillets are to be fried add 1 tablespoon milk.
2. Put a pile of dry, sieved crumbs on to a square of absorbent paper; get out a palette knife and a coating brush.
3. Season the clean, dry fish, and dredge it lightly with flour; brush off any that is loose.

4. With the fingers lower one piece at a time into the egg, brush the egg over all surfaces then lift the piece with knife and brush, drain it and lower it quite flat on to the crumbs.

5. Holding the paper, roll the fish gently till coated with crumbs.

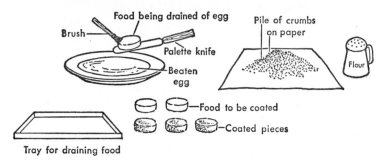

Fig. 39. COATING WITH EGG AND CRUMBS

6. With the fingers lift the coated fish on to the table.

7. When all pieces are coated, press on the crumbs with the dry palette knife. Sift the crumbs back into their container and use the square of paper for draining after frying.

Coating with Batter (see Fig. 40)

Suitable for small pieces of fish before frying.

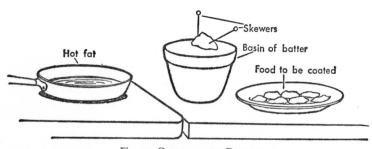

Fig. 40. COATING WITH BATTER

Batter I.

> 2 oz. self-raising flour   pinch of salt
> 4 tablespoons water

1. Mix the flour and water to a smooth cream that will coat the back of spoon; use a small basin so that the batter is deep enough to cover the fish.

2. Make the fat hot in the frying-pan and arrange the fish, batter and 2 skewers or a fork and skewer on a plate alongside the pan.
3. With the 2 skewers or fork and skewer lift one piece of fish at a time, dip it right under the batter and then lower it carefully into the fat without splashing.

(The two pointed tools are used so that they shall not drag the coating-batter off the fish.)

Batter II. Fritter Batter

    2 oz. flour (plain)   pinch of salt
    3-4 tablespoons tepid water   1 egg-white
    2 teaspoons olive oil or cooking oil

1. Mix the flour, salt, oil and water to a smooth batter that will coat the back of the spoon thickly.
2. Whip the egg-white to a stiff foam and with a metal spoon fold it into the batter.
3. Use the batter at once as for Batter I.

Batter III, with yeast

    4 oz. flour   ¼ oz. yeast
    ¼ teaspoon salt   ¼ pint milk or water
    ½ oz. margarine

1. Warm and sieve the flour with the salt.
2. Rub in the margarine, warm the milk to blood-heat.
3. With a teaspoon of warm milk work the yeast to a cream, then stir in the remaining milk, and stir all the liquid into the flour to make a coating batter.
4. Beat the batter till it is stringy, cover it and keep it in a slightly warm place for ¾ hour to rise.
5. Check the consistency which should coat the back of the spoon.
6. Coat and fry the fish as for Batter I.

To Fry Fish (pp. 8, 9, 125)

Cooking time   4-10 minutes

Fillets, cutlets or steaks of white fish, or small, whole white or oily fish.
1. Clean, trim, dry and season the fish, and coat it with one of the coatings above.

2. Put enough frying-oil, clarified dripping, white cooking-fat or lard in a frying-pan to come half-way up the fish.

3. *To test the fat.* Cut a small piece of stale white bread to use for testing the heat of the fat. Heat the fat steadily and then fry the bread on one side only; it should be browned in 30 seconds for thin pieces of fish or 50 seconds for pieces $\frac{1}{2}$ inch to 1 inch thick or any fish coated in batter.

4. Fry the fish till golden-brown on one side, then turn it once only and fry the other side. Allow 2-3 minutes each side for thin pieces or 4-5 minutes each side for pieces $\frac{1}{2}$ inch to 1 inch thick.

5. Put the pieces in one at a time, allowing a pause for the fat to heat again after each addition.

6. *Drain* the fried fish on absorbent paper and serve it hot, on a dish-paper to absorb any remaining fat.

7. *Serve* with lemon sections and perhaps a rather strongly-flavoured sauce in a sauceboat.

Note, For deep frying use fat at 340° F. for batter coating, or 360° F. for egg and crumbs.

To Bake Coated Fish ('*Oven-frying*')

Oven 375° F. or Gas No. 5-6

Cooking time   10 mins. to $\frac{3}{4}$ hour

Use any white fish; whole, filleted or in cutlets.
>   Dripping or cooking fat
>   Beaten egg and crumbs for coating
>   Seasoned flour

Garnish: Parsley and small sections of lemon

Sauce: $\frac{1}{2}$ pint of well-flavoured sauce to 4 helpings, e.g. parsley, anchovy, shrimp or tomato

1.   Have the fish cleaned and if necessary skinned.
2.   Season the fish and dredge it with flour.
3. (*a*) Small fillets, fold in three or roll head to tail, skin side inside.
   (*b*) Fillets of large fish, cut in neat portions.
   (*c*) Whole haddock, truss with a long skewer to an S shape (Fig. 41).
   (*d*) Whole whiting, curl and fix the tail in the mouth.
   (*e*) Whole flat fish, trim fins—the head may be removed.
4.   Coat the fish in egg and crumbs (see p. 235 and Fig. 39).
5.   Heat the dripping in a roasting tin to hazing point, put the fish in and either turn it over in the fat or baste it; $\frac{1}{4}$ inch depth of dripping is sufficient.

6.   Bake small fillets 10-15 minutes.
          large fillets and cutlets 20 minutes.
          large cuts or whole fish 10 minutes to the pound + 10 minutes.
7.   Dish the fish in a hot dish, garnish and serve the sauce separately
     or poured round the fish.

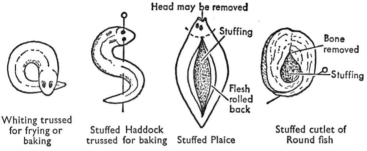

Fig. 41. METHODS OF STUFFING FISH

To Stuff and Bake Fish (Fig. 41)

Before being coated and baked in fat, as above, the fish may be stuffed.
To each 1 lb. of fish allow 2 tablespoons crumbs for veal stuffing (p. 354).
Fillets of flat fish: spread stuffing on the skinned side and roll them from
     head to tail; stand them upright.
Fillets of large fish and Boned Herring or Mackerel: cut the fillets in neat
     pieces and spread the stuffing smoothly on the skinned side or sand-
     wich equal pieces together with stuffing; 2 boned herring or mackerel
     may be sandwiched.
Whole round fish: fill the cavity with stuffing and stitch it or close it with
     a skewer, form the letter S with a haddock (see Fig. 41) and skewer
     it into shape, put a whiting's tail in its mouth and fix it there with its
     sharp teeth (see Fig. 41).
Whole flat fish, e.g. plaice: on the white side of the fish make an incision
     down the backbone and begin to fillet each side of this cut till an oval
     pocket is made; press the stuffing into the pocket and smooth it over
     the top (see Fig. 41).
Cutlets or steaks: with a sharp knife, remove the bone. Make the stuffing
     into a ball and press this into the hole where the bone was, wrap the
     ends of a cutlet round the stuffing and fix them with a little skewer or
     a cocktail stick.
     Coat, baste with hot fat and bake the fish as for 'Baked Coated Fish'
     allowing 5 to 10 minutes longer.

To Grill Fish

White Fish

Use cutlets or steaks, cut 1 inch thick from fairly firm, large fish such as cod or hake, or small flat fish.

1. Clean and dry the fish; tie or skewer cutlets into a neat shape.
2. Score whole fish on both sides: the black skin may be removed.
3. Brush the fish liberally with oil or melted margarine, then dredge it with flour and shake off any loose flour. The oil keeps the fish from getting dry and the flour gives it a golden-brown finish.
4. Have the grill moderately hot.
5. Grill the fish until it is golden-brown and cooked, turning it only once.

Herring or Mackerel

1. Clean, dry, remove the heads and close the opening with a small skewer; score the fish on both sides.
2. Wash, dry and trim kippers.
3. Brush the fish with a little oil or melted margarine but do not dredge them with flour as they brown readily.
4. Grill medium-sized fish for 4 to 5 minutes each side.

Maître d'Hôtel butter may be served with grilled fish:

½ oz. butter   pepper, salt, lemon juice
2 teaspoons chopped parsley

1. Mash and work all ingredients together.
2. Shape the butter into a neat cake and keep it cool.

To Poach Fish

Fillets, cutlets, steaks or whole fresh fish.

Poaching on Top Heat

1. Clean, dry and season the fish, sprinkle it with lemon juice and fold fillets in three or roll them.
2. Have enough boiling fish-stock, milk or salted water to come half-way up the fish in a shallow pan only just large enough to hold it.
3. Remove the pan from the heat, put the fish in and baste it with the hot liquid; cover the fish with greased paper and a lid.
4. Simmer the fish very gently, allowing the liquid to bubble slowly at one side of the pan, for 10 to 15 minutes for small, thin fillets or for 10 minutes to each pound and 10 minutes over for large pieces.

5. Use all the liquid in a well-flavoured coating sauce. Keep the fish hot while the sauce is being made; coat and garnish the fish.

Poaching in an Oven   325° to 330° F. or Gas No. 3

1. Clean, dry, season and pack the fish into an ovenware dish, pour 2 or 3 tablespoons fish stock, white wine or milk round it and cover the dish with greased, greaseproof paper or foil.
2. Bake the fish for 15 minutes for small fillets or 10 to 15 minutes per pound and 10 minutes over for larger cuts. Use all liquid in a sauce.

To Steam Fish

For small fillets or thin cutlets steam the fish on a plate (see Fig. 5).
1. Grease the plate and a square of paper to cover it, heat the plate over the saucepan of boiling water.
2. Clean, season and sprinkle the fish with lemon juice.
3. Arrange the pieces on the hot plate, cover them with greaseproof paper and a saucepan lid.
4. Steam the fish for 10 to 20 minutes turning it over when half cooked.

For large pieces of fish wrap them in greased cookery parchment or greaseproof paper or foil and steam them in a perforated steamer.
1. Steam the fish for 10 to 15 minutes per pound and 10 to 15 minutes over.
2. Add any liquid that runs from the fish to the sauce.

White Fish (Poached or Steamed) with Sauce

Any white fish—filleted or in cutlets

Some examples of :	Sauce	Garnish
	Anchovy	Parsley and lemon
	Caper	Hard-boiled egg or gherkin and lemon
	Cheese— see Fish 'Mornay'	
	Egg	Parsley or gherkin
	Mushroom	One or two whole mushrooms and parsley
	Parsley	Lemon
	Shrimp	Whole shrimps and lemon
	Tomato	Gherkin or rings of hard-boiled egg

To Poach Smoked Fish

Poaching is a good way of cooking smoked fish as it makes the flesh plump and moist and removes some of the salt.

1. Wash and trim the fish and put it into a roasting-tin, grill pan or frying-pan; pour on to it enough boiling water almost to cover it.
2. Cook it over gentle heat or in a slow oven for 5 to 10 minutes for haddock, or 3 to 5 minutes for kippers; turn the fish over at half-time if it is very thick.
3. Drain the fish and serve it with a few small pats of butter.

Kippers may be cooked by slipping them into a large jug, pouring in boiling water to cover them and keeping them hot for 4 or 5 minutes with no actual simmering.

MISCELLANEOUS RECIPES FOR FISH

Fish and Cheese (*Fish 'Mornay'*)

Cooking time   30-40 minutes

Fillets or cutlets of white fish
>   Pepper, salt, lemon juice
>   To 4 helpings, $\frac{1}{2}$ pint coating white sauce using $\frac{1}{2}$ fish stock, half milk
>   2-3 oz. grated cheese
>   1 dessertspoon fresh breadcrumbs
>   *Optional extra:* Border of mashed potato

1. Prepare and season the fish; fold thin fillets in three; steam or poach the fish and arrange it neatly in a shallow oven-dish. Remove skin, and bones from cutlets.
2. Make the sauce, adding the fish-liquid, and all but two tablespoons of the cheese; season it to taste.
3. Coat the fish and strew the top of the sauce with the remaining cheese and the crumbs.
4. If required pipe the potato round the edge.
5. Brown in a hot oven or under a moderate grill.

Fish Charlotte   *4 helpings*

Oven 400° F. or Gas No. 7

Cooking time   30 minutes

$\frac{3}{4}$ lb. smoked haddock or golden fillet

$\frac{1}{2}$ pint white coating sauce using $\begin{cases} \frac{1}{4} \text{ pint liquid from haddock} \\ \frac{1}{4} \text{ pint milk} \end{cases}$

3 oz. fresh breadcrumbs
3-4 tomatoes
salt, pepper, nutmeg
$\frac{1}{2}$ oz. margarine

1. Grease a deep oven-dish.
2. Make the crumbs, poach the fish for 10 minutes only, in boiling water, drain the fish and slice the tomatoes.
3. Make the sauce.
4. Sprinkle the dish with crumbs and in it put the fish, tomatoes, sauce and crumbs in layers, finishing with crumbs.
5. Melt the margarine and sprinkle it over the crumbs.
6. Bake until golden-brown and very hot.

Kedgeree   *3 to 4 helpings*

Cooking time   20-30 minutes

$\frac{1}{2}$ lb. smoked haddock   salt, pepper (cayenne if liked)
4 oz. Patna rice   1 teaspoon curry powder
$\frac{1}{2}$ teaspoon chopped parsley   a little grated nutmeg
1 oz. margarine
To garnish: 1 hard-boiled egg

1. Poach the haddock, drain and flake it, removing bones and skin.
2. Boil the rice, about 10 minutes until it is only just cooked and not at all sticky, drain it, rinse it with boiling water and drain it again.
3. Melt the margarine and in it re-heat the rice and haddock, shaking and tossing them to keep them loose. Season it to taste.
4. Slice the egg, pile the kedgeree high and loosely in a hot dish. Arrange the egg round it and sprinkle it with chopped parsley.

Fish Cakes   *8 fish cakes*

$\frac{1}{2}$ lb. cooked fish or canned herring, pilchards or Grade III salmon
$\frac{1}{2}$ lb. cooked potato   2 teaspoons chopped parsley
$\frac{1}{2}$ oz. margarine   a little white sauce or beaten egg to bind
salt, pepper
lemon juice   *Coating* $\begin{cases} \text{beaten egg} \\ \text{breadcrumbs} \end{cases}$

1. Remove bones and skin from cooked fish but not from tinned fish.
2. Flake and mash the fish on a plate.
3. Melt the margarine in a saucepan and in this mash the potato, then add the fish and mash and beat the mixture smooth.
4. Season it and add lemon juice and parsley to taste, then add just enough sauce or beaten egg to make it possible to shape the mixture.
5. On a floured surface form the mixture into a long roll and cut 8 cakes. Neaten the shape of the cakes.
6. Coat them with egg and crumbs (see p. 236 and Fig. 39).
7. Fry in fat that browns bread in 20 seconds, i.e. 380° F., and serve them.

Fish Pie   *4 helpings*

Oven 400° F. or Gas No. **7**

Cooking time   30-45 minutes

> ½ to 1 lb. cooked, raw or canned fish
> salt, pepper, lemon juice   1 lb. potatoes
> 2 teaspoons chopped parsley   ½ oz. margarine
> ¼ pint white coating sauce   a little milk
> a little beaten egg to brush
> *Optional extras:* 1 hard-boiled egg or 1 or 2 tomatoes

1. Grease a pint-sized pie-dish.
2. Boil the potatoes, chop the parsley, make the sauce, hard boil the egg.
3. Flake the cooked or raw fish; include the skin and bones of canned fish.
4. Slice the egg or tomato and line the sides of the dish with either.
5. Mix fish and sauce, season them and add parsley and lemon juice to taste.
6. Drain, dry and mash the potatoes, season them and add margarine and milk to make a spreading mixture.
7. Put the fish mixture in the pie-dish cover it with potato and smooth the top with a wet knife. Mark the top neatly with the tip of the knife or a fork.
8. Bake for 30 minutes if cooked fish is used, 45 minutes if raw fish; turn down the heat when the top is brown.

Fish Pudding *2-3 helpings*

Cooking time ¾-1 hour

½ lb. white fish filleted	1 egg
1 oz. stale bread without crusts	2 teaspoons chopped parsley
2 oz. margarine	a little grated lemon rind
¼ pint milk or fish stock	salt, pepper, lemon juice

To coat: ½ pint parsley, anchovy or egg coating sauce

1. Grease a ¾-pint basin and prepare a steamer.
2. Heat the milk or fish stock with the margarine, into this put the bread, cover it and soak it. Skin the fillets and flake them.
3. Mash the bread in the liquid and when cool add the fish and the egg and beat the mixture smooth. Season it and add lemon and parsley.
4. The mixture should drop easily from the spoon.
5. Steam it in the basin over water that only simmers, until the pudding is firm in ¾ to 1 hour.
6. Turn out the pudding and coat it with sauce, garnish it with parsley.

Russian Fish Pie *4 helpings*

Oven 400° F. Gas No. 7.

Cooking time ¾ hour

6 oz. flaky or rough puff pastry

Filling { ½ lb. filleted white fish
2 tablespoons white coating sauce
1 hard-boiled egg

salt, pepper, lemon juice
2 teaspoons chopped parsley
beaten egg to brush the top

1. Make the pastry, roll it to an 8-inch square, trim the edges and roll the trimmings to make 4 long leaves.
2. Slice the egg; flake the fish into large pieces.
3. Mix the fish, sauce, seasoning, lemon and parsley and pile this mixture in the middle of the pastry, arrange the slices of egg flat on top.
4. Damp the edges of pastry with egg and fold the square to an envelope shape overlapping the edges a good ½ inch.
5. Brush the top with beaten egg, make a hole in the top to let steam escape, arrange the leaves to cover joins and brush them with egg.
6. Bake for ¾ hour, reducing heat once the pastry is golden-brown.

Note: ½ lb. short pastry may be used instead of flaky but this pie is not 'Russian'.

RECIPES FOR HERRINGS AND MACKEREL

Boiled Herrings and Mackerel

Cooking time 7 minutes

> 1 herring or mackerel for each person
> water to cover them
> 4 tablespoons salt to each pint
> *To serve:* Mustard sauce, see p. 346

1. Clean the fish and remove their heads (Fig. 36).
2. Choose a fish-kettle or any large pan and in it boil enough water to cover the fish, add the salt.
3. Put the fish on the drainer of the fish-kettle or tie them loosely in a cloth and lower them into the brine.
4. Boil the fish for 7 minutes, drain them and serve them with the sauce handed separately.

> *Note.* The brine is so strong that it prevents the fish from breaking or losing flavour in the water. This recipe originally used sea-water and was used by fishermen at sea.

Soused Herrings or Mackerel

Oven 325°-300° F. Gas No. 2

Cooking time 1 hour

> 1 herring or mackerel to each person
> equal measures of vinegar and water to cover them
> to 2 fish $\left\{\begin{array}{l}\text{1 teaspoon salt} \quad \text{2 cloves} \\ \text{6 peppercorns} \quad \text{1 sliced onion} \\ \text{1 bay leaf}\end{array}\right.$

1. Clean and bone the fish (Fig. 36), roll them from head to tail and pack them into a deep oven-proof dish, so closely that they cannot unroll and with tails up.
2. Half fill the dish with vinegar then fill up with water just to cover the fish.
3. Put in the spices, salt and onion and cover the dish with a lid or foil.
4. Bake for 1 hour in the slow oven.
5. Leave the fish to cool in the liquid.

Note. Roes may be cooked and served separately, e.g. grilled on toast, or rolled inside the fish.

See also Fried Fish coated in Oatmeal, Baked Stuffed Fish, both suitable for herrings and mackerel.

Frozen Fish

Frozen fish will require about an hour to thaw at room temperature, or 5 minutes in its wrapping immersed in tepid water. Once thawed it is used as any other filleted fish.

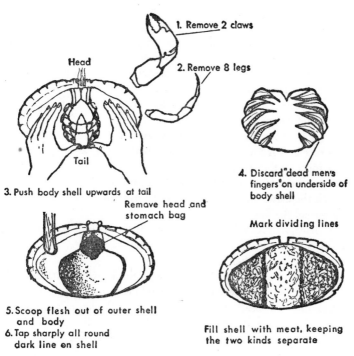

Fig. 42. PREPARING A CRAB

To Dress a Crab   *2 helpings from a* 1½ *lb. crab* (Fig. 42)

1 crab	salad cream or French dressing
pepper, salt, lemon juice	chopped parsley or paprika pepper
For dishing: Green salad	

Crabs are bought ready cooked and may be dressed by the fishmonger but he will charge for this service.

Choose a medium-sized crab rather than a very large one as there is more meat in proportion to size and the white meat is more tender in a medium crab.

A female crab has a very wide tail and under the tail there may be a little red 'coral' or spawn, which is edible.

To dress a crab. See Fig. 42

1. Have ready two basins, one for white flesh and one for soft, creamy brown meat. Have ready also paper or a small waste-bin for the refuse.
2. Twist off the claws and the legs, close to the body.
3. With the tail towards you, press the tail up with the thumbs until it breaks free from the outer shell, then lift out the inner body framework.
4. Remove and discard the small, transparent stomach bag which will be left in the main shell just under the head.
5. Remove the pale fawn, feathered 'dead men's fingers' from the body shell: all the rest of the meat is edible.
6. With a teaspoon handle or skewer scoop out the white flesh from the leg sockets and from the inside of the body shell, keeping white and brown meat in the separate bowls.
7. Scoop all the meat from the outer shell or carapace.
8. Crack the claws with nut-crackers or a hard blow with a weight and scoop out all the flesh.
9. Tap sharply all round the shell just inside the dark line and lift off the inner piece of shell which should come away easily.
    Scrub and dry the shell.
10. Mix pepper, salt and lemon juice with the brown meat, and a little salad cream or French dressing with the white meat.
11. Pack the meat neatly into the shell putting the larger amount at the sides and the smaller amount in the middle.
12. Outline the dividing line with chopped parsley or red paprika pepper.

14

MEAT

To Prepare Meat for Cooking

1. Scrape the outer layer of fat to remove any dust, and strip off outer skin that is shrivelled or soiled.
2. Wipe cut surfaces with a clean, damp cloth or wet-proof paper; whole joints with little cut, lean surface may be washed and dried.
3. Soak salt meat for 2-6 hours in cold water: the time depends on the degree of salting.
4. Have any chopping or sawing of bones or boning of joints done by the butcher who will usually do this willingly and efficiently.
5. Trim off excessive fat, not required on the meat for cooking, and chop or mince it to be rendered for dripping.

To Prepare Offal for Cooking

1. Wash the offal in slightly salted water and dry it on absorbent paper or clean cloth.
2. *Hearts:* Cut away the walls of large blood-vessels but leave the fleshy flaps intact. Soak the hearts for 5 to 10 minutes in salt water and rinse them to remove blood from inside. Keep them whole if they are to be stuffed or slice them for stewing.

Kidneys: Remove the skin before washing them, cut them almost in half from the rounded side towards the core, cut out the core with scissors.

For grilling, skewer the two halves open, for stewing or soup, cut the kidney in suitable-sized pieces. Fig. 43.

Liver: Have the liver sliced expertly by the butcher. Remove the outer skin and with scissors cut out all blood-vessels.

Sweetbreads: Blanch the sweetbreads, see p. 14, then plunge them into cold water, this hardens the fat which can be removed with a stainless knife.

Tongue: Tongues are usually salted by the butcher to cleanse them; they must therefore be soaked in cold water for 1 to 2 hours to remove some of the salt. The trimming of a tongue is done after cooking when the food-pipe and wind-pipe, the skin and tiny bones are easy to remove. Before cooking only excessive fat at the root need be removed.

Tongues that have not been salted should be soaked in salt water for 1-2 hours and blanched to cleanse them.

Tripe: Tripe is usually sold 'dressed', that is cleaned and almost completely cooked; it may be blanched for extra cleansing.

Heads: Have the head split by the butcher; have pig's head salted. Scour teeth and nostrils with salt, cut away spongy bone from nostril, soak the head in salt water and blanch it as for tongue.

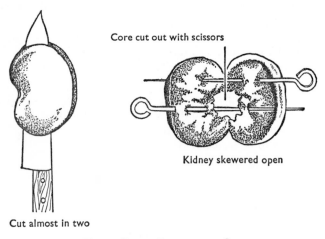

Core cut out with scissors

Kidney skewered open

Cut almost in two

Fig. 43. KIDNEY PREPARED FOR GRILLING

To Bone Joints

Meat is boned to make it into a more compact shape, and to make room for stuffing. The butcher will usually do this free of charge and always more quickly and efficiently than an amateur. If boning must be done at home here are some rules.

Rules for Boning

1. Use a pliable, very sharp knife of a size that can be easily manipulated.
2. Keep the fingers always behind the knife and cut away from the person.
3. Find out the shape of the bone first and follow its shape with the knife.
4. Keep the knife against the bone and, holding it flat, scrape the meat away; hold the flesh in the other hand and roll it away from the bone as it is freed.

Boning Breast of Mutton or Veal. (Fig. 44)

1. Lay the breast hollow side up and notice a flap of flesh (the diaphragm), a thick edge to the breast bone where the ribs join and sawn-off ribs joined near the breast bone.
2. Slip the knife under the diaphragm and without cutting it, fillet it off the long strips of cartilage lying under it. Fig. 44. 1.
3. Score through all the joints of the ribs and break them on the edge of the table. Fig. 44. 2.
4. Working from the cut edge of the breast slip the point of the knife all round each short rib bone and cut it off at the broken joint. Fig. 44. 3.
5. Scrape the meat off the strips of cartilage and cut them out.
6. Turn the breast over and fillet the flesh off the breast bone. Fig. 44. 3.
7. Fillet inside and between the rib endings of the breast bone and keep this meat to add with the stuffing.
8. Trim off any unwanted fat.
9. Turn the breast diaphragm upwards and spread it with stuffing from the thick end to the inner edge of diaphragm. Fig. 44. 4.
10. Roll it from the thick end. Fig. 44. 5.
11. Skewer and tie it into a neat roll.

Boning a Shoulder of Mutton

1. Free the meat from the blade bone up to the joint, turning the meat inside out as it is freed.
2. Free the meat all round the shank bone, exposing two joints. It is easy to do this if the flesh is slit where it lies nearest the bone.
3. When work from each end reaches the larger joint the bone can be pulled out and the cavity stuffed.
4. The slit end may have to be stitched together with thick cotton and a large darning-needle.

Boning Leg of Mutton

Work from either end as for shoulder.

METHODS OF COOKING MEAT

Roasting

Meat is usually roasted in an oven nowadays but, although strictly speaking this should be called 'baking' the older term is more popular.
Roasting Meat may be done in several different ways:

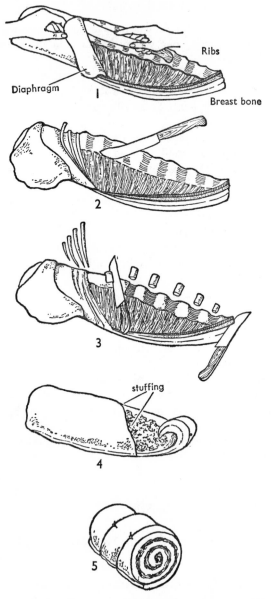

Fig. 44. Boning and Stuffing Breast of Lamb or Veal

1. *The Cold Oven Method for Electric or Gas Cookers*

The joint is put into a cold oven which is then heated to 400° F., Gas No. 7; the meat begins to cook as the oven heats up and the slow rise of temperature ensures that the meat is tender. This is the method used in any automatically-controlled oven.

2. *Searing Method*

The joint is put into a very hot oven, 450° to 500° F., Gas No. 9-10 for 20 minutes to 'sear' the outside and to develop the savoury flavour characteristic of roast meat, the heat is then reduced to cook the joint without over-hardening it. This method produces a good flavour but does not increase the tenderness of the meat; it is suitable for tender joints.

3. *Slow Roasting*

The joint is put into a cold or cool oven and baked at 325° to 350° F., Gas No. 2 to 4 and cooked for one-and-a-half times or twice the usual time. This method is useful for making meat tender but it does not develop the flavour as fully as the quicker methods: it is valuable to the cook who must be out of the house for a short time and who has no automatic-timing device on her cooker.

4. *Roasting by Temperature*

A special meat thermometer is used; it has a sharp spike which is stuck into the thickest part of the joint, before cooking begins and registers the internal temperature of the meat. The joint is cooked sufficiently when the temperature reaches:

140° F.	for 'underdone' beef
150° F. to 168° F.	„ well cooked beef
160° F.	„ veal
170° F. to 175° F.	„ mutton and lamb
180° F.	„ pork

This method removes uncertainty from roasting.

Rôtisserie or Spit-roasting

Some gas or electric cookers have a mechanically rotated spit on which a medium-sized joint can be impaled, and kept turning, under a hot grill or in a hot oven. This is a modern return to true roasting.

To Roast or Bake Meat

For methods, see p. 90; for suitable cuts, see p. 97.

Time-table

Kind of meat	1. Cold oven method	2. Searing and 4. Rotisserie methods	3. Slow oven method
	Oven heat: Cold to 400° F. Gas No. 7	450° to 500° F. Gas No. 9 to 10 for 20 minutes then 350° F. or Gas No. 4 for remaining time	325° to 350° F. Gas No. 2 to 4
	Allow 20 minutes for heating oven	Allow no time for heating	Allow 20 minutes for heating oven
Beef: Thick cuts	20 minutes per pound	+ 20 minutes	30-40 minutes per pound
Thin cuts	15 ,, ,, ,,	+15 ,,	25 to 30 ,, ,, ,,
Mutton: Thick cuts	25 ,, ,, ,,	+25 ,,	40 to 50 ,, ,, ,,
Thin cuts	20 ,, ,, ,,	+20 ,,	30 to 40 ,, ,, ,,
Lamb: Thick cuts	20 ,, ,, ,,	+20 ,,	30 to 40 ,, ,, ,,
Thin cuts	15 ,, ,, ,,	+15 ,,	25 to 30 ,, ,, ,,
Pork: all cuts	30 ,, ,, ,,	+30 ,,	45 to 60 ,, ,, ,,
Veal: Thick cuts	30 ,, ,, ,,	+30 ,,	45 to 60 ,, ,, ,,
Thin cuts	25 ,, ,, ,,	+25 ,,	40 to 50 ,, ,, ,,
	If a covered roasting-tin is used or if the meat is covered with foil allow an extra 20 to 30 minutes		

Method:

1. Weigh the prepared joint and work out the time needed to cook it.
2. Tie or skewer it into shape if necessary, put it into a roasting-tin, preferably on a grid so that hot air can circulate round it.
3. If the joint has little fat or if potatoes are to be baked round it put one or two tablespoons of dripping on it.
4. Put the joint into the oven, see chart above, and bake it for the calculated time.
5. Very lean joints may be basted every 20 to 30 minutes but basting is not necessary for joints with plenty of fat or for roasting any joint in a heat-controlled oven.
6. Bake potatoes round the joint for ¾ to 1 hour, basting them well with the fat in the tin.
7. Dish the joint and keep it hot while the gravy is being made. As well as gravy serve the following accompaniments with roast meat:

Meat	Accompaniments	Special Points
Beef	Yorkshire pudding horse-radish sauce	Beef should be served slightly underdone—pink and juicy inside.
Mutton	Red currant jelly or onion sauce	Mutton should be well cooked without being dry. Mutton may be stuffed with veal stuffing or sage and onion stuffing (p. 354).
Lamb	Mint sauce	As mutton.
Pork	Apple sauce, sage and onion stuffing	The gravy should be thick. Brush crackling with oil or milk to make it crisp but not hard.
Veal	Bacon rolls, sections of lemon, veal stuffing (p. 354)	Veal and pork should be well cooked.

To Make Gravy

Dish the meat and potatoes and keep them hot.

Thin gravy

1. Pour off the dripping from the roasting-tin, carefully keeping back any sediment or meat juices.

2. Dredge the tin with enough flour to absorb the fat that clings to the tin.

3. Stir the flour well and over gentle heat, brown it a little, stirring all the time.

4. Stir in water in which vegetables have been cooked, or stock or water, allowing $\frac{1}{2}$ pint for 6 helpings. Boil the gravy, skim it to remove grease, season it to taste with pepper, salt and meat or vegetable extract if necessary, and, if too pale, add to it a little gravy-browning off a skewer.

Thick gravy. Make this as for thin gravy but keep 1 *tablespoon* of fat in the tin, and stir in *one level tablespoon* flour for $\frac{1}{2}$ *pint gravy.*

Serve thick gravy with pork and all stuffed joints.

5. Strain the gravy only if it has lumps in it, as straining may remove some savoury flakes of extractives.

To Roast Meat in a Saucepan ('Pot Roast' or 'Pan Roast')

See p. 10.

Suitable cuts: any compact joint, preferably with a covering of fat,
    such as: breast of mutton, boned, stuffed and rolled,
    brisket of beef,   „   „   „   „
    fillet end of leg of mutton,
    topside,
    stuffed sheep's heart.

Time is calculated as for oven roasting with a minimum of 50 minutes for sheeps' hearts or any joint of 1 lb. to 2 lb.

1. Choose a strong saucepan and melt in it enough dripping to give a depth of ¼ inch.
2. Make the dripping smoking hot and in it brown the meat on all sides.
3. Reduce the heat and cook the meat gently for the calculated time, turning it every 15 to 20 minutes.
4. Potatoes may be roast round the meat for ¾ hour.

When the meat is cooked it is lifted out and dished, the fat is drained off and gravy can then be made in the saucepan.

To Boil Meat

For suitable cuts, see p. 97.

It has been found by experiment that all meat, whether salt or fresh, is more tender and retains more extractives and therefore more flavour if 'boiling' is begun in cold rather than boiling water.

For a good flavour use barely enough to cover it and simmer the meat gently.

Time-table for Boiling Meat

Salt Beef,	large joints	25 minutes per lb. +25 minutes after boiling-point
	small ,,	minimum time of 1½ hours
Bacon and Ham,	large ,,	30 minutes per lb.+30 minutes after boiling-point
	small ,,	minimum 1½ hours
Mutton,	large ,,	20 minutes per lb.+20 minutes after boiling-point
	small ,,	minimum 1 hour 20 minutes
Salt Pork,	large ,,	30 minutes per lb. +30 minutes
	small ,,	minimum 1½ hours
Tongue, Ox		3½ to 4½ hours
Sheep's		3 to 3½ hours
Lamb's		2½ to 3 ,,
Boiling fowl		2 to 3 hours, depending on the age of the bird

Meat	Accompaniments	Special Points
Salt beef	Carrots, turnips, onions, $\frac{1}{4}$ lb. of mixed vegetables per helping. Suet dumplings, p. 356, $\frac{1}{2}$ oz. flour per helping Mustard sauce, p. 346, $\frac{1}{2}$ pint per 4 to 6 helpings	Soak the joint in cold water for 1 to 2 hours to remove unwanted salt
Bacon and ham	Root vegetables may be served as for salt beef, often omitted. If served hot; mustard, parsley or tomato sauce, pp. 346-50, and boiled butter or haricot beans or dried peas, p. 146. Rasping crumbs are pressed on to the outer fat surface, or this may be studded with cloves.	Scrape off the 'rust' and soak the joint as for beef. When cooked peel off the rind and if it is to be served cold put the joint back into the cooking water to cool; this prevents it getting dry.
Mutton	Vegetables as for beef. Spices and dumplings may be omitted. Caper sauce, p. 346.	
Salt or 'Pickled' pork	Vegetables as for beef. Parsley sauce and pulses as for bacon or ham	Soak as for salt beef.
Tongue	Vegetables as for beef may be cooked with tongue or omitted. Tongues are usually pressed: reduce $\frac{1}{2}$ pint of cooking liquid to $\frac{1}{4}$ pint and dissolve in it $\frac{1}{4}$ oz. gelatin. Lamb's or sheep's tongues may be served hot in a brown sauce, p. 347.	Have ox tongue salted by the butcher; cleanse all tongues by blanching them. When cooked skin them and remove lining of gullet and wind pipe and the tiny bones found in the root. Press tongues in a suitable cake tin, which is filled up with the gelatin solution, with a plate and heavy weight on top.
Boiled fowl	Béchamel, parsley, Italian, p.348, mushroom, p. 348, or tomato sauce. Veal, celery, chestnut or sweet corn stuffing, p. 355.	Stuff and truss the bird. Serve it whole or carved, coated with the sauce which should be made with cooking liquor or half liquor and half milk. Use lemon juice instead of vinegar in the cooking liquid.

General Method

1. Weigh the meat and work out the cooking time.
2. Fasten the joint into a compact shape with skewers or string.
3. Put the meat into a pan just large enough to hold it and any vegetables or dumplings that may be added later.
4. Barely cover the joint with cold water and to each quart add:

> 2 level teaspoons salt
> 1 tablespoon vinegar
> 2 level teaspoons brown sugar
> 1 clove, 2 allspice berries ⎫
> $\frac{1}{2}$ bay leaf   ⎬ if liked
>   ⎭

5. Bring the water very slowly to boiling-point then simmer it gently for the calculated time
6. Whole root vegetables (quartered if very large) should be added $1\frac{1}{2}$ hours before the end of cooking-time.
7. Dumplings should be added 20 minutes before the end. Some of the cooking liquid may be used for sauce.

Dish the meat with vegetables, dumplings and a little cooking liquid round it on the dish.

Keep the cooking liquid to use for soups, remembering that it will be very salt from ham, bacon or salt beef.

To Braise Meat (Fig. 2). See p. 7.

For suitable cuts of meat, see p. 97.

Time-table

Beef, tough cuts	3 to $3\frac{1}{2}$ hours
,, fairly tough cuts	$2\frac{1}{2}$,,
,, ,, tender	2 ,,
Lamb and Mutton fairly tough cuts	$1\frac{1}{2}$ to 2 hours
tender ,,	$1\frac{1}{4}$ to $1\frac{1}{2}$,,
chops	$\frac{3}{4}$,,
Veal	$1\frac{1}{2}$ to 2 ,,
Rabbit (depending on age)	$1\frac{1}{2}$ to 2 ,,
Boiling fowl ,, ,, ,,	2 to $2\frac{1}{2}$,,
Lamb's or sheeps' hearts	$1\frac{1}{2}$,,
Liver, lamb's or sheep's	$\frac{3}{4}$ to 1 hour
,, Ox	1 to $1\frac{1}{4}$ hours

General Recipe

To 1 lb. to 2 lb. meat:

Mirepoix	*Optional:*
1-2 onions	*Veal Stuffing* (see p. 354) from 3
2-3 carrots	to 4 tablespoonfuls crumbs
1 small turnip	*Vegetables to braise round meat:*
1-2 sticks celery	potatoes
1 oz. dripping	*or* celery
1 oz. streaky or scrap bacon	*or* young carrots
a bunch of herbs	*or* small leeks
1 bay leaf	*or* ,, onions
a few peppercorns	*or* mushrooms
$\frac{1}{2}$ to 1 pint stock or water	

To thicken the stock:

2 level teaspoonfuls arrowroot to each finished $\frac{1}{2}$ pint liquid
Meat extract or yeast extract, gravy browning

General Method

1. Prepare the meat and vegetables.
2. Choose a strong saucepan, large enough to hold the meat easily and in it melt the dripping and fry the bacon gently.
3. Cut the vegetables in slices $\frac{3}{4}$ inch thick and make sure that there are enough slices to cover the bottom of the saucepan to a depth of 1 inch at least.
4. Lift out the bacon and if the meat is lean brown it quickly in the hot fat then lift it out. Do NOT fry meat that has plenty of fat.
5. Fry the vegetables till they are brown then pour in almost enough stock or water to cover them, add the herbs and spices and bring the liquid to simmering-point.
6. Put the meat on the mirepoix, cover any cut surface with the bacon, baste the meat with the hot liquid and cover it with greaseproof or parchment paper or foil.
7. Put on the lid, putting a weight on it to keep it fitting closely.
8. Simmer the liquid gently for the required time, basting the meat with the hot liquid every 20 to 30 minutes. The simmering may be well done in a slow oven.
9. If stuffing is to be served either stuff the joint, e.g. breast of mutton or veal, or brisket of beef, or make the stuffing into balls the size of small

walnuts and dredge them with flour, they can then be braised round the meat for ¾ hour.

To braise vegetables round the meat, prepare them as usual then tie leeks or celery into small bundles with clean string or tie such small vegetables as mushrooms or small carrots and onions in a square of muslin; baste them with the hot liquid and allow the following times:

Old carrots, leeks, celery	1½ hours
young carrots	1 hour
potatoes	1 ,,
onions	1 ,,
mushrooms	¾ to 1 hour

1. *To dish the braise.* Lift out the meat and if it has a coating of fat over the outside, e.g. loin of mutton, brown it lightly under a moderate grill or in a hot oven. Serve it on a hot dish with braised vegetables and balls of stuffing round it; keep it hot.

2. Strain the liquid into a measure and serve the mirepoix vegetables in a separate vegetable dish or use them later for a soup.

3. Make up the liquid to ½ pint or boil it fast in the braise saucepan to reduce it to ½ pint.

4. Thicken the liquid with arrowroot, season it to taste, add a little meat extract or yeast extract and gravy browning if necessary; it should glaze the back of the spoon and should be a rich brown and very savoury.

5. Baste this glaze over the meat and vegetables and pour the rest round the dish.

6. Chopped parsley gives a little bright colour on the braised vegetables.

To Fry Meat. See p. 8.

General Method

1. Wipe the meat and remove any outside skin or unwanted fat.

2. Beat the meat with a rolling-pin or steak-hammer to make it tender by bruising the fibres; it may also be rubbed with lemon juice or treated with a preparation of the enzyme of pawpaw (see p. 90) to increase its tenderness. This treatment is not applied to internal organs or to bacon.

3. Fry any accompaniments such as potatoes, onion-rings or tomatoes before the meat and keep them hot.

4. Heat enough fat to come barely half-way up the pieces when all are in the pan: for liver and sausages use only enough fat to grease the pan.

5. *Test the heat of the fat* with a small piece of bread which should brown

on one side in 15 seconds for steak or uncoated mutton and for pork; in 20 seconds for veal and for meat coated in egg and crumbs.

6. Put one piece of meat into the fat at a time, using two tools such as a fish slice and palette knife to prevent splashing: wait for a few seconds before adding another piece so that the fat regains the right heat.

7. Turn each piece once only as soon as the first side is brown, when all pieces are turned reduce the heat and fry gently till the meat is cooked.

8. *Test the meat* by pressing it with the flat of a knife: when cooked no red juice should be squeezed out, beef and liver should just cease to feel spongy; lamb, mutton, pork and veal should feel firm.

9. Drain the pieces by standing them against the edge of the frying-pan. Dish at once on a hot dish.

Time-table for Frying Meat

Meat	Time	Accompaniments	Special points
(All cuts being under 1 inch thick)			
Lamb chops Mutton „	10-15 minutes	Thick gravy. Fried potatoes, tomatoes or mushrooms	Serve fairly well done, juicy but not pink inside.
Lamb cutlets Mutton „	8 to 10 minutes	Brown or tomato sauce. Mashed or new potatoes, seasonable vegetable	Cutlets may be coated in egg and crumbs.
Steak, 1 inch ¼ inch	7 to 10 minutes 3 to 4 „	Fried onion-rings or tomatoes or mushrooms. Gravy and fried potatoes if liked	Serve slightly under-done, pink and juicy inside.
Pork chops	15 minutes	Thick gravy, fried apple slices or apple sauce	Serve well cooked but not dry.
Veal ½ inch ⅛ inch	10 minutes 4 to 5 „	Brown or tomato sauce. Bacon rolls, slices of lemon. Mashed or new potatoes, seasonable vegetable	Veal is often coated with egg and crumbs or it may be dipped in flour to give it a brown coating; serve well cooked.
Bacon	3 to 5 minutes	Eggs, sausages, tomatoes, smoked haddock, etc.	Remove rind and rust. To prevent rashers curling snip the edges of the fat. Overlap the lean over the fat of the next rasher in a cold, dry pan. Fry gently till the fat is turning golden and is slightly crisp.
Gammon rashers ¼ inch thick	7 to 10 minutes	Fried apple slices, tomatoes or or mushrooms	Snip the edges of the fat to prevent it curling. Fry gently.

Time-table for Frying Meat—cont.

Meat	Time	Accompaniments	Special points
Kidneys	4 to 5 minutes	Bacon and fried bread or toast	Skin, wash and cut them open length-wise, leaving them joined at the core on the inward curve. Cut out the core, serve them under-done.
Liver, calf's, pig's or lamb's	5 to 7 minutes	Bacon and thickened gravy	Have the liver sliced by the butcher to $\frac{1}{2}$ inch thick; remove skin and blood vessels; coat with flour. Fry the bacon first and keep it warm; fry the liver quickly and serve it slightly underdone.
Sausages, 8 to the 1 lb.	20 to 30 minutes	Mashed potatoes, thick gravy, fried tomatoes or apple slices or apple sauce.	Use enough dripping or lard to grease the pan. Fry the sausages slowly to prevent bursting, turning them till they are brown all over, firm and beginning to shrink.
Chipolata sausages	15 to 20 „	May be served with bacon and eggs or in a 'mixed fry' with bacon and chops or steak	
Chicken, joints: breast, wing and thigh	15 to 20 minutes	Fried $\frac{1}{4}$ bananas, bacon rolls. Canned sweet corn, hot, or sweet-corn fritters	Trim the joints. Flour the joints, coat them in egg and crumbs and fry gently.

To Grill Meat

For suitable cuts, see p. 97.

General Method

1. The butcher will cut steaks and chops to the right thickness and the only trimming needed will be of excessive fat; some fat is needed to baste the meat during grilling.

2. To make the meat tender beat it as for frying; mutton, lamb and pork may be brushed with lemon juice but this would spoil the red colour of beef; any meat may be treated with papayin extract if toughness is suspected.

3. Brush the meat all over with salad oil, olive oil, frying oil or melted dripping.

4. Heat the grill till it is glowing red, grease the grid bars with a piece of fat cut from the meat.

Have all accompaniments ready before beginning to grill the meat:

> fry potatoes and keep them warm,
> make maître d'hôtel butter and keep it cool, (p. 240)
> wash watercress,
> oil and grill small whole tomatoes or large mushrooms below the grid bars, beginning them 5 to 10 minutes before the meat; large, half tomatoes may be steamed on a plate or baked for 10-15 minutes.

5. Grill the meat under fierce heat, turning it with tongs or a spoon and palette knife every few minutes until done.
6. When cooked the meat should just cease to feel spongy.
7. For very thick pieces of meat heat may be reduced after 10 minutes.
8. Dish the meat as soon as it is cooked, putting the parsley butter on it at once.

Time-table

Meat	Time	Accompaniments and variations in method
Steak 1 to 1½ inches	7 to 12 minutes	Maître d'hôtel butter, steamed, baked or grilled tomatoes, French fried potatoes, watercress; optional, grilled mushrooms. Steak should be served underdone—pink and juicy inside.
Chops, 1 to 1½ inches	10 to 15 minutes	Accompaniments as for steak.
Cutlets	7 to 10 minutes	Mutton and lamb should both be served moderately well done, juicy but no longer pink inside.
Pork chops 1 to 1½ inches	15 to 20 minutes	Apple sauce or grilled tomatoes. Pork chops should be brushed with lemon juice ½ hour before grilling. Pork should be served well cooked.
Bacon rashers	3 to 5 minutes	Have the grill at moderate heat only, do not oil.
Gammon „ ¼ inch thick	5 to 7 minutes	Have the grill at moderate heat only, oil the lean. Snip the edges of the fat to prevent the rashers curling. Serve with tomatoes or apple sauce.
Sausages	15 to 20 minutes	Have the grill at moderate heat, do not oil or prick the sausages. Serve with bacon, tomatoes or apple sauce.
Kidneys	5 to 6 minutes	Serve with grilled bacon and maître d'hôte butter.
Liver	5 to 6 minutes	Have liver cut thick, remove all blood vessels and skin. Serve with grilled bacon.

To grill chicken see p. 287.

Mixed Grill. This includes steak or chop, sausage, bacon, kidney, tomato or mushroom.

    Time must be worked out for each item and pieces requiring longest grilling started first; bacon may be grilled first and kept warm; sausages may be finished under the other meat. Fat from bacon and sausages should be poured away from the grill-pan as it may catch fire. Accompaniments are served as for grilled steak.

Kebabs. These are collections of small pieces of meat, bacon, etc., threaded on skewers and grilled; one skewerful is served to each person.

    Each skewer should hold:

all well oiled
{
1 or 2 1-inch cubes of lean, tender mutton
1 or 2 bacon rolls
1 or 2 button mushrooms
¼ kidney
1 small sausage in two halves
1 small whole tomato
optional: slices of onion or small whole onion
    1 or 2 bay leaves
}

    Time for kebabs is calculated for the meat needing most cooking, usually the mutton and sausages.

To Stew Meat or to Cook Meat in a Casserole

For suitable cuts, see p. 97.

There are two methods of stewing, starting with pan and liquid cold for a 'cold water stew' or starting by frying the meat in hot fat before adding liquid for a 'fried' or 'brown stew'.

Cold Water Stew or 'Cold Start' Casserole

This is a better method than its name suggests, in fact it is the best way to soften really tough meat such as shin of beef: it is also suitable for any other stewing-meat, see p. 97. *The success of this method* depends on using a small amount of water so that the gravy is rich in flavour and in bringing the stew very slowly to simmering-point so that the meat does not shrink and become hard

Basic Recipe   *4 helpings*

1 lb. meat
1½ level tablepoons flour
salt and pepper
½ pint water
optional: chopped parsley to garnish

about ½ lb. root vegetables for
    flavour, e.g. carrot, turnip,
    onion, celery, or parsnip
optional: bunch of herbs

General Method

1. Wipe the meat, remove unwanted fat and outside skin.

2. Beat the meat to bruise the fibres.

3. Cut the meat into mouthful-sized pieces or into helpings, cutting across the fibres to shorten them.

4. Put the meat into the saucepan or casserole, add the seasoned flour, put on the lid and shake the meat about in the flour till it is coated.

5. Add the water and begin cooking on low top heat or in an oven at Gas No. 3 or 325° F.: this gives the meat a little extra time of cooking while vegetables are prepared.

6. Prepare the vegetables, slice them neatly, and add them to the hot stew.

7. Cook the stew till the meat is tender (see times below) then taste and season the gravy.

8. Serve the stew in a covered dish—very hot.

Name of stew and kind of meat	Time	Variation of recipe	Variation of method
Beef Casserole, shin stewing steak	3½ to 4 hours 2½ to 3½ hours	1 onion, 1 carrot; 1 small turnip or ½ parnsip or 2 sticks celery	If time is short treat the meat with papayin extract (see p. 90) or add 2 tablespoons vinegar or 2 tomatoes to make meat tender in less than suggested time.
Brazilian Casserole, beef	As above	As above, and add 3 to 4 tablespoons vinegar. Omit 3 to 4 tablespoons water.	If possible soak the meat in the vinegar for ½ hour before cooking.
Exeter Stew, beef	As above	2 oz. veal forcemeat	Make the forcemeat into balls the size of walnuts and cook these on top of the meat.
Sea Pie stewing beef, neck of mutton	2½ to 3 hours 2 to 2½ hours	Add 4 oz. suet pastry to the basic recipe (suet pastry, see p. 356)	As soon as the stew begins to cook make the pastry and, using the lid as a guide, shape it to fit the stewpan; rest it on top of the stew so that it cooks in the steam; keep the lid on. The 'pie' may be cooked on top heat or in an oven.

Name of stew and kind of meat	Time	Variation of recipe	Variation of method
Hotpot, Winter neck of mutton, stewing beef or jointed rabbit	2½ to 3 hours	Add 1 lb. potatoes to the basic recipe; use only about ¼ pint water	Pack the meat, flour, seasoning and vegetables into a deep casserole, add water to come about half-way up; begin cooking the stew. Peel and slice the potatoes ½ inch thick, arrange them neatly overlapping to cover meat and vegetables completely; season them and dot them with a few tiny pieces of fat trimmed from meat. Keep the lid on until the last ½ hour of cooking then remove it and brown the top of the potatoes.
Note *Lancashire Hotpot* should be made from mutton; the neck joints should stand upright in the pot		Lancashire Hotpot used to have oysters added and may also include mushrooms	
Hotpot, Summer neck of lamb or stewing-veal	1½ to 2½ hours	Use summer vegetables for flavour: ½ lb. mixed young carrots, turnips, spring onions, broad or runner beans or peas; a sprig of mint, and 1 lb. new potatoes	Leave the new potatoes whole if they are small; cut them in halves if they are medium sized and slice them if they are large, cook the hotpot as above but only just long enough to make the meat tender.
Liver Hotpot calf, lamb or sheep liver ox liver	1½ to 2 hours for vegetables 20 to 30 minutes 1 hour	1 lb. liver instead of the meat in winter or summer hotpot	Prepare the hotpot as above but omit the meat at first, and toss the flavouring vegetables in the seasoned flour. So that the liver shall not be overcooked, insert it into the flavouring vegetables by lifting the layer of potatoes aside and cook it for the stated time.
Irish Stew neck or breast of mutton, cut up by the butcher	2 to 2½ hours	½ lb. onions as the only flavouring vegetable omit flour, use ¾ pint water; add 2 lb. potatoes	Slice the onions thin, and half the potatoes ½ inch thick, add these to the seasoned meat and cover with the water—the sliced potatoes will thicken the gravy. The rest of the potatoes are kept whole and cooked on top of the stew after the first hour of cooking. To serve Irish stew, lift out the whole potatoes and arrange them round the dish, then the pieces of meat in the middle; mash and beat smooth the sliced potatoes; taste and season this potato gravy and pour it over the meat.

Name of stew and kind of meat	Time	Variation of recipe	Variation of method
Fricassée of Veal or Rabbit or Chicken; stewing-veal, jointed rabbit, or boiling fowl, jointed	1½ hours 1½ to 2 hours 2 to 2½ hours	1 onion, 2 oz. mushrooms instead of usual vegetables; add bunch of herbs, a strip of lemon rind and 2 teaspoons lemon juice *For the sauce:* 1 oz. margarine 1 oz. flour ¼ pint liquor from meat ¼ pint milk *Garnish:* bacon rolls fried croutons of bread chopped parsley	Stew the meat till tender with onion, mushrooms and flavouring herbs but with no thickening, and sufficient water barely to cover. When the meat is cooked, drain it and the mushrooms; make the sauce (see p. 345), return the meat and mushrooms to the sauce and re-heat them. Dish the stew and garnish it.
Stewed Tripe Tripe 'dressed' that is, cleansed and cooked by the butcher	1 to 1½ hours	½ lb. onions instead of vegetables in basic recipe, nutmeg *Sauce* as for Fricassée of Veal *Garnish:* chopped parsley	Cut the tripe in 2-inch squares. Slice the onions; stew both with seasoning in water barely to cover, until quite tender. Drain off the liquid, make the sauce, return the tripe and onion to the sauce and re-heat: season well.
Stewed Sweetbread calf's 'heart' or 'throat' sweetbread or 1 set lamb's sweetbreads	1½ to 2 hours 1 hour	To each ½ lb. sweetbread, ¼ pint sauce as for Fricassée of Veal, with the same flavouring	As for Fricassée of Veal but omitting onion and mushroom if it is for an invalid.

BROWN OR FRIED STEWS

For suitable cuts, see p. 97, omitting leg and shin of beef and scrag neck of mutton.

Basic Recipe *4 helpings*

1 lb. meat

¾ oz. dripping

1 carrot

1 onion

½ small turnip

¾ oz. flour

½ pint water or stock

optional: bunch of herbs

to brown the gravy, a piece of brown onion skin

salt and pepper

General Method

1. Prepare the meat, cut it in mouthful-sized pieces or in helpings. If time is short make the meat more tender as for fried meat.

2. Prepare the vegetables and slice the onion.

3. Heat the dripping till it hazes and in it fry the meat turning it rapidly until it is just brown all over, then lift it out.

4. Fry the onion slowly and meanwhile slice the carrot and turnip, add these and fry all until they are golden-brown.

5. Stir in the flour and fry it very gently till it is pale fawn: avoid over-frying as this makes the flour bitter.

6. Stir in the liquid and continue stirring till it boils.

7. Remove the pan from the heat and add the meat.

8. Simmer the stew very gently till the meat is tender. The stew may be transferred to a casserole and finished in a slow oven, Gas No. 1-2 or 300° to 320° F.

Name of stew and kind of meat	Time	Variations of recipe and method
'Haricot' Mutton or Ragoût of Mutton use mid-neck mutton or lamb	1½ to 2 hours	The name of this stew does not mean that it contains haricot beans though there is no reason why beans should not be cooked in any meat stew. 'Haricot' is also the name of a thick meat stew.
Ragoût of Steak, use stewing steak, buttock steak or skirt	2½ to 3 hours	
Beef Olives, use buttock steak	2 to 2½ hours	Cut the buttock steak in pieces about 3 inches by 4 inches then cut these to ½ inch thickness. Spread the pieces with 2 oz. veal forcemeat and roll them up: fix them with cocktail sticks.
Ragoût of Rabbit	1½ to 2 hours	Have the rabbit jointed, soak the joints in salt water for 1 hour or blanch them; dry them before cooking. ¼ lb. salt pork improves a rabbit stew.
Stewed kidney, use ox kidney	2 hours	Wash, skin and cut up the kidney; omit carrot and turnip. 2 oz. mushroom may be added for flavour.
Stewed Oxtail	3½ to 4 hours	Have the tail jointed by the butcher, remove outside fat, and blanch the meat. Dry the pieces. Add a bunch of herbs, a blade of mace, a bay leaf. Do not thicken the sauce until the oxtail is cooked; thicken it by stirring in blended flour. During the long cooking needed to make oxtail tender the liquid is so much reduced that it might be too thick if flour were added at the beginning.
Stewed stuffed Hearts 2 large sheeps' hearts or 4 small lambs' hearts; ½ tablespoon stuffing for each heart	2 to 3 hours	Trim and stuff the heart (see p. 249). Serve one small lamb's heart or ½ large sheep's heart per person. The flesh of the heart is very firm and requires long stewing to make it tender.

SPECIAL RECIPES FOR STEWING MEAT

Curry   *4 helpings*

Cooking time   1½ to 2 hours

1 lb. stewing veal or lean mutton, both without bone
or 1 small boiling fowl
or 1 rabbit

Accompaniments:
4-6 oz. Patna rice, boiled and dry
chutney
some or all of the following:
sliced tomato
sliced cucumber
grapefruit sections
sliced banana
salted nuts

½ *pint curry sauce:*
1 small onion
½ cooking-apple
½ oz. margarine or vegetable fat or oil
½ oz. curry powder
½ oz. flour
½ pint stock, vegetable water or coconut infusion
1 teaspoon black treacle
2 teaspoons lemon juice
1 teaspoon chutney

To make coconut infusion:
Simmer 1 oz. dessicated coconut for 5 minutes in ½ pint water. Strain and press out all the liquid.

1.   Cut the meat into mouthful-sized pieces or neat, small joints.
2.   Chop the onion finely and the apple coarsely.
3.   Melt the fat in a saucepan and in it fry the onion very gently without browning.
4.   Stir in the curry powder and flour and fry these for a few minutes.
5.   Add the apple, chutney, black treacle, lemon juice and liquid and stir the sauce till it simmers.
6.   Add the meat and let it stew very gently until it is tender in 1½ to 2 hours. Half an hour before serving the curry begin preparing the rice.
7.   *To boil Rice for Curry. The aim* is to cook the rice till it is just tender and to serve it so that the grains are separate and loose.
     To each ounce of rice about ½ pint water
     1 teaspoon salt
(a) Wash the rice in a strainer under the cold tap until the water no longer runs cloudy, or blanch it (see p. 14), to remove all loose starch.

(b) Have the salted water boiling fast in a rather deep pan, sprinkle in and stir the rice till it boils again. Boil it briskly without a lid until it is just tender when a grain is pinched or bitten, in 10 to 12 minutes. The water must boil briskly to prevent the rice sticking to the pan.

(c) Drain the rice, pour boiling water through it, rest the strainer over the pan which should have ½ inch boiling water in it; cover the rice closely with absorbent paper and keep it hot for 10 minutes shaking it gently once or twice to let out the steam.

8. While the rice is boiling and drying prepare the accompaniments and dish them in small dishes or bowls to hand with the curry.

9. Dish the curry in one hot, covered dish, and the rice in another; garnish the rice with lemon or paprika pepper.

Gulyas or Goulash   *4 helpings*

Cooking time   1 to 2 hours

1 lb. stewing steak or veal	¼ pint water
¾ oz. dripping or lard	¾ lb. small potatoes
2 onions	⅛ pint yoghurt *or*
2–4 teaspoons paprika pepper	3 tablespoons milk soured
2 large tomatoes *or*	with 1 teaspoon vinegar
¼ pint tinned tomato	¾ oz. flour
salt	*Optional additions:* 1 teaspoon caraway seeds, 1 green pepper
	Garnish: chopped parsley

1. Cut the meat into 1-inch cubes, slice the onion thin, skin and cut up fresh tomatoes.

2. Heat the fat and fry the meat quickly till just brown then remove it and fry the onion gently till soft; stir in the paprika pepper and caraway seeds, if used.

3. Add the tomatoes, water and salt, replace the meat and simmer the stew for 1 to 1½ hours for veal or 1½ to 2 hours for beef, until the meat is tender. ¾ hour before serving put the potatoes on top of the stew.

When the meat is tender lift off the potatoes and stir into the stew the flour, blended with the yoghurt or sour milk, replace the potatoes and continue cooking for 5 minutes.

4. Taste and season the goulash and serve it in a casserole, sprinkled with chopped parsley.

If the pepper is used it must be emptied of seeds, shredded and added just before the thickening.

Chinese Stewed Pork   *4 helpings*

Cooking time   1 hour

1 lb. streaky pork	2 teaspoons lemon juice
½ pint water	1 teaspoon chutney
1 level teaspoon Marmite	½ teaspoon brown sugar
or 2 teaspoons soy sauce	½ lb. white cabbage

1. Cut the pork into 1-inch cubes and simmer it for ½ hour in the water.
2. Mix the Marmite with a scant tablespoonful of the hot liquid, then drain off the rest of the liquid and keep it; do not dilute soy sauce.
3. Add the savoury sauce to the pork and turn the pieces till they are brown all over, heating very gently.
4. Add the lemon juice, sugar and chutney and stir the mixture for 2 or 3 minutes.
5. Put back the liquid and bring it to simmering-point.
6. Shred the cabbage, add it to the pan, lifting the pork on top of it, cook the whole for a further 20 minutes.
7. Taste, season and serve the dish in a casserole.

Savoury Liver   *4 helpings*

Oven 350° F. or Gas No. 4

Cooking time   ¾ to 1 hour

¾ lb. ox, calf or sheep liver	¼ pint fresh breadcrumbs
1 or 2 onions	1 tablespoon chopped parsley
½ tablespoon seasoned flour	½ teaspoon dried mixed herbs
4-6 rashers bacon	pepper, salt, nutmeg
under ¼ pint stock or water	

1. Have the liver sliced by the butcher; remove the skin and blood-vessels.
2. Scald the onions.
3. Dip the liver in the seasoned flour and pack the slices close together in a shallow fireproof dish.
4. Chop the onions very fine and mix them with the crumbs, herbs and seasoning.
5. Cover the liver with the crumb mixture and arrange the bacon to cover the crumbs.
6. Pour in enough stock or water to cover the liver and to come half-way up the crumbs.

7. Cook the dish in a moderate oven for 1 hour for ox liver or ¾ hour for other kinds.

Liver Risotto   *3-4 helpings*

Cooking time   About 45 minutes

1 oz. margarine	4 oz. rice
1 onion	bunch of herbs or ½ teaspoon mixed herbs
1-2 oz. streaky bacon	2 tomatoes or 2 tablespoons tomato juice
¼ lb. liver	about ¾ pint stock or stock substitute

To hand separately, 2 to 4 tablespoons grated cheese

1. Chop the onion fine and sweat it in the maragarine for 5 minutes.
2. Chop the bacon and fry it till clear, chop the liver and fry it gently for 3 minutes.
3. Add the rice and cook it for a further 2 to 3 minutes.
4. Add scalded, skinned tomatoes or tomato juice and ¼ pint stock and the herbs.
5. Simmer the risotto gently without a lid, stirring it frequently and adding more stock gradually to keep it moist, with the rice grains loose and slippery.
6. Continue cooking until the rice is quite tender and the risotto is still moist in about 45 minutes.
7. Taste and season it and serve it very hot in a deep dish with grated cheese sprinkled thickly over it at the last minute or handed with it.

   Note. There are many recipes for risotto, this is a simple one in which kidney or raw, boned chicken may be used instead of liver.

MEAT DISHES TO SERVE COLD

Pig's Head Brawn   *4-6 helpings*

Cooking time   3 hours

½ pig's head	bunch of herbs
¼ to ½ lb. shin of beef	6 peppercorns, a blade of mace,
1 onion	2 cloves
salt	4 allspice berries, 1 bay leaf
cold water to cover	*or* 1 tablespoon whole pickling spices

1. Soak the head in salt water, overnight if possible.
2. Scour the nose, mouth, throat and ears with salt and a small stiff brush.
3. Blanch and rinse the head.
4. Cut the shin of beef in 1-inch cubes.
5. Simmer the half head, the beef, spices, herbs and onion in water barely to cover them, adding 1 teaspoonful salt to each quart. Cook for 3 hours.
6. Drain the meat in a colander, returning the liquid to the pan.
7. Lift the bones out of head which should be very tender. Put the bones back into the liquid and let it boil quickly to reduce to half to three quarters of a pint.
8. Meanwhile, skin the tongue, lift away all cartilage, returning this also to the pan, and cut the meat into neat cubes.
9. Put the meat into a basin, pie-dish or cake-tin.
10. Strain the reduced liquid over the meat to fill the pie-dish and leave it till quite cold.
11. When cold turn the brawn out and serve it with salad.

Galantine of Beef   *4-6 helpings*

Cooking time   2 hours

½ lb. minced stewing steak	pepper, salt
¼ lb. pork sausage meat	¼ teaspoon ground allspice
or fat bacon *or* 2 oz. of each	1 beaten egg
3 oz. bread crumbs	about ¼ pint stock
Gelatine glaze: ¾ oz. gelatine	½ teaspoonful gravy browning
⅛ pint water	1 teaspoonful meat extract or Marmite

1. Grease a 1-lb. size cocoa or other cylindrical tin or a trough-shaped cake-tin or a 12-inch square of linen cloth or aluminium foil.
2. Chop the bacon if it is to be used.
3. Mix all the ingredients together, beating them smooth and adding enough stock to give a soft, dropping consistency.
4. Press the mixture carefully into the tin, leaving no air spaces, and cover it with foil or greased greaseproof paper: *or* form it into a roll and tie it firmly at each end in a cloth or square of foil.
5. Steam the galantine for 2 to 2½ hours or simmer it, preferably in a pan of stock, for 2 hours.
6. Press the roll between two plates or put a lid or a plate on the tin and put a 2-3 lb. weight on top. Leave till quite cold.

7. *To make the Glaze.* Put the water in a small basin, stir in the gelatine and stand the basin in boiling water; stir till the gelatine is dissolved then add the extract and the browning. The glaze should be very dark brown.
8. Stand the cold galantine on a cake rack and paint it thickly with the hot glaze.
9. When the glaze has set the top of the galantine may be decorated with thin slices of radish, cucumber or gherkin.
10. Serve the galantine with salad.

Galantine of Veal

Galantine may be made using minced stewing-veal instead of steak; a sliced hard-boiled egg may be added when the galantine is being shaped.

Jellied Meat Mould   *4-6 helpings*

Oven 325° F. or Gas No. 3

Cooking time   2½-3 hours (beef); 1½-2 hours (veal)

1 lb. shin or stewing-steak	a bunch of herbs
or 1 lb. stewing-veal	a strip of lemon-rind
¼ lb. bacon	6 peppercorns, a blade of mace
1 tablespoon lemon juice	1 clove, 2-3 allspice berries
or 2 teaspoons vinegar	*or* 2 teaspoons whole pickling spices
about ¼ pint water or stock	salt
¼ oz. gelatine	1 hard-boiled egg (optional)

1. Rinse a 1-pint basin or plain mould with water.
2. If the hard-boiled egg is to be added, slice it and arrange it on the bottom and sides of the mould.
3. Cut the meat and bacon in ¼- to ½-inch cubes and squares. Tie the herbs and spices in a small piece of muslin.
4. Put the meat and bacon into the mould but do not pack it down.
5. Pour in stock or water barely to cover the meat, add the salt, tuck in the bag of flavourings and cover the whole with foil or several layers of greaseproof paper.
6. Steam the mould or cook it in a slow oven, beginning at Gas No. 3 and reducing to 1 after ¾ hour or 325° F. to 275° F. allowing 3 hours for shin; 2-2½ hours for steak or 1½ to 2 hours for veal.
7. When the meat is tender, drain off half the liquid, cool it slightly and stir in the gelatine, stir it over gentle heat or a waterbath until it is

dissolved, add it to the mould and leave it to get quite cold, making sure that the meat is just covered.

8. When cold turn out the mould and serve it with salad.

Potted Meat

Oven 300° F. or Gas No. 1 or 2

Cooking time 2 to 2½ hours

½ lb. stewing steak
¼ lb. calf, sheep or pig liver
4 rashers of streaky bacon
Melted margarine or butter to cover
Grease a ¾-pint oven-ware casserole or basin

pepper, salt
¼ teaspoon powdered allspice
1 dessertspoon water

1. Line the sides of the basin with bacon and keep 2 rashers for the top.
2. Cut the meat in 2 or 3 pieces, press these into the basin and add the seasoning and water.
3. Cover the basin closely with foil, or greaseproof paper and a saucepan lid.
4. Bake the meat in a slow oven for 2-2½ hours until very tender.
5. Mince all the meat and either rub it through a wire sieve or pound it smooth.
6. Taste and re-season it if necessary, and beat into it all its own gravy and fat.
7. Press the meat firmly into a clean, dry basin or glass tongue jar, smooth the top and cover it with melted butter or margarine.
8. Keep the potted meat in a cold place for not more than 3 days. Serve it cut in slices with thin toast or as a sandwich spread.

DISHES USING MINCED BEEF

Fresh Mince   *2-3 helpings*

Cooking time   About 1¼ hours

½ lb. minced beef
1 small onion
½ oz. dripping
½ oz. flour or medium oatmeal
salt and pepper

¼ pint stock or water
1 teaspoonful savoury sauce
or ketchup
or 1 teaspoonful vinegar
and 1 tomato

Garnish: { Triangles of toast or fried bread
chopped parsley

1. Chop the onion finely, scald, skin and cut up the tomato.

2. Heat the dripping in a saucepan and in it fry the onion gently till soft and beginning to brown.

3. Fry the minced meat more quickly for 2 minutes, separating the pieces with two forks.

4. Remove from the heat and stir in the flour, then the liquid, salt and savoury sauce.

5. Bring the mixture very slowly to simmering-point and simmer it with a lid on, for 1 hour or until tender. Do not allow it to boil and stir it occasionally to prevent it sticking.

6. Taste and season the mince and serve it sprinkled with chopped parsley and with a border of triangles of toast or fried bread.

Note. Mince may also be served within a border of macaroni or spaghetti or of mashed potato.

Hamburgers (Fresh Mince Cakes)   *4 cakes*

Cooking time   15 minutes

$\frac{1}{2}$ lb. minced chuck or buttock steak
1 small onion   optional, $\frac{1}{2}$ egg   salt and pepper
To fry, dripping or vegetable fat or oil
To serve (optional), fried tomatoes or apple slices or onion rings.

1. Grate the onion.

2. Mix the minced meat with the other ingredients, beating it smooth and pressing it well together.

3. Divide the mixture into four and, with a lightly floured hand and a palette knife, shape the pieces into round cakes $\frac{3}{4}$ inch thick. Press the cakes firmly into shape as the only binding agent is the meat juice which will coagulate during cooking. If tomato, apple or onion is to be served fry this first and keep hot.

4. Heat $\frac{1}{8}$ inch fat in a frying-pan until it will brown a piece of bread in 15 seconds then put in the hamburgers one at a time and fry them at this heat for 2 minutes each side then reduce the heat and fry them very gently for a further 10 minutes or until they are just firm.

5. The hamburgers may be served in hot, toasted soft rolls.

Hamburgers with Barbecue Sauce

Cooking time   10 minutes for sauce and 20 minutes for hamburgers

Hamburgers as in the above recipe.

Barbecue sauce

1 small onion	1 teaspoon Worcester sauce
½ oz. margarine	½ teaspoon salt
2 tablespoons tomato ketchup	pinch of pepper
1 dessertspoon vinegar	4 tablespoons water

To garnish: 4 thick slices of tomato, grilled for 1 minute

1. To make the sauce, grate the onions, mix all the ingredients in a small saucepan and simmer them for 10 minutes.
2. Make the hamburgers as in the previous recipe.
3. Put them in the grill pan without the grid and pour the sauce over them; leave them for 20-30 minutes.
4. Heat the grill and grill the hamburgers for 2 minutes each side under strong heat, then reduce the heat and grill them for a further 15 minutes, basting them frequently and turning them once.
5. Serve hot with the sauce poured over them and with a slice of tomato on top of each.

Meat Loaf   *4-6 helpings*

Oven 350° F. Gas No. 4

Cooking time   ¾ to 1 hour

1 lb. minced beef	1 egg
4 oz. fresh breadcrumbs	½ teaspoonful mixed herbs
¼ pint stock or water	salt and pepper
1 small onion	¼ teaspoon ground allspice
1 teaspoon savoury sauce, e.g. Worcester sauce	

To coat: rasping crumbs
To serve: ½ pint tomato sauce (p. 350) or brown sauce (p. 347)

1. Grease a trough-shaped tin 6 inches long, and dust it with rasping crumbs.
2. Grate the onion, mix the minced beef with all the other ingredients to give a soft, dropping consistency.
3. Press the mixture into the tin, leaving no air spaces.

4. Cover the tin with foil or greaseproof paper and bake it for $\frac{3}{4}$ to 1 hour until just firm to the touch in a moderate oven.

5. Meanwhile make the sauce.

Turn out the loaf and pour the sauce round it.

Spaghetti with Meat Sauce (Spaghetti alla Bolognese)
4-6 helpings

Cooking time   50 minutes

$\frac{1}{2}$ lb. spaghetti $\frac{1}{2}$ oz. margarine, butter or olive oil
2 teaspoons salt

$\frac{1}{2}$ lb. minced steak	$\frac{1}{4}$ pint stock
1 oz. vegetable fat or oil	$\frac{1}{4}$ pint pulped tomato (fresh or
1 small onion	tinned)
2 oz. mushrooms	$\frac{1}{2}$ teaspoon meat or yeast extract
1 small stick of celery	$\frac{1}{2}$ teaspoon Worcester sauce
1 oz. flour	pepper and salt

To hand separately: $\frac{1}{4}$ lb. dry grated cheese

1. Grate or finely chop the onion, celery and chop the mushrooms.

2. Heat the fat in a saucepan and gently fry the grated vegetables for 5 minutes, then stir in the flour.

3. Add the tomatoes, bruise them and cook them for 2 or 3 minutes. Add the stock, savoury sauce, seasoning and minced meat and simmer the whole, covered, for $\frac{3}{4}$ hour. Taste and season it.

4. After 20 minutes boil the spaghetti in 2 to 3 pints of water with 2 teaspoons of salt; keep it boiling briskly without a lid.

5. When the spaghetti is soft in about 20 minutes drain it, add the margarine, butter or oil to the pan, return the spaghetti to the pan and lightly shake it to take up the fat.

6. Dish the spaghetti round the edge of a deep dish, pour the meat sauce in the middle and hand the grated cheese separately.

MEAT DISHES WITH BATTER

Meat Filled Pancakes   *4 helpings*

Cooking time   Abour 1 hour

$\frac{1}{4}$ lb. fresh meat mince (p. 275)
$\frac{1}{4}$ pint pancake batter (p. 383)
$\frac{1}{2}$ pint brown or cheese or tomato sauce (pp. 347, 350)

1. Prepare the mince as on p. 257.
2. Make the sauce.
3. While these two are cooking make the batter and fry 5 to 8 small, thin pancakes, keep these hot in a deep serving dish.
4. When the mince is ready fill the pancakes, rolling them round the mince.
5. Lay them in the serving-dish and pour the hot sauce over them.
6. If cheese sauce is made sprinkle the top with 2 tablespoons of grated cheese and ½ tablespoon of breadcrumbs and brown it under a moderate grill (pp. 345-6).

'Toad in a Hole' (Sausages in Batter)   *4 helpings*

Oven 400° F. or Gas No. 7

Cooking time   50 minutes

> ½ pint pancake batter (p. 383)
> ½ lb. sausages

1. Heat the oven.
2. Skin the sausages: soak them in cold water for 5 minutes to soften the skins; slit the skins lengthwise with a sharp knife or scissors and, holding one edge of skin, shake and roll the sausage out of its skin.
3. Put the sausages in an oven-ware dish and bake them for 5 minutes until the fat runs from them and the dish is hot.
4. Make the batter and pour it over the hot sausages.
5. Bake in the hot oven for 45 minutes until the batter is well risen, brown and crisp.
6. Serve at once.

   Note. 'Toad in a Hole' may also be made with 4 small mutton chops in ½ pint batter: trim most of the fat from the chops and put about one ounce of the trimmings to heat in the baking-dish, baste the chops with the melted fat and then bake them for 5 minutes before adding the batter.

Individual Toads in a Hole or Sausage Puffs

Recipe as above. Using 4 deep patty tins 4 inches across or 8-12 smaller ones.

1. Prepare oven, sausages and batter as above.
2. Divide the sausage between the tins, heat them as above, pour an equal amount of batter into each tin.
3. Bake for 30 minutes in the oven at 400° F., Gas No. 7.

RE-HEATED MEAT DISHES

As most butchers will cut any weight of all qualities of meat it is not necessary for any household to have much left-over cooked meat. A wise shopper, when buying a joint for roasting, chooses one that will serve her family for one hot meal and perhaps one cold salad meal, thus avoiding the disadvantages of re-heating meat. The two chief disadvantages are the readiness with which meat becomes hardened and indigestible when it is reheated and the danger of its becoming a vehicle of food-poisoning (see Chapter 3).

If re-heated meat is to be not only palatable but also digestible and safe there are certain rules that must be followed.

RULES FOR RE-HEATING MEAT

1. The meat to be re-heated must still be fresh, having been stored correctly for not more than two days after cooking.
2. Liquid as stock or gravy and extra seasoning and flavouring must be added to replace the moisture and extractives lost during the first cooking.
3. Meat that has already been overcooked cannot be made digestible when re-heated.
4. All ingredients added for flavour must be cooked and, like the meat, in fresh condition.
5. Meat must be re-heated quickly so that it reaches a safe temperature as soon as possible, remembering that bacteria can multiply very rapidly in a warm, moist mixture.
6. Meat must only be re-heated not re-cooked or the proteins will become hard and the dish indigestible.
7. Meat must never be re-heated a second time.
8. In order to make the meat moist and to re-heat it quickly it must be minced.
9. If the meat mixture is to be fried or baked it must be protected from the dry heat with a coating of egg and crumbs or batter or a covering of mashed potato or pastry.

TO PREPARE MEAT FOR RE-HEATING

1. Carve the meat from the bone, make stock with the bone (see p. 220).
2. Trim away all gristle and skin and all but a little fat; add the gristle to the stock and melt the fat (see p. 121).
3. Mince the meat putting a dry bread crust through the mincer to clear it of the last shreds of meat.

General Recipe. Cold Meat Mince

½ lb. lean cooked meat or corned beef

1 small onion	¼ to ½ pint stock or gravy
½ oz. dripping	pepper and salt
½ oz. flour	savoury sauce to taste (optional)

1. Grate or finely chop the onion and fry it till quite soft in the dripping.
2. Mince the meat.
3. Stir the flour into the dripping and fry it a little.
4. Add the liquid and bring the sauce to the boil, stirring it the while.
5. Simmer the sauce for 5 or 10 minutes.
6. Off the heat stir in the meat, season and taste the mixture.
7. Over moderate heat stir the mixture to heat it thoroughly without boiling. Serve the mince as for Fresh Meat Mince.

   Note. The amount of liquid added may be varied according to the dryness of the meat.

Cold Meat Cakes, Croquettes or Cutlets   *3-4 helpings*

Cooking time   5 minutes

General recipe using only ⅛ to ¼ pint of liquid to ½ lb. meat
To coat: egg and breadcrumbs (Fig. 39)
To fry: dripping or vegetable fat or oil
To serve: ½ pint brown, curry or tomato sauce (see pp. 347, 349, 350)

1. Prepare the mince mixture as in the previous recipe, using only enough liquid to give a paste that will not drop from the spoon.
2. Cool the mixture on a wet plate, covered with greased paper, foil or pliofilm.
3. Make the ½ pint sauce.
4. Divide the cool mixture into six or eight pieces.
5. On a floured board with floured hand and a palette knife shape them into round cakes ¾ inch thick or short, thick sausages or cutlets.
6. Coat the cakes twice with egg and crumbs (Fig. 39).
7. Fry them for just long enough to brown them all over in fat that will brown a piece of bread in 20 seconds, i.e. 380° F.; drain them on paper.
8. Dish them on a dish paper with the sauce handed separately.

K

Shepherd's Pie　*4 helpings*

Oven 400° F. Gas No. 7

Cooking time　30 minutes

> *General recipe* using $\frac{1}{4}$ pint liquid to $\frac{1}{2}$ lb. meat
> add 1 to $1\frac{1}{2}$ lb. mashed potato (p. 323)

1. Cook the potatoes and, when ready, mash them with seasoning, margarine and milk.
2. Prepare the mince as in the general recipe and put it in a 1 pint pie-dish.
3. Cover the top with potato, smooth the mashed potato with a palette knife and mark it neatly with a fork or the tip of a round-ended knife.
4. Sprinkle or brush the top with melted dripping.
5. Bake the pie at the top of the oven to brown the potato crust.

15

POULTRY

To choose Poultry. Notice that there is no discoloration of the skin and flesh and no unpleasant smell. The body and legs should be plump and rounded, the end of the breast-bone should be pliable and the feet soft and smooth if the bird is young.

A poulterer will always dress any poultry or game-birds that he sells and there are plenty of frozen, oven-ready birds on the market but home-reared birds often have to be prepared at home.

Plucking

1. Pluck the bird as soon as it is killed, while still warm, or if this is not possible, plunge it into water just below boiling-point, for 10 seconds.
2. Keep the bird's head hanging down.
3. Pull the feathers out without breaking the skin, pulling them against the way they lie.
4. Gather the feathers carefully into a large paper bag or a kitchen dust-bin.

Stubbing

Remove short, pin-feathers with the point of a knife and the thumb, washing them off the fingers in a bowl of water.

Singeing

Singe off hairs with a gas-taper or a wooden spill (wax or paper spills make too much black smoke).

Drawing

Protect the table with newspaper, have a bowl of water ready to rinse the fingers and a basin of salt water for the giblets.
Draw the leg sinews by making a slit down the inside of the leg below the 'knee', inserting a skewer under each sinew in turn and pulling them all out.
Cut off the legs 1 inch below the 'knee', scald the feet and the stumps in boiling water for 10 seconds, then scrape off the hard outer skin. Cut off the claws.

Draw the internal organs

1. Slit the skin up the back of the neck loosen it all round the neck and cut it round below the head.
2. Turn the flap of skin over the breast.
3. Wrap the head in newspaper, twist it off and discard it.
4. Cut off the neck close to the body and keep it in the salt water.
5. Loosen the crop and wind-pipe from the neck skin.
6. With the bird on its back insert the first finger in the breast cavity and loosen all the organs.
7. Make a cut horizontally above the vent and about 2 inches long, do not pierce the intestine.
8. With the fore-finger, loosen the organs from the vent-end, then hook the first and middle finger over the gizzard, which can be felt as a hard lump, and pull steadily until all the entrails are drawn out.
9. Cut away the skin all round the vent.

Prepare the giblets

Keep the neck, gizzard, heart and liver and feet. Wrap the rest of the organs in paper and discard them.

1. Remove the green, gall-sack from the liver without breaking it and cut away any liver that is stained green with gall as the gall is very bitter.
2. Cut through the dark red flesh of the gizzard to the silver skin, peel the flesh off the sack of stones.
3. Remove fat from all giblets and wash them in salt water. Use the giblets to make gravy or chop liver and add it to stuffing or roast it for 10 minutes with the bird.

Wash and dry the bird inside and out.

Stuff the bird at the neck-end rounding the stuffing to fill the hollow of the wish-bone, draw the skin over the stuffing (this may be done after trussing by lifting the flap of neck-skin).

Trussing (Fig. 45)

(a) With a trussing-needle and string

1. Lift the legs and press the upper joint downwards and towards the head, pass the needle right through the body, at the angle of the drum-stick and thigh and draw it out at the same point on the opposite side.
2. Fold the wing-tips inwards to secure the flap of skin, then pass the needle through the lower wing-joint, then the upper wing-joint and

in reverse order through the wing-joints on the other side, the two ends
of string now meet and are tied firmly in a bow.
3. Slip the needle through the skin below the tip of the breast-bone,
draw the string through and remove the needle; wind the string round
the ends of the legs and the tail and tie it firmly.

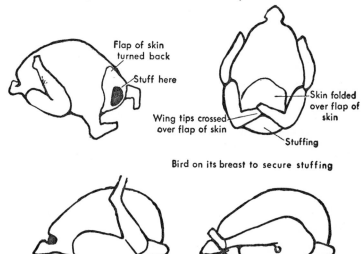

Fig. 45. TRUSSING A CHICKEN

(b) With skewers, if no trussing-needle is available

1. Pass a long skewer through the lower wing-joint into the angle
between thigh and drumstick through the body and out through the
same joints, in reverse order, on the other side.
2. Fasten the neck skin with a short skewer.
3. Tie legs and tail firmly together.

Other birds are trussed in a similar way, a turkey is often stuffed from
both ends using two different stuffings and game-birds are not stuffed.

To Roast Poultry

1. Follow any of the methods for roasting meat (p. 253) but, for all
but spit-roasting, cover the breast with fat bacon and cover or wrap

the bird with two or three layers of greased greaseproof paper or foil.

2. For the last 10 minutes of cooking, remove wrapping and bacon, baste the breast and dredge it with a very little flour.

3. Brown the breast at the top of the oven.

Special Method of Roasting Chicken

Oven 380° to 400° F. Gas No. 6 to 7

1. Heat the oven and heat to hazing-point about 2 tablespoons of bacon, sausage or pork-dripping, in a roasting-tin.

2. Lay the chicken on one side of the breast in the hot fat and baste it well.

3. Cook the chicken for $\frac{1}{3}$ total time in this position, $\frac{1}{3}$ of the time on the other side of the breast and the last $\frac{1}{3}$ on its back; each time the bird is turned baste it thoroughly.

Note. This method allows the juices to run into the breast and keeps the flesh from getting dry without bacon or wrapping.

Timing. Allow 20 minutes to the pound and 20 minutes over for methods 1, 2 and 4 (p. 253) and for special method; 30 minutes per pound for slow roasting.

Accompaniments for Roast Poultry

Kind of Poultry	Accompaniments	Special points
Chicken	Veal or other suitable stuffing (pp. 354-5). Bread sauce. Thin gravy. Sausages, bacon-rolls, potato crisps, French, lettuce salad or Brussels sprouts or green peas.	Stuff the bird from the neck end. Bake the sausages for 30 to 40 minutes and the bacon-rolls for 10 to 15 minutes with the chicken. Make gravy by rinsing out the roasting-tin with giblet-stock and skimming off the fat, using no flour.
Duck	Sage and onion or prune stuffing. Orange salad or peas. Thick gravy. Apple, orange or cranberry sauce.	Stuff the duck from the vent end.
Goose	Sage and onion or prune stuffing. Apple or cranberry sauce. Thick gravy.	Stuff the goose from the vent end.
Turkey	Veal, chestnut, prune or sausage-meat stuffing. Bread or cranberry sauce. Thin gravy. Hot ham or boiled bacon or bacon-rolls.	Stuff turkey from both ends.

Suggested Order of Work for Roasting Poultry

1. Prepare the bird if necessary. (A frozen bird should be thawed slowly for 12 to 24 hours in a cool larder or a refrigerator.)
2. Prepare giblets and make giblet stock.
3. Make stuffing and breadcrumbs for bread-sauce.
   Preparations 1 to 3 may well be done the day before cooking.
4. Stuff, truss and roast the bird.
5. Begin bread-sauce, make bacon-rolls, prepare sausages, cut and fry potato crisps and prepare salad plant or vegetables.
6. Bake sausages, finish bread-sauce and keep it hot.
7. Bake bacon-rolls and cook a green vegetable if served.
8. Dress the salad.
9. Dish the bird and make the gravy.

For Boiled Fowl, Braised Fowl, Fricassée of Chicken, Fried Chicken, Curry of Chicken, Chicken Pie, see the appropriate sections.

Grilled Chicken *4 helpings*

Cooking time 25 minutes

> 1 small, young roasting chicken or 4 quarter chickens
> 3–4 tablespoons melted butter or cooking oil
> salt and pepper   optional, 1 tablespoon lemon juice

1. Cut the chicken in 2 halves through the breast bone, using a large knife and a weight to hammer it through the bone. Cut each half in two, between wing and leg.
2. Skewer each piece flat.
3. Mix seasoning, lemon juice and oil and marinate the chicken in this for an hour or two or overnight. If butter is used this must be melted and brushed over the joints just before grilling.
4. Heat the grill to moderate heat; remove the grid from the grill pan.
5. Put the joints in the grill pan and baste all the liquid over them, arrange them wrong side up.
6. Grill for 10 minutes on wrong side, turn baste and grill right side for 15 minutes.
7. Serve hot with green salad.
   Note. Barbecue sauce, p. 277, may be used as for Hamburgers.

16

MEAT DISHES WITH PASTRY

MEAT WITH SUET PASTRY

Steak and Kidney Pudding *4 helpings*

Cooking time 2½ to 4½ hours

> 6 oz. suet pastry (p. 356)
> *Filling*

1 lb. stewing steak, skirt or shin	¼ teaspoon pepper
1 sheep's kidney or ¼ lb. ox kidney	1 teaspoon salt
1 tablespoon flour	2 tablespoons water

1. Grease a 1½ pint basin and greaseproof paper to cover it.
2. Prepare a steamer.
3. Make the pastry and with it shape a lid and line the basin (see Fig. 46).

Roll pastry to a round to cover the basin, cut out a ¼

Join the edges in the basin. Roll a round for the lid

Line the basin with pastry

Fruit Pudding to be turned out, join on top. Sides neat.

Meat Pudding, served in basin, edges tucked down the sides.

Fig. 46. LINING A BASIN WITH PASTRY

4. Prepare the steak and the kidney; cut the steak in strips about 1 inch wide and 3 inches long; cut the kidney and some of the fat in small pieces.

5. Toss all the meat in the flour and seasoning.

6. Roll a piece of kidney or fat inside each strip of meat.

7. Pack the meat into the lined basin; it should fill it and be piled a little above the rim. Pour in the water.

8. Turn the edge of the pastry lining inwards over the meat, damp this edge and press the lid firmly on, tuck the edge of the lid down inside the basin. This pudding is not turned out of the basin so the top must be neat.

9. Twist the greaseproof cover at the edges to form a cap.

10. Steam the pudding for a minimum of 2½ hours if fairly tender steak is used or 4½ hours for shin of beef.

Note. To shorten cooking time a small round may be cut from the bottom of the lining so that heat can reach the meat sooner.

To serve the pudding, fold a table napkin diagonally and pleat the triangle lengthways to match the depth of the basin. Wrap and pin the napkin round the basin to keep it hot.

Send to table about ¼ pint boiling water to be poured into the pudding to make more gravy when the first helping is cut.

Meat Roly Poly   *3 helpings*

Cooking time   2½ to 3 hours

   6 oz. suet pastry (p. 356)
   Filling
   ½ lb. minced beef   ⎫ or ½ lb. lb. minced lean bacon
   1 rasher streaky bacon ⎬ or ½ lb. sausage-meat
   1 small onion   ⎭ pepper, salt
   1 teaspoon flour   ½ teaspoon mixed herbs (optional)
   1 tablespoon water   ½ pint brown or tomato sauce

1. Grease a 12-inch square of greaseproof or cooking-parchment or foil or a pudding-cloth.

2. Prepare a steamer.

3. Make the pastry (p. 356), roll it to an oblong and damp the edges.

4. Chop the onion finely and mix the filling.

5. Spread the filling on the pastry, roll it up keeping the edges neat.

6. Roll the pastry in the greased covering paper, foil or cloth; secure the ends by twisting or tying with string.

7. Steam the roll for 2½ to 3 hours.

8. Serve it with brown or tomato sauce.

MEAT WITH SHORT PASTRY

Cornish Pasties   *4 portions*   Fig. 47

Prepare and
divide filling

Roll rounds of pastry, put filling across
the middle, damp the edges

Seal the edges and flute them

North Cornish   South Cornish

Fig. 47. SHAPING CORNISH PASTIES

Oven 380°-400° F. or Gas No. 6

Cooking time   50 minutes

½ lb. short pastry (p. 359)	pepper, salt
6 oz. chuck steak	1 tablespoon water
2 oz. kidney or liver	½ very small swede turnip
4 oz. potato	(optional, but a really Cornish
1 small onion	addition)

1. Make the pastry, divide it into four and roll each piece to a round about 6 inches across.
2. Cut the meat into ¼-inch thick strips, the liver or kidney into small pieces; dice the potatoes and turnip and chop the onion finely.
3. Mix the filling, add seasoning and water.
4. Pile ¼ mixture on to each round of pastry, damp the edges, fold the pastry in half and press the edges firmly together, knock up the edge.

5. *To shape the pasties as in north Cornwall:* set the pasty on edge with the join on top. Flute this edge with the thumb and fingers. With a skewer make a hole in the fluting to allow steam to escape.

To shape pasties as in south Cornwall: fold the cut edge neatly back on to the pasty and flute it with a spoon handle or the back of a knife.

6. Brush the pasties with beaten egg or milk.

7. Bake them for 20 minutes at 380° to 400° F. and then at 325° F. for the remaining $\frac{1}{2}$ hour to cook the meat without overcooking the pastry.

MEAT WITH SHORT, FLAKY OR ROUGH PUFF PASTRY

Meat Pie, General Recipe   *4 helpings* Fig. 48

Oven 380° F. to 425° F. Gas No. 6-8

Total Cooking time $1\frac{1}{2}$ to $2\frac{1}{2}$ hours

> 4 to 6 oz. pastry for a pint-sized pie-dish (pp. 359, 362)
> *Filling*
> 1 lb. meat   1 tablespoon flour
> pepper and salt   2 tablespoons water

General Method:

1. Make the pastry and leave it to cool and relax.

2. Prepare the filling and fill the pie-dish completely, packing the filling in firmly and rounding it above the edge of the pie-dish; if there is not enough filling use a pie-lifter, an egg-cup or a peeled, raw potato, flattened at the bottom and trimmed to the required size.

3. Roll the pastry to $\frac{1}{4}$ inch thickness for short pastry or just under $\frac{1}{2}$ inch for the flaky pastries.

4. Roll it to the shape of the pie-dish but with a 1 inch margin on 3 sides or three-quarters of the circumference.

5. Cut a strip $\frac{3}{4}$ inch wide from this margin—the extra width all round the main piece allows for rounding over the filling.

6. Damp the rim of the pie-dish, and press the strip of pastry on to it; the ends will meet but should be trimmed to fit with no overlap.

7. Damp the strip, lift the main piece of pastry on the rolling pin and lower it into position without stretching it or allowing it to sag into the dish.

8. Press the edges firmly together.

Roll pastry to size

Fill pie dish, put on ¾ inch strip of pastry

Damp the edge and cover the pie

Trim the edge

Flake or knock up the edge

Flute the edge

DECORATIONS FOR SAVOURY PIES

Leaves

Tassel

Fig. 48. COVERING A PIE-DISH

9. Trim the edges with a sharp knife held at a slant so that the pastry is a little wider at the top than at the edge of the pie-dish, this is to allow for shrinkage during baking.

10. Flake or knock up the edge with the knife held horizontal and the pastry kept in place on the edge of the dish with the back of the fore-finger. This is not necessary for the flaky pastries as they rise naturally in flakes.

11. Flute the edge with the back of the knife, setting the width of the flutes at about 1 inch (to indicate a savoury filling) with the tip of the thumb.

12. Brush the top with beaten whole egg, diluted with a little milk.

13. Make a neat hole to allow steam to escape—a little 'chimney' made of greaseproof paper draws off the steam more effectively.

14. Decorate the top of the pie with leaves of pastry or, for short pastry, with a tassel (see Fig. 48).

Cooking the Pie

Short Pastry

As short pastry cannot be cooked for much more than an hour without becoming too dry, the meat must usually be partly cooked and then cooled before being covered with short pastry.

1. Cook the meat with as little liquid as possible:

    (a) in a stewpan on top-heat for 1 to $1\frac{1}{2}$ hours
    (b) in a pie-dish, covered with foil in a slow oven for 1 to $1\frac{1}{2}$ hours
    (c) in a pressure cooker for 10 to 20 minutes

2. Bake the pie for 20 minutes at 380° F. or Gas No. 6, then reduce the heat to 325° to 340° F., Gas No. 2 to 3 and bake the pie on a lower shelf for the remaining 30 to 40 minutes.

Flaky and Rough Puff Pastry

Except for very tough meat such as shin of beef the flavour and texture are both improved by cooking the meat entirely under the crust, but the crust cannot be baked for much over $2\frac{1}{2}$ hours without getting hard.

Bake the pie for 20 minutes at 400° to 425° F. or Gas No. 7 until the pastry begins to turn golden then reduce heat to 300° to 325° F., Gas

No. 1 to 2 and bake the pie on a lower shelf until the meat is tender in 1 to 2 hours. For baking that must exceed 1½ hours the pastry must be covered with greaseproof paper, damp on the upper side, or with foil to prevent it getting too hard.

For all meat pies pour a little hot stock or water into the pie when it is cooked, using a funnel inserted in the steam-hole; this is to make more gravy, as extra liquid cooked in the pie would make the crust sodden underneath.

Various Fillings for Meat Pies

Name of pie and kind of filling	Time to cook the meat	Variation of method
Steak and Kidney 1 lb. chuck steak, skirt or shin 1 sheep's or ¼ lb. ox, kidney 1 tablespoon flour, seasoning 2 tablespoons water	Chuck steak } 2½ Skirt } hrs. Shin, 3½ to 4 hours	Cut the steak in thin strips about 1 by 3 inches, and the kidney in small pieces. Roll steak round the kidney.
Veal and Ham 1 lb. stewing veal 2–4 oz. fat, streaky bacon, grated rind and juice ½ lemon 1 level teaspoon mixed herbs, pepper, salt, 2 tablespoons water 1 hard-boiled egg, optional	1½ to 2 hours	Cut meat in mouthful-sized pieces, dice the bacon. Mix all ingredients. Arrange slices of hard-boiled egg round the sides of the pie-dish.
Fitchet Pie ½ lb. lean streaky bacon or pork ½ lb. cooking apples ½ lb. potatoes 1 onion pepper and a very little salt 1 dessertspoon brown sugar ¼ pint stock Usually short pastry	1½ hours	Slice potatoes ½ inch thick, onions very thin and quartered apples ½ inch. Dice the pork or bacon in about ¼ inch pieces. Arrange layers of potato, sprinkled with seasoning, apple sprinkled with sugar, onion and pork in the pie-dish, pour in stock.
Medley Pie ½ lb. streaky pork or bacon ½ lb. cooking apples 2 onions ¼ teaspoon chopped or powdered sage pepper and salt	1½ hours	Dice the bacon to ¼ inch size, slice the quartered apples, chop the onion finely. Mix the ingredients, add no liquid as the juice runs from the apples.

Various Fillings for Meat Pies—cont.

Name of pie and kind of filling	*Time to cook the meat*	*Variation of method*
'Squab' Pie 1 lb. lean mutton, cut from the neck ½ lb. cooking apples 1 oz. brown sugar ½ oz. raisins ⅛ teaspoon mixed spice ½ tablespoon flour 1 onion pepper and salt	1½ to 2 hours	Cut the meat in neat rounds about ½ inch thick. Chop apple roughly and onion finely. Mix all the ingredients. Add no liquid—the apple juice will be enough
Mutton Pie 1 lb. lean mutton, cut from the neck 1-2 oz. mushrooms ½ teaspoon mixed herbs pepper, salt ½ tablespoon flour 2 tablespoons stock or water	1½ to 2 hours	Cut the mutton in neat pieces, chop the onion finely and the mushrooms roughly. Mix all the ingredients. Add the liquid.
Chicken Pie 1 chicken or boiling-fowl of medium size or 1 lb. chicken joints 2-4 oz. streaky bacon 1 small onion ¼ teaspoon mixed herbs 1 teaspoon chopped parsley grated rind ½ lemon 1 clove, pepper, salt ¼ to ½ pint stock, preferably made from chicken carcase and giblets. Optional: the chicken liver	1½ hours for chicken 2½ hours for boiling fowl	Bone the chicken or joint it and cut large joints in half Chop the onion. Mix all the flavourings; arrange the chicken in layers, sprinkled with the flavourings. Pour in about ⅛ pint stock. When cooked add hot stock to fill the pie-dish.
Rabbit Pie 1 medium-sized rabbit or 1 lb. rabbit joints 2-4 oz. streaky bacon 1 onion ¼ teaspoon mixed herbs ⅛ teaspoon grated nutmeg 1 tablespoon flour pepper and salt	1½ to 2 hours	Bone the joints or cut them into half. Chop the onion.

Individual Meat Pies

Any of the above fillings may be used in small, one-portion pies with short or flaky pastry. Use 1 oz. pastry to each 1 oz. of filling, cook the filling for all but $\frac{1}{2}$ hour of the required time and bake the little pies in large patty-tins or small oven-ware dishes for $\frac{1}{2}$ hour.

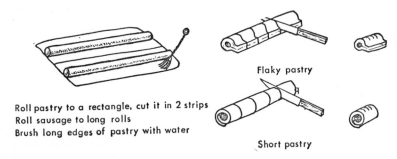

Roll pastry to a rectangle, cut it in 2 strips
Roll sausage to long rolls
Brush long edges of pastry with water

Flaky pastry

Short pastry

Fig. 49. Shaping Sausage Rolls

Sausage Rolls   *8 large or 12 small rolls*   Fig. 49

Oven 380° F. to 425° F. Gas No. 6 to 8

Cooking time $\frac{1}{2}$ hour

> 8 oz. short pastry or 6 oz. flaky or rough puff pastry (pp. 359, 362)
> 8 oz. sausages or sausage-meat

1. Make the pastry.
2. Skin the sausages and roll them on a floured board to two long rolls.
3. Roll the pastry to an oblong about 7 inches wide and $\frac{1}{8}$ inch thick.
4. Cut the oblong into two strips lengthways; put a roll of sausage on each.
5. Damp one edge of each strip (Fig. 49)

With short pastry

Roll the dry edge of the strip of pastry over the sausage to overlap the damp edge, press the join firmly under the roll.

With flaky or rough puff pastry

1. Fold the pastry in half lengthways, sausage inside, press the cut edges together at the side of the roll.
2. Brush the pastry with beaten egg, cut it into suitable lengths and slash the tops of the rolls with a sharp knife or scissors.
3. Bake the rolls at 380° to 400° F. for short pastry; 400° to 425° F. for flaky and rough puff pastry, for the first $\frac{1}{4}$ hour then at 325° to 350° F. for the second $\frac{1}{4}$ hour.

Raised Meat Pies, Hot Water Pastry *4 helpings* Fig. 50

Oven 360° to 375° F. Gas No. 5

Baking time $1\frac{1}{2}$ hours for veal; 2 hours for pork

Hot Water Pastry

This pastry must be firm enough before baking to keep its shape with no more support than a strip of paper; the flour therefore is partly cooked by mixing it with boiling water so that the starch grains burst, stiffen the pastry and absorb the melted fat.

This pastry is almost always used with a meat filling, though one country recipe fills it with gooseberries.

Recipe for Hot Water Pastry

$\frac{1}{2}$ lb. flour   6 tablespoons or $\frac{3}{16}$ pint water
3 oz. lard   or milk and water mixed
                                        $\frac{1}{2}$ level teaspoon salt

1. Sift the flour into a warm basin.
2. Boil the liquid with the lard and salt and stir it, boiling, into the flour, using a wooden spoon.
3. Beat it only until it forms a ball then cool it a little.
4. When it has cooled slightly knead the pastry smooth, flatten it to a thin cake to cool more quickly.
5. Wrap it in plastic film or foil to prevent it drying and leave it till just cold but still pliable.

FILLINGS FOR RAISED PIES

Pork Pie

$\frac{3}{4}$ lb. pork ($\frac{2}{3}$ lean, $\frac{1}{3}$ fat)
$\frac{1}{4}$ teaspoon mixed dried herbs including sage
$\frac{1}{8}$,,   pepper
$\frac{1}{2}$,,   salt
$\frac{1}{4}$ pint stock to be added after baking

Veal and Ham Pie

$\frac{1}{2}$ lb. stewing veal   1 teaspoon chopped parsley
$\frac{1}{4}$ lb. streaky bacon $\frac{1}{4}$,,   mixed herbs
grated rind $\frac{1}{2}$ lemon   pepper and salt
Optional: 1 hard-boiled egg $\frac{1}{4}$ pint stock to be added after
                                      baking

1. Have pork minced by the butcher.
2. Cut veal into small dice, leave bacon rashers whole and use them to line the pastry case.
3. Mix the filling with the seasoning and herbs and pack it into the pastry case without any liquid.

To Raise a Pie

1. Over a 2 lb. Jam-jar (Fig. 50)

1. Grease a double strip of greaseproof paper, 2 inches deep when folded and long enough to go loosely round the jar; have 2 pins ready.
2. When the pastry is just cold but still pliable, cut off a quarter and knead and roll this to a round, larger than the base of the jar, to form the lid. Knead and roll the larger piece to a round about $\frac{3}{4}$ inch thick.
3. Turn the jam-jar upside down and press the pastry on to it to cover the bottom and three-quarters of the sides. Avoid stretching the pastry, take care to keep it the same thickness all over, and keep the lower edge even.
4. Use the palm of the hand and clasp the hands round the sides to get a smooth, close fit.
5. Turn the jar open end up and slip the pastry off directly on to a baking-tray.
6. Re-shape the case as needed, using the knuckles at the bottom and fingers up the sides.

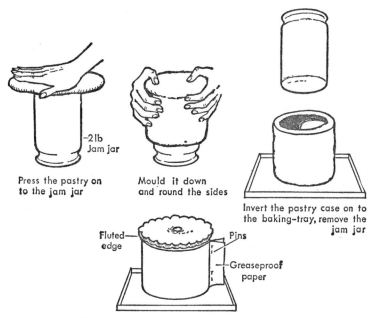

Press the pastry on
to the jam jar

Mould it down
and round the sides

Invert the pastry case on to
the baking-tray, remove the
jam jar

Fluted—
edge

Pins

—Greaseproof
paper

Fig. 50. Shaping a Raised Pie over a Jam-jar

7. Strap the greaseproof paper round outside, drawing the pie into a good shape, pin the paper in position; leave ½ inch pastry above the paper.

8. Pack the filling in carefully.

9. Brush the edge of the lid with beaten egg and press this to the upper edge of the pie between finger and thumb.

10. Hold the edges between finger and thumb to knock them up, and flute them.

11. Brush the top with egg; if liked a scrap of pastry may be kept to cut leaves or rounds for decoration. Make a hole to let out the steam.

12. Bake the pie at 350° to 360° F. Gas No. 5 reducing the heat after ¾ hour.

13. Half an hour before the pie is done, peel off the paper, brush the sides with egg and put the pie back in the oven to crisp the sides.

To Mould a Pie in a Tin

A special raised-pie mould is made with hinged sides which clip round the base, but as this is an expensive item a cake-tin will do instead.

1. Grease a cake-tin of about 5 inches diameter with a loose bottom.

2. Have the pastry cool—it need not be quite cold—make a lid and roll the larger piece to a round as above.

3. Press the pastry into the shape of the tin, working from the bottom up, using knuckles on the bottom and fingers up the side and keeping the pastry of uniform thickness. Raise the pastry $\frac{1}{2}$ inch above the tin.

4. Fill the pie, seal the lid on with beaten egg, knock up and flute the edge.

5. Glaze the top with egg, make a hole to let out steam.

6. Bake the pie in the tin, otherwise as above.

7. Half an hour before the pie is done remove the tin by standing it on a jam-jar, easing the side and gently drawing it down.

8. Brush the sides with egg and put the pie back in the oven to brown.

17

CHEESE DISHES, MEATLESS AND VEGETARIAN DISHES

Cheese Pudding *3-4 helpings*

Oven 350° to 360° F. Gas No. 4-5
Baking time 30-40 minutes

¼ pint (2 oz.) stale bread
½ pint milk
½ oz. margarine

1 to 2 eggs
salt, pepper, mustard
1½ to 2 oz. grated cheese

1. Grease a pint-sized pie-dish.
2. Cut the crust off bread, before weighing it, or make breadcrumbs.
3. Boil the milk, add to it, in the saucepan, the margarine and bread, put on the lid and soak the bread ½ hour.
4. Separate yolk from white of egg. Grate the cheese.
5. Add yolk(s) to the slightly cooked milk mixture, season it and stir in the cheese.
6. Whisk the white(s) stiff and with a tablespoon fold it into the mixture.
7. Bake the pudding at once until it is golden-brown, well risen and just set.
8. Serve it at once.

Cheese, Bread and Butter Pudding *3 helpings*

Oven 350° to 360° F. Gas No. 4-5
Baking time 30-40 minutes

2 oz. thin slices bread and butter.
½ pint milk
1 egg

1½ to 2 oz. grated cheese
pepper, salt, made mustard

1. Grease a pint-sized pie-dish.
2. Warm the milk, and stir it into the beaten egg, season this mixture with a little pepper and salt.
3. Spread the bread and butter with a very little made or French mustard then press the grated cheese on top.

4. Arrange the bread neatly in the pie-dish, strain the warm milk and egg over it, leave it to soak for $\frac{1}{2}$ hour.

5. Bake the pudding till brown and just set.

Macaroni or Spaghetti Cheese   *3 helpings*

Cooking time 20–30 minutes. Grilling time 3–4 minutes

3 oz. macaroni or spaghetti	salt, pepper, made mustard
$\frac{1}{2}$ pint milk or $\frac{1}{4}$ pint milk and	3 oz. grated cheese
$\frac{1}{4}$ water from boiling the macaroni	$\frac{1}{2}$ tablespoon breadcrumbs
$\frac{1}{2}$ oz. margarine	Dice or small triangles of
$\frac{1}{2}$ oz. flour	toast or fried bread

Optional additional flavouring ingredients:
2 oz. fried bacon (not for vegetarians)
1 hard-boiled egg
1 small onion
2 to 4 tomatoes and $\frac{1}{2}$ oz. margarine

1. Grease the sides of a shallow oven-ware dish to hold 1 pint.

2. Boil the macaroni or spaghetti in plenty of salted water, without a lid: the water must boil steadily to toss the macaroni up and prevent it sticking to the pan; the lid is left off to prevent it boiling over. Cook the macaroni for 20 to 40 minutes, spaghetti for 20–25 minutes, until either is quite soft.

3. Meanwhile chop and fry the bacon and put it in the bottom of the dish, or chop the onion finely and cook it till quite soft in the margarine; chop the hard-boiled egg to be added to the sauce later; or scald, skin, slice and cook the tomatoes in the margarine till soft, turn them out of the pan to be added to the sauce later. Drain the macaroni.

4. Make a thin sauce with the margarine, flour and liquid, leaving the cooked onion (if used) in the saucepan.

5. Stir the macaroni or spaghetti into the sauce, and re-heat it if necessary, season the sauce to taste and add tomatoes if these are used.

6. Stir in all but 2 level tablespoons of cheese and turn the mixture into the dish. Heat the grill. Make the toast and cut it neatly or fry cut bread.

7. Mix the cheese and crumbs and sprinkle them evenly over the sauce; make sure that all sauce is covered or it will form brown blisters under the grill.

8. Grill fairly quickly until the top is browned and crisp.

Savoury or Spanish Rice   *3 helpings*

Cooking time about 20 minutes. Grilling time 3-4 minutes

3 oz. rice (preferably Patna)	¼ teaspoon made mustard
2 large tomatoes, raw or canned	2 oz. grated cheese
1 onion	1 level tablespoon breadcrumbs
½ oz. margarine	*Optional* { 1 tablespoon chopped parsley
1 level teaspoon curry powder	½ small sweet pepper
1 teaspoon chutney	

1. Have ready a shallow oven-ware dish to hold ¾ pint.
2. Boil the rice till just soft in 7 to 12 minutes, drain it.
3. Chop the onion fine, scald and skin the tomatoes and cut them up roughly. Wash the seeds out of the pepper and cut it in fine shreds.
4. Fry the onion gently in the margarine till soft, add the pepper and tomatoes and cook them till soft.
5. Stir in the rice and all other ingredients except cheese, crumbs and parsley, and re-heat the mixture; taste and season it.
6. Stir in ⅔ cheese, turn the mixture into the dish and heat the grill.
7. Mix the rest of the cheese with the crumbs and sprinkle these evenly over the top.
8. Brown it under the grill.
   If parsley is used arrange it in thick lines across the top.

Tomato and Cheese Pancakes   *3-4 helpings*

Cooking time to fry pancakes
to cook filling 10 minutes
to make sauce
Grilling time 3-4 minutes

¼ pint pancake batter (p. 383)	
Filling:	
2 oz. mushrooms	1 small onion (optional)
3 medium tomatoes	pepper and salt
½ oz. margarine	1-2 teaspoons breadcrumbs
Coating:	
½ pint white coating sauce	2 teaspoons breadcrumbs
2 oz. grated cheese	

1. Have ready a deep oven-ware pie-plate, 1 pint size, set it on a saucepan ¼ full of boiling water to get hot.

2. Chop the onion; wipe and chop the mushrooms; scald, skin and cut up the tomatoes, and fry all these till quite soft in the margarine, season the mixture and add enough crumbs to absorb any juice.

3. Make the batter and fry it as 7 to 8 small, thin pancakes; keep these hot, as they are ready, in the hot dish covered with the saucepan-lid.

4. When all are fried slip them on to the lid, fill one at a time with the savoury filling and pack them neatly in the hot dish.

5. Make the sauce, add ⅔ cheese, taste and season the sauce and with it coat the pancakes. Heat the grill.

6. Sprinkle the rest of the cheese mixed with the crumbs evenly over the top and brown the top under the grill.

CHEESE AND VEGETARIAN DISHES WITH PASTRY

Cheese Flan or 'Quiche Lorraine'

Oven 350° to 360° F. Gas No. 5

Baking time　35 to 40 minutes

> 4 to 5 oz. short pastry (p. 359)
> *Filling:*
> 1 small onion　　　　　　　　½ oz. margarine
> 2 rashers streaky bacon (omit for vegetarians)
> ½ pint milk　　　　　　　　　pepper and salt
> 2 eggs　　　　　　　　　　　2 oz. grated cheese

1. Make the pastry and with it line a deep, 7-inch sandwich tin, flan ring or a 1 pint size, deep oven-ware pie-plate (Fig. 64).

2. Chop the onion very fine and the bacon in small squares.

3. Fry the bacon and onion gently in the margarine until both are quite tender, turn them into the pastry case.

4. Beat the egg, stir in the milk, seasoning and most of the cheese, pour this mixture into the case, and sprinkle the top with the rest of the cheese.

5. Bake the flan until it is just set and golden brown on top.

Vegetable Pie   *4 helpings*

Oven 380° F. Gas No. 6, then 325° F. Gas No. 2 or 1
Cooking time   20 minutes stewing, 40 minutes baking

> *For 1 pint pie-dish:*
> 4 to 5 oz. cheese pastry (p. 361)
> ¼ pint cooked or canned haricot or butter beans
> ¾ to 1 lb. mixed vegetables, e.g. 3 or 4 of the following:
> onion, parsnip, tomato,
> carrot, mushrooms, leek,
> celery, cauliflower
> 1 oz. margarine or 2 tablespoons cooking oil
> 1 tablespoon flour   pepper, salt
> 1 hard-boiled egg   bunch of herbs

1. Prepare and slice the vegetables thinly.
2. Make the fat or oil hot and fat-steam the vegetables, adding the hardest first and omitting tomato, cook them for 20 minutes then cool them on a plate.
3. Make the pastry, hard boil the egg.
4. Add seasoning to the vegetables, sprinkle them with the flour, and pack them into the pie-dish with the beans, herbs, cut up tomato and any juice from the pan: arrange slices of hard-boiled egg on top.
5. Cover the pie and bake it as usual.

CHEESE SNACKS AND SAVOURIES

Cheese Biscuits and Straws

Oven 400° F. Gas No. 7
Baking time   4 to 7 minutes

> Cheese pastry made from either recipe, p. 361

1. Roll the pastry very thin.
2. For biscuits cut it into small rounds or ovals or, with a knife, into squares, fingers or diamond shapes; prick the biscuits. For straws cut the pastry into strips 3 to 4 inches wide then cut ¼-inch wide straws across the strips. Straighten the straws on the baking tray with the knife. Cut a few rings about 1 inch across. As the pastry shrinks and rises during baking, the biscuits and straws should be cut a little larger than necessary.
3. Bake quickly until they are a pale golden colour, firm and risen.

Cheese Straws from Pastry Scraps

Oven 400° F. Gas No. 7
Baking time　5 to 7 minutes

> Scraps of short or flaky pastry
> Grated cheese, if liked, a little cayenne pepper

Roll the pastry very thin, sprinkle it all over, liberally, with grated cheese, fold it in three and again roll it thin. Cut 5-inch strips and cut these into ½-inch wide straws. Twist the straws, holding them at each end.

Bake them as above for 5 to 7 minutes.

Cheese Fingers (Cheese d'Artois)

Oven 400° F. Gas No. 7
Baking time　10 to 15 minutes

> About 4 oz. scraps of flaky or rough puff pastry
>
> *Filling* { 2 oz. grated cheese
> 1 oz. margarine
> a little cayenne pepper or mustard
> beaten egg

1. Roll the pastry very thin to a neat rectangle and cut it in halves.
2. Brush one half with a little beaten egg.
3. Melt the margarine, stir into it the grated cheese and cayenne pepper or mustard and enough beaten egg to make a paste that can be spread easily.
4. Spread the cheese mixture over the egg on half pastry, lift the other half to cover the cheese, and roll it very lightly.
5. Trim the edges and brush the top with beaten egg. Cut neat fingers or diamonds about 1 by 2 inches.
6. Bake the fingers till well risen and golden-brown.

Cheese Dreams

> Thin slices of bread and butter.
> *Filling:*
> 2-3 oz. grated cheese　　　　pinch of cayenne or mustard
> ½ oz. margarine　　　　a little chutney, savoury sauce
> a little grated nutmeg　　*or* Marmite
> 　　　　if liked, a small piece of onion
> *shallow fat* for frying

1. If onion is used chop it very fine and fry it till soft in the margarine.
2. Mix all the ingredients with the melted margarine, taste and season the mixture.
3. Make sandwiches with a thick layer of the filling, cut them into neat fingers.
4. Fry them in shallow fat till crisp and golden; drain them well, serve them hot.

Cheese Fondue or Cheese Dip

A cheese fondue may be either a soft, creamy mixture into which fingers of toast or bread are dipped or a baked mixture rather like a soft soufflé. There are many recipes for either kind, here are two simple ones.

(1) Cheese Fondue for Dipping

$\frac{1}{2}$ lb. cheese (odd, dry scraps grated)
$\frac{1}{4}$ pint cider or white wine or $\frac{1}{2}$ pint white coating-sauce (p. 345)
pepper, salt, a very little cayenne pepper
if liked, a clove of garlic
Fingers of toast or slices of French bread

1. Grate the cheese which may be of several different kinds.
2. Make the toast; crush the garlic and rub it round a flame-proof casserole.
3. Make the white sauce if this is to be used.
4. Mix the cheese into the cider, wine or sauce, heat it gently, stirring it all the time until it is melted and creamy and season it well. Keep the fondue warm over very gentle heat such as a dish-warmer with a wax 'night light'.

(2) Baked Cheese Fondue

Oven 350° F. Gas No. 4
Baking time   35 to 40 minutes

3 oz. breadcrumbs	3 oz. grated cheese
$\frac{1}{2}$ to 1 oz. margarine or butter	2 eggs
$\frac{1}{2}$ pint milk	if liked, a clove of garlic
salt, cayenne pepper	

1. Heat the milk, add the fat and breadcrumbs; season the mixture, crush the garlic and rub it round an oven-ware pie-dish or casserole (1 pint size).

2. Cool the mixture a little, separate the yolks from the egg-whites, beat the yolks then the cheese into the crumb mixture.

3. Whisk the egg-whites stiff and fold them into the mixture.

4. Bake the fondue until it is well risen and golden-brown but only lightly set.

Serve it at once.

Home-made 'Processed' Cheese for Salad or Sandwiches

dry scraps of cheese, if liked, a little chopped chives or spring onion

a little melted margarine ($\frac{1}{2}$ oz. to 4 oz. cheese)

a little milk, salad cream or bottled tomato sauce

1. Grate the cheese fine.

2. Melt the margarine and work it into the cheese, and chives or onion, if used.

3. Add the chosen liquid, a few drops at a time, and work it very firmly into the cheese until a smooth, rather stiff paste is made.

4. Roll the cheese into balls, and if liked press these into chopped nuts, or use the mixture as a sandwich spread.

Welsh Rarebit   *2 helpings or 8 to 10 small savouries*

Grilling time 5-7 minutes

3 oz. grated cheese	1 tablespoon melted butter or
$\frac{1}{4}$ teaspoon made mustard	margarine
salt and cayenne pepper	1 to 2 tablespoons milk, beer,
2 fairly large slices of	cider
buttered toast	

1. Make the toast, butter it and keep it hot.

2. Melt the fat, stir into it the cheese, seasonings and enough liquid to make a soft paste.

3. Either heat the mixture very gently till the cheese melts, then spread it on the toast, *or* spread it on the toast, make it smooth and grill it rather slowly until it is golden-brown all over.

Serve it at once.

For Buck Rarebit

1. Poach one egg for each helping, keep them warm in hot water after poaching.

2. Make the rarebit as above, drain the eggs and dish them on top of the cheese mixture.

VEGETARIAN CROQUETTES

Basic recipe using thick binding sauce

Example: **Hard-Boiled Egg Croquettes** *4 helpings*

Main Ingredient:	4 hard-boiled eggs
Binding sauce	⎧ 1 oz. margarine or vegetable cooking fat or oil ⎨ 1 oz. flour ⎩ $\frac{1}{4}$ pint milk or vegetable water
	$\frac{1}{2}$ egg, pepper and salt
For coating:	beaten egg and crumbs
For frying:	vegetable frying oil
To serve:	$\frac{1}{2}$ pint tomato or cheese or curry sauce

Basic Method

1. Chop the main ingredient fine.

2. Make the thick sauce by the roux method.

3. Add to it the chopped main ingredient, the seasoning and beaten egg, cook it a little to set the egg.

4. Spread the mixture on a wet plate, cover it with greased paper and smooth the top. Leave it till cold and set.

5. Cut it into 8 pieces, shape each to a short, thick sausage-shape or a small, flat cake like a fish cake, using a little flour.

6. Coat the cakes, twice if possible, with beaten egg and crumbs (see p. 235 and Fig. 39).

7. Fry in deep fat at 380° F. or in shallow fat that will brown bread in 20 seconds; drain them.

8. Serve hot with the sauce handed separately.

Two Variations of Basic Method

Name of croquettes	Alternative main ingredients	Variation of Method
Macaroni Cheese Croquettes	2 oz. macaroni 3 oz. grated cheese	Boil the macaroni till soft, chop it in ⅛-inch lengths.
Nut Croquettes	4 oz. mixed nuts 2 oz. breadcrumbs 1 small onion	Chop the onion and fry it till soft in the fat, before making the sauce. Chop the nuts.

Lentil, Bean or Pea Croquettes *4 helpings*

4 oz. lentils, butter beans, haricot beans or dried peas
½ teaspoon mixed herbs   ½ oz. margarine or vegetable fat
1 teaspoon chopped parsley   1 oz. breadcrumbs
salt and pepper   ½ egg
1 oz. grated cheese

1. Soak beans or peas overnight.
2. Boil the pulse in 1 pint salted water until quite soft, drain them, reserve the liquid and dry the pulse a little in the saucepan.
3. Rub beans or peas through a wire sieve or beat lentils smooth.
4. Add the fat, herbs, cheese, seasoning and breadcrumbs. Beat in the ½ egg and if necessary a little of the cooking-water to give a moist paste that is stiff enough to shape into croquettes, taste and season it. Shape, coat and fry the croquettes as for the basic recipe.

Serve with sauce handed separately.

Nut or Lentil Roast

The same mixtures used for Nut Croquettes or Lentil Croquettes can be made into one roll, coated twice in egg and crumbs, and baked in hazing hot vegetable fat, basting it well. The roast should be served with a sauce as for croquettes.

Semolina Fillets *3-4 helpings*

2 oz. semolina (good weight)   salt and pepper
½ pint milk   a pinch of ground nutmeg
1 oz. margarine or vegetable fat   ½ egg
2 oz. grated cheese

To coat: beaten egg and breadcrumbs.
To fry: vegetable frying oil
To garnish: sections of lemon
To serve: tomato or curry sauce

1. Cook the semolina in the milk until very thick; add the fat.
2. Add the cheese and season very well, beat in the egg.
3. Cool the mixture as for other croquettes but do not try to reshape the 8 triangles when it is divided.
4. Coat the triangular fillets and press the edges to neaten them.
5. Fry and serve as for croquettes.

Hard-Boiled Egg Curry   *4 helpings*

½ pint curry sauce (p. 349)
4 hard-boiled eggs
4 oz. Patna rice and other accompaniments for curry (p. 269)

1. Make the curry sauce and simmer it for 1 hour.
2. Boil the eggs for 7 minutes, not quite hard, remove the shells and put the whole, peeled eggs into the sauce.
3. Keep the curry hot, but not simmering, for 20 minutes to allow the eggs to take up the curry flavour.
4. Serve the curry with rice and other accompaniments.

Vegetable Curry   *4 helpings*

½ pint curry sauce (p. 349)
¾ lb. mixed vegetables, e.g. artichokes, celery, cauliflower, carrots, parsnip, tomato
¼ pint cooked or canned haricot or butter beans
Rice and accompaniments as usual

1. Make the curry sauce.
2. Prepare the vegetables and cut them in neat slices or pieces.
3. Cook the harder vegetables very gently in the curry sauce for about an hour or until they are tender; add cauliflower, tomato and beans later and allow them 20 minutes only.
4. Serve the curry as usual.

18

EGG DISHES

To Boil Eggs

Put the eggs into enough boiling water to cover them, keep them simmering gently and time them.

The length of time needed depends partly on the age of the eggs; new-laid eggs requiring longer to set than eggs one or two weeks old, and partly on personal taste for soft-boiled or well set eggs.

Allow $3\frac{1}{2}$ minutes for soft-boiled eggs up to 5 minutes for a firm set or for really new-laid eggs.

To 'Coddle' Eggs

This gives a soft but evenly-set result.

Boil enough water to cover the eggs, put the eggs in and at once remove the pan from direct heat. Cover it and keep it in a warm place for 5 minutes.

To Fry Eggs (usually with Fried Bacon)

To each egg, 2 teaspoonfuls bacon fat or butter or frying-oil

1. If bacon is served fry it first, keep it warm on a serving-dish and add lard if there is not enough fat.
2. Have the fat moderately hot so that a drop of egg-white coagulates quickly but without spurting.
3. Break one egg into a cup, basin or saucer and slide it carefully into the pan; tilt the pan slightly so that the egg lies in a pool of hot fat at one side of the pan, lower the pan as soon as the white sets in shape.
4. Fry the egg gently and push the white inwards to prevent it spreading. To cook the upper side of the egg either baste it with hot fat from the pan or turn the egg over with a fish slice giving a quick turn of the wrist.
5. If several eggs are to be fried the first should be almost set before the next is added to the pan.

To Bake Eggs

Oven 325° F. Gas No. 3
Baking time 7 to 15 minutes

1. Grease, with butter or margarine, a small oven-ware cup for each egg, or hollow out large baked potatoes, cut in halves.
2. Slip an egg into each cup, sprinkle it with salt and pepper and put a tiny pat of butter or margarine, or a teaspoonful of cream from the top of the milk, or a spoonful of tomato sauce, on each egg.
3. Bake them till just set in the moderate oven.

If the oven is in use at a higher temperature set oven-ware cups in a roasting-tin with a little water in the bottom.

To Poach Eggs

The aim is to keep the white in a compact shape; this is not easy with either really new-laid or rather stale eggs. The water must be almost at boiling-point but with very little bubbling which would break up the white before it could coagulate.

1 tablespoon salt in each pint of water slightly raises the boiling-point and makes it possible to have the water hot enough without any movement; the salty flavour is usually liked.

1 tablespoon vinegar in one pint water speeds up coagulation by chemical means but gives the eggs a flavour of vinegar.

Method

1. Make the toast, butter it and keep it hot; for other ways of serving poached eggs see below.
2. Grease a frying-pan or shallow stewpan and pour in enough boiling water to cover the eggs, add the salt or vinegar and put the pan over low heat so that it bubbles very gently at one side only.
3. (a) Slide one egg at a time into the water and gently stir round it to draw the white together round the yolk.
   (b) *or* put a greased, 2- to 2½-inch round cutter into the pan and slide the egg into this; by either method as soon as one egg is just set in shape another can be added, the cutter being lifted off and used for the next egg if only one is available.

(c) *Another method, for poaching several eggs at once*, is to plunge them, in their shells, into a pan of boiling water for exactly 10 seconds, using a strainer to make this easy. The eggs are cracked one at a time and lowered directly into the pan for poaching, with neither salt nor vinegar; as the white will have begun to set in the shape of the shell the eggs can all be poached at once without losing shape.

4. Poach the eggs for 3½ to 5 minutes until the white and yolk are just set.

5. Lift them out with a draining spoon or fish-slice, drain them for a second or two and if necessary trim the edges of the white. Dish the eggs on the buttered toast or other cooked food.

Other ways of dishing poached eggs are on fried bacon, on mashed potato, on cooked spincah, on savoury rice, on spaghetti, on smoked haddock or on Welsh rarebit, when it is called 'Buck Rarebit'.

To Scramble or Butter Eggs

To each egg:	1 tablespoon milk
	salt and pepper to taste
	¼ to ½ oz. butter, margarine or frying oil
and for dishing:	a slice of buttered toast

1. Make the toast, butter it and keep it warm in the serving-dish.

2. Beat the eggs with the milk and seasoning.

3. Melt the fat over moderate heat, pour in the egg mixture and cook it fairly quickly, stirring hard all the time and scraping it off the bottom of the pan, until it is all set to a creamy consistency. Pile it at once on the toast; if it is not dished quickly the heat of the pan may overcook and curdle the last of the egg.

Other ingredients that may be added to Scrambled Eggs:

    1. Grated cheese, 1 tablespoonful to each egg

    2. Cooked, flaked, smoked haddock, 1 oz. to each egg

    3. Cooked, chopped bacon or ham, ½ to 1 oz. to each egg

All these may be added to the raw egg mixture as the cooking time is so short that these cooked ingredients are only re-heated, not overcooked.

    4. *'Polish' Egg or Egg and Tomato*

      To each egg: 1 small tomato, pepper and salt to taste

             ½ oz. butter or margarine

Scald, skin and slice the tomato and cook it in the fat for a few minutes, till just soft, then add and cook the egg as for Scrambled Egg.

Eggs with Cheese Sauce (Eggs au Gratin or 'Eggs Mornay')
2-4 helpings

> 4 eggs
> ½ pint white coating sauce (p. 345)
> 2-3 oz. grated cheese   pepper, salt
> 1 tablespoon fresh crumbs   ⅛ teaspoon cayenne or mustard

1. Grease an oven-ware baking-dish of 8 to 9 inches diameter or 4 individual baking-cups and heat them in an oven or under a moderate grill.
2. Make the white sauce and keep it hot.
3. Break the eggs and slide them into the hot dish where they should begin to set.
4. Stir all but 2 tablespoons of cheese into the hot sauce, taste and season it.
5. Coat the eggs with the hot sauce, sprinkle the remaining cheese, mixed with crumbs evenly over the top.
6. Brown the top, in a hot oven, 425° F. Gas No. 7-8, for 3 minutes, or under a moderate grill.

   By the time the cheese is browned the eggs will be cooked. The oven would only be suitable if it were already in use.

Scotch Eggs   *1 egg per helping*

To each egg: 1 sausage or 2 oz. sausage-meat
To coat: beaten egg and crumbs
To fry: shallow or deep fat

1. Hard boil, cool and shell the eggs and dust them lightly with flour.
2. Skin sausages and shape them into flat, round cakes.
3. Wrap each egg in sausage meat, pressing out all cracks and keeping the meat to an even thickness.
4. Coat them with egg and crumbs, twice if possible.
5. Heat the fat: shallow fat to come half-way up the eggs, until it will brown bread in 50 seconds, or deep fat to 340° F.
6. Fry the eggs over moderate heat for 7 to 10 minutes until the raw sausage is cooked.
7. Cut the eggs in halves with a sharp knife.
8. Serve cold with salad or hot with a juicy vegetable such as tomatoes.

OMELETS

Savoury or French Omelet *1-2 helpings*

For a 7-8-inch omelet- or frying-pan:

> 3 eggs, salt and pepper to taste
> ¾ oz. cooking fat or clarified butter
> *or* 3 teaspoons olive oil or cooking oil
> *Optional:* 2 teaspoons chopped parsley
> and/or ½ teaspoon mixed herbs

If possible keep a pan specially for omelets, never wash it but clean it with dry salt and soft, clean paper, wiping out all the salt.

1. Prove the omelet pan (see p. 384), clarify butter (if used), see p. 14.

2. Beat the eggs slightly and season them.

3. Have ready a hot serving-dish and a palette knife.

4. Heat the fat or oil till tiny ripples can be seen on the surface in a good light; keep the pan over strong heat.

5. Pour the egg slowly into the hot fat: as it touches the fat it should set and must be lifted off the bottom of the pan constantly with the palette knife so that more liquid flows into the hot fat.

6. When the whole mixture is creamy loosen it round the edge, take the pan off the heat and tilt it sharply so that the omelet rolls down it to fold in three. Press it into a crescent shape with the palette knife.

Invert the omelet on to the hot dish and serve it at once.

Filled Savoury Omelets

General Method

Cook the filling separately and keep it hot.

Make the savoury omelet and when the mixture is creamy put the filling across the middle and fold the omelet over it.

Dish the omelet in the usual way.

Varieties of Savoury Omelet

Kind of omelet	Additions to 3-egg omelet	Variations of method
Cheese Omelet	1 oz. grated cheese pinch of cayenne, 1 tablespoon cream from top of the milk.	Mix the extra ingredients into the beaten egg
Haddock Omelet	2 oz. cooked, smoked haddock a little grated nutmeg	Flake the cooked haddock and mix it with the beaten egg.
Spanish Omelet	2 tablespoons olive oil instead of ¾ oz. fat; one tomato 1 tablespoon shredded sweet pepper 1 small onion, 1 small potato	Chop the onion, dice the potato and fry them till golden in the oil; scald, skin and cut the tomatoes in strips discarding all juice and pips, shred the pimento and add these to the oil and fry them a few minutes. Cook the omelet with the oil and the mixture in the pan. Do not fold the omelet but brown it lightly under a moderate grill.

Fillings for Savoury Omelets

Kind of omelet	Recipe for filling	Method for filling
Kidney Omelet	1 sheep's kidney ½ oz. margarine or butter 2 tablespoons water 1 teaspoon flour salt and pepper	Prepare the kidney and cut it in small dice. Melt the fat and in it fry the kidney for a few minutes; sprinkle in the flour and stir in the water. Stew the kidney gently for 20 to 30 minutes. Season the mixture.
Mushroom Omelet	2 to 4 oz. mushrooms ½ oz. butter or margarine 1 teaspoon flour 2 tablespoons water salt, pepper, lemon juice ¼ teaspoon Marmite	Wash dry and chop the mushrooms. Melt the fat and fat-steam the mushrooms for 10 minutes. Blend the flour with the water and stir it into the mushrooms; cook the mixture until the mushrooms are quite soft. Taste it and season it.

Sweet or Soufflé Omelet   *1–2 helpings*

Oven 350° F. Gas No. 4
Baking time   15 minutes

2 eggs	⅛ teaspoon vanilla essence
1 oz. caster sugar	1 tablespoon jam
caster sugar for dredging	

1. Prove the omelet-pan (p. 384) and warm a serving-dish, heat the oven.
2. Separate yolks from whites of egg.
3. Beat the yolks with the sugar until they are pale yellow and thick and add the vanilla.
4. Warm the omelet-pan and grease it.
5. Whisk the egg-whites until they are stiff, then fold them into the yolks and sugar.
6. Pour the egg mixture into the pan and cook it over very low top-heat for 1 minute to set the underside then put the pan into the middle of the oven.
7. Bake the omelet for 15 minutes when it should be golden, set and very light.
8. While the omelet is baking warm the jam over hot water, and dredge a square of paper with caster sugar.
9. Turn the omelet upside down on to the paper, mark the underside across the middle with the back of a knife.
10. Spread the warm jam over one half, lifting the other half by means of the paper, fold the omelet in half,
     Dish and serve it at once.

BAKED SOUFFLÉS

Baked soufflés are not difficult to make but ingredients must be weighed accurately; egg-whites must be whisked stiff and baking-time and temperature must be exact.

Basic Recipe   *3–4 helpings*

Oven 350° F. Gas No. 3–4
Baking time   40 to 45 minutes large; 15–20 minutes small

1 oz. margarine or butter	3 eggs or 3 yolks and 4 whites
1 oz. flour	flavouring
¼ pint milk	

Basic Method

1. Grease a 1½-pint or 6-inch soufflé case or deep casserole or 4 to 6 small cases (paper soufflé cases may be used ungreased).
2. Make a thick sauce by the roux method, with the fat, flour and milk; use a 1½-2 pint saucepan and leave the sauce in it to cool a little.
3. Beat the yolks into the cooled sauce and add flavourings to taste.
4. Whisk the egg-whites stiff and with a tablespoon fold them into the sauce mixture, lightly but completely.
5. Pour the mixture into the case and at once bake it in the middle of the oven. Fold a table napkin in a 'water-lily' fold (p. 22).
6. As soon as the soufflé is golden-brown, very light and just set, it must be served in the case. If, unavoidably, it cannot be eaten immediately, it should be kept in the oven, turned off if it is electric or to Gas No. ¼ or 'low'. As soon as the soufflé is taken from the oven it begins to shrink; a folded table napkin keeps the soufflé warm and hinders shrinkage.

Variations of Recipe for Baked Soufflés

Name of Soufflé	Additional ingredients	Variation of method
Cheese	(omit ½ oz. flour) (Add) 2 oz. dry grated cheese; salt, pepper and a very little cayenne pepper to taste.	Serve with a French salad, see p. 340.
Chocolate	1 oz. chocolate 1 oz. sugar ¼ teaspoon vanilla essence	Melt the chocolate in 1 tablespoon milk and beat it smooth, mix it with the milk for the sauce.
Coffee	1 teaspoon instant coffee-powder or coffee essence 1 oz. sugar, ⅛ teaspoon vanilla essence.	Mix the coffee-powder with the flour before making the sauce.
Lemon	Grated rind of 1 lemon 1 oz. sugar	Serve all sweet soufflés with a suitable sweet, hot sauce.
Vanilla	1 oz. sugar, ½ teaspoon vanilla essence.	

BAKED FRUIT SOUFFLÉS
Basic Recipe
Oven 340°-350° F. Gas No. 4
Baking time   30 to 40 minutes

stiff purée from 1 lb. fruit
sugar to sweeten   2 eggs or 2 yolks and 3 whites
lemon or orange to flavour

1. Grease a 1½-pint oven-ware soufflé case or deep casserole.
2. Make the fruit purée, sweeten it and add lemon or orange rind and juice to taste.
3. Beat the yolks into the mixture.
    Whisk the whites stiff and fold them into the purée.
4. Bake in the middle of the oven until well risen, just set and golden on top. Serve at once with cream or custard.

Variations of Recipe

Name of soufflé	Special ingredients	Variation of method
Apple	1 lb. cooking apples rind and juice ½ lemon 2–3 oz. sugar pinch of ginger or ground cinnamon, if liked	Bake the apples, remove pulp and beat it smooth.
Apricot or any stewed fruit with a good flavour	6 oz. dried apricots, soaked, stewed and drained *or* 1 lb. stewed or canned apricots juice ½ lemon, 3–4 oz. sugar	Rub the drained apricots through a nylon sieve.
Banana	1 lb. bananas without skins (4 to 6), rind and juice of ½ orange, 2 teaspoons lemon juice caster sugar to sweeten	Mash the bananas smooth, beat into them the juice, caster sugar to taste and grated orange rind. Beat in the yolks until the mixture is pale and a little thickened.

Note. For a very light soufflé the yolks are sometimes omitted and used for custard; 3 whites must then be used.

Baked Lentil Soufflé   *3 helpings*

Baking as for Basic Recipe, p. 318

¼ pint lentils	evaporated milk	pepper, salt, cayenne
¾ pint water	3 eggs or 2 yolks	¼ teaspoon mixed dried herbs
1 oz. margarine	and 3 whites	2 tablespoons dry, grated
⅛ pint cream or		cheese

1. Prepare the case as for Basic Recipe, p. 318
2. Stew the lentils in the water till soft, then drain them and press them through a wire sieve.
3. Add the fat, cream, seasonings and cheese.
4. Now follow the Basic Recipe.

19

VEGETABLES

To cook and serve vegetables so that their important nutrients—minerals and Vitamins C and the B Group—are conserved certain rules should be followed for all vegetables, see Chapter 7:

1. Use them as fresh as possible.
2. Prepare them just before cooking, do not soak them unless absolutely necessary.
3. Cook them in the least amount of water and for the shortest time needed to soften them.
4. Keep the liquid in which they are cooked and use it either with the vegetable, made into a sauce or for gravy or soup.

POTATOES

To Prepare Potatoes for Cooking

1. Scrub them.
2. When possible cook them in their skins: if skins are to be removed, peel old potatoes very thinly; scrape new potatoes; remove 'eyes' from both kinds.
3. Rinse them in clean water and cook them at once. If they *must* be left for a while keep them in water with 1 tablespoon salt to each quart.

To Boil Potatoes

Cooking time   20 to 40 minutes

1. Choose even-sized potatoes. Put on a kettle of water.
2. Put them into a saucepan which they half or two-thirds fill.
3. Add 1 teaspoon salt to each pound, and a sprig of mint for new potatoes.
4. Pour on boiling water not quite to cover them.
5. With the lid on simmer them gently until soft when tested with a skewer; 20-30 minutes for new potatoes, 30-40 minutes for large old ones.
6. Drain the water away through the lid.

7. Return the pan to very low heat and gently shake it to drive off steam; for 1 or 2 minutes only for new potatoes; until they are floury for old ones.

8. *To serve.* Add ½ oz. margarine or butter to each pound new potatoes. Add chopped parsley to both kinds, with a sprig of fresh mint or a little mint chopped with the parsley for new potatoes.

To Bake Potatoes in their Skins

Oven 350°-400° F. Gas No. 4-6
Cooking time 50 minutes to 1¼ hours

1. Choose large, equal-sized potatoes.
2. Score the potatoes all round with the point of a knife or prick them to let out steam.
3. Put them on open oven-shelves and then light the oven. Bake till soft when pinched.
4. To keep the skins soft grease them with dripping or rub them with greased paper, such as wrapping from margarine or lard or wrap them in clean, dry paper.
5. *To serve.* Pile them in a wooden bowl or in a table-napkin on a serving-dish. Hand butter or margarine with them.

Baked Potatoes with Cheese

To each large potato   ¼ oz. margarine   pepper and salt
                1 oz. grated cheese   1 tablespoon milk

1. Score the potatoes; bake them, cut them in half by the scoring-line.
2. Scoop out the cooked potato leaving the skin unbroken.
3. Mash the potato in a bowl and beat in the other ingredients, taste and season.
4. Pile the mashed potato back into the skins, mark the top all over with a fork.
5. Sprinkle a little melted margarine on the surface and put them back into the hot oven to brown.

Baked Potatoes in Fat

Oven 400°-425° F.
Cooking time 10 minutes to boil, 40 to 45 minutes to bake

1. Choose equal-sized potatoes, about the size of a large egg.
2. Boil them gently for 10 minutes (save the water for cooking a green vegetable for the same meal) drain and dry them.

3. Have dripping haze-hot—usually round a roast joint.

4. Roll the potatoes in the fat and baste them so that they are coated with fat.

5. Bake them in a moderately hot oven; turn and baste them after 20 minutes.

To Mash Potatoes (Also called 'Creamed' potatoes)

Cooking time As for boiling + 5 minutes

1. Boil and dry the potatoes.

To each pound potatoes: ½ oz. margarine   pepper, salt
                        2-3 tablespoons   a little grated nutmeg
                             milk   (optional)

2. Mash the potatoes in the saucepan with a potato-masher, the end of a rolling-pin, or fork, breaking up all lumps, or press them through a potato ricer.

3. Draw the potatoes to one side of the saucepan, heat the fat and milk in the empty space.

4. Add seasoning then beat the potatoes with the hot liquid, adding more milk if needed, until they are white and fluffy.

5. Pile them in a hot dish; neaten the pile with a knife or fork and, if liked, sprinkle it with chopped parsley.

Potato Croquettes or Potato Balls

Duchesse Potato mixture (p. 324)
To coat: egg and crumbs   *To fry:* shallow or deep fat

1. Make the duchesse mixture as above keeping it rather firm.

2. Divide it into pieces the size of a large walnut, dredge these with flour, roll them into balls and coat with egg and crumbs. Fry them in deep fat at 380° F. or in shallow fat that will brown bread in 15 seconds.

Casserole of Potatoes

Oven 325°-350° F. Gas No. 2-4 or top heat
Cooking time 30 to 45 minutes

     1 lb. old potatoes   ¼ pint milk
     ½ to 1 oz. margarine   pepper and salt

1. Peel the potatoes and slice them ½ inch thick.

2. Melt the fat in a casserole or saucepan and 'fat-steam' the potatoes in it for 5 to 10 minutes, in the oven or on top heat.

3. Add seasoning and the milk, bring this to boiling-point, cover the potatoes with greased paper or foil and simmer them gently for 20 minutes on top heat or 30 minutes in an oven.

4. When cooked the potatoes should have absorbed all the milk and should be soft and creamy. They may be mashed if liked.

Note. This is a good way of cooking potatoes when the whole meal is cooked in an oven.

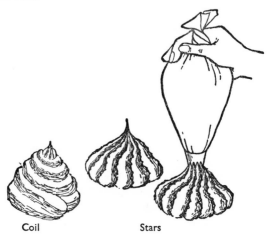

Coil   Stars

Fig. 51. Piping Duchesse Potatoes

Duchesse Potatoes (Fig. 51)

Oven 350°-400° F. Gas No. 4-6

Cooking time   ½ hour to boil, 15 minutes to bake

½ lb. potatoes	pepper, salt, grated nutmeg to taste
½ oz. margarine	1 egg-yolk or ½ beaten egg
1 tablespoon cream (top of the milk)	

1. Boil, thoroughly dry and 'rice', or rub the potatoes through a wire sieve (mashing with a fork or masher does not give a smooth enough result).

2. In the saucepan melt the margarine, beat the potatoes into it and season them.

3. Add the egg, and beat this in smoothly, add a little cream only if the mixture is dry.

4. Put the potato mixture into a forcing-bag with a large star pipe and pipe large rosettes, stars or zig-zag finger-shapes on to a greased oven-tray.

To Fry Potatoes

Chipped Potatoes

1. Choose waxy potatoes of medium size. Peel them.
2. Slice them $\frac{1}{4}$ to $\frac{1}{2}$ inch thick, cut the slices in $\frac{1}{4}$- to $\frac{1}{2}$-inch thick strips.
3. Fold the strips in a clean cloth or thick absorbent paper, to dry them.
4. Heat deep fat to 330° F. or shallow fat until it browns bread in 40 seconds (p. 8).
5. Put a few chips at a time into the fat, using a basket with deep fat; when the pan is half full add no more, keep the chips moving gently with a draining-spoon until they are soft but not brown, lift them out and fry the next half panful in the same way.
6. When all are thus fried heat the fat to 375° F. or to brown bread in 15 seconds and re-fry them for 2 or 3 minutes until they are crisp and golden. Drain them on absorbent paper.
7. Serve them at once, very hot and sprinkled with salt.

Potato Crisps or Straws (*French Fried*)

Crisps. Cut unpeeled potatoes in slices about $\frac{1}{32}$ inch thick using a potato slicer or 'mandolin' if possible.

Straws. Cut slices of peeled potatoes $\frac{1}{8}$ inch thick, then cut the slices to strips as thin as matchsticks.
2. Dry the crisps or straws in a cloth (see 'Chipped Potatoes').
3. Fry them in deep fat at 320° to 330° F. until quite crisp and golden (see Fig. 3).
4. Crisps are almost impossible to fry in shallow fat, but straws may be so fried in fat that browns bread in 50 seconds.
5. Drain the potatoes on absorbent paper; they may be kept warm without becoming limp, and may be stored in a tin for future use.
6. Serve them hot, sprinkled with salt.

These crisps are the correct kind to serve with *a grill, with roast chicken or game.*

Sauté Potatoes

To 1 lb. potatoes: 1 to 2 oz. butter, margarine or cooking fat or oil
seasoning
1. Boil the potatoes in their skins until barely cooked, or use left-over cooked potatoes.
2. Dry them slightly, peel them and slice them $\frac{1}{4}$ inch thick.

3. Heat the fat in a frying-pan until the sediment begins to turn golden-brown.

4. Put in the potatoes gradually and shake and turn them over fairly strong heat until they are crisp, golden-brown and have absorbed the fat. Season them.

5. Serve very hot, sprinkled, if liked, with chopped parsley.

TO COOK GREEN VEGETABLES

To Prepare Green Vegetables for Cooking

1. Remove damaged outer leaves and tough, fibrous stalks.

2. Soak only close-hearted vegetables, such as cabbages, cauliflowers or brussels sprouts, for not more than 10 minutes in cold water with 1 tablespoon salt to each quart. The salt reduces the loss of soluble nutrients and also kills insects quickly.

3. Wash open-leaved vegetables and also the soaked ones under running water, separating the leaves and making sure that all grit and insects are washed away.

4. Shred or cut them according to kind, see below.

General Method for Boiling Green Vegetables

1. Quarter fill with boiling water a saucepan just large enough to hold the vegetables.
Add 1 teaspoon salt to each pint.

2. Add the vegetables a handful at a time, so that the water hardly goes off the boil.

3. Put the lid on when all are in and boil them steadily until the stalks are tender when pierced with a skewer.

4. Drain the vegetables in a colander, shake but do not squeeze them; keep the water for gravy, sauce or soup.

5. Serve the vegetables at once in a covered dish.

See chart on p. 327.

TO COOK ROOT, BULB AND STEM VEGETABLES

To Prepare Root Vegetables for Cooking. For bulbs and stems, see chart below

1. Scrub them (except beetroot, see below).

2. Remove their skins by scraping off thin skins, peeling thick, tough ones.

3. Rinse them in clean water; if they cannot be cooked at once add 1 tablespoon salt to each quart water and keep the vegetables under water.

Name of vegetable	Cooking time	Special points
Brussels sprouts	10 to 15 minutes	Cut large sprouts in half before soaking, slit the stalk of all sprouts.
Cabbage	10 to 20 minutes	Cut in 4 before soaking, open out the leaves when washing. Separate and shred stalks with a sharp knife, cook them for 3 minutes; shred the dark outer leaves, cook them for a further 3 minutes; lastly shred inner leaves and cook these for a further 4 to 14 minutes till all is tender.
Spring cabbage or spring greens	7 to 10 minutes	Do not soak, but open out the leaves and wash them. Cook the shredded stalks 4 minutes before the shredded leaves
Cauliflower	20 to 30 minutes	Break the cauliflower into sprigs and slice the stalk or hollow the stalk and leave the head whole. Use all but the fibrous stalks. Cook the cauliflower with the stalk down in the water. Serve coated with white sauce made with $\frac{1}{2}$ cooking water, $\frac{1}{2}$ milk; or sprinkle the cooked cauliflower with French dressing or lemon juice.
Curly Kale	10 to 20 minutes	Wash the kale under running water. Discard really tough stalks, shred usable stalks and large leaves, keep small inner leaves whole. Cook as cabbage.
Sprouting broccoli	10 to 15 minutes	Treat as curly kale—keeping all flower sprays whole
Spinach	5 to 10 minutes	Wash the leaves in at least 3 changes of water till all grit is removed.
		Strip off fibrous stalks and mid-ribs except for certain varieties which have tender stalks.
		Pack the leaves rather firmly into an empty saucepan with only the water left on them after rinsing.
		Heat gently till the juice flows, turning the spinach so that all gets heated. Cook gently till soft.
		Drain the spinach, chop it roughly and toss it in the saucepan with a little margarine and salt.

General Method I. Boiling

1. Put the vegetables, whole or quartered, into the saucepan, pour in boiling water, not quite to cover them, and add 1 teaspoon salt to each pound vegetables.

2. Simmer them very gently till tender when pierced with a skewer.

3. Drain them, keep the water for use in gravy or soup.

4. Toss the vegetables in a little melted margarine in the pan; or coat them with sauce.

5. Serve them sprinkled with chopped parsley.

General Method II. Conservatively Cooked or in a Casserole

To each 1 lb. vegetable: ½ oz. margarine   salt
                            ⅛ to ¼ pint boiling water   chopped parsley

1. Slice the vegetables if mature, or leave them whole or cut in four if young and tender.
2. Melt the fat in a saucepan or in a casserole in the oven, in it sweat or fat-steam the vegetables for 5 to 10 minutes; keep the lid on.
3. Add the boiling water, ¼ pint for top heat, ⅛ pint for oven-cooking; add 1 teaspoon salt to each lb. vegetable.
4. Simmer the vegetables very gently till tender in 20 to 30 minutes on top, or 30 to 40 minutes in a slow oven.
5. If cooked in the oven cover them with greased paper under the lid.
6. Serve the liquid with the vegetables. Sprinkle them with chopped parsley.

Note. This method is far better than boiling both for flavour and nutritive value of the vegetable. It is also quicker as a rule.

Casserole of mixed vegetables could include any mixture of roots, bulbs and stem vegetables.

SOME SPECIAL RECIPES USING VEGETABLES

Asparagus

To 25 heads of asparagus: 1 oz. butter
                             a few drops of lemon juice

1. To prepare asparagus: cut off the hard white ends, cutting all the sticks to the same length. Scrape the sticks gently from the bud to the end, rinse them. Tie the sticks in bundles.
2. Put the asparagus in a wide, shallow pan, barely cover it with boiling water and simmer it very gently, keeping the buds right off the source of heat. Add no salt until the asparagus is tender, salt in the cooking water spoils the flavour.
3. Test the asparagus with a skewer inserted just below the bud.
4. Lift the bundles out on a fish-slice and drain them.
5. Serve it on a folded table napkin, hand the butter melted, flavoured with pepper, salt and lemon juice and served in a small sauceboat.

Kind of vegetable	Cooking time	Special points
Artichokes, Jerusalem	40 to 60 minutes	Scrape artichokes under water and keep them until cooked in water containing a tablespoon vinegar. Cook them, just covered with boiling water containing 2 teaspoons lemon juice per pound. Coat with white sauce. Method II is suitable; add lemon juice before sweating.
Beetroot	1 to 2 hours	Neither scrub nor peel; rinse off earth, leave 1 inch leaf-stalk. Cover with cold water, simmer till the skin can be rubbed off.
Beetroot, quick method	20 to 30 minutes	Scrub, peel, slice beetroot thinly. Add $\frac{1}{4}$ pint boiling water per pound and simmer till soft. Drain off half the remaining liquid and add vinegar to cover the slices. Cool the beetroot in this liquid.
Carrots	20 to 40 minutes, depending on age	Scrape them; slice them thinly unless quite young and small, use Method II. Add 1 teaspoon sugar per pound.
Celery (a stem)	40 to 60 minutes	Remove green leaves, broken or very tough outer sticks; trim the soiled part off the root but use the firm centre of the root. Save the heart to eat raw. Scrub the sticks. Scrape off brown or damaged patches. Method I tie the sticks in bundles, cutting them to equal lengths. For Method II cut the sticks in $\frac{1}{2}$- to 1-inch lengths. Serve coated with white sauce made with half celery water, half milk.
Parsnips	30 to 50 minutes, shorter time after they have been in frosty ground	Scrape or peel according to size and shape. Slice them $\frac{1}{4}$ inch thick for Method II. Cut in thick chunks for Method I. By this method they may be mashed with fat and milk as potatoes. Parsnips may also be baked in fat as potatoes.
Salsify	40 to 50 minutes	Prepare and cook as Jerusalem artichokes, serve coated with white sauce.
Turnips, white and swede	20 to 30 minutes by Method II 45 minutes to 1 hour by Method I	Peel them thickly to remove all the hard fibrous skin. Slice them $\frac{1}{4}$ inch thick and cook them by Method II for good flavour and texture. If cooked whole or cut in four by Method I they may be served with sauce or mashed as potatoes.

Bulb Vegetables

Onions	20 to 30 minutes by Method II 40 to 60 minutes by Method I	Peel off the papery skin and one white layer, do not wash or keep in water. Cook by either method or roast in their skins. If boiled they may be coated with white sauce.

Kind of vegetable	Cooking time	Special points
Leeks	40 to 60 minutes	Cut off the roots, remove one outer layer, cut off shrivelled or dark green tops. Split the leeks to ½ inch from the root, turn the leaves back and wash to remove all grit. Cook whole, tied in bundles, by Method I; serve coated with white sauce.

Seed and Fruit Vegetables

Kind of vegetable	Cooking time	Special points
Beans, Broad	15 to 30 minutes	Shell them if mature; if very young they may be cooked whole, pod and all, remove only the stalk and the tip and strip off the string at the side if it is tough enough to pull off. Boil them. Serve them in a pouring parsley sauce or toss them in a little butter.
Beans, French	10 to 15 minutes	Remove stalk and tip and any string that can be stripped off. Boil them whole in very little water. Toss them in butter before serving.
Beans, Runner	5 to 10 minutes	When very young these may be treated as French beans. When mature remove stalk and tip and strip off the string at each side, using a vegetable parer. Do not use any with a hard inner skin. Snap them into short lengths with the fingers or cut them diagonally. Boil them, toss them in butter before serving.
Green Peas	10 to 15 minutes	Shell them, rinse them. Boil peas in very little water, adding 1 teaspoon sugar to each pound of peas and a sprig of mint. Toss them in a little butter before serving.
Tomatoes	5 to 15 minutes	Wash them, cut in halves at right angle to the stalk. *Bake* them: sprinkle with salt and pepper, put a flake of margarine on each half, pack them into a greased fireproof dish, cover with greased paper or foil, bake them in a moderate oven. *Fry* them: cut side down for 2–3 minutes; cut side up till soft, fry gently. *Grill* them: whole small ones for preference. Prick them and grill them slowly. *Steam* them: prepare them as for baking, put them on a greased plate, covered.
Vegetable Marrow	30 to 40 minutes	Peel the marrow, cut it in half lengthways and into convenient lengths, scoop out the seeds with a spoon. *Bake* it: cut it into 2-inch squares. Heat in a casserole 1 oz. margarine for each pound of marrow. Shake the pieces in the fat, bake them covered, in a slow oven. *Cook it conservatively:* cut in 1- to 2-inch squares. *Steam* it: in a perforated steamer; serve it coated with white sauce.

Sweet-Sour Beetroot, Hot

1 lb. cooked beetroot	salt, pepper
1 small onion	1 teaspoon sugar
½ oz. margarine	1 teaspoon grated horseradish
½ oz. flour	*or* bottled horseradish sauce
3 to 4 tablespoons yoghurt	1 tablespoon chopped parsley

1. Peel the beetroot and shred it on the coarse side of a grater.
2. Chop the onion finely.
3. Melt the fat and in it fry the onion, without browning it, till clear and quite soft.
4. Stir in the flour, and then the yoghurt and boil the mixture.
5. Add the beetroot and heat it gently, stirring it frequently.
6. Add the horseradish, sugar and seasoning to taste, adding more yoghurt if it is too sweet.
7. Pile it in a hot dish, decorate the top with lines of chopped parsley.

Sweet-Sour Cabbage

1 lb. white cabbage	salt and pepper
1 oz. bacon	a little grated nutmeg
½ oz. margarine	¼ pint boiling water
1 small onion	1 cooking apple or 2 tomatoes
½ oz. flour	

1. Chop the bacon and fry it in the margarine for 2 or 3 minutes.
2. Chop the onion finely and fry it till soft, with the bacon.
3. Shred the cabbage, add it to the onion and bacon, shake and stir it to mix the fat with it.
4. Add the boiling water and 1 teaspoon salt; simmer the cabbage till it is almost tender.
5. Peel and chop the apple or skin and cut up the tomatoes, add this to the cabbage and continue cooking till all are soft.
6. Sprinkle in the flour and stir it till it thickens, simmer the whole for two minutes.
7. Season and add nutmeg to taste.
Serve at once.

Sweet-Sour Red Cabbage

Cooking time   1 to 1¼ hours

1 lb. red cabbage	1 tablespoon brown sugar
1 small onion	2 teaspoons lemon juice
1 oz. margarine	1 to 2 tablespoons vinegar
2 small or 1 large cooking apple	salt and pepper

1. Chop the onion finely and fry it gently till soft, in the margarine.
2. Shred the cabbage and add it and shake it in the fat for a few minutes.
3. Chop and add the apple and add the sugar, stir and shake the pan over low heat for 10 minutes until juice is running from apple and cabbage.
4. Add lemon juice, vinegar and 1 teaspoon salt and simmer the cabbage very gently till it is tender in about 1 hour.

Vegetables Au Gratin (With Cheese)

Suitable vegetables: celery, cauliflower, leeks, onions, vegetable marrow or potatoes, or a mixture of root vegetables including potatoes.

1 lb. vegetables
½ pint cheese sauce (p. 346)
2 tablespoons extra grated cheese
2 teaspoons breadcrumbs

1. Boil the vegetable till tender, drain it and keep it hot in a shallow fireproof dish. Make the surface of the vegetable smooth.
2. Make the sauce with ¼ pint vegetable water and ¼ pint milk, season, add the cheese and taste it.
3. Coat the hot vegetable with the cheese sauce.
4. Mix the extra grated cheese with the crumbs and strew this all over the sauce.
5. Brown under a moderate grill.

Macedoine or Mixture of Vegetables for Garnish

Equal amounts of: carrots, cauliflower,
                    turnips, cut runner beans,
                    shelled peas, ½ oz. margarine to each lb.

1. Cut the carrot and turnip into ¼-inch to ½-inch dice.
2. Cut the beans into ½-inch diamond shapes.

3. Break and cut the cauliflower into very small sprigs.

4. Have a pan with ½ pint boiling water for each pound of mixed vegetables and add 1 teaspoon salt.

5. Add the carrots first and cook them for 3 minutes, add turnips and cook both for another 3 minutes, then add the cauliflower, the runner beans and the peas, just allowing the water to re-boil after each addition.

6. Cook the panful for another 5 to 10 minutes till all the vegetables are tender.

7. Drain and gently shake the vegetables with ½ oz. margarine for each pound.

8. Serve the vegetables as a border round fried or stewed meat.

Vegetable Marrow with Tomatoes

Oven 325° to 350° F. Gas No. 2-4
Cooking time ¾ to 1 hour

1 lb. marrow	1 small onion (optional)
½ to 1 lb. tomatoes	pepper and salt
1 oz. margarine	chopped parsley

1. Peel the marrow, remove the seeds, cut the flesh into 1-inch squares.

2. Scald, skin and quarter the tomatoes.

3. Melt the fat in a saucepan or casserole and cook the tomatoes in it till the juice runs freely.

4. Add the marrow and 1 teaspoon salt, cover it with greased paper or foil and the lid and cook it in a slow oven or on gentle top heat till tender in ¾ to 1 hour.

Stewed Mushrooms

Cooking time 20 to 30 minutes

½ lb. mushrooms	¼ pint stock
1 oz. margarine	2 teaspoons arrowroot
2 teaspoons lemon juice	pepper and salt
chopped parsley	

1. Wash the mushrooms quickly under running water, rub the skins dry on paper, scrape the stalks. Do not peel mushrooms.

2. Melt the margarine and in it sweat the mushrooms very gently for 10 minutes.

4. Add the stock and bring it to the boil, add ½ teaspoon salt and simmer the whole till the mushrooms are just tender.

5. Blend the arrowroot with lemon juice and a little water, stir it in and bring it to the boil.

6. Season to taste.

7. Serve sprinkled with chopped parsley.

STUFFED VEGETABLES

Stuffed Marrow (Fig. 52)

Stuff peeled, hollowed sections

Stuff half-marrow, cover it with the other half

Fig. 52. STUFFED MARROW

1 medium-sized marrow

Filling { ½ lb. fresh or cooked mince (as on p. 275 or p. 281)
{ 2 oz. fresh crumbs

To bake: a little melted margarine or dripping

To serve: ½ pint brown or piquant or tomato sauce

1. Peel the marrow, halve it lengthways or cut in sections and scoop out the seeds.
2. Steam it till not quite tender.
3. Meanwhile prepare the mince as on p. 275 or p. 281.
4. Add the crumbs to the cooked mince to stiffen the mixture.
5. Pile the stuffing into one half marrow, cover it with the other half.
6. Melt the fat in a roasting-tin, lift the marrow into it and baste it well.
7. Bake for 20 minutes in a moderately hot oven.
8. Serve on a hot dish with sauce poured over and round it.

Alternative method. Fill the two halves separately. Coat the mince thickly with dry crumbs and baste the tops with hot fat. Bake as above.

Stuffed Onions

Oven 350° to 375° F. Gas No. 5-6
Cooking time   1 hour to boil, 20 minutes to bake

     1 Spanish onion for each helping

Filling for 4 onions:	½ quantity ham or liver stuffing (p. 354)
To cook in:	a little melted dripping or margarine
To serve:	½ pint brown or piquant sauce (pp. 347-8)

1. Boil the onions till tender in about 1 hour.
2. Make the stuffing; begin the sauce to add the onion liquid to it later.
3. Drain the onions and with a vegetable peeler and teaspoon handle loosen and pull out the centre of each onion, leaving a hole at least ¾ inch across.
4. Chop the centres and add them to the sauce or the stuffing.
5. Fill the holes with stuffing, pressing it well down and mounding the tops.
6. Melt a little fat in a tin, baste the onions and bake them in a moderate oven for about 20 minutes.
7. Serve them with the sauce poured over and round them.

Stuffed Tomatoes (Fig. 53)

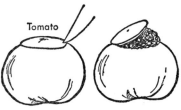

Tomato

Mark and cut out	Scoop out and stuff
the rounded end	the tomato

Fig. 53. STUFFED TOMATO

Oven 325° to 350° F. Gas No. 3-5
Cooking time   15 to 20 minutes

     1 large tomato for each helping

Filling for 4 tomatoes:	½ quantity ham or liver stuffing (p. 354)
To cook:	a little melted margarine
For dishing:	4 rounds fried bread the same size as tomatoes

1. Wash and dry the tomatoes.

2. Mark the end away from the stalk of each with a 1-inch round cutter.

3. Cut round these circles with a sharp-pointed knife; remove the round of tomato and scoop out the juice and pips inside, leaving a completely hollow fruit.

4. Cut 4 rounds from a slice of bread ¼ inch thick, use the scraps in the stuffing.

5. Make the stuffing and pack it into the tomatoes.

6. Sprinkle the top with melted margarine.

7. Pack the tomatoes close together in a small greased tin or fireproof dish.

8. Bake them in a moderate oven until they are just soft, bake the 'lids' as well.

9. Fry the rounds of bread till crisp and golden.

10. Dish each tomato on a round of fried bread with its lid aslant on the stuffing.

Stuffed Sweet Peppers (Fig. 54)

Oven 330° to 350° F. Gas No. 3-5
Cooking time   40 to 45 minutes

1 pepper to each helping

Filling for 3 peppers: 2 oz. raisin and nut stuffing using rice (p. 355)
a little olive oil

1. Scald peppers leaving them for 3 to 5 minutes in the near-boiling water. With a sharp-pointed knife cut all round the base of the stalk (Fig. 54).

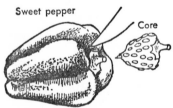

Fig. 54. STUFFED SWEET PEPPERS

2. Draw out the stalk and the core and wash all seeds out of the inside as they are too hot to eat. Stuff the peppers and brush them with olive oil.

3. Pack them into an oven-ware dish or casserole that just fits them, cover them with foil or a lid.

4. Bake them till they are soft.

20

SALADS

Certain food-plants are known as salad-vegetables but in addition to these a salad may be made of almost any mixture of raw, cooked or even pickled, vegetables, fruit and nuts. The important thing to remember about any salad is that it must be refreshing: this is achieved by having all the ingredients fresh and crisp; by arranging the salad attractively; making the most of the colours of the ingredients and, above all, contriving to keep it looking unhandled.

A salad may be an accompaniment to a meat or vegetarian dish—even hot ones such as grilled steak or roast chicken, which are often served with French salad, or it may be a complete main course in which case it must contain some cold, protein food such as cheese, eggs, meat or fish.

A salad should be served with a salad-dressing, partly to increase its refreshing taste and partly because the oil or fat contained in the dressing helps, during digestion, to convert carotene to Vitamin A.

Some Suitable Ingredients for Salads

Salad vegetables	Method of preparation and special points
Chicory	Strip off damaged leaves, wash. Do not separate leaves but halve lengthways or slice thickly.
Endive	Remove coarse outer leaves, wash under running water, drain and shake dry in a salad-basket or a cloth.
Lettuce	As for endive but separate the leaves, handle very gently to avoid bruising the tender leaves.
Mustard and Cress	Hold the tiny leaves in small bunches and shorten the stalks, wash the cress upright in its punnet or hold it in bunches to wash it; avoid getting it loose and tangled.
Watercress	Remove damaged leaves, coarse stalks and any rootlets. Clean the stalks by rubbing with salt to remove tiny, invisible grubs and wash the watercress in two changes of water.

Salad vegetables	Method of preparation and special points
Cucumber	Wash the skin if it is not to be removed. Peeling cucumber is a matter of personal taste. Slice it very thinly.
Radishes	Trim off leaf-stalks and roots and wash them, rubbing the skins clean with the fingers.
Spring Onions	Cut off roots and tough, dark tops; remove the outer layer, wash them.
Tomatoes	It is usually wise to remove the skins in case they have been sprayed with insecticide. To do this scald the tomatoes for 30 seconds then drop them into cold water to make them firm again. If skins are not removed wash them thoroughly. Cut in sections or slice them.

Other vegetables, these are prepared as for cooking:

Green, used raw

Cabbage	The white heart only is used, shredded finely.
Cauliflower	The flower only, broken into minute flowerets or chopped.
Brussels sprouts	Shredded.
Spinach	Shredded.

Root vegetables used raw		*Vegetables used cooked*
Beetroot, young	grated	Beetroot
Carrot	grated	Beans, broad, French or runner
Celery	whole or cut up	Carrots
		Cauliflower
Turnip, young	grated	Celery
Mushrooms, button	peeled, sliced or chopped	Mushrooms
		Peas
		Potatoes, preferably new
		Turnips

Fruits	*Pickles*	*Herbs for flavouring*
Apples	Capers	Basil, Borage
Bananas	Gherkins	Chervil, Chives
Dates	Olives	Fennel, Garlic (sparingly)
Grapes	Walnuts	Marjoram, Mint

Fruits	*Herbs for flavouring*
Grapefruit	Parsley, Rosemary (sparingly)
Oranges	Savoury, Sage (sparingly)
Pineapple	Tarragon, Thyme
Raisins	
Sultanas	
Walnuts	

RULES FOR MAKING SALADS

1. All the vegetables used must be perfectly fresh.
2. Wash them, drain them and shake off all surface water.
3. To keep green plants fresh, put them in a covered vessel and store them in a cool place preferably a refrigerator.
4. Prepare salads just before serving them or if this is not possible, keep them closely covered in a refrigerator for as short a time as possible.
5. The dressing must be added to green salads at the last moment before serving as the acid and oil together quickly make the leaves limp.
6. Avoid a very wide mixture of ingredients—three or four of contrasting textures and colours are usually more attractive than a very wide variety; small amounts of herbs or other vegetables can be added for flavour. Prepare all the ingredients before beginning to mix.
7. Keep some of the bright-coloured ingredients separate from the mixture to make a decoration.

SOME SUGGESTED MIXTURES FOR SALADS

'English' or Summer Salad

lettuce	cucumber
watercress	tomatoes
or mustard and cress	*or* radishes

hard-boiled egg optional

Handed with the salad an egg-or-cream dressing

1. Serve this salad in a deep bowl, which can be lined with lettuce leaves.
2. Shred any rather coarse lettuce leaves and mix these with some of the sliced ingredients, but keep small leaves whole and arrange that some of all the ingredients can be seen on top of the salad.

French Salad

This always indicates a salad made of one, or at most two, salad-plants basted with, or tossed in, French dressing. Some examples are:

Chicory with dressing made with lemon juice
Cucumber
Lettuce, round or cos
Tomato with chopped parsley and other herbs if liked
Watercress

Fruit and Green Salads

These may be served with either French or creamy dressings and there are many possible mixtures; a few suggestions are:

Lettuce or endive with pineapple and chopped nuts
Lettuce, watercress or chicory with skinned grapefruit sections
Lettuce or chicory with banana and chopped nuts or grapes
Lettuce, watercress, celery and skinned sections of orange
Lettuce, endive or chicory with chopped apple and raisins, or dates
Lettuce, banana, grated carrot and seedless raisins

Potato Salad

¾ lb. new potatoes	1 tablespoon vinegar
1-2 spring onions	1 tablespoon chopped parsley
or 2 teaspoons chopped chives	1 teaspoon chopped mint
¼ pint thick cream or egg dressing	*Garnish:* Tomato or radish and watercress

1. Cook the potatoes carefully without breaking them, drain them.
2. While warm cut them in ¼-inch slices or in ¼-inch to ½-inch dice, and either add the dressing at once or baste them with vinegar. This is to keep their flavour fresh and to enable them to absorb the flavours of the other ingredients.
3. Chop the onions or chives, the parsley and mint and lightly mix these into the dressing; then add potatoes.
4. Dish, and decorate the edges only with sprigs of watercress and small sectors of tomato or radishes.

WINTER SALADS

To make when green salad-plants are dear or scarce.

Cabbage Salad

½ lb. white heart of cabbage	2 tablespoons raisins
1 raw carrot or small cooked beetroot	1 tablespoon chopped parsley or watercress leaves
1 celery heart	French dressing or lemon juice

1. Shred the cabbage finely, grate the carrot or beetroot, chop the celery.
2. Reserve some grated carrot or beetroot for decoration, mix all the other ingredients lightly with the dressing, pile the salad loosely in a shallow dish and decorate it.

Beetroot and Celery Salad

1 medium cooked beetroot	½ bunch watercress
1 small celery heart	a few walnuts or sprigs of raw cauliflower
1 apple (dessert or cooker)	cauliflower
French dressing	2 teaspoons chopped parsley

1. Dice or slice the beetroot, chop the apple, celery, nuts or cauliflower and parsley.
2. Mix the salad lightly and decorate it with watercress and beetroot.

Raw Vegetable Salad

2 raw grated carrots	2 or 3 sticks of celery or
1 ,, ,, beetroot	¼ cauliflower
1 teaspoon chopped parsley	1 small grated turnip
a little watercress	
French or creamy dressing	

1. Grate the root vegetables, keeping the colours separate, chop the celery or cauliflower.
2. This kind of salad looks well arranged in wide stripes, one for each ingredient, with parsley or watercress to separate the colours.
3. Baste it with French dressing or hand a thick dressing separately.

SALAD DRESSINGS

French Dressing

2 parts olive oil, or salad oil   salt, pepper, dry mustard ⎱ to
1 part vinegar or lemon–juice   sugar   ⎰ taste
       a few drops Worcester sauce (optional)

1. The easiest way to make this dressing is to measure and mix it in a graduated medicine bottle, but any smallish, clean bottle can be used.
2. Shake the ingredients hard until the oil is emulsified giving the dressing a cloudy look.
3. Serve it at once as the emulsion is only temporary.

Thick or Creamy Dressings
English Salad Dressing

1 yolk of hard-boiled egg   2 teaspoons vinegar
1 tablespoon olive oil   1 teaspoon Worcester sauce
$\frac{1}{8}$ teaspoon made mustard   pepper and salt to taste
2 tablespoons cream, evaporated milk or top of the milk

Sieve the egg-yolk (the white may be chopped and added to the salad) and work into it gradually the seasonings, oil and vinegar. Whip the cream or evaporated milk and fold it in last. (Top of the milk will not whip.)

Evaporated Milk Dressing

2 tablespoons evaporated milk   pepper, salt, made mustard to
1 tablespoon vinegar   taste
or lemon juice $\frac{1}{4}$ teaspoon sugar

Add $\frac{1}{2}$ tablespoon vinegar to the milk and whisk the two together until they are thick and frothy, then stir in the other ingredients until it tastes right, adding the rest of the vinegar or lemon juice to taste.

    Condensed milk may be used with double the quantity of vinegar and no sugar.

White Sauce Dressing

$\frac{1}{4}$ pint coating white sauce, preferably Béchamel (see p. 347)
$\frac{1}{2}$ oz. margarine   pepper and salt
1 egg-yolk $\frac{1}{8}$ teaspoon made mustard
1-2 tablespoons vinegar $\frac{1}{4}$ teaspoon sugar if liked

1. Add the margarine to the hot sauce, cook the yolk in the sauce without boiling it.
2. Cool the sauce with wet paper over the surface to prevent a skin forming.
3. Gradually whisk in the vinegar and season the dressing to taste.
4. For a really smooth, glossy result wring the dressing through wet muslin.
5. With chopped parsley, chives, mint and tarragon this dressing is very good with potato salad.

Yoghurt Dressing

½ bottle yoghurt	salt and pepper ⎤ to
⅛ teaspoon sugar	mixed mustard ⎦ taste

Mix the ingredients together; yoghurt is usually sour enough for most tastes but a few drops of vinegar or lemon may be added if liked.

Mayonnaise

1 egg yolk	¼ pint olive (or salad) oil
¼ teaspoon dry mustard	1–2 tablespoons vinegar or
¼ teaspoon salt	lemon juice
a little pepper	*Optional*, a few drops
1 teaspoon caster sugar	Worcester sauce

1. Have the oil and yolk cold but not just out of the refrigerator.
2. Using a small egg whisk or a rotary beater and a small basin, beat the dry seasonings into the yolk; this makes the addition of oil easier and helps to stabilize the emulsion of oil in egg yolk.
3. Put the oil in a small jug or in a bottle with two grooves cut in the cork and trickle it, drop by drop, into the yolk, at the same time beating it vigorously; if a rotary beater is used add 1 dessertspoon oil at a time.
4. Once the emulsion begins to thicken, pour the oil in a thin continuous trickle and keep up the vigorous beating.
5. When the emulsion is too thick to beat easily thin it by adding a little vinegar, drop by drop.
6. Beat in the rest of the oil, thinning the emulsion with vinegar as needed. The finished mayonnaise should be as thick as double cream.
7. Taste and adjust the seasoning.
   Electric Blender. Use whole egg and add vinegar with the seasonings, then pour in oil in a steady stream with blender running.

21

SAUCES, STUFFINGS
OR FORCEMEAT

Sauce-making is a most important part of cooking because a good sauce is designed to bring out the flavour of the food with which it is served; to add extra flavour to it and by its consistency to provide a pleasant contrast to the texture of more solid food.

Sauces must therefore be seasoned and flavoured with great care; they must be tasted to check the flavour and tested for the right consistency.

A sauce may be part of the dish as in a brown stew or a fricassée; it may coat such food as fish or vegetables or it may be served as an accompaniment, to be poured from a sauce-boat: in every case it must taste very good by itself.

To Test the Consistency
A coating sauce, at boiling-point, must coat the back of a wooden spoon and only just settle to its own level in the saucepan. It must be used at once and the food to be coated must be hot if the coating is to be smooth.

A pouring sauce, at boiling-point, must glaze the back of a wooden spoon and of course pour easily; if it must be kept hot cover it with wet greaseproof paper to prevent a skin forming.

The Amount of Sauce to Serve
Coating sauce: ½ pint to coat 4 helpings of fish or vegetable
Pouring sauce ⎱
Gravy   ⎰ ½ pint for 4 to 6 helpings

General Proportions of Thickening for Sauces

	Coating sauce	Pouring sauce	Thick gravy or thin sauce
To 1 pint liquid	⎰2 oz. flour ⎱2 oz. fat	1½ oz. flour 1½ oz. fat	1 oz. flour 1 oz. fat
or	1½ oz. cornflour, custard powder or other starch	1 oz. cornflour, etc.	½ oz. cornflour, etc.

SAVOURY WHITE SAUCES

Basic Recipes

Coating sauce

   1 oz. margarine or butter
   1 oz. flour

Pouring sauce

   ¾ oz. margarine or butter
   ¾ oz. flour

   ½ pint milk, or ¼ pint milk and ¼ pint meat, fish or vegetable liquor
   ½ teaspoon salt
   2 or 3 shakes pepper

Method I. Roux

1. Make a 'roux' with the fat and flour, that is melt the fat, stir the flour into it and stir it over low heat for 1 or 2 minutes.
2. Remove the pan from the heat, gradually stir in half the liquid, beat it smooth, then stir in most of the rest. Lumps will form if the liquid is added too quickly or stirring is slow.
3. When the uncooked sauce is quite smooth, return the pan to the heat, bring the sauce slowly to boiling-point, stirring it vigorously all the time. Lumps will form if heating is too rapid or stirring is slow.
4. Test the consistency and add the remaining liquid if necessary.
5. Season, flavour and taste the sauce.

Method II. Beurre manié

'Beurre manié' is French for kneaded butter; the 'kneading' is best done with a spoon.
1. Soften the fat in a basin with a wooden spoon, then work the flour into it to form a paste.
2. Bring the liquid almost to boiling-point, remove the pan from the heat and with an egg-whisk, whisk a little of the flour-fat-paste at a time into the hot liquid.
3. When the sauce is smoothly whisked return the pan to the light, and with a wooden spoon stir it till it boils.
4. Test, season and taste the sauce as above.

M

Variations of White Sauce

Name of sauce	Additions to Basic recipe	Variation of method
Anchovy sauce	2 teaspoons anchovy essence 1 teaspoon lemon juice a few drops of red colouring (optional)	Use all fish stock if possible or milk and fish liquor.
Caper sauce	2 tablespoons capers, roughly chopped 2 teaspoons vinegar from the capers	Use liquor from boiled mutton or, for a fish dish, fish stock or milk and fish liquor
Cheese sauce	Use all milk 2 heaped tablespoons dry, grated cheese ¼ teaspoon made mustard a small shake of cayenne pepper	A cheese coating sauce is generally sprinkled with 1 to 2 tablespoons extra cheese and 1 teaspoon fresh crumbs, then browned under the grill.
Egg sauce	1 hard-boiled egg, chopped	Add the chopped egg to the hot sauce and re-heat it. Season it very well.
Herb sauce	2 heaped tablespoons mixed fresh herbs, finely chopped, e.g. basil, chives, fennel, tarjoram, parsley, savory, tarragon, thyme or any mixture of some of these.	Add the chopped herbs to the hot sauce and simmer it for 1 or 2 minutes.
Maître d'Hôtel sauce	1 tablespoon finely chopped parsley 2 teaspoons lemon juice extra ½ oz. butter	For serving with fish, use ½ fish stock and half milk, whisk in the butter. This sauce should have enough finely chopped parsley to make it really green.
Mushroom sauce	2 oz. mushrooms 1 teaspoon lemon juice ¼ teaspoon Marmite	Chop the mushrooms finely and cook them gently in the margarine for 10 minutes without drying them. Make the roux as usual.
Mustard sauce	1 teaspoon dry mustard or 1 tablespoon French mustard 1-2 tablespoons vinegar 1 teaspoon sugar	Use liquor from boiled beef or, for a fish dish, fish stock.
Onion sauce	1 Spanish or 2 English or French onions, boiled and chopped	Boil the onion and use the liquid with milk for the sauce.

For a quick method chop the onion finely and cook it in the fat until absolutely soft in 10 to 15 minutes, then make the roux in the usual way, add all milk or ½ milk, ½ stock.

Name of sauce	Additions to Basic recipe	Variation of method
Parsley sauce	½ tablespoon finely chopped parsley	Add the parsley to the boiling sauce and cook it 1 minute.

Name of sauce	Additions to Basic recipe	Variation of method
Piquant White sauce	1 onion, chopped 2 teaspoons vinegar, tarragon if possible 2 teaspoons chopped parsley 2 gherkins, chopped ½ teaspoon French mustard	Cook the chopped onion till quite soft in the fat, then make the roux. Add all other ingredients to the hot sauce.
Shrimp sauce	2 oz. picked shrimps 1 teaspoon lemon juice ½ „ anchovy essence Use fish stock if possible	If shrimps are bought frozen or in a carton, wash them to remove salt; chop the shrimps.
Watercress sauce	½ bunch watercress 1 teaspoon lemon juice	Plunge the watercress in boiling water; dry it, chop it finely discarding coarse stalks; simmer it in the finished sauce for 2 minutes. Serve with fish or vegetarian dishes.
Special White sauce:	Use all milk	
Béchamel sauce	½ small carrot 1 bay leaf 1 small onion 6 peppercorns ½ stick celery piece of blade mace 2 tablespoons cream or top of the milk	Slice the vegetables, cover them and the spices with cold milk, bring them slowly to boiling-point, remove the pan from heat, cover it and infuse the liquid for ½ hour. Strain the milk and use it to make the white sauce. Stir the cream into the boiling sauce after seasoning it.
'Mock Holland-aise' or Dutch sauce	½ pint béchamel sauce as above 1 egg yolk 2 teaspoons lemon juice	Make the sauce; mix the egg-yolk with the cream; stir the lemon juice into the sauce, add the yolk-cream mixture to the sauce and cook it without boiling. Serve the sauce at once, it cannot be kept hot.

BROWN SAUCES

Basic Recipe, Pouring Sauce

¾ oz. dripping
1 small carrot
1 small onion
¾ oz. flour
a few shakes of pepper

½ pint stock
½ teaspoon meat extract, yeast extract or savoury sauce
a piece of brown skin of the onion
½ teaspoon salt

1. Melt the dripping, slice the onion and carrot and fry them in the dripping till they are golden-brown.

2. Stir in the flour and fry it slowly till it is fawn-coloured.

3. Add the liquid and stir it till it boils, add the other ingredients and simmer the sauce gently for 20 to 30 minutes.

4. Strain the sauce, taste, reseason and if necessary colour it with a few drops of gravy-browning added off the end of a skewer.

Variations of Brown Sauce

Name of sauce	Additions to recipe	Variation of method
Italian sauce	1 extra onion or shallot 1 oz. lean bacon, chopped 2 tomatoes, fresh or tinned 1 oz. mushrooms, whole 2 teaspoons chopped parsley 1 teaspoon vinegar 1½ tablespoons olive oil	Use olive oil instead of dripping; fry the bacon in the oil with the carrot and onion; add whole mushrooms and tomatoes with the stock and simmer the sauce till mushrooms are soft, strain the sauce, lift out mushrooms; chop them and return them to the sauce; add vinegar and chopped parsley last.
Mushroom sauce, brown	2 oz. mushrooms ¼ teaspoon Marmite 1 teaspoon lemon juice	Cook the mushrooms whole and unskinned in the sauce; strain the sauce; when they are tender, lift them out, chop them and return them to the sauce; add Marmite and lemon juice last.
Piquant sauce	1 oz. mushrooms 1 blade mace, 1 bay leaf, 2 teaspoons Worcester sauce 1 tablespoon vinegar 1 „ capers } chopped 2 gherkins	Add mushrooms whole, the mace and bay leaf with the stock, and simmer the sauce till mushrooms are soft. Strain the sauce, chop the mushrooms, return them to the sauce, add all the other ingredients and simmer the sauce 5 minutes.

MISCELLANEOUS SAUCES. SAVOURY

Apple Sauce, for Roast Pork, Duck or Goose   *8 helpings*

1 lb. cooking apples   ½ oz. butter or margarine
a thin strip of lemon rind   1 oz. sugar or more, to taste
2 tablespoons water

1. Peel, quarter, core and slice the apples roughly.
2. Stew them with the fat and water, adding the lemon-rind.
3. When the apples are soft, lift out the rind and beat the apple pulp smooth with a wooden spoon or pass it through a nylon sieve.
4. Add sugar to taste.

Bread Sauce, for Roast Chicken or Turkey

¼ pint stale, white breadcrumbs
or 1-inch thick slice from a large loaf

1 onion	2 cloves
1 blade mace	4 peppercorns
1 bay leaf	½ pint milk

½ oz. butter or margarine or 1 tablespoon cream
salt to taste

1. Put the onion and spices in a pan with the milk, bring the milk slowly to boiling-point, cover the pan and keep it in a warm place to infuse the milk for ½ hour.
2. Strain the milk, return it to the saucepan and add the breadcrumbs or the slice of bread with the crusts cut off rather thick.
3. Soak the bread in the hot milk for 15 minutes then, if a slice is used, mash it with a potato masher or a fork; re-heat the sauce.
4. Taste and season the sauce and stir in the butter or cream.

Cranberry Sauce for Roast Turkey

½ lb. cranberries	*or* ¼ lb. cranberries
about ¼ pint water	¼ pint water
	½ lb. cooking apples

sugar to taste, 2–4 oz.

1. Stew the cranberries in the water till they 'pop', add more water if necessary.
2. Rub them through a nylon sieve.
3. Sweeten and re-heat the sauce.

Curry Sauce

1 small onion	½ pint water
½ cooking apple	1 oz. desiccated coconut
½ oz. margarine	1 teaspoon black treacle
½ oz. curry powder	1 ,, chutney
½ oz. flour	2 ,, lemon juice

1. Make an infusion of the coconut by simmering it for 5 minutes in the water; strain it and squeeze out all the liquid.
2. Chop the onion finely and the apple coarsely.
3. Fry the onion gently in the margarine till it is beginning to soften.
4. Stir in the curry powder and cook it for a few minutes, then stir in the flour, add the liquid and the apple and stir the sauce till it simmers.
5. Add the other ingredients and simmer the sauce for $\frac{3}{4}$ to 1 hour.
This sauce is not strained so all pieces of fruit and onion should be soft.

Horseradish Sauce for Roast Beef

2 tablespoons grated horseradish	2 teaspoons vinegar
$\frac{1}{4}$ pint thin white sauce, cold	1 teaspoon lemon juice
or $\frac{1}{8}$ pint top of the milk or thin cream	$\frac{1}{2}$,, sugar

1. Grate the horseradish.
2. Mix all the ingredients together.

Note. Horseradish is difficult to buy in some towns so commercial horseradish sauce may be used diluted, for economy, with sauce or top of the milk.

Mint Sauce

2 rounded tablespoons finely chopped mint	2 tablespoons boiling water
	2 tablespoons vinegar
1 tablespoon caster sugar	

1. Chop the mint very fine with half the sugar.
2. Put it and the rest of the sugar in a small sauce-boat.
3. Add the boiling water and leave it to cool.
4. Add the vinegar last.
This sauce should be thick with very finely chopped mint.

Tomato Sauce

1 small onion	$\frac{1}{2}$ pint liquor from canned tomatoes or stock
1 small carrot	
1 oz. bacon scraps	4 to 5 medium sized tomatoes, canned or fresh
$\frac{1}{2}$ oz. margarine	
$\frac{1}{2}$ oz. rice flour or cornflour	a piece of blade mace
	pepper, salt, sugar and lemon juice to taste

1. Slice the onion and carrot and dice the bacon, cut up fresh tomatoes.
2. Fry the bacon for a minute or two then fry the onion and carrot without browning them.
3. Add the tomatoes and cook them for 2 or 3 minutes.
4. Stir in the rice flour or cornflour, add the stock or tomato juice and stir the sauce till it simmers. Add the mace.
5. Simmer the sauce for ¾ hour; rub it through a nylon or fine wire sieve.
6. Re-heat, add pepper, salt, sugar and lemon juice to taste.

Quick Tomato Sauce

½ pint canned tomato juice   ½ oz. cornflour

salt, pepper
grated nutmeg
sugar
lemon juice
} to taste

1. Blend the cornflour with a little of the juice, boil the rest of the juice and stir it into the blended cornflour. Stir it for 5 minutes simmering, season and flavour it to taste.

SWEET SAUCES

Basic Recipe, Pouring Sauce Thickened with Cornflour, Custard Powder or Arrowroot

½ pint milk, fruit juice or water
½ oz. cornflour or custard powder or ¼ oz. arrowroot
½ to 1 oz. sugar
½ oz. margarine, optional
flavouring

General Method

1. Blend the starch powder with 2 tablespoons of cold liquid, boil the rest of the liquid with the sugar and the margarine if used.
2. Stir the nearly boiling liquid into the starch mixture.
3. Rinse the saucepan, return the sauce to it and boil the sauce for 1 minute stirring it all the time.
4. Add the flavouring.

Name of sauce	Additions to recipe	Variation of method
Butterscotch sauce	4 oz. brown sugar 1 oz. butter rind and juice $\frac{1}{2}$ lemon use $\frac{1}{2}$ pint water	Dissolve the sugar in $\frac{1}{4}$ pint of the water, add the butter and lemon rind and boil the whole for 5 minutes. Blend the starch with the other $\frac{1}{4}$ pint water, thicken the sauce as usual; add the lemon juice.
Caramel sauce	2 oz. Lyle's Golden Syrup* 1 tablespoon warm water 2 or 3 drops vanilla *(one make of syrup has been found to curdle the milk)	Heat the syrup in a dry saucepan until it is a deep golden-brown; add the water at once and cool the caramel a little. Add the milk and heat it gently to dissolve the caramel. Thicken the sauce as usual.
Chocolate sauce	2 oz. plain chocolate or 1 tablespoon cocoa and 1 oz. extra sugar a few drops vanilla essence $\frac{1}{4}$ teaspoon instant coffee powder water or milk may be used	Melt the chocolate slowly with 2 tablespoons milk or water; or blend the cocoa and sugar with the starch and instant coffee, if used. Thicken the sauce as usual.
Coffee sauce	3 teaspoons instant coffee powder 2 or 3 drops of vanilla essence brown sugar for sweetening	Blend the coffee powder with the starch.
Ginger sauce	1 tablespoon Golden Syrup $\frac{1}{2}$ teaspoon ground ginger a strip of lemon rind 1-2 teaspoons lemon juice	Add syrup and lemon rind to the milk when boiling it. Add lemon juice last.
Lemon sauce	rind of $\frac{1}{2}$, juice of 1 lemon deduct 2 tablespoons from half pint water 2 oz. sugar	Infuse thinly peeled rind 5 minutes in boiling water. Add lemon juice last.
Orange sauce	rind of half, juice of 2 oranges $\frac{1}{4}$ pint water, sugar to taste	As for Lemon Sauce.

Fruit, Jam and Syrup Sauces

Fruit sauce	$\frac{1}{2}$ pint juice from tinned or stewed fruit, e.g. cherries, pineapple, apricot, prunes sugar to sweeten if needed 1 or 2 teaspoons lemon juice $\frac{1}{4}$ oz. arrowroot 2 tablespoons of fruit whole or diced if suitable, e.g. whole, stoned cherries or dice of pineapple	Thicken the juice with arrowroot, sweeten and add lemon juice to taste.

Name of sauce	Additions to recipe	Variation of method
Jam sauce	2 tablespoons jam ¼ pint water, ¼ oz. arrowroot 1 to 2 teaspoons lemon juice sugar to sweeten	Heat the jam with the water, thicken with arrowroot as usual. Add lemon juice and sugar to taste. If there are pips in the jam strain the liquid.
Marmalade sauce	As Jam sauce	As Jam sauce: do NOT strain it.
Syrup sauce	2 tablespoons Golden Syrup ¼ pint water 2 strips lemon rind ¼ oz. arrowroot 2 teaspoons lemon juice If liked ¼ teaspoon ground ginger	Infuse the lemon rind in the water for 5 minutes, add the syrup, thicken the sauce as usual add lemon juice last. If ginger is used mix it with arrowroot before blending.

Hard Sauce

2 oz. butter   a few drops lemon juice
3 oz. icing sugar   1 drop almond essence
½ to 1 oz. ground almonds 1 to 2 drops vanilla essence

1. Cream the butter; sieve the icing sugar, cream the two together till soft and white.
2. Work in the ground almonds and the lemon juice and essences; serve the sauce piled up in a small dish.

Brandy or Rum Butter

As for Hard sauce using soft brown sugar, omitting ground almonds, flavouring with 1 teaspoon brandy or rum.

STUFFINGS OR FORCEMEAT

Stuffing or forcemeat is used mainly to add flavour to meat, fish or vegetables, but it may also make these foods a little more substantial or filling, it may in some cases add fat and protein to the dish or it may be useful in filling a hollow space in a vegetable or a boned cut of meat or fish.

The two standard stuffings of British cookery—veal stuffing or sage and onion stuffing—are only two among many possible kinds, a few varieties of which are given below.

Basic Recipe

2 oz. breadcrumbs	$\frac{1}{2}$-1 beaten egg
$\frac{1}{2}$-1 oz. margarine or chopped	pepper and salt
suet	flavouring additions (see below)

General Method

1. Crumb the bread, or cut off crusts, soak the bread in the beaten egg, and when soft mash it smooth with a fork.

2. Chop the shredded suet finely or mash the margarine into the bread with a fork. In some recipes the margarine is melted and used to cook some of the flavouring ingredients.

3. Mix all ingredients together, flavour, season and taste the mixture. The flavour should be very good and the consistency slightly sticky but firm enough to shape into a ball.

Name of stuffing	Additions to Basic recipe	Variation of method
Veal Stuffing for chicken, veal or any purpose	1 tablespoon chopped parsley $\frac{1}{2}$ teaspoon mixed chopped herbs grated rind of $\frac{1}{2}$ lemon	
Sage and Onion for pork, and goose	1 large cooked onion, chopped 2 teaspoons chopped sage	Cook the onion sliced thickly in a very little boiling water for 20-30 minutes or chop it finely and cook it in the margarine till soft in 10 minutes.
Apple and Celery for chicken, veal, pork	1 oz. bacon or cooked ham or tinned luncheon meat 1 small onion 1 medium cooking apple 2 sticks celery heart	Chop the bacon or ham. Chop the onion finely and cook it for 10 minutes in the margarine with raw bacon if this is used. Chop the apple and celery.
Ham or Liver for chicken or vegetables	4 oz. cooked ham or tinned meat *or* { 2 oz. bacon 2 oz. liver (calf's, lamb's or chicken's) } 2 teaspoons chopped parsley $\frac{1}{2}$ „ mixed herbs grated rind $\frac{1}{2}$ lemon	Chop the meat or bacon and liver and, if raw, cook them for 2 or 3 minutes in the margarine. 1 small onion and 2 or 3 mushrooms may also be chopped and cooked in the margarine.
Prune, for chicken, veal, pork, duck or goose	6 to 8 large cooked prunes 1 small cooking apple $\frac{1}{16}$ teaspoon spice—nutmeg or cinnamon 1 oz. chopped nuts grated rind and juice $\frac{1}{2}$ lemon	Stone and chop the prunes, chop or mill the nuts, chop the apple.

Name of stuffing	Additions to Basic recipe	Variation of method
Mushroom for meat, fish or vegetables	2 oz. mushrooms 1 oz. bacon	Chop the bacon and mushrooms and cook them in the margarine slowly for 10 to 15 minutes
Raisin and Nut, for any meat or vegetable	2 oz. seedless raisins 2 oz. chopped nuts 1 teaspoon chopped parsley 2 oz. bacon ⎫ 1 small onion ⎭ optional	If bacon and onion are used chop them and cook them in margarine.
Shrimp for white fish	2–3 oz. picked shrimps 1 small onion 1 teaspoon chopped parsley rind and juice ½ lemon ½ teaspoon anchovy essence	Wash the shrimps to remove salt, chop them finely. Chop the onion finely and cook it in the margarine.

Note. For all the above stuffings 2 oz. rice may be substituted for the breadcrumbs. The rice should be boiled till quite soft and slightly sticky, then drained.

Two Special Stuffings

Chestnut Stuffing, for poultry or veal

    1 lb. chestnuts or ½ lb. chestnut flour

    ½ pint stock   ½ teaspoon sugar

    1 oz. butter or margarine   a pinch of powdered cinnamon

    ¼ teaspoon Marmite   pepper and salt

1. Boil the chestnuts for 10 minutes, then taking a few out of the water at a time, shell and skin them.
2. Stew the chestnuts in stock till soft in 20 to 30 minutes, drain them.
3. Mash them or rub them through a wire sieve.
4. Melt the butter, dissolve the Marmite in a little of the stock, add these with the seasoning, spice and sugar.
5. Add enough of the stock to make a slightly sticky mixture.

Sweet Corn Stuffing, for poultry, meat or fish

    1 small tin sweet corn   1 teaspoon chopped parsley

    1 very small onion   rind and juice of ½ lemon

    ½ oz. butter or margarine   pinch of ground nutmeg

    pepper and salt   ½ beaten egg

    1 oz. breadcrumbs

1. Chop the onion finely and cook it in the fat for 5 minutes.
2. Drain the sweet corn and add it to the onion; cook it for 5 minutes more.
3. Add all the other ingredients and bind them with the egg.

22

PASTRIES

Note. In recipes using any pastry, the weight given always refers to the weight of flour used, e.g. '¼ lb. short pastry' means made from ¼ lb. flour.

SUET PASTRY

General Proportions

½ suet to flour, plain or self raising
5 level teaspoons baking-powder to each 1 lb. plain flour
2 ,, ,, salt ,, ,, ,, flour
½ pint water to each 1 lb. flour or 1 tablespoon to each oz.

Basic Recipe

¼ lb. fresh beef suet or shredded suet
½ lb. plain or self-raising flour
2½ level teaspoons baking-powder (omit for self-raising flour)
¼ pint or 8 tablespoons water

Note. For a very light, friable result, 2 oz. flour may be replaced by 2 oz. fresh, fine breadcrumbs.

1. Sieve the flour, baking-powder and salt.
2. Remove any blood-vessels and skin from *fresh suet*, keeping it in large lumps.
3. Roll the suet in the measured flour, and shred it on the coarse section of a grater.
4. Sprinkle the flakes with more of the flour and chop them till they look like fine breadcrumbs.
5. For the best and shortest result from *shredded suet*, chop it with a little of the flour till it also looks like breadcrumbs.
6. Mix the suet well into the flour.
7. Pour in most of the water and mix the pastry to a soft, elastic but not sticky dough, adding the rest of the water if needed.
8. Turn the ball of dough on to a floured board or work-surface, it should leave the basin absolutely clean.

9. With floured fingertips knead the pastry lightly until it is evenly mixed and quite smooth; knead it to the required shape.

10. Press and roll it to the required size and shape.

11. Steam puddings for $1\frac{1}{2}$ hours at least; simmer $\frac{1}{2}$ oz. dumplings for 20 minutes. The long time is needed to shorten the pastry as it takes about an hour to melt the suet. Dumplings can only be given the short time because as they are cooked in liquid, they disintegrate with longer looking.

TO USE SUET PASTRY

1. To Line a Basin (see Fig. 46)

Allow 8 oz. pastry and $1\frac{1}{2}$ lb. filling for a 2-pint basin

„ 6 „ „ „ I „ „ „ „ $1\frac{1}{2}$ „ „

„ 4 „ „ „ $\frac{3}{4}$ „ „ „ „ $\frac{3}{4}$ to 1 pint basin

1. Grease the basin and greaseproof paper, foil or a cloth to cover it.

2. Knead the pastry to a round ball; press and roll it to a round, large enough to line the basin with $\frac{1}{2}$ inch over, all round.

3. Cut a $\frac{1}{4}$ sector from the round, knead and roll this to fit the top of the basin for the lid.

4. Damp one of the cut edges and carefully lift the larger piece of pastry into the basin, taking care not to stretch it.

5. Press it gently into the shape of the basin, working with knuckles then fingertips from the bottom upwards, until the basin is completely lined, with $\frac{1}{2}$ inch extra pastry all round.

6. Press the cut edges firmly together till the join disappears.

7. Fill the basin, damp the top edge of the pastry.

Put the lid on. If the pudding is to be turned out the lid is put on to the filling and the lining edges are pressed on top of it.

If the pudding is not to be turned out (a meat pudding) turn the lining edges inward over the filling and press the lid over them. Twist and roll the edges of the greased paper or foil to make a well-fitting cap.

2. To Make a Layer Pudding

1. Grease basin and cover as in method above.

2. Knead and shape the pastry to a roll wider at one end than the other.

3. Cut 4 to 6 slices, grading them so that they are a little thicker at the wide end than at the narrow.

4. Roll the pieces to rounds of the same thickness (about $\frac{1}{4}$ inch) but of

varying sizes; the smallest goes to the bottom of the basin the largest is the lid, filling is spread on all layers except the lid.
5. Cover with the greased cover.

3. To Make a Roly-Poly

1. Grease a square of greaseproof paper, foil or a cloth.
2. Knead the pastry to a brick-shape.
3. Press and roll it to an oblong $\frac{1}{4}$ inch thick; keep the edges straight by pressing them between the rolling-pin and the knife; gently pull the corners square.
4. Spread the filling over the pastry, right up to the near short edge, but leaving $\frac{3}{4}$-inch margin on all other edges, as for Swiss roll, see Fig. 72.
5. Damp the three margins.
6. Roll the pastry from the near, short edge, lifting it slightly so as not to squeeze out any filling.
7. Roll the roly-poly in the greased cover; twist the ends of paper or foil or tie the ends of a cloth with string.

GENERAL RULES FOR PASTRY-MAKING, SHORT, FLAKY, ROUGH PUFF

Shortening power of fat, see p. 125.

Choice of flour (see p. 132). Plain flour is used for a correct result; if self-raising flour is used the pastry will not be true to type.

Choice of fat (see p. 125). A mixture of lard and margarine or butter is usually found to be satisfactory though other fats may be used successfully.

Keep everything cool. Keep fat in the refrigerator or cool larder till needed, use freshly-drawn cold water, iced if possible; handle pastry as little as possible and only with cool fingertips; rinse the hands first in cold water; lift and shape the pastry as far as possible with a rolling-pin and palette knife.

Use the correct proportions. Too much fat will make the pastry difficult to mix, too little fat will obviously make plain, 'unshort', tough pastry; too much water will make the pastry sticky to handle and usually tough or limp when baked; too little water will make short pastry too short and crumbly and in flaky pastry it will make a dough that is not sufficiently elastic to stretch easily and will therefore not produce light pastry.

Knead the pastry only just enough to mix it smoothly; for short pastry the kneading may be firm as the small amount of water does not develop much gluten and so does not toughen the dough; for the flaky pastries, with a high proportion of water, kneading must be very gentle.

Allow pastry to 'rest' or 'relax' in a cool place to allow fat to harden and gluten to soften after it has been kneaded and rolled. Make pastry before preparing filling; leave richer pastry in a cool place for at least ¼ hour before baking it—longer in warm weather.

Pastry made on one day and kept wrapped in foil or plastic sheeting in a cool place for use next day is easy to handle and is generally shorter and lighter than usual.

Bake pastry in a fairly hot oven so that the water is quickly turned to steam to puff up the pastry; the starch grains burst and absorb the fat as soon as it melts and the pastry sets in its risen state. Too cool an oven allows fat to melt and run out of rich pastry before it can be absorbed and it dries and toughens the dough before it is risen. Too great heat hardens pastry before it has time to rise.

Reduce the oven temperature once the pastry is risen, set and beginning to turn golden-brown to avoid making it over-hard. For very long baking, as for a meat pie, the pastry may be covered after the first hour with foil or greaseproof paper, damped on top, to keep it from getting over-dry and hard.

Tins or dishes need not be greased before lining them with pastry, the fat in the pastry prevents it sticking; the edge is often damped to fix the pastry to the dish.

SHORT PASTRY

General Proportions

½ fat to flour
1 teaspoon salt to each pound flour
4 to 5 tablespoons water to each pound flour or just over 1 teaspoon water to each ounce flour

The variation in the amount of water is necessary because all flour does not have the same moisture-content, nor does it all absorb the same amount of water.

Basic Recipe

Oven 380° F. Gas No. 6

$\frac{1}{2}$ lb. plain flour (pastry flour if possible)

$\frac{1}{4}$ lb. fat $\begin{cases} \text{2 oz. margarine or butter} \\ \text{2 oz. lard} \end{cases}$

$\frac{1}{2}$ level teaspoon salt

8 to 10 teaspoons cold water

1. Sieve the flour with the salt.
2. Drop the fat into the flour and there cut it into thin slices.
3. With the fingertips pinch and rub the fat into the flour; keep the hands well above the bowl to aerate the flour.

Stop rubbing in as soon as the mixture looks like fine breadcrumbs or earlier if the fat begins to melt.

In hot weather rubbing in may be done with a fork.

4. Measure in most of the water and mix firmly with a round-ended knife, this is cooler than the fingers and easier to withdraw than a spoon. When the pastry begins to hold together finish mixing with two fingers and a thumb to get the 'feel' of the pastry to find if it needs the rest of the water and to draw it together into a firm ball. If the right amount of water is added little gluten is developed and the pastry may therefore be kneaded firmly without toughening it (Fig. 55).

Turn edges of pastry   With fingertips rock   Turn the pastry round
to the middle   the pastry firmly   and repeat the rocking

Fig. 55. KNEADING SHORT PASTRY

5. Knead the pastry until it is perfectly smooth and evenly mixed. Leave the pastry to rest while the filling is prepared. Before beginning to roll the pastry knead it approximately to the shape required—a round or an oblong.
6. On a lightly floured board, with a lightly floured rolling-pin press the pastry to the right shape and then roll it with short, light movements of the rolling-pin, always away from the worker.

Turn the pastry, not the rolling-pin, to alter the shape, so that equal pressure is exerted on each end of the rolling-pin. Roll the pastry to the required thickness and shape.

7. Bake at 380° F. or Gas No. 6 for 15 to 20 minutes, then if the filling needs longer cooking reduce the heat to 325° to 350° F. Gas No. 2-4.

8. *Glazing.* Short pastry is generally baked without a glaze, fruit pies only being dredged after baking with caster or icing sugar, but for some covered tarts white of egg and caster sugar may be used and savoury pies are often brushed with beaten egg or milk.

Variations of short pastry recipe	*Variations of method*
Rich short pastry (flan pastry)	
½ lb. flour	Add sugar to flour before rubbing in fat.
4-5 oz. fat	The amount of water must vary with the
1 oz. caster sugar	size of the egg-yolk.
¼ teaspoon salt	Reduce oven-heat after ¼ hour as this pastry
1 egg yolk	browns more quickly than usual owing
about 1 tablespoon water	to the sugar.
Biscuit crust	
½ lb. flour	Add no extra water.
4 oz. fat	The more sugar the more quickly will this
2 to 4 oz. sugar	pastry brown; bake it at 350° F. Gas
1 small beaten egg (about 2 tablespoons)	No. 4.
Cheese pastry	
Add to the basic recipe:	
2 to 4 oz. dry grated cheese	Add the grated cheese after rubbing in fat.
pinch of cayenne pepper	Use plainer version for vegetarian pies, the
Optional: beaten egg to bind (2 tablespoons)	richer version for cheese biscuits or straws.

Quickly Made Short Pastry using 'Ready Creamed' Cooking fat or Cooking oil

½ lb. flour, plain   ½ level teaspoon salt
¼ lb. cooking fat or 8 tablespoons cooking oil
2½ tablespoons cold water

1. Sieve the flour and salt on to a plate.
2. Put 2 heaped tablespoons flour into the mixing bowl, make a well in it and add the water and the fat or oil.
3. With a fork whisk the mixture lightly together for $\frac{1}{2}$ minute.
4. Gradually work in the rest of the flour with the fork.
5. Knead and roll as usual but work very gently indeed if oil is used.
6. The oil pastry is rather soft and is better used as a lining for tarts than as a covering.
7. Bake as usual.

Flaky and Rough Puff Pastry

These two pastries are interchangeable in use, the recipe is the same for both, the method of folding and rolling is similar and both are baked at the same temperature. The difference lies in the method of adding the fat and only personal preference or personal skill need decide which to choose.

Both these pastries, when well made, should consist of a series of short, crisp flakes of pastry with air spaces between. To bring about this result a rather high proportion of water is added so that plenty of steam is produced to puff up the pastry and so that the dough is soft and elastic enough to allow it to stretch and rise. Acid, in the form of lemon juice or sour-milk whey is added to soften the gluten to make it still more elastic. The fat is added in firm pieces which, during rolling, are flattened to thin flakes; the pastry is folded and rolled several times to enclose layers of air as well as to distribute the fat. During baking the air expands and the fat, as it melts and is absorbed by the flour, leaves more air spaces and so the flaky result is achieved by the steam, the air and the method of adding the fat.

General Proportions

$\frac{2}{3}$ to $\frac{3}{4}$ fat to plain flour
$\frac{1}{2}$ teaspoon salt
4 teaspoons lemon juice } to each pound flour
$\frac{1}{2}$ pint water to each pound flour *or* 1 tablespoon to each ounce.
or $\frac{1}{2}$ pint whey from sour milk, omitting lemon juice.

Basic Recipe

½ lb. plain flour

6 oz. fat ⎰ 1-2 oz. lard
⎱ 5-4 oz. margarine or butter

¼ teaspoon salt

2 teaspoons lemon juice

approximately ¼ pint or 8 table-⎫ *or* ¼ pint whey from sour milk
spoons cold water ⎭

Method common to both pastries

1. Sieve the flour and salt.
2. Rub in ¼ of the total fat using all or most of the lard.

Method for Flaky Pastry (Fig. 56)

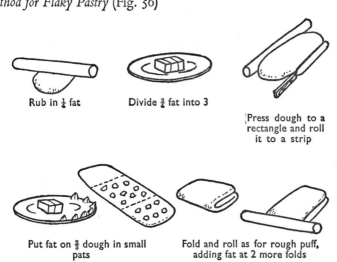

Rub in ¼ fat   Divide ¾ fat into 3

Press dough to a
rectangle and roll
it to a strip

Put fat on ⅔ dough in small
pats

Fold and roll as for rough puff,
adding fat at 2 more folds

Fig. 56. FLAKY PASTRY

3. Add the lemon juice and most of the cold water and make a soft, pliable, but not sticky dough, using a palette knife for mixing, only adding all the water if necessary.

4. Turn the dough on to a lightly floured board, and knead it very lightly, just enough to mix it thoroughly and smoothly. Wrap it in plastic film or foil.

5. Leave the dough to relax in a cool place for 20 minutes, if time allows.

6. Cut the firm, cold fat into three and cut one-third of it into small, flat pieces.

7. Press and roll the cooled dough to a long, narrow strip, $\frac{1}{4}$ inch thick : use as little flour as possible on board and rolling-pin; straighten the edges of the dough with the knife and the rolling-pin, pull the corners square and do all this very gently, with as little fingering as possible.

8. Mark the strip of dough into thirds, arrange the little pats ($\frac{1}{3}$ of the remaining fat) over $\frac{2}{3}$ of the strip. Fold the strip in three, with the plain section inside.

9. Turn the folded pastry, a quarter turn, so that the fold is to the left. Seal the open edges with the rolling-pin and straighten the edges so that they fit. Press and roll once more very gently. Use just enough flour to keep the pastry from sticking. If it should stick underneath, lift it on the rolling-pin. Scrape the board clear, and lightly re-flour it. If it should stick to the rolling-pin, scrape this clear, re-flour it and also lightly flour the sticky patch on the pastry.

10. Repeat the addition of fat, the folding and rolling twice more, then fold the pastry once more and leave it to relax before rolling it to shape (4 rollings in all).

Method for Rough Puff Pastry (Fig. 57)

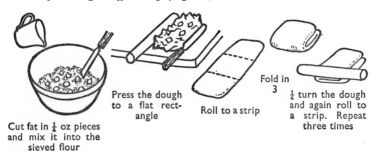

Cut fat in $\frac{1}{4}$ oz pieces and mix it into the sieved flour

Press the dough to a flat rect-angle

Roll to a strip

Fold in 3

$\frac{1}{4}$ turn the dough and again roll to a strip. Repeat three times

Fig. 57. ROUGH PUFF PASTRY

3. Cut the cold, firm fat into rather flat, $\frac{1}{4}$-oz. pieces and drop these into the sieved flour.

4. Add the lemon juice and most of the water and with a palette knife press the mixture gently together, taking care not to break the pieces of fat.

5. When the whole is just bound together in a rather rough mass, with the addition of the remaining water, if necessary turn it on to a lightly

floured board and press it into a brick shape with palette-knife and rolling-pin.

6. Press the pastry gently into a long strip, using palette knife and rolling-pin frequently to straighten the edges.

7. Fold the strip in three and roll it exactly as for flaky pastry except that there is no more fat to add; repeat the folding and rolling three times more (4 rollings in all).

Glaze the pastry with beaten egg for a savoury dish, with white of egg and caster sugar for a sweet dish.

Bake both pastries at 400° F. Gas No. 7 for 20 minutes reducing the heat after that time to 325° to 350° F. Gas No. 2-4 to cook the filling.

To use Trimmings of Flaky or Rough Puff Pastry

Pile the scraps, quite flat, one on top of the other and do not knead them —awkward shapes may be folded. Press gently and roll to shape. The aim is to keep the flaky nature of the pastry even when using up scraps.

PUFFS AND TURNOVERS USING FLAKY OR ROUGH PUFF PASTRY

Apple Turnovers   *6 large or 8 small helpings*

Oven 400° F. Gas No. 7
Baking time   35 to 40 minutes

> 6 oz. flaky or rough puff pastry
> ½ lb. apple filling as for Plate Apple Tart (p. 395)
> egg-white and caster sugar

1. Make the pastry, prepare the filling.
2. Roll the pastry very thin to an oblong twice as long as it is wide (for 8 turnovers).
3. Cut 8 squares and put filling on half of each piece, diagonally, leaving a margin.
4. Damp the edges, fold each square to make a triangle, press and flake the cut edges.
5. Brush the turnovers with egg-white and dredge them with caster sugar. Cut several slits in the top with scissors.
6. Bake them, reducing the heat to 325° to 330° F. Gas No. 3 after 25 minutes. Serve them hot or cold.

Alternative fillings. Other fruit with sugar to sweeten, jam, lemon curd or mincemeat.

Banbury Puffs, Eccles Cakes, Coventry God-cakes, Hawkshead Cake or Chorley Cakes (Fig. 58)

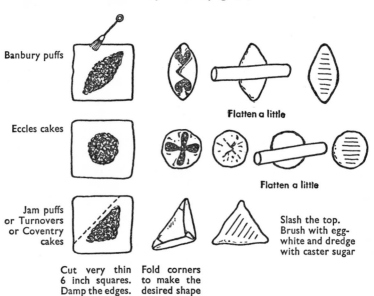

Banbury puffs

Eccles cakes

Flatten a little

Flatten a little

Jam puffs or Turnovers or Coventry cakes

Cut very thin 6 inch squares. Damp the edges.

Fold corners to make the desired shape

Slash the top. Brush with egg-white and dredge with caster sugar

Fig. 58. PUFFS AND TURNOVERS WITH FLAKY OR ROUGH PASTRY

These are all cakes traditionally made in the districts that gave them their names, the filling of all is similar but the shapes and sizes vary: Banbury puffs are boat-shaped, Eccles and Chorley cakes round, Coventry God-cakes triangular and all these are small while Hawkshead Cake is the size of a dinner-plate.

6 oz. flaky or rough puff pastry

Filling

1 oz. butter or margarine	4 oz. currants
$\frac{1}{2}$ oz. flour	$\frac{1}{2}$ oz. chopped peel
1 tablespoon lemon juice (or brandy)	2 oz. brown sugar
$\frac{1}{8}$ teaspoon cinnamon	$\frac{1}{2}$ egg or 1 yolk

Method for the Filling

1. Make a thick sauce with the fat, flour and liquid, add the fruit, sugar and cinnamon and last the beaten egg.
2. Cool the mixture before using it.
   Roll the pastry to a very thin oblong and cut 6 or 8 squares (no trimmings).

To shape Banbury Puffs (or cakes)

1. Put the filling diagonally across the middle of each square, damp the edges and gather them over the filling, shaping a 'boat' with two pointed ends; press the join, turn the puffs over, roll them lightly with a rolling-pin.
2. Brush them with white of egg, dredge with caster sugar and slash each three times with a sharp knife.

Eccles and Chorley Cakes. Shape these in the same way but gather them into rounds.

Coventry God-cakes. Shape these as for Apple turnovers.

Cream Horns   10–12

  Trimmings of flaky or rough puff pastry (about 4 oz.)
  Jam $\frac{1}{8}$ to $\frac{1}{4}$ pint whipped cream or mock cream

1. Lightly grease 10 to 12 cream-horn moulds.
2. Roll the pastry very thin to an oblong and cut strips 1 inch wide.
3. Beginning at the pointed end wind the pastry spirally round the mould, overlapping the layers $\frac{1}{8}$ inch. Trim the top edge.
4. Put them on a baking-tray and lightly brush them with beaten egg-white.
5. Bake the horns for 7 to 8 minutes at 400° F. Gas No. 7.
6. Cool them, then put a small teaspoonful of jam in each.
7. Pipe a whirl of cream in each horn.

Vanilla Slices   8

  Trimmings of flaky or rough puff pastry (about 4 oz.)
  $\frac{1}{4}$ to $\frac{1}{2}$ pint confectioner's custard (p. 451) or mock cream (p. 452)
  jam (optional) glacé icing, 4 oz. sugar; or icing sugar to dredge.

1. Roll the pastry very thin, lift it carefully on to a baking-tray and mark it into neat fingers about 2 inches by 3 inches and all the same size.

2. Bake it until crisp and golden in about 10 minutes.

Cool the pastry and cut it into the marked shapes, keeping any crumbs or trimmings.

3. Spread a little jam on half the fingers then sandwich pairs together with a thick layer of the custard or cream. Ice the tops or dredge them with icing sugar.

4. Crush the crumbs and sprinkle them on the ends of the iced fingers.

To Make Patties from Flaky and Rough Puff Pastry

1. Roll the pastry to $\frac{1}{8}$ inch.

2. Cut out rounds about 2 inches across, or whatever size is needed, but make allowance for shrinkage during baking.

3. From half the rounds cut out the centres with a cutter about $\frac{3}{4}$ inch across.

4. Damp the rings, press them firmly on to the rounds and prick them lightly to prevent uneven rising.

5. Cool the patties at least 15 minutes before baking them.

6. Bake them for 15 to 20 minutes until well risen and crisp, baking the small rounds as well if these are needed as lids.

7. If there is any undercooked pastry in the middle cut it out.

8. These patties may be filled with jam, fruit or cream, or they may be used for savoury fillings.

CHOUX PASTRY FOR ÉCLAIRS AND CREAM BUNS

Choux pastry is a good example of the use of steam as a raising-agent; it consists of a thick binding sauce called 'panard' into which eggs are beaten and in its raw state it contains a fairly high proportion of water which turns to steam and puffs the pastry up to three or four times its original size during baking. This pastry is so soft that it cannot be rolled to shape but must be piped and is designed to make quite hollow éclairs or buns which are filled with whipped cream when cold.

A cream bun looks rather like a small cabbage, hence the French name 'choux'.

Recipe for Choux Pastry   *16 to 20 éclairs, 12 cream buns*

Oven 400° F. Gas No. 7

Cooking time   30 to 40 minutes

2½ oz. flour
2 to 2¼ oz. margarine or
 butter
¼ pint milk or water

6 oz. chocolate or coffee
 icing

⅛ teaspoon salt
¼ teaspoon sugar
¼ teaspoon vanilla essence
2 eggs

¼ pint cream

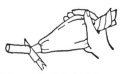

Piping with a ¾ inch plain pipe.
Cut to the right length with a
wet knife

Split the éclairs and
fill them with a small
pipe

Dip the éclairs in icing.
Scrape the trail of icing
on edge of pan

Fig. 59. PIPING AND ICING ÉCLAIRS

Have ready a greased baking-tray and a forcing bag and pipe.

1. Warm the flour then sieve it on to a square of paper that can be held comfortably in the hand.
2. Boil the liquid with the fat, salt and sugar.
3. When it is boiling fast, draw the pan off the heat, at the same time beating in all the flour.
4. Beat the panard only until it is smooth and beginning to leave the sides of the saucepan; further beating may separate the fat out of the flour paste.
5. Cool the panard to blood heat in the saucepan, add the vanilla.
6. Beat the eggs and beat them gradually into the panard and beat the whole mixture vigorously. The paste should now be smooth, glossy and stiff enough to stand in peaks when drawn up with the spoon. If the eggs are small a little more beaten egg may be needed, if very large all the beaten 2 eggs may not be needed.
7. Put the mixture into a large nylon or cotton bag with a plain pipe about ¾ inch diameter and pipe finger shapes, 2½ to 3 inches long for éclairs, or round balls 1½ to 2 inches across for cream buns, keeping the shapes about 2 inches apart on the tin (Fig. 59).

8. Bake the pastry in the upper half of the oven and do not open the door for 20 minutes as a draught may make them collapse.

When well risen and brown they may be moved down to a lower shelf in the oven or the heat may be reduced and they are then baked until they are quite crisp at the side as as well as on top.

9. As soon as they are cooked make a little slit on the side of each pastry and if there is any soft paste inside scoop it out with a teaspoon handle.

10. When quite cold fill them with whipped cream, mock cream or confectioner's custard and ice the tops with coffee or chocolate icing or dust cream buns with icing sugar (Fig. 59).

Choux pastry must be eaten the day it is baked as it soon becomes limp and sodden.

23

HOT PUDDINGS

MILK PUDDINGS

The method used to mix the cereal into the milk depends on the size of the grain.

Basic Recipe for Milk Puddings *4 helpings*

1 pint milk	flavouring of cinnamon stick, bay leaf or a
1½ oz. grain	strip of lemon or orange rind, cooked in the
1 oz. sugar	pudding *or* nutmeg grated on top

Long Method for Whole or Large Grain, Baked

Rice, Barley Kernels or Large Tapioca

Oven 350° then 300° F. Gas No. 4, then 1 or 2
Cooking time 2 to 2½ hours

1. Heat the oven.
2. Grease the top rim of a 1-pint pie-dish.
3. Wash whole grain unless it is bought ready cleaned and sealed.
4. Put the grain, sugar and flavouring into the pie-dish, pour in the milk.
5. Bake it at moderate heat for 20 minutes then at low heat for 1½ to 2 hours until the grain is soft, the milk creamy and the skin golden-brown.

Method for Medium or Crushed Grain and a Quicker Method for Large Grain, Baked

Small Sago, Seed Tapioca, Semolina and Flaked Grains. Also Macaroni

Oven 350° F. Gas No. 3-4
Baking time 30 to 45 minutes

1. Heat the oven.
2. Grease the top of a 1-pint pie-dish.
3. Heat the milk in a deep saucepan and when it is almost boiling sprinkle in and stir in the grain, the sugar and whole flavouring.

4. Simmer the pudding, stirring it occasionally, for 10 minutes for medium grain or 15 to 20 minutes for large grain, until the grain is soft.

5. Turn into the pie-dish and bake it for 30 minutes for medium grain and 40 to 50 minutes for large grain or 1 hour for macaroni.

Method for Powdered Grain, Baked

Arrowroot, Cornflour, Custard Powder, Farola, Ground Rice, Powdered Barley

Oven 350° F. Gas No. 3-4
Baking time   20 to 30 minutes

1. Heat the oven. Grease the pie-dish.
2. Mix the powdered grain and sugar to a thin cream with cold milk.
3. Boil the rest of the milk and stir it into the cereal.
4. Rinse the pan, return the pudding to it and stir it while it boils for 1 minute for powders or till clear for Farola and ground rice.
5. Turn the pudding into the pie-dish and bake it till creamy and golden on top.

Cornflour Mould

Use Basic Recipe for Milk Pudding.

Flavouring of: 1 tablespoon cocoa using 1¼ oz. cornflour ⎱ blended
              or 2 teaspoons instant coffee powder ⎰ with the
                                                        cornflour

         or vanilla essence or lemon or orange rind

Follow the method for powdered grain pudding but cook the mixture for 5 to 7 minutes in the saucepan, stirring all the time, add the essence when cooked. Rinse a mould with cold water and turn the mixture into it quickly. If the mould is to be coloured add a few drops of colouring to the milk before making the mould.

Leave the mould to get quite cold before turning it out.

Serve it with stewed fruit or jam.

Mould Made with Large or Medium Grain

Use Basic Recipe
            with ⎰ 1 pint milk
                 ⎱ 2 oz. grain

Follow the method for the particular grain but cook it in the saucepan for from 10 minutes for ground rice to 2½ hours for whole rice; a double saucepan should be used for this long cooking.

To Add an Egg to Medium or Powdered Grain Puddings

Oven 350° F. Gas No. 3-4
Baking time   30 minutes

Cook the grain in the usual way in a saucepan, cool it slightly.
Separate the yolk and white of one egg for each pint of milk.
Add the yolk to the cooled pudding.
Whisk the white to a froth stiff enough to be held upside down without falling.
With a tablespoon lightly fold the white into the pudding and turn it into a greased pie-dish.
Bake it till brown and puffed up, in about 30 minutes.

CUSTARDS AND CUSTARD PUDDINGS

For the effect of heat on eggs, see p. 107.

Baked Custard   *2-3 helpings*

Oven 325° to 350° F. Gas No. 2-4
Baking time   40 to 45 minutes

½ pint milk	½ oz. caster sugar
1 egg	2-3 drops vanilla essence or a little grated nutmeg

Heat the oven, grease the top rim of a ½-pint pie-dish.
Beat the egg with the sugar and 2 tablespoons milk.
Heat the rest of the milk till it steams, then stir it into the egg mixture.
Strain the custard into the pie-dish, add the flavouring.
If, because of other cooking, the oven is over 330° F., stand the pie-dish in a baking-tin with ½-inch warm water.
Bake the custard for 40 to 45 minutes or until set.
To test it, slip the tip of a knife into the middle of the custard, press the edges of the slit and if no liquid milk is squeezed up the custard is set.

Caramel Custard   *3-4 helpings*

Steam   50 to 75 minutes

3 eggs	Caramel { 3 oz. granulated sugar
½ pint milk	{ 6 tablespoons water
½ oz. caster sugar	1 tablespoon hot water
2-3 drops vanilla essence	

1. Prepare a steamer as for Cabinet Pudding; grease a round of paper for the top of custard.
2. Put the sugar and water for the caramel in a small, thick saucepan and dissolve it very slowly over gentle heat; it must not be stirred, nor must the pan be shaken until the sugar is dissolved or it will crystallize out and become insoluble.
3. Wrap a fourfold strip of cloth or thick paper round a soufflé tin or a metal basin to protect the hands. Do NOT grease the basin.
4. When the sugar is dissolved boil the syrup until it turns a rich, golden-brown, at once add 1 tablespoon hot water and pour it into the tin or basin.
5. Rest the basin on the edge of the saucepan and slowly roll it round till it is completely coated with caramel; leave it to cool.
6. Prepare the egg and milk as for Baked Custard and strain it into the mould.
7. Steam the custard very gently as for Cabinet Pudding until it is firm in the centre. The water must not boil at any time during steaming.
8. When set, loosen the top edge all round with a finger, tilt the mould to let the custard draw away from the sides; invert the dish over the custard and then turn the tin upside down on the dish. Wait until liquid caramel runs from the tin then lift it off carefully.

Stirred Custard or Custard Sauce

½ pint milk	a few drops of vanilla essence
2 yolks or one egg	½ oz. sugar

1. Beat the egg with the sugar and 2 tablespoons milk.
2. Heat the rest of the milk until it steams, then stir it into the egg mixture.
3. Rinse the saucepan and strain the custard into it.
4. Take the mixing-basin to the cooker, and stir the custard over moderate heat, testing it frequently to find if it will coat the spoon.

5. As soon as the custard has thickened turn it out of the saucepan into the basin so that the heat of the pan cannot continue to cook it, cooking must be stopped as soon as the eggs are just coagulated or the custard will curdle.

6. Serve the custard at once if it is wanted hot as it cannot be kept warm.
   Serve custard with stewed fruit or as a sauce with many puddings.

Cornflour Custard

Thicken the milk with 1 tablespoonful of cornflour, cool it a little then make the custard with it as above.

Bread and Butter Pudding   *3 helpings*

Oven 330° to 350° F. Gas No. 2-4
Baking time   30 to 40 minutes

> 1½ buttered, thin slices from a large loaf
> ½ pint milk   ½ oz. caster sugar
> 1 egg   1 oz. currants or sultanas
>   optional 1 tablespoon marmalade

1. Heat the oven, grease the top rim of a ¾-pint pie-dish. Wash and drain the fruit.
2. Spread the bread and butter with marmalade, if used, and cut it into neat squares or triangles.
3. Arrange half the pieces of bread and butter on the bottom of the pie-dish, put the dried fruit on top and then a neat layer of bread and butter on top.
4. Prepare the egg and milk as for Baked Custard, strain it over the bread and leave the pudding to soak for 20 to 30 minutes.
5. Bake it as for Baked Custard, using a high shelf to brown the top.
   Note. About 3 oz. stale cake may be sliced, buttered and used instead of bread; gingerbread is particularly good.

Cabinet Pudding   *3-4 helpings*

Steaming   40 minutes to 1 hour

> ½ pint milk   3 small sponge cakes
> 2 eggs   *or* 8 Savoy fingers
> ½ oz. sugar   *or* ⅓ to ½ Swiss roll
> 6 glacé cherries   a few drops vanilla essence

1. Grease a ¾-pint basin and a paper to cover it.

2. Wash and halve the cherries and arrange a few halves in a pattern on the bottom of the basin.

3. Slice the sponge cake or Swiss roll to about ¼ inch thick, shorten the Savoy fingers to fit the basin, arrange the cake neatly round the bottom and sides of the basin, break up the trimmings and put them in the middle.

4. Prepare eggs and milk as for Baked Custard, add vanilla essence and strain it into the basin. Cover the pudding and leave it to soak for ½ hour.

5. *Steam it* in a double steamer with the water only simmering below, or stand the basin on a thick pad of paper at one side of a large saucepan with simmering water to come half-way up it; set the other side of the pan over low heat and only allow the water to simmer gently at that side. Steam the pudding very gently for 40 minutes to 1 hour till just firm in the centre. Turn it out.

Serve it with jam or fruit sauce.

Queen of Puddings　　*4 helpings*

Oven 350° F. Gas No. 4 then 300° F. Gas No. 1-½
Baking time　　30 minutes + ½ to 1 hour

2 oz. or ¼ pint breadcrumbs (about 1-inch thick slice of a large loaf)

½ oz. margarine	½ oz. sugar
½ pint milk	grated rind ½ lemon or 2 or 3
2 egg yolks	drops vanilla essence
Meringue	2 tablespoons jam
2 egg whites, 3 to 4 oz. caster sugar	

1. Grease the top rim of a 1-pint pie-dish . Heat the oven.

2. Make the crumbs or cut off the crust rather generously and leave the slice of bread whole.

3. Boil the milk with the margarine, drop the bread into it, add sugar and lemon rind, put a lid on the saucepan and leave it to soak for 20 to 30 minutes.

4. Beat the yolks into the bread and milk and turn the mixture into the pie-dish.

5. Bake it till it is just set in 20 to 30 minutes.

6. When set take it from the oven, spread the jam on top of it Reduce the oven heat.

7. Whisk the egg whites stiff, then whisk in 2 teaspoons of sugar and finally fold in the rest of the sugar with a tablespoon. Pile the meringue on top of the pudding.

8. Put it back into the cool oven to dry the meringue and make it crisp. If the oven is kept very cool the meringue can be kept quite white but the flavour is far better if it dries to a fawn colour.

Poor Knight's Pudding

2 to 3 slices from a large loaf, cut ½ to ¾ inch thick
¼ pint milk   1 beaten egg
1 teaspoon caster sugar   cooking fat or oil for frying
¼ teaspoon powdered   Hot jam to sandwich the bread
    cinnamon   caster sugar and cinnamon
or ¼ teaspoon vanilla essence

1. Cut the bread in neat fingers, remove tough crusts.
2. Add the sugar and flavouring to the milk and soak the bread in it, on a plate, for ½ hour, then drain it thoroughly.
3. Beat the egg and turn it on to a plate. Prepare a paper with caster sugar and cinnamon.
4. Heat the fat till it will brown bread in 30 seconds. Have paper ready for draining.
5. Dip the bread into the egg, coat it thoroughly then lift it into the hot fat, one piece at a time until the pan is reasonably full.
6. Fry the bread till it is golden-brown, turn it and brown the other side.
7. Drain on soft paper; toss the bread in the cinnamon and sugar. If liked, sandwich with hot jam.
8. Serve hot.

Junket   *4 helpings*

1 pint milk   1 tablespoon sugar
            1 teaspoon essence of rennet

1. Have ready a large fruit bowl or 4 individual bowls or glasses.
2. Warm the milk and sugar to blood heat (testing a little on the inner side of the wrist it should feel just warm) (or to 100° F. on a thermometer).
3. Pour it into the large bowl and stir in the rennet, or add the rennet and then divide it between the 4 bowls.

N

4. Keep the junket in a warm place to give the enzyme time to act, in about 20 minutes. When set the junket may be chilled.

Note. If rennet is added to hot milk, or chilled too soon, it will not set the junket. Junket can be made with milk that has been boiled (and cooled) but a little extra rennet should be added.

STEAMED PUDDINGS

PUDDINGS WITH SUET PASTRY

Fruit Pudding   *3 helpings*

Cooking time   1½ to 2½ hours

> 4 oz. suet pastry (p. 356)
> ¾ lb. fruit   2 to 3 oz. sugar

1. Prepare a steamer.
2. Grease a ¾- to 1-pint basin and a square of greaseproof paper to cover it.
3. Make the pastry and line the basin (see Fig. 46), if time is short cut a small square out of the pastry at the bottom of the basin so that heat can penetrate to the fruit.
4. Prepare the fruit, if it is large cut it up so that it can be packed closely in the lined basin; put the sugar in the middle so that it will not make the pastry sticky. Add 1 tablespoon water unless the fruit is juicy.
5. Cover the fruit with pastry, keeping the join on top as this pudding will be turned out of the basin.
6. Twist the greaseproof paper round the edge of the basin to form a cap.
7. Steam the pudding for 1½ to 2½ hours; the longer time gives a shorter pastry with a golden crust.
8. Turn the pudding out on to a hot dish and serve it with custard sauce.

Layer Puddings   *4 helpings*

Cooking time   2 to 2½ hours

> 6 oz. suet pastry (p. 356)
>
> *Fillings:*
> 3 tablespoons jam or marmalade, *or* 3 tablespoons mincemeat,
> *or* 3 tablespoons syrup with 1½ tablespoons breadcrumbs

or for *Delaware Pudding:*

    1 small cooking apple ⎤
    2 tablespoons raisins   ⎬ chopped
    1 tablespoon peel   ⎦
    1 tablespoon Golden Syrup
    2 tablespoons brown sugar

1. For making Layer Pudding, see p. 357.
2. Cover and steam the pudding 2 to 2½ hours.
3. Turn it out and serve it with custard sauce.

Roly-Poly Puddings   *4 helpings*

Cooking time 2 to 2½ hours

    6 oz. suet pastry (p. 356)
    Fillings:
    2-3 tablespoons jam *or* 3 tablespoons syrup with 1 tablespoon
       breadcrumbs
   or 3 tablespoons mincemeat

1. Make the pastry and shape the roll, see p. 358.
2. Wrap it in greased paper, foil or pudding-cloth and steam it 2 to 2½ hours.
3. Unroll it and serve it with custard sauce.

SUET SPONGE PUDDINGS

Basic Recipe   *4-6 helpings*

Steaming 1½ to 2½ hours

    6 oz. plain flour   ⎫ *or* self-raising flour
    1½ level teaspoons baking-powder ⎭
  or 3 oz. plain flour and 3 oz. breadcrumbs ⎫ recommended for
    1 level teaspoon baking-powder   ⎭   really light pudding
    ½ level teaspoon salt   1½ oz. sugar
    3 oz. suet   ⎧ 1 small egg
    8 tablespoons milk   *or* ⎨ 6 tablespoons milk
                        ⎩

General Method

1. Prepare a steamer, grease a 1- to 1½-pint basin and a square of grease-proof paper to cover it.

2. Shred and chop the suet, see p. 356, using some flour.

3. Sieve flour and powdered ingredients.

4. Mix dry ingredients.

5. Mix liquid ingredients. Check the recipe.

6. Mix the pudding to a soft consistency that drops easily from the spoon.

7. Turn it into the greased basin which it should two-thirds fill.

8. Steam the pudding for $1\frac{1}{2}$ hours when it will be just cooked or $2\frac{1}{2}$ hours for a really spongy, friable result.

9. Turn the pudding out and serve it with $\frac{1}{2}$ pint hot sauce.

Variations

Name of pudding	Additional ingredients	Suitable sauce (see pp. 325-3)
College	3 to 4 oz. mixed currants, raisins, sultanas $\frac{1}{2}$ oz. chopped peel, use the egg $\frac{1}{2}$ teaspoon mixed spice	Cornflour, custard or syrup sauce
Date	3 to 4 oz. dates, grated rind $\frac{1}{2}$ lemon $\frac{1}{4}$ level teaspoon ground ginger, optional	Lemon- or ginger-flavoured cornflour sauce
Fig	4 oz. figs (soaked overnight in $\frac{1}{2}$ pint water) Chop the figs	Use the soaking water to make a lemon cornflour sauce
Jam or Syrup	2 to 3 tablespoons jam or golden syrup in the bottom of the basin.	Jam or syrup sauce
Lemon or Orange	grated rind of 2 lemons or 2 oranges Use the egg	Lemon or orange sauce using the juice
Marmalade	2 tablespoons marmalade, grated rind $\frac{1}{2}$ lemon, 2 oz. raisins, use the egg Instead of baking-powder, $\frac{3}{4}$ level teaspoon bicarbonate of soda	Marmalade sauce
Raisin or Sultana	3 to 4 oz. of the dried fruit $\frac{1}{2}$ level teaspoon grated nutmeg, optional.	Custard or cornflour sauce
'Spotted Dick'	3 to 4 oz. currants, $\frac{1}{2}$ to 1 oz. chopped peel	Custard or cornflour sauce
Syrup Sponge Ginger	1 tablespoon golden syrup 1 teaspoon ground ginger $\frac{1}{2}$ tablespoon black treacle Use brown sugar, insteadof baking-powder, use $\frac{3}{4}$ level teaspoon bicarbonate soda	Lemon cornflour sauce or syrup sauce or custard sauce

Christmas Pudding   *1 large pudding (2-pint basin) or 2 medium (1-pint basins)*

Steaming time   5 to 6 hours

¼ lb. sultanas	1 level teaspoon mixed spices
¼ lb. currants	½ level teaspoon salt
2 oz. raisins	grated rind 1 lemon
2 oz. mixed peel	½ medium cooking apple (2 oz.)
3 oz. suet	2 eggs
5 oz. breadcrumbs	1 tablespoon black treacle
2 oz. flour	6 tablespoons ale, cider or milk
¼ level teaspoon bicarbonate of soda	(optional) 2 oz. chopped almonds
¼ lb. moist brown sugar	

1. Prepare the fruit.
2. Grease the basin and double greaseproof paper or greaseproof and foil to cover it. Prepare the steamer.
3. Shred and chop the suet, make the crumbs.
4. Sieve the flour with powdered ingredients and mix in other dry ingredients.
5. Peel and shred the apple.
6. Mix the apple and the liquid ingredients.
7. Mix the pudding to a soft consistency that falls easily from the spoon.
8. Three-quarters fill the basins, cover them.
9. Steam the puddings for 5 to 6 hours.
10. When cooked, cover it with clean greased paper and tie it down; store the pudding in a cool, dry, airy larder. It can be kept for a year and more.
11. To use the pudding, re-steam it for at least 1½ hours. If it has got dry with storage baste it with a tablespoon or more of ale, cider or milk.
12. Serve it with egg-custard sauce or brandy butter.

STEAMED PUDDINGS FROM CAKE MIXTURES
Rubbing-in Method

Basic Recipe   *4-5 helpings*

Cooking time   1½ to 2½ hours

6 oz. self-raising flour
or 6 oz. plain flour with 1½ level teaspoons baking-powder
3 oz. granulated or brown sugar   3 oz. margarine, flavouring
1 large, or 1½ standard, eggs, about 4 tablespoons milk

General Method

1. Prepare a steamer, grease a pint-size basin and a square of greaseproof paper to cover it.
2. Make the cake mixture (see p. 432) mixing it to a consistency that will fall easily from the spoon, i.e. softer than the similar cake mixture.
3. Turn it into the basin, cover it by rolling the edge of the paper to form a cap.
4. Steam it for $1\frac{1}{2}$ hours when it will be just cooked or for $2\frac{1}{2}$ hours for a light pudding with a crisp, golden crust.
5. Turn it out on to a hot dish and serve with it $\frac{1}{2}$ pint hot sauce.

Examples

Name of pudding	Additional ingredients	Sauce
Date, Raisin or Currant pudding	2 to 3 oz. fruit $\frac{1}{4}$ teaspoon grated nutmeg *or* grated rind $\frac{1}{2}$ lemon	Lemon-cornflour or custard
Jam or Patriotic pudding	2 large tablespoons jam in the bottom of the basin	Jam or custard
Chocolate pudding	Use 5 oz. flour with 1 oz. cocoa	Chocolate or custard

Creaming Method

Basic Recipe   *4-5 helpings*

Steaming time $1\frac{1}{2}$ to $2\frac{1}{2}$ hours

Ingredients	Plain	Medium	Rich
Flour	6 oz. self-raising or 6 oz. plain	4 oz. plain	4 oz. plain
Baking-powder	2 level teaspoons	$1\frac{1}{4}$ level teaspoons	1 level teaspoon
Fat	3 oz. margarine	$2\frac{1}{2}$ to 3 oz. margarine	4 oz. butter or margarine
Caster sugar	3 oz.	$2\frac{1}{2}$ to 3 oz.	4 oz.
Eggs	$1\frac{1}{2}$ or 2 small	$1\frac{1}{2}$ to 2 standard	2
Milk	about 4 tablespoons	2 to 3 tablespoons	about 2 tablespoons

General Method

Follow the method for Creaming Method, Cakes (p. 437) and prepare the pudding as for Rubbing-in Method, Puddings above.

Some Recipes for Puddings Made by Creaming Method

Name of pudding	Additional ingredients	Special points
Beresford pudding	grated rind 2 oranges 1 oz. breadcrumbs	Medium or rich recipe Serve with a sauce made from orange juice
Canary pudding	grated rind 1 lemon	Plain, medium or rich. Serve with lemon sauce
Cassel or Castle pudding	grated rind ½ lemon or ¼ teaspoon vanilla essence	Use individual dariole moulds (8 to 10), steam 1 hour or bake them 20 minutes in moderate oven. Serve with jam sauce
Cherry pudding	2-3 oz. glacé cherries grated rind ½ lemon or ¼ teaspoon vanilla essence	Plain or medium recipe, serve jam sauce
Chocolate pudding	1 oz. cocoa instead of 1 oz. flour	Serve chocolate sauce
Pineapple pudding	1 tablespoon chopped canned pineapple with 1 tablespoon juice	Medium mixture Make a sauce with juice of canned pineapple and 2 tablespoons of the fruit chopped
Prince Albert pudding	½ lb. prunes, 2 oz. bread-crumbs and 2 oz. flour (instead of 4 oz. flour)	Medium or rich mixture. Line the basin with soaked, stewed prunes and make a sauce with ½ pint prune juice
Sultana pudding	2 to 4 oz. sultanas, grated rind ½ lemon or ¼ tea-spoon vanilla essence	Plain or medium mixture, serve with jam sauce

---

PUDDINGS MADE WITH BATTER

Yorkshire Pudding-or-Pancake Batter

4 oz. flour   1–2 eggs
¼ teaspoon salt   ½ pint milk
        optional 1 teaspoon cooking oil

Method of Mixing

1. Sieve the flour and salt into a deep mixing bowl.
2. With the back of a wooden spoon make a deep hole or 'well' in the flour by pushing it up the sides of the basin.
3. Drop the egg into the well, add half the milk and begin mixing.
4. Beat the egg and milk so that the mixture washes round the sides of

the well and gradually draws the flour into the liquid. Beat rapidly until all is mixed, it should now be a smooth, thick cream.

5. Lightly beat in the rest of the milk and the batter is ready to use at once.

Baked Batter Pudding   *6 helpings*

Oven 400° to 425° F. Gas No. 7
Baking time   ¾ hour or 20 minutes for small ones

> ½ pint batter   1 oz. cooking fat
> *To serve:* hot syrup or jam

Put the fat into a wide, oven-ware dish about 9 inches by 7 inches, or 6 to 8 large, deep bun-tins.

Heat the fat in the oven until it just begins to give off a haze.

Pour the batter into the hot fat.

Bake it in the upper part of the oven until well risen, brown and very crisp.

Serve it at once with hot syrup or jam.

Yorkshire Pudding to Serve with Roast Beef   *6 helpings*

Make this like Baked Batter but use 1 oz. dripping instead of cooking fat.

Fruit in Batter

> ½ pint batter   4 oz. raisins or sultanas
> 1 oz. cooking fat   *or* { ½ lb. raw, fresh fruit
>   { 1 to 2 oz. sugar

Make this like Baked Batter, but put the fruit (rolled in the sugar if used) into the haze-hot fat before adding the batter.

Pancakes   *4 helpings*

> ½ pint batter   caster sugar
> lard for frying   lemon juice
> *To serve:* cut sections of lemon

1. Burnish a small frying-pan with dry salt on a pad of soft, clean paper, dust all the salt out.

2. *Prove the pan.* Heat in it a piece of lard the size of a hazel-nut, run this well round the pan until it begins to smoke then wipe it all out with clean, soft paper.

3. *Have ready:* Lard in a small basin, the batter in a jug with a spoon;

a piece of paper dredged with caster sugar; lemon juice and sugar dredger; a plate over a pan of hot water to keep the pancakes hot; a fork.

4. *To fry the pancakes:* Put a small piece of lard into the frying-pan, heat it till it just smokes then pour it out into the basin; stir the batter and pour enough of it into the pan to cover it thinly. Cook the pancake over moderate heat until it can be shaken free in the pan and is golden underneath.

5. *To toss the pancakes:* Hold the handle of the frying-pan comfortably with the thumb on top, toss the pancake forward and up and catch it in the pan, cooked side up.

6. Cook the second side till it puffs up off the pan.

7. Turn the pancake out upside down on to the paper, dredge it with sugar.

8. Sprinkle it with lemon juice and roll it up with the fork and keep it hot on the plate with the saucepan-lid over it.

9. When all the pancakes are fried serve them dredged with sugar and with a section of lemon for each helping.

Other Fillings for Pancakes. Apple purée, jam, marmalade, orange juice instead of lemon.

Fruit Fritters *3 helpings*

Deep fat at 340° F. or shallow fat

3 dessert apples	fritter batter	
or 3 bananas	*or* yeast batter	p. 237

or any firm dessert fruit or well-drained tinned fruit
caster sugar

1. Make the batter, leave it to rise 30 to 45 minutes for yeast batter; omit the white of egg for fritter batter.

2. Heat deep fat, prepare a draining-tray with absorbent paper.

3. Peel, core and slice the apples $\frac{1}{2}$ inch thick; peel bananas, cut them in half lengthways then across.

4. Fold the whisked egg white into the fritter batter.

5. Have deep fat at 340° F. or shallow fat hot enough to brown a piece of bread in 40 seconds.

6. With a fork and a skewer or 2 skewers dip one piece of fruit at a time into the batter, to coat it and immediately into the hot fat; continue until the pan is reasonably full and turn the fritters frequently till they are golden and crisp (Fig. 40).

7. Drain them and serve them dredged thickly with caster sugar.

HOT PUDDINGS WITH FRUIT

To Prepare Fruit for Cooking or Serving in Fruit Salad

Apples	Wash, peel thinly, quarter and remove cores; for use raw, at once rub with lemon or put them into fruit juice or syrup: for stewing leave them in thick pieces or quarters.
Apricots	Wash, remove stalks; for fruit salad halve them and remove stones.
Bananas	Cut off the stalks, peel them and strip off the 'strings', rub with lemon or use them at once.
Bilberries	Wash and remove stalks.
Cherries	Wash, remove stalks; stones may be removed with a cherry stoner, or a skewer.
Damsons	Wash, remove stalks; remove stones during stewing with a draining spoon.
Gooseberries	Wash, top and tail them with scissors or a short knife.
Grapes	Wash, remove stalks, with a small sharp knife make a slit in each and prise out the pips.
Melon	For fruit salad either slice, remove seeds and peel thickly then dice; or cut the top off the melon, remove seeds, and scoop out the flesh with a teaspoon.
Plums	See Apricots.
Peaches	To skin them scrape the skin with the back of a knife or scald them for 30 seconds in boiling water then cool them in cold water: the skins will come off easily. Halve and remove stones, slice them for fruit salad.
Pears	See Apples.
Pineapple	Cut off the leaves, slice the pineapple, cut the core out of each slice and cut off the brown skin and the brown 'eyes' below the skin.
Oranges	For fruit salad, with a saw-knife peel them right through rind, pith and thin, inner skin, work over a plate to catch the juice; the juicy ball that remains may be cut in slices with a sharp knife; or the sections of fruit can be slipped out of the skin with a knife and the centre skin crushed with a wooden spoon to squeeze out the juice (Fig. 60).

Soft Berries and Currants | Wash them either with a spray nozzle on the tap or by dipping them in and out of water in a colander, drain them on absorbent paper; instead of washing strawberries may be wiped with damp, absorbent paper. Remove currants from the strings with a fork; pull out the 'plugs' of raspberries, strawberries and blackberries.

Rhubarb | Cut off the leaves and thick ends of the sticks, wipe the sticks with damp cloth or paper, cut in lengths.

With a saw-knife remove the rind and pith

Slip the sections from the skin

Fig. 60. PREPARING AN ORANGE FOR FRUIT SALAD

To Stew Fresh Fruit

Cooking time   5 to 30 minutes

    1 lb. fruit   2 to 4 oz. granulated sugar
    ¼ pint water

1. Prepare the fruit.
2. Put the water and sugar in the saucepan, dissolve the sugar.
3. Add the fruit as soon as the syrup begins to boil and cook just below simmering-point until it is just tender when tested with a teaspoon.

   Note. Very juicy fruit may be cooked with 1 or 2 tablespoons water.

To Stew Fruit in the Oven

Put the fruit and sugar in a casserole, add the water boiling, put on the lid and cook it at the bottom of a moderate oven 350° F. Gas No. 4 or in a slow oven until tender in 20 to 30 minutes.

   Note. Stewing pears stewed in the oven require 1 to 2 hours and are ready when they turn dull pink.

Stewed Apple Purée

Cooking time   10 to 30 minutes

> 1 lb. cooking apples   ½ oz. butter.
> 1 to 2 tablespoons water   3 to 4 oz. sugar
> flavouring of lemon rind and cinnamon or ginger

1. Put the apples with the water and butter in a covered saucepan and cook them gently till the juice begins to flow, then a little more quickly; shake the pan and stir the pulp occasionally.
2. Add the sugar when they are almost cooked.
3. Beat them smooth with a wooden spoon or rub them through a nylon sieve.

Rhubarb and Orange

Oven 300° to 320° F. Gas No. 1-2
Cooking time   15 to 30 minutes

> 1 lb. prepared rhubarb   4 oz. brown sugar or golden
> 1 dessertspoon water   syrup
> grated rind and juice of 1 small orange

Put the cut up rhubarb with the water and sugar or syrup in a casserole, grate the orange rind on to it and cover the casserole.

Cook it in the slow oven till just soft.

Add the orange juice to the hot rhubarb when it is cooked.

To Stew Dried Fruit

Whole fruit, e.g. prunes and figs,   ½ lb. fruit ⎫ ½ pint water
Halved fruit, e.g. apricots, peaches, pears, 6 oz. fruit ⎬ 1 to 2 oz. sugar
Sliced fruit, e.g. apple rings   4 oz. fruit ⎭ flavouring of lemon or orange rind, cinnamon stick, clove or bay leaf

1. Wash the fruit and soak it overnight in the water, adding the flavouring if used.
2. Stew the fruit in the soaking-water without any sugar, as for fresh fruit.
3. When cooked stir in the sugar. If liked add lemon or orange juice.

To Bake Apples   *1 apple per serving*

Oven 350° F. Gas No. 4
Baking time   45 minutes to 1¼ hour

> Apples. Filling of brown sugar with flavouring of lemon rind or
> spice; mincemeat, chopped dates, raisins, honey and
> chopped nuts, or stiff jam.

1. Wash the apples, remove the cores, cut ½ inch off the bottom of each
core and use it as a stopper to prevent the filling running out.
2. Run a sharp knife all round the middle of the skins.
3. Put the apples in an oven-ware dish and press the filling tightly into
the middle of each, using a teaspoon handle.
4. Pour 2 to 3 tablespoons water into the dish so as to keep any juice from
drying.
5. Bake until the apples are foamy and soft right through.

Pears may be baked but they are better with the cores left in and they
will need 2 hours at least.

Apple Amber (without pastry)   *4 helpings*

Oven 350° then 300° F. Gas No. 4 then No. 1
Baking time   20 minutes +½ to 1 hour

1 lb. cooking apples	flavouring of grated rind and juice ½ lemon
1 tablespoon water	¼ teaspoon ground cinnamon
½ oz. butter or margarine	2 egg-yolks
2 oz. sugar	1 tablespoon cake crumbs, bread-crumbs or crushed cornflakes
Meringue: 2 egg whites	4 oz. caster sugar

1. Grease a pint-size pie-dish or pie-plate.
2. Stew the apples with the water, butter, sugar and flavouring; or bake
them whole.
3. Beat the apple pulp smooth, add lemon juice (butter if the apples
were baked), crumbs and lemon juice, taste and sweeten if necessary.
4. When slightly cooled beat in the egg-yolk and turn the mixture into
the dish.
5. Bake it in the moderate oven till just set in about 20 minutes. Reduce
the oven heat.
6. Make the meringue as for Queen of Puddings (p. 376).
7. Dry the meringue till crisp in the cool oven.

Apple Charlotte ('Brown Betty') *4 helpings*

Oven 325° to 350° F. Gas No. 2-4
Baking time   1¼ to 1½ hours

1 lb. cooking apples	1 oz. brown sugar
3 oz. or 8 tablespoons	2 tablespoons golden syrup
breadcrumbs	1 tablespoon water

rind and juice ½ lemon

1. Grease a ¾-pint pie -dish.
2. Put the syrup, sugar, water and grated lemon rind into a small saucepan and warm them gently.
3. Make the crumbs, peel the apples and slice them very thinly or shred them on a coarse grater.
4. Arrange thin layers of crumbs and thicker layers of apple in the pie-dish, pressing them well down, and finishing with a layer of crumbs. The mixture should be piled well above the edge of the dish as it shrinks during cooking. Clear the mixture inwards from the top rim.
5. Add lemon juice to the syrup and baste it carefully over the crumbs: do not let it run on to the edge of the dish.
6. Bake the charlotte until the apple is soft and the top is golden-brown. Serve with custard sauce.

Notes. 3 oz. thin slices of bread and butter may be used instead of crumbs. Other juicy fruits, e.g. rhubarb, plums, apricots may be chopped and used instead of apples.

Apple Flapjack *4 helpings*

Oven 325° to 330° F. Gas No. 2-3
Baking time   ¾ to 1 hour

1 lb. cooking apples
2 oz. granulated sugar
Flapjack:

4 oz. rolled oats	2 oz. moist brown sugar
2 oz. margarine	2 tablespoons golden syrup

1. Grease a pint-size pie-dish.
2. Peel and thinly slice the apple and pack it into the pie-dish with the sugar in the middle.
3. Warm the syrup, fat and sugar in a saucepan and when the fat is melted, stir in the rolled oats.

4. Spread this mixture over the apple and roughen the top slightly with a fork.

5. Bake the pudding until the apple is soft and the top is golden and crisp.

Note. Other fruit may be used instead of apples.

Eve's Pudding   *4 helpings*

Oven 325° to 340° F. Gas No. 2-3:
Baking time   1¼ hours

1 lb. cooking apples	2 oz. sugar
Cake mixture:	
4 oz. flour ⎱	*or* 4 oz. self-raising flour
1¼ level teaspoons baking-powder ⎰	
2 oz. sugar	1 egg
2 oz. margarine	grated lemon rind or vanilla
2-3 tablespoons milk	essence

1. Grease a pint pie-dish.
2. Prepare the cake mixture by rubbing-in or creaming method but do not add the liquid to rubbing-in mixture or flour to creamed mixture.
3. Peel and slice the apple thinly, pack it tightly into the pie-dish with sugar in the middle.
4. Finish the cake mixture and spread it over the apple.
5. Bake in the cool oven so that the fruit cooks in the same time as the cake.
6. Serve the pudding with custard sauce.

Note. Other fruit may be used instead of apple.

Upside Down Pudding

Oven 325° to 340° F. Gas No. 2-3
Baking time   1¼ hours

To line the tin: 1 oz. margarine, 1 oz. soft brown sugar
drained canned or bottled fruit,
e.g. pineapple, apricots, sliced peaches
or halved plums and a few cherries

Cake mixture: 4 oz. of plain or medium creamed cake mixture, or
quickly made mixture (pp. 432, 438, 441)

1. Use a deep 8-inch sandwich tin.
2. Cream the 1 oz. margarine and 1 oz. brown sugar and spread the mixture round the sides and over the bottom of the tin.
3. Drain the fruit well and arrange a pattern of fruit on the bottom of the tin, keeping it as flat as possible.
4. Make the cake mixture and spread it over the fruit.
5. Bake the pudding till risen, firm and lightly brown.
6. Turn it out on to a large plate.

See also Baked Fruit Soufflés (p. 319).

SWEET DISHES WITH PASTRY

Apple Balls or Dumplings   *1 apple per helping* (Fig. 61)

Put the apple, smoother end down, on a round of pastry

Press the pastry up round the apple, add the filling when it is nearly covered, seal the top

Invert the apple ball on the baking tray

Fig. 61. SHAPING APPLE BALLS

Oven 380° to 400° F. Gas No. 6
Baking time   40 to 45 minutes

To each medium-sized cooking apple:

> 2 oz. short pastry
> about 1 teaspoon brown sugar
> flavouring of lemon rind, clove or cinnamon as liked

1. Make the pastry, divide it into 2 oz. pieces, one for each apple.
2. Knead the pieces to rounds and roll them out, 1 inch larger all round than the apples.
3. Peel and core the apples and put one on each piece of pastry, stalk end upwards.
4. Shape the pastry up round the apple, pressing out all creases with the fingers.

5. When the pastry has almost covered the apples fill the centre hole of each with sugar and add the flavouring.

6. Damp the edges of the pastry, draw the edges over the hole and press them firmly together.

7. Turn the apple balls smooth side up, brush them with water and dredge them with caster sugar. Make a small hole in the side of each with a skewer.

8. Bake them on a greased baking-tray for 15 minutes at 380° F. then reduce the heat and bake them for the remaining ½ hour at 325° F. until the pastry is crisp and golden and the apple quite soft.

American Apple Balls   *3 helpings* (Fig. 62)

Cover the apple with thin strip of pastry, 1 inch wide, wound spirally

Fig. 62. AMERICAN APPLE BALLS

Oven 380° F. Gas No. 6
Baking time   40 to 45 minutes

> 3 medium cooking apples
> 4 oz. short pastry
> *Syrup:*
> ½ pint water, 3 oz. brown sugar, golden syrup or honey
> apple cores and peels, grated rind ½ lemon
> 1 teaspoon lemon juice, a pinch of cinnamon if liked

1. Wash, peel and core the apples, rub them with cut lemon to keep them white.

2. Put the peels, cores, sugar, syrup or honey and flavouring with the water into a saucepan and simmer them steadily.

3. Grease the sides of an oven-ware dish that fits the apples.

4. Make the pastry, knead and roll it very thin to a long strip, 3 inches wide.

5. Cut three strips 1 inch wide using a pastry wheel if possible.

6. The syrup by now should be reduced to half its volume. If it has not, boil it hard until it is sticky, then strain it.

7. Beginning at the top of each apple press the pastry firmly round it in a spiral, overlapping the edges and leaving a little hole at the top. The pastry should not cover the bottom of the apple.

8. Put the apples in the dish and baste the syrup over them evenly, pour the rest into the dish.

9. Bake them at 360° F. for 15 to 20 minutes, then reduce the heat, baste them every 10 minutes or so with the syrup.

10. To finish them put a spoonful of red jam or jelly on top of each.

Fruit Pie (or Tart) (Fig. 48)

Oven 380° to 400° F. Gas No. 6
Baking time 35 minutes.

> 4 oz. short pastry
> 1 lb. fruit   2 to 4 oz. sugar
> 1–2 tablespoons water for hard fruit

1. Make the pastry

2. Prepare the fruit, put half of it in a 1-pint pie-dish then add the sugar and cover it with the other half of the fruit. If the sugar touches the pastry it makes it soft and sticky underneath. The fruit should rise in a mound above the edge of the dish to hold up the crust.

3. Roll the pastry to the shape of the pie-dish with a 1-inch margin on three sides.

4. Cut a ¾-inch strip from these three sides, damp the edge of the pie-dish and press the strip on to it; trim the ends so that they meet without overlapping.

5. Damp the strip, lift the pastry on the rolling-pin and lower it on to the pie.

6. Press the edges without stretching the pastry; trim and knock up the edge then flute it.

7. Make a neat round hole in the top of the crust, fit a little roll of greaseproof paper into it to act as a chimney to draw off the steam.

8. Stand the pie-dish on a baking-tray and bake the pie for 15 minutes at 380° F. to set the crust and to begin browning it, then move the pie lower in the oven and reduce the heat to cook the fruit.

9. Bake the pie till the crust is crisp and golden-brown and steam is puffing out of the hole showing that the fruit is cooked.

10. Dredge the top of the pie with sugar.

Bottled or Canned Fruit in a Pie

1. The juice must be drained off and used for other sweet dishes.
2. The fruit is too soft to support the crust during baking, therefore a pie-raiser should be used.

Covered Plate Pies or Tarts (*Top and bottom crust*)

Oven 380° F. Gas No. 6
Baking time ¾ to 1 hour

Use a flat, oven-ware or enamel plate as the bottom crust is not easy to cook completely in a deep plate.

For an 8- to 8½-inch plate: 6 oz. short, flaky, or rough puff pastry.
¾ lb. fruit (or other suitable filling)

1. Divide the pastry into 2 pieces, one slightly smaller than the other, knead each to a smooth ball.
2. Roll the smaller piece very thin, shaping it carefully to a round to fit the plate and with it line the plate; press any air bubbles out from the centre to the edge. Roll the other piece to a round for the cover.
3. Put the filling on and smooth it to a flat dome, damp the edges.
4. Put the other round on top, press the edges, trim, flake and flute them. Cut neat slits in the top with scissors or make a neat hole in the middle to let out steam. Trimmings may be cut in tiny rounds and used as decoration.
5. The crust may be brushed with white of egg or very little milk and dredged with caster sugar.
6. Bake the tart for ¾ to 1 hour, reducing the heat after 15 minutes to 350° to 330° F. Gas No. 4-3.

Fillings for Covered Tarts

Name of tart	Recipe for filling	Method of preparing filling
Apple (Dutch or spiced)	¾ lb. cooking apples, 2 oz. brown sugar 1 oz. flour, ¼ teaspoon cinnamon grated rind ½ lemon, 1 tablespoon water optional, 1 oz. raisins or sultanas	Mix the dry ingredients. Peel and thinly slice the apple; toss the slices in the dry ingredients. Fill the tart, then baste the water over the filling.

Name of tart	Recipe for filling	Method of preparing filling
Cherry (or other juicy fruit)	¾ lb. fruit (stoned if possible) 2 oz. sugar, 2 level tablespoons cake crumbs	Prepare the fruit and mix it with the sugar. Put the cake crumbs on the bottom pastry, to absorb juice, and the fruit over them.
Mint (Yorkshire)	1½ oz. currants, 1½ oz. raisins 1 oz. chopped peel, 2 oz. brown sugar 1 tablespoon chopped mint ⅛ teaspoon mixed spice ½ oz. margarine	Mix the sugar, spice and mint Arrange layers of fruit, mint mixture then fruit and add the margarine in thin shavings on top.
Yorkshire Treacle	¼ pint breadcrumbs ¼ pint mixed cake-fruit, e.g. sultanas, raisins, 1 medium cooking apple 2 tablespoons golden syrup ⅛ teaspoon ground cinnamon ⅛ ,, ,, ginger rind and juice ½ lemon	Mix the dry ingredients together. Peel and coarsely grate the apple and mix all with the lemon juice and syrup

Mince Pies

Mincemeat to fill 3 1 lb. jam jars

½ lb. fresh beef suet   ¼ lb. mixed peel
½ lb. cooking apples   1 to 2 oz. almonds
½ lb. raisins   grated rind ½ lemon
½ lb. sultanas   juice ½ lemon
½ lb. currants   ¼ to ½ level teaspoon mixed spice
(optional) 2 to 4 tablespoons   ½ lb. brown sugar
      brandy

1. Shred the suet and chop it fine, peel, quarter and core the apples, prepare the fruit.
2. Put the apples, dried fruit and suet through a mincer with a fine cutter.
3. Blanch and chop the almonds and add them with the flavourings; mix the mincemeat well.
4. Pack it into clean, dry jars and tie it down as for jam.

Note. Butter or margarine may be used instead of suet to make a mincemeat that will need little cooking as a filling. The soft fats may be added melted but cool to the other ingredients.

For 6 to 8 Mince Pies

4 oz. flaky or rough puff pastry (8 pies)
or 4 oz. short pastry (6 pies)
about 6 tablespoons or ½ lb. mincemeat

Use shallow patty- or bun-tins.

1. Roll the pastry very thin, cut rounds to fit the tins for the tops, then cut rounds one size larger to line the tins, re-rolling the scraps as necessary.

2. Fill the pies with mincemeat, damp the edges of the lids and press them on; flake the edges.

3. Brush the tops with white of egg and dredge them with caster sugar; make a neat hole with a skewer in the top of each pie.

4. Bake them for 25 to 30 minutes at 400° F. Gas No. 7 for flaky or rough puff pastry, or 380° F. Gas No. 6 for short pastry, reducing the heat when the pastry begins to brown.

Open Tarts (Fig. 63)

4 oz. pastry to line an 8-inch deep pie-plate or sandwich-tin.
5 oz. pastry if a lattice-work cover is to be made.

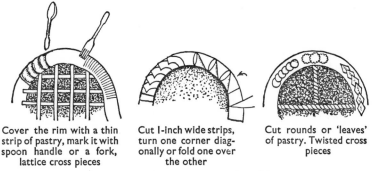

Cover the rim with a thin strip of pastry, mark it with spoon handle or a fork, lattice cross pieces

Cut 1-inch wide strips, turn one corner diagonally or fold one over the other

Cut rounds or 'leaves' of pastry. Twisted cross pieces

Fig. 63. Some Decorations for Open Tarts

The crust under the filling is cooked most easily in a metal pie-plate but oven-glass is often preferred because it looks nicer and if a small piece of pastry is cut out of the middle the heat can penetrate to cook both filling and pastry lining.

For some fillings it is necessary to bake the pastry 'blind' for 15 to 20 minutes before adding filling.

To Bake Blind

1. Line the plate or tin with pastry, carefully press out any air bubbles from the centre to the edge, prick the bottom and sides with a skewer or a fork, decorate the edge so that the pastry is double.

2. Grease a square of greaseproof paper, large enough to fit the plate

with the corners free for lifting it; put this greased side down on to the pastry and cover it with a layer ($\frac{1}{4}$ inch deep) of haricot beans, rice or bread-crusts. (Margarine or butter wrapping-papers are the right size.)

3. Bake the pastry at 360° to 370° F. Gas No. 5 for 15 to 20 minutes, till the pastry is set, then remove the paper and beans.

4. For an empty pastry shell, finish drying it at 325° to 330° F. Gas No. 3 until the centre is as firm as the edge.

If the tart is to have a filling cooked in it it needs no drying.

Jam Tart

Use a shallow plate or sandwich-tin.

1. Line the pie-plate, trim the edge.

2. Use the trimmings to cut a decoration for the edge, or cut and fold the edge so that the pastry is double on the edge of the plate (a single layer of pastry would be dry and hard when baked).

3. Fill the centre of the plate with jam allowing room for it to bubble up during cooking.

4. With the hands roll the trimmings to a long thin sausage, then roll this thin and cut strips $\frac{1}{8}$ inch wide for a lattice or $\frac{1}{4}$ inch wide for twisted cross-pieces: arrange the lattice or cross-pieces, trim the ends, damp them and press them on to the pastry just above the jam.

Fillings for Open Tarts

Name of tart	Recipe for filling	Special method
Almond or Bakewell	2 oz. butter or margarine 2 oz. caster sugar, 1 egg 1 oz. ground almonds 1 oz. cake crumbs a few drops almond and vanilla essence, 2 teaspoons lemon juice 1-2 tablespoons jam or lemon curd	Line a deep pie-plate and spread the bottom with jam or lemon-curd. Make the filling as for a creamed cake mixture, p. 438. Bake the tart 40 to 45 minutes at 350° F. Gas No. 4. When cold the top may be iced with glacé icing (3 oz. sugar).
Apple cheesecake	1 large baked apple ($\frac{1}{2}$ lb.) 1 oz. butter or margarine 3 oz. brown sugar, 2 eggs grated rind $\frac{1}{2}$ lemon, $\frac{1}{8}$ teaspoon cinnamon	Partly bake the pastry blind. Remove the pulp from the apple and while hot beat the butter into it, add the sugar, beaten egg and flavourings. Bake the filling for 30 to 35 minutes at 330° F. Gas No. 3.

Name of tart	Recipe for filling	Special method
Cheesecake (Yorkshire)	¼ lb. cottage cheese or curd drained from 2 pints sour milk 2 oz. butter or margarine, 1 oz. currants 1½ oz. caster sugar, 1 egg 1 teaspoon grated lemon rind, 1 teaspoon lemon juice, a little grated nutmeg	Sieve the curd with the butter, add the fruit and sugar then beat in the egg, and add flavourings. Bake for 35 to 40 minutes beginning at 380° F. Gas No. 6, and reducing to 330° F. Gas No. 3, after 15 minutes.
Custard tart	½ pint milk, 2 eggs ¾ oz. sugar, a little grated nutmeg	Make the pastry with 1 teaspoon caster sugar in 4 oz. flour and partly bake it blind. Bake the custard filling at 350° F. Gas No. 4 for 30 to 35 minutes.
Lemon curd	4 oz. caster sugar, 3 oz. butter 1 oz. ground rice, 1 egg rind and juice ½ lemon	Partly bake the pastry blind. Cream the fat and sugar, add the ground rice then beat in the egg and lemon. Bake the filling 20 to 30 minutes at 330° F. Gas No. 3.
Lemon meringue	¾ oz. cornflour, ¼ pint water ½ oz. butter or margarine, grated rind, and juice 1 lemon, 1 oz. sugar, 2 egg-yolks *meringue:* 2 egg-whites 4 oz. caster sugar	Bake the pastry blind. Blend and cook the cornflour with the water as for a mould, adding the fat during cooking. While hot, gradually beat in the lemon juice then add the grated rind, sugar and yolks. Bake the filling for 20 minutes at 350° F. Gas No. 4, then reduce oven heat to 300° F. Gas No. 1. Make the meringue (p. 445), pile it, or pipe it, over the lemon filling, dredge it with caster sugar and dry it in the cool oven till crisp.
Orange	3 oz. caster sugar, 3 oz. butter or margarine, 2 eggs grated rind 1 orange, 1½ oz. cake crumbs 2 teaspoons cornflour mixed with the juice of 1 orange	Cut a piece of pastry from the centre of the plate. Cream the fat and sugar, beat in the egg and orange rind then the cake crumbs, and cornflour blended with the juice. Bake for ¾ hour at 350° F. Gas No. 4, reducing to 320° F. Gas No. 2 when golden.

Name of tart	Recipe for filling	Special method
Treacle	¼ pint golden syrup 2 tablespoons rolled oats or breadcrumbs grated rind and juice ¼ lemon optional, ¼ teaspoon ground ginger	Cut a piece from the centre of the pastry lining. Mix all the ingredients, cover the filling if liked with a lattice-work or cross-pieces of pastry. Bake for 40 to 45 minutes at 350° F. Gas No. 4, reducing the heat as necessary.
Treacle custard	¼ pint golden syrup 1 beaten egg flavouring as above	As above.
West Riding pudding or Welsh cheesecakes	1 to 2 tablespoons jam 4 oz. butter or margarine 4 oz. caster sugar, 2 eggs 4 oz. flour, ½ level teaspoon baking-powder grated rind ½ lemon	Cut a large round from the centre of the pastry lining. Make the filling as a creamed cake mixture. Bake at 350° F. Gas No. 4 for ¾ to 1 hour, reducing the heat when browned. 30 minutes for Welsh cheesecakes.

Tartlets

All the above recipes may be used for tartlets, using half the filling to 3 oz. pastry for 10 to 12 patty- or bun-tins (rolling the pastry very thin). Bake tartlets for 20 to 25 minutes at the same temperature as the large tart.

To bake tartlet cases blind: cut rounds of pastry a size larger than the patty-tins; turn the tins upside down, press the pastry firmly over the tins and prick the upper surface. Bake for 7 to 10 minutes at 350° F. Gas No. 4, then turn them the other way up and drop the pastry shells into the tins to bake the filling.

Tartlets may be served for tea as small cakes or 'pastries'. Fruit tartlets are filled and finished like a fruit flan.

FRUIT FLANS

In England, a fruit flan is an open tart made from a rich, short pastry with a filling of fruit arranged in a decorative pattern and glazed with a thick syrup, apricot glaze or melted jelly; in France where it originated, this kind of tart is called 'une tourte' and 'flan' denotes a custard tart.

To Line a Flan-ring (see Fig. 64)

4 oz. rich short crust (p. 361) will line a 7-inch flan-ring; a sandwich-tin may be used but care is needed to turn the cooked pastry out without breaking it.

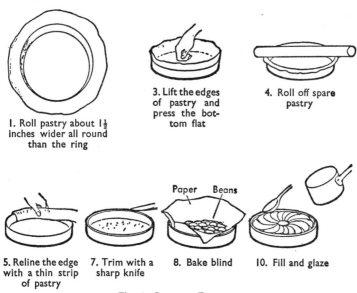

1. Roll pastry about 1½ inches wider all round than the ring

3. Lift the edges of pastry and press the bottom flat

4. Roll off spare pastry

Paper   Beans

5. Reline the edge with a thin strip of pastry

7. Trim with a sharp knife

8. Bake blind

10. Fill and glaze

Fig. 64. LINING A FLAN-RING

1. Roll the pastry to a round about 1½ inches larger all round than the flan-ring, to allow for lining the sides with about ¾ inch margin.
2. Put the flan-ring on a baking-sheet turned upside down to make it easy to remove the cooked pastry shell.
3. Lower the round of pastry into the ring, lift the edges to stand upright and gently smooth out any air-pockets from the centre outwards and up the sides.
4. Roll the rolling-pin across the top of the ring to cut off spare pastry.
5. Roll the trimmings to a long thin sausage-shape and roll this to ⅛ inch thick; cut a strip to line inside the edge of the flan to give a thick, firm layer of pastry that will stay upright during baking.
6. Damp the strip and press it on to the pastry lining, bending its top edge out over the rim; trim the ends to fit and press the join smooth.
7. Trim the edge with a sharp knife held flat against the top of the ring.
8. Prick the bottom and sides and bake the flan blind, see p. 397. When

Fillings for Fruit Flans

Filling	Recipe	Method for filling
Canned fruit, or home-bottled or firm stewed fruit	½ a large can, or 1 medium can firm fruit, ¼ pint syrup from the can 1½ level teaspoons arrowroot sugar and lemon-juice to taste a little colouring to match the fruit if liked	Drain the fruit on a nylon sieve, then arrange it in a neat pattern to fill the flan case completely, more than one kind of fruit may be used. Blend the arrowroot and just bring it to boiling-point as for any starch thickening, taste and add lemon or sugar as necessary, colour it with a few drops of colouring if liked. When the syrup is cool it should be of a coating consistency. Coat the fruit with syrup, basting it from the outside edge to the centre, using a tablespoon. Prick out any bubbles and leave the syrup to set.
Raw fruit, e.g. strawberries or raspberries	¾ lb. sound, large berries, with 4 or 6 smaller, or mis-shapen fruits cut up and cooked in the ¼ pint water with 2 oz. sugar. Use this syrup as above	Prepare and wipe the fruit, arrange it in a pattern in the flan case and coat it as above.
Apple flan	1 lb. cooking apples, 2 to 4 oz. sugar, 1 eating apple or an extra cooking apple, ⅛ teaspoon ground ginger or cinnamon, grated rind ½ lemon, ¼ oz. butter *Glaze:* 2 tablespoons red jelly (preserve) or apricot glaze (p. 448)	Stew the 1 lb. apples with the butter and the flavourings, adding only enough water to prevent it sticking. Add sugar to sweeten and beat the pulp smooth. Put the cooked flan-case on an oven-ware plate and fill it with the pulp. Peel, quarter and slice the eating-apple very thin; arrange the slices in a pattern over the pulp, dredge them thickly with caster sugar and put the flan into a slow oven 325° F. Gas No. 3 for 8-10 minutes to soften the sliced apple and melt the sugar. Warm the jelly or apricot glaze and baste it over the top. Serve the flan cold.

the pastry is firm after 15 to 20 minutes remove the flan-ring as well as the paper and beans or crusts.

9. Finish baking the pastry in a cooler oven, 325° F. Gas No. 2-3 until it is as firm in the centre as at the edge.

10. Cool the flan on a cooling rack, then dish it on a flat, round plate before filling it as the weight of fruit might crack the pastry if it were lifted after filling.

24

COLD SWEETS

Apple or Banana Snow *2 helpings*

2 cooking apples	juice $\frac{1}{2}$ to 1 lemon
or 2 bananas	colouring if liked
1 to 2 tablespoons caster sugar	1 egg-white; cherries to decorate

Bake the apples, without coring them, until quite soft, remove the skins and cores.

Beat the pulp smooth or rub it through a sieve.

Peel and mash the bananas.

Add lemon juice and enough sugar to sweeten the fruit.

Whisk the egg-white to a froth, stir the fruit into it and then whisk all together until it is a stiff foam. A little colouring may be added to tint the foam pale pink or pale green.

Pile the snow into grapefruit glasses and decorate them with pieces of glacé cherry.

Apricot or Prune Jelly *(packet jelly)* *4 helpings*

$\frac{1}{2}$ lb. prunes
or 6 oz. dried apricots $\Big\}\frac{3}{4}$ pint water

$\frac{1}{2}$ inch cinnamon stick   sugar to taste
or rind $\frac{1}{2}$ lemon   lemon juice to taste

1 pint-size packet jelly, lemon for apricots, raspberry for prunes
cherries, angelica or almonds $\Big\}$ for decoration
mock cream

Soak the prunes or apricots with the water, cinnamon or lemon rind, overnight.

Stew the fruit till very soft, drain off the juice into a measure and at once drop the jelly squares into it and stir them till dissolved.

Remove prune-stones and chop the fruit with a stainless knife, keeping 3 or 4 whole fruit for decoration.

Stir the fruit into the jelly, sweeten it and add lemon juice.

Turn it into a mould or grapefruit glasses and leave till quite cold and set.

Decorate with prunes or apricots, with cherries or almonds to replace their stones, and diamonds of angelica for leaves, and with mock cream.

Fruit Condé *2-3 helpings*

½ pint rice mould (p. 372)	2 to 3 halves of dessert or
or tinned rice pudding	canned peaches, or pears or
flavouring of cinnamon,	6 to 9 halves of apricots or
orange or lemon rind or	large plums
vanilla essence	2 tablespoons evaporated milk

Glaze: 2 tablespoons sieved jam or apricot glaze (p. 448).
Decoration: Angelica and mock cream (p. 452).

Cook the rice with the flavouring or add vanilla to the tinned rice pudding.

Prepare the apricot glaze or heat and sieve the jam.

Stir the evaporated milk into the cold rice mould and half fill the grapefruit glasses with the rice.

Arrange the fruit on the rice, coat the fruit with warm jam or glaze. Put them in a cold place to chill.

Decorate them with leaves of angelica and a border of mock cream.

Fruit Fool *3 helpings*

	⌈ 1 lb. soft or stone fruit, fresh or canned
½ pint fruit purée from ⎨	2-4 tablespoons water
	⌊ *or* 4 tablespoons syrup from the can
sugar to taste	¼ pint egg custard sauce (p. 374)
lemon juice if needed	*or* 1 bottle yoghurt
to taste	*or* ¼ pint evaporated milk, chilled

1. Prepare and stew the fruit to a pulp.
2. Rub it through a nylon sieve and sweeten it and add lemon juice as needed.
3. If yoghurt is used omit lemon juice and make the fruit very sweet to counteract the acid flavour of yoghurt.

If evaporated milk is used, whip the chilled milk till it is slightly thick and frothy.

Cool the custard.
4. Mix the cold custard or the yoghurt or evaporated milk gently into the fruit purée; taste the fool and re-sweeten if necessary.
5. Serve it in individual glasses or bowls.

Fruit Mould, soft, to serve in glasses   4 *helpings*

1 pint fruit purée from $\begin{cases} \text{1 lb. fruit, fresh or canned} \\ \frac{1}{4} \text{ pint water or juice from the can} \end{cases}$

1½ oz. seed tapioca, sago, semolina *or* 1 oz. cornflour or arrowroot
Lemon juice to taste   sugar to taste

1. Choose well-flavoured fruit such as raspberries, currants, blackberries or apricots.
2. Stew the fruit in the water till pulpy, and drain off the juice through a nylon sieve.
3. Cook the cereal in the fruit juice as for a milk mould, p. 372.
4. Sieve the fruit and stir it into the hot, cooked cereal.
5. Sweeten the mixture, add lemon juice if needed.
6. Cool the mixture a little then dish it in individual glasses or bowls.
7. Sprinkle the top of each with caster sugar to prevent a skin forming.
8. If possible serve it with cream (whipped or 'mock').

Fruit Salad   4-5 *helpings*

1 lb. of a good mixture of fruit in season, including canned fruit
½ pint syrup from canned fruit, *or* water with 4 oz. sugar
rind and juice of ½ to 1 lemon   1 bay leaf or clove
                                  or ½-inch cinnamon stick

1. Choose a mixture of fruit with a variety of colours, textures and flavours.
2. Prepare fresh fruit in the usual way, see p. 386. Rub apples with the cut lemon as soon as they are peeled.
3. Put the sugar and water in a saucepan, add to it any apple or pear peelings, stones, inner skin of oranges and a few strips of orange or lemon rind, removed with a vegetable peeler, with other flavouring as liked.
   Bring the syrup to boiling-point, put on the lid and leave it to infuse for 20 minutes.
4. Prepare the rest of the fruit and cut it in neat pieces, slicing apples very thinly.
   Suit the size of the fruit to the method of serving, cutting them rather small for grapefruit glasses but larger for a large bowl.
5. Put the fruit in a mixing bowl and pour the hot syrup over it. Leave it to cool, covered. Serve in one bowl or in individual glasses.
   Most hard fruits taste better if kept in syrup overnight, but soft berries and bananas lose their colour and become pulpy and should be added just before serving.

Fruit in Jelly (*packet jelly*)   *5-6 helpings*

Time to set   1 hour in chilling compartment or 2 hours in refrigerator

> To a 1 pint jelly, about ½ pint fruit, fresh or canned
> Lemon juice to taste

1. Choose a mixture of fruit or 1 or 2 kinds only, cut them into rather small pieces, so that they are still recognizable and attractive.
   Drain canned fruit.
2. Melt the jelly square by putting it into a pint measure and filling this to ¾ pint with boiling syrup from the can or boiling water. Add lemon juice and cool it.
3. *If there is time* arrange fruit to form a pattern in the bottom of the mould, cool a little jelly on ice and just cover the fruit with it; leave it to set.
   Add half the fruit and half the jelly, leave this to set then add the other half of each. When the mould feels cold put it in the refrigerator.
   If there is plenty of time fruit can all be arranged, one layer at a time, allowing the jelly of each layer to set before putting in the next.
   If time is short, divide the fruit between 5 to 6 grapefruit glasses and cover it with cool, liquid jelly.
4. Serve the jelly with mock cream or whipped cream.
   To turn out the jelly, dip the mould in water uncomfortably hot to the hand, invert the dish over it and holding tight with both hands give one sharp jerk to loosen the jelly.

Honeycomb Mould (*packet jelly*)   *4 helpings*

> 1 pint-size packet jelly
> ¼ pint water
>
> custard from { ½ pint milk
>   2 egg-yolks
>
> 2 egg-whites

1. Boil the water in a small saucepan, drop the jelly squares into it and stir them till they dissolve.
2. Make custard sauce with the egg-yolks and milk, see p. 374. Cool both liquids.
3. When the jelly is beginning to get syrupy and the custard is cold, whisk the eggs to a stiff foam.
4. Whisk the jelly a little, whisk into it the cold custard.
5. Fold the stiffly whipped whites into the mixture and turn it into a rinsed, pint mould or into individual glasses, leave it to set.
6. Turn out the pint mould as for Fruit in Jelly.

Swiss Jelly (*packet jelly*)   *4 helpings*

$\frac{3}{4}$ pint fruit juice from canned fruit
or water

1 pint packet jelly	a little lemon juice
$\frac{1}{8}$ pint evaporated milk	$\frac{1}{3}$ Swiss roll

1. Rinse a pint-size plain mould or basin with cold water.
2. Dissolve the jelly square in half the fruit juice (hot) or hot water, add the lemon and the other half of the liquid cold. Cool the jelly.
3. Slice the Swiss roll thinly.
4. Pour a little of the cool jelly into the bottom of the mould and put a slice of Swiss roll on it; dip slices of Swiss roll in jelly and arrange them round the sides of the mould, leave them for the jelly to set.
5. Whip the evaporated milk, fold it into the cool, liquid jelly with any trimmings of Swiss roll and pour the mixture carefully into the mould.
6. Leave it to set and turn it out as for Fruit in Jelly.

Summer Fruit Pudding   *4 helpings*

1 lb. soft fruit with a bright colour and good flavour,
  e.g. currants, raspberries, blackberries or damsons
$\frac{1}{4}$ pint water; sugar to sweeten
stale bread or sponge cakes $\frac{1}{2}$ pint cold custard to serve with it.

1. Stew the fruit with the sugar and water till soft; there should be plenty of good juice
2. Line a 1-pint size basin neatly and closely with thin slices of bread, or sponge cake and cut a round to fit the top.
3. Pour the hot, stewed fruit into the lined basin, putting a layer of scraps of bread in the middle and covering it with the round of bread.
4. Put a saucer and a 2 lb. weight on top and leave the pudding till cold. Turn it out.

Trifle   *4 helpings*

3 to 4 small sponge cakes, or 4 slices ($\frac{1}{2}$-$\frac{3}{4}$ inch thick) Swiss roll
jam
$\frac{1}{4}$ to $\frac{1}{3}$ large can fruit or its equivalent
about $\frac{1}{4}$ pint fruit juice, a little lemon juice to taste
if liked, 1 to 2 tablespoons sherry

To coat: $\frac{3}{4}$ pint cornflour custard, p. 375, or powder custard
To decorate: glacé cherries or almonds or neat pieces of fruit
  angelica and whipped or mock cream

1. Split sponge cakes, spread them with jam and cut them in neat pieces to fit into 1 large or 4 individual bowls or glasses.

2. Add lemon juice and sherry, and sugar if needed, to the juice and baste this over the cake. Arrange the fruit all over the top, making the surface flat.

3. Leave the trifle to soak, covered, for at least ½ hour.

4. Make the custard and cool it without allowing a skin to form; it should be thick enough to coat the back of the spoon but should just settle to its own level. Coat the trifles and leave them to chill.

5. Arrange a neat decoration on a plate, and whip the cream.

6. Pipe cream round the edge and in a pattern on top and decorate the trifle.

COLD SWEETS USING GELATINE

Rules for using Powdered Gelatine

1. *Measure the gelatine accurately*, 4 level teaspoons = ½ oz.
   If the gelatine is packed in envelopes make sure that the envelope contains ½ oz. or follow the manufacturers' recipes.

2. *Allow ½ oz. gelatine to 1 pint* as a rule, but for acid juice such as lemon juice, or in hot weather, or if there is no refrigerator and time is short, allow ¾ oz. to 1 pint.

3. *Dissolve the gelatine* in warm water by heating it gently, without boiling it, and stirring it with a bright metal spoon, so that it is easy to see, in the spoon, if all the gelatine is dissolved. Boiling spoils the flavour of gelatine and reduces its setting power.

4. *If the jelly is made with milk* the gelatine must be dissolved in ⅛ pint (4 tablespoons) water for each ½ oz. and added while hot to the milk mixture. The simplest way to do this is to put the measured water in a small basin, stand the basin in boiling water then stir in the gelatine and continue stirring till it is all dissolved. If this strong solution is not stirred thoroughly into the milk mixture at once, it is likely to set in 'ropes' which will not set the mould.

5. *Pour a gelatine mixture into moulds* when it is cold and only just liquid.
   To cool the mixture stand the bowl in a colander, pack ice cubes round it and stir it gently and often; if ice is not available stand the mixing bowl in cold water and allow longer time.

6. *Moulds for jellies.* For large moulds metal is best as, being a good conductor of heat it is quickly warmed in hot water which melts a little jelly and so allows it to slip out.

o

All jellies may be served in individual glasses or waxed paper trifle cases or paper soufflé cases.

7. *To set jellies.* Gelatine sets quickly at low temperatures and more slowly at room temperature, therefore allow ½ to ¾ hour in the chilling or ice compartment, 1 hour in the main cabinet of a refrigerator or 2 to 3 hours in a cool larder. Jellies kept overnight in a refrigerator will get too stiff and will need 1 hour at room temperature to make them soft and palatable.

8. *To turn out a jelly,* loosen the top edge all round with a finger, dip the mould into water uncomfortably hot to the hand, then invert the serving dish over it, grasp both firmly with both hands and give a sharp jerk to loosen the jelly.

Orange or Lemon Jelly   *3 helpings*

Orange:	⅜ pint water	*Lemon:*	½ pint water
	rind 2 oranges		rind 2 lemons
	2–3 oz. sugar		3 oz. sugar
	½ oz. gelatine		½ oz. gelatine
	⅜ pint orange juice		¼ pint lemon juice
	juice 1 lemon		

Optional decoration: Whipped cream or 'mock' cream (p. 452), leaves of angelica

1. Scrub the fruit and roll them hard to free the juice.

2. Peel the rind off with a vegetable peeler to include no bitter, white pith.

3. Dissolve the gelatine and sugar and infuse the rinds in the water over gentle heat: do not allow it to boil. Put on the lid and keep the liquid warm for ¼ hour to extract flavour from the rinds; then cool it.

4. Squeeze the fruit juice, add it to the gelatine mixture and strain the whole.

5. Taste, and sweeten the jelly if necessary; colour it if liked with a few drops of orange colouring.

6. Mould the jelly when it is beginning to get syrupy, chill it till set.

7. Turn out and decorate the jelly with piped cream and leaves of angelica if liked.

GELATINE MOULDS WITH MILK, EGGS AND FRUIT PURÉE

Basic Recipe *4 helpings*

1 pint milk, or custard or fruit purée
sugar to sweeten, flavouring
½ oz. gelatine in ⅛ pint (4 tablespoons) water

Some Recipes for Egg and Milk Moulds

Name of mould	Variations of recipe	Variations of method
Milk jelly	Flavour milk strongly with cocoa, coffee or vanilla, add dissolved gelatine to slightly warm milk.	Dissolve instant coffee or boil cocoa in a very little milk.
Chocolate 'Cream'	2 oz. block chocolate or 2 tablespoons cocoa, 1 pint milk, 2 eggs, vanilla essence, sugar to sweeten, whipped cream to decorate.	Dissolve chocolate or boil cocoa in a little milk, make custard with ½ pint, add cold milk, sweeten and flavour, add gelatine. Use individual glasses.
Egg-lemon jelly	¾ pint water, ¼ pint lemon juice, rind 2 lemons, 6 oz. sugar, 2 eggs. Optional: omit ¼ pint water, add ¼ pint sherry.	Peel lemons with vegetable peeler. Dissolve gelatine and sugar and infuse the lemon rind in the water. Make a custard with this liquid and the eggs, cool it and stir in the lemon juice and sherry.
Fruit mould	¾ pint fruit purée from 1 lb. fruit (fresh, bottled or canned), ¼ pint water or juice, sugar and lemon juice to taste. ¼ pint evaporated milk, or cream or egg custard.	Sweeten the fruit purée and add lemon juice to taste, dissolve and add gelatine, cool the mixture. Fold in the cream, half-whipped, or the evaporated milk whipped till thick, or the egg custard, cold.
Honeycomb mould	1 pint milk, 2 eggs, 1 oz. sugar, flavouring of vanilla or coffee *or* rind and juice 2 lemons, 4 oz. sugar.	Make a custard with ½ pint milk, egg-yolks (grated lemon rind) and 1 oz. sugar, add (extra sugar) flavouring and cold milk. When cold fold in lemon juice and stiffly whipped egg-whites.

If a curdled effect is liked the custard may be brought just to boiling-point and the mixture may be moulded warm.

General Method

1. Prepare the liquid ingredients, for example, make custard or stew and sieve fruit and cool them, or whip evaporated milk, or ½ whip cream.
2. Mix the cooled liquids.
3. Dissolve the gelatine in the water (see note on dissolving gelatine) and stir the hot solution into the cooled liquid.
4. Lastly whip and fold in egg-whites.

Lemon Sponge   *4-6 helpings*

⅛ pint (4 tablespoons) lemon juice
½ pint water   2 oz. sugar
rind 2 lemons   2 egg-whites
½ oz. gelatine

1. Dissolve the gelatine and sugar and infuse the lemon rind in the water over low heat, leave this mixture covered for ¼ hour. Strain it and leave it till quite cold and beginning to thicken; to cool it quickly stand the basin over ice.
2. Add the strained lemon juice and the whisked egg-whites.
3. Whisk all together till quite stiff and either mould the jelly or pile it in a glass dish a little at a time, whisking between additions.

Lemon or 'Milanese' Soufflé   *3-4 helpings*

2 eggs   ¼ pint double cream or evaporated milk
2 oz. caster sugar   ¼ oz. (2 level teaspoons) gelatine
1 lemon   2 tablespoons water

To decorate ⎰ whipped cream ('mock' or fresh) 2 to 3 tablespoons
              ⎨ leaves of angelica
              ⎱ optional, crystallized violet

1. Firmly tie a double band of greaseproof paper round a ½ pint china or glass soufflé case, so that the paper stands 2 inches above the rim of the case; or use individual serving glasses with no paper band.
2. Separate yolks from whites of eggs, grate the lemon rind finely on to the yolks.
3. Put the yolks, sugar, lemon rind and juice in a mixing bowl set over a saucepan quarter full of boiling water on very low top heat.
4. Whisk the yolk mixture steadily till it is slightly thick, pale yellow and foamy.
5. Remove it from the hot water and whisk it till cool.

6. Dissolve the gelatine in the cold water, in a basin standing in the hot water in the saucepan.

7. Whip the cream till the whisk just makes a trail, or the evaporated milk till thick and frothy, add this to the egg-yolk mixture, then stir in the hot gelatine solution.

Whisk the egg-whites stiff.

8. With a tablespoon fold the whisked whites lightly into the egg mixture until it is just smooth and frothy.

9. Pour the mixture at once into the case or glasses. Set it in the refrigerator for 1 hour or in the chilling compartment for $\frac{1}{2}$ hour.

10. Decorate the top.

Orange Soufflé

Make this exactly as Lemon Soufflé using orange rind and juice instead of lemon.

Cold Chocolate or Coffee Soufflé

$\frac{1}{4}$ pint milk	1–2 oz. sugar
2 oz. sweetened chocolate	$\frac{1}{4}$ oz. (2 level teaspoons) gelatine
or $\frac{1}{2}$ oz. cocoa	2 tablespoons water or cold coffee
or 4 level teaspoons instant coffee	$\frac{1}{4}$ pint double cream
powder	or evaporated milk
$\frac{1}{4}$ teaspoon vanilla essence	2 eggs

To decorate: chopped nuts, chocolate vermicelli, grated chocolate and/or whipped fresh or 'mock' cream (p. 452)

1. Prepare the soufflé case as for Lemon Soufflé.

2. Melt block chocolate in 1 tablespoon of milk over low heat; or blend cocoa with a little milk and boil it; or dissolve coffee powder in a little hot milk.

3. Add the rest of the milk and 1 oz. sugar.

Separate yolks from whites of the eggs.

4. With the yolks, milk and sugar make a custard (p. 374) and at once strain it into a mixing bowl, add vanilla and more sugar if needed and cool it.

5. Dissolve the gelatine in the water or coffee and stir it, hot, into the cool custard, cool it again till beginning to thicken.

6. Whip the cream, whisk the egg-whites and fold them in as for Lemon Soufflé.

7. Pour the mixture into the case and chill it.

8. Decorate it when set.

25

BREAD AND YEAST MIXTURES

Good home-made bread is easy to make and, contrary to popular belief, it need not take very long; the whole operation can, in fact, be completed in 2 hours, of which only 20 minutes is spent on the actual handling.

The most important thing to remember is that *yeast 'works' best, that is it produces new cells and gives off carbon dioxode, at 80° F.* In order to arrive at this temperature, all the ingredients may be warmed very slightly or, if time is short, the flour may be used at room temperature (about 60° F.) and the water at blood heat (98° to 99° F.); a suitably warm place must be selected for the rising period, such as the plate-warming compartment of a cooker or the plate rack above it, and the baking-tins must be kept slightly warm to the touch while the dough remains cool and clammy feeling.

If time is very short the amount of yeast may be increased by half in each recipe and the rising time curtailed.

Dried baker's yeast may be used in all the following recipes (see p. 162).

Basic Recipe for Bread   *2 loaves of about 10 oz. weight*

Oven 450° F. Gas No. 8-9
Time to rise   40 to 50 minutes; *time to bake*   35 minutes

> 1 lb. flour, 'strong' plain *or* wholemeal *or* ½ wholemeal, ½ plain
> 2 level teaspoons salt   ½ oz. yeast
> ½ pint water

1. Warm the baking-tins, grease them lightly and dredge them with flour.
2. Sieve the flour (slightly warmed) with the salt into a warm bowl.
3. Boil ¼ to ⅓ of the water and add it to the cold remainder.
4. Add 2 teaspoons of the water to the yeast and soften it to a cream, then stir in half the water.
5. Make a deep hole or 'well' in the flour, pour the yeast and water into it, rinse the yeast basin with the other half of the water and add it.
6. Mix with the hand to make a soft, elastic dough, using more water if necessary. Beat the dough hard with a clawing movement until, in 2 or 3 minutes, the fingertips are clear of dough (Fig. 65).

Turn it out of the bowl on to a floured board or table-top and knead it.

To knead bread, lift one end of the dough and rub it heavily over the other end, using the base of the palm; keep turning the dough and repeating this movement vigorously for about 5 minutes. When kneaded enough the dough will be most elastic and smooth (Fig. 65).

8. Divide the dough and shape 2 loaves:

For a coburg loaf, knead the dough lightly to a ball, cut a deep cross with a sharp knife.

For a cottage loaf, cut off ¼, shape one small and one larger ball: with one finger make a hole in the larger ball, pull out the small ball till it is pear shaped and press the pointed end into the hole. Flour the handle of a wooden spoon and push it right through both balls, then pull it out sharply.

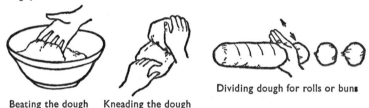

Beating the dough   Kneading the dough   Dividing dough for rolls or buns

Fig. 65. MAKING YEAST MIXTURES

For a tin-loaf, knead the dough edges to the middle, into a roll, then press the ends of the roll to the middle. Drop the oblong dough smooth side up into the tin, do not touch the top but allow it to fill out the corners as it rises.

9. Set the bread to rise at 80° F. for 40 to 45 minutes or until the loaves have doubled their size.

10. *Finishing the crust:* for a soft crust brush the top with flour;
for a crisp crust do nothing to it;
for a hard crust brush the top with cold water.

11. Bake the bread in the upper half of the hot oven.

12. *To test the bread when baked,* turn it out of the tin and knock the bottom crust, if it is done the crust will be hard and will sound hollow.

13. If the loaves are not quite done leave them out of the tins, set them on their sides and put them back in the oven to harden the bottom crust.

14. Cool the bread on a wire rack.

Note. Wholemeal bread may have ½ oz. brown sugar and ½ oz. fat added for a short, 'nutty' result.

Bloomer   Coburg   Boat shape   Huffkin   Bap

Fig. 66. LOAVES

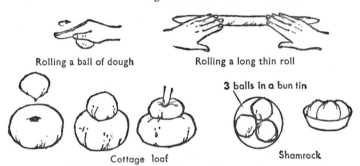

Rolling a ball of dough   Rolling a long thin roll

3 balls in a bun tin

Cottage loaf   Shamrock

Fig. 67. SHAPING ROLLS FROM BALLS OF DOUGH

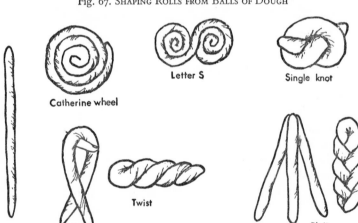

Catherine wheel   Letter S   Single knot

Twist   Plait

Fig. 68. SHAPING ROLLS FROM LONG, THIN ROLLS OF DOUGH

Hard Rolls (Figs. 67, 68)

Oven and Recipe as for bread

Time to rise 20 to 25 minutes; *time to bake* 20 minutes

Warm and grease a baking-tray.

Mix and knead the dough as for bread.

Divide ½ lb. dough into 8 pieces.

To shape rolls: small cottage, coburg and tin 'loaves' can be shaped as bread, for other quickly-made shapes roll each piece of dough to a long, finger thick 'sausage' (Figs. 67, 68):

> tie a single knot
> tie a double knot
> coil the roll like a catherine wheel
> coil the roll in an S shape
> twist the ends like a skein of wool
> *or* cut the roll in 3, roll the pieces thin and plait them.

MILK BREAD

Basic Recipe

Oven 450° F. Gas No. 8-9

Rising time ¾ to 1 hour ⎫ *or single rising as for bread*
Proving 15 to 20 minutes ⎭

1 lb. plain flour, strong if possible	½ oz. yeast
2 level teaspoons salt	½ pint milk
1 to 2 oz. lard or other fat	1 egg (optional)

1. Grease the tins or baking-tray.
2. Make and knead the dough as for bread.
3. *Rising.* This dough may be shaped before rising as for bread but this softer, richer dough keeps a better texture and shape if set to rise in the mixing bowl before being shaped.

For this long method, after beating the dough till it leaves the fingers, draw it up and grease the mixing bowl below it; smooth the top of the dough and grease it also to keep the dough from forming a dry crust.

Cover the bowl with a plate and set it to rise at 80° F. until it has doubled in size.

4. Turn the dough on to a floured surface, knead it as for bread, shape it into loaves or rolls and set it again in the warm place to 'prove', that is to rise again until doubled in size (Fig. 65).

The kneading after rising is called 'knocking back'.

Bake milk loaves or milk rolls as for their bread equivalent.

Glaze for Milk Bread and Rolls

> For a short but not shiny crust, brush with melted margarine after baking.
> For a brown, shiny glaze brush with beaten egg before baking.

For a sweet, crisp glaze for fruit bread, brush after baking with a solution of 1 tablespoon sugar in one tablespoon milk, then put back in the oven for 2 or 3 minutes to dry.

For soft rolls, dust them with flour before baking and cool them wrapped in a cloth.

VARIATIONS OF MILK BREAD RECIPE

Currant bread   Add 1 oz. sugar and 2-4 oz. currants (or sultanas), shape into 2 loaves, bake in tins, use a sugar glaze.

Cornish Splits   Omit the egg. Divide 1 lb. into 18 to 20 and shape as balls, set them close together, flatten them a little. Glaze with fat after baking.

Dinner rolls   Divide 1 lb. into 16, shape fancy rolls (see Figs. 67, 68, 69). Brush with egg.

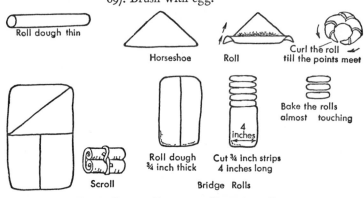

Roll dough thin

Horseshoe   Roll   Curl the roll till the points meet

Roll dough ¾ inch thick   Cut ¾ inch strips 4 inches long   Bake the rolls almost touching

Scroll   Bridge Rolls

Fig. 69. SHAPING ROLLS FROM ROLLED-OUT DOUGH

Bridge rolls   Roll the dough to ¾-inch thick oblong: cut it into 3-inch wide strips and then into ¾-inch wide fingers, roll the fingers a little and taper the ends. Put the rolls close together on the baking-tray so that as they rise the sides touch and so keep the side crusts soft (Fig. 69). Do not separate to cool them and cool them wrapped in a clean cloth.

'Huffkins' (Kent)   Divide 1 lb. into 12 to 16 and shape oval, flat cakes, flour them, then make a hole in the middle with one finger (Fig. 66).

Scots Baps   Divide as for huffkins but make the flat cakes round, flour them and make 2 holes in each.
Cool huffkins and baps in a cloth (Fig. 66).

SWEET DOUGH FOR BUNS

Basic Recipe

Oven 400° to 425° F. Gas No. 7
Rising time 1 hour + 15 minutes; *baking time* 15 to 30 minutes

½ lb. strong plain flour	1 oz. margarine or cooking fat
½ level teaspoon salt	1 egg
1 oz. sugar	scant ¼ pint milk
½ oz. yeast	(optional) ½ level teaspoon mixed spice

Make the dough, beat it, set it to rise, knock it back and prove it as for Milk bread. The shaping and baking can be varied as follows.

VARIATIONS OF BASIC RECIPE

Lancashire Teacakes   Shape the dough into 4 flat, round cakes. Bake them on a greased baking-tray for 20 to 25 minutes. Glaze them with melted margarine after baking.

Yorkshire Teacakes   Add 2 oz. currants or sultanas and 1 oz. chopped peel. Shape as Lancashire Teacakes.

Glaze after baking with sugar and milk glaze.

Serve teacakes split and buttered, fresh from the oven or toasted.

Plain Currant Buns   Add 2 oz. currants and if liked ¼ teaspoon mixed spice. Shape 8 round balls, bake them 15 to 20 minutes, glaze them after baking with sugar and milk.

Hot Cross Buns   Knead in 1 oz. sugar, 1 oz. fat, 3 oz. currants or sultanas after the first rising, shape 8 round balls, mark these with a cross before proving. The cross may be made with a knife or with narrow strips of short pastry.

Glaze the buns after baking with sugar and milk.

Dough Cake   Grease a 7- to 8-inch round cake tin; use ¾ oz. yeast in the dough. Knead into the dough after rising, 2 oz. brown sugar, 2 oz. margarine, 6 to 8 oz. dried fruit, 1 oz. chopped peel. Prove for 20 to 30 minutes. Bake for ¾ to 1 hour, reducing the heat to 350° F. Gas No. 4 after 20 to 30 minutes when well browned. Ice if liked with thin glacé icing, p. 450.

*Chelsea Buns
and Swedish
Tea Ring*

Make the dough with 1½ eggs and 3 tablespoons milk. Prepare separately 2 oz. margarine, 2 oz. caster sugar, 2 oz. currants or sultanas, ½ level teaspoon spice.

After the dough has risen, knock it back and roll it to a rectangle, ½ inch thick; spread the butter in pats over ⅔ of it and fold as for flaky pastry; roll it to a 10-inch square. Mix spice, sugar and fruit and spread this over the dough. Damp the edges and roll the dough tightly, pressing the long edge firmly.

For Chelsea Buns. With a knife dipped in warm water cut 10 to 12 slices, set these close together on edge in a greased roasting-tin or Yorkshire pudding tin

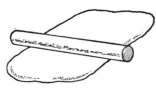

Roll the dough to a rectangle. Add fat as for flaky pastry. Fold and roll again

Spread the dough with sugar, spice and currants and roll it up

Cut I inch slices and stand them on the cut side

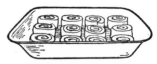

Pack the buns close together in a deep tin

Fig. 70. SHAPING CHELSEA BUNS

about 11 by 9 inches. Prove and bake them and while warm ice them with thin glacé icing made from 3 oz. icing sugar.

For Swedish Tea Ring. Lift the roll on to a greased baking-tray, and curl it into a ring. Join the ends of the ring firmly together. With scissors cut ⅔ through the ring at ½-inch intervals; press the strips alternately inwards to the centre and outwards. Prove 20 to 30 minutes, bake 25 to 30 minutes.

While warm ice with glacé icing as for Chelsea Buns.

Doughnuts *8-10*

Deep frying fat at 330° F.
Frying time 15 minutes for each panful

$\frac{1}{4}$ lb. strong plain flour	$\frac{1}{4}$ oz. yeast
$\frac{1}{2}$ oz. caster sugar	$\frac{1}{2}$ egg
$\frac{1}{2}$ oz. margarine	2 tablespoons milk

2 tablespoons caster sugar and $\frac{1}{4}$ teaspoon cinnamon to roll them in

1. Warm the milk to blood heat; cream the yeast with a few drops of it and mix the beaten egg with yeast and milk.
2. Mix flour and sugar and rub in the margarine.
3. Mix all to a soft but not sticky dough and set it to rise for 1 hour.
4. Knock the dough back, roll it out to $\frac{1}{3}$ inch thick, cut it into rounds with a $2\frac{1}{4}$- to $2\frac{1}{2}$-inch round cutter and cut a round out of the centre with a $\frac{3}{4}$-inch cutter.
5. Put the doughnuts on a greased baking-sheet and prove them for 15 minutes.
6. When the fat is at 330° F. or when it will brown bread in 50 seconds, lower the doughnuts in one at a time, pausing a minute before adding another, adding only as many as can be turned easily. Keep them frying slowly and turning frequently until they are golden and crisp.
7. Drain them over the fat then lift them into the caster sugar and cinnamon.

Babas or Savarin *4-6 helpings*

Oven 425° F. Gas No. 6-7
Baking time 15 to 30 minutes; *rising time* 40 minutes + 20 minutes

$\frac{1}{4}$ lb. strong plain flour	$\frac{1}{4}$ oz. yeast
1 teaspoon caster sugar	$2\frac{1}{2}$ oz. butter or margarine
2 small eggs	1 oz. currants
3 to 4 tablespoons milk	

Syrup: 4 oz. granulated sugar } *or* juice from tinned fruit
$\frac{1}{2}$ pint water
juice $\frac{1}{2}$ lemon   suitable flavouring of rum or orange or lemon rind

1. Sieve the warmed flour with the sugar. Grease the tins.
2. Cream the yeast with a little of the warm milk, mix it with the rest of the milk and the beaten egg.

3. Beat the liquid into the flour to make a thick batter, beat this for 5 minutes or until it leaves the fingertips clean.

4. Cover the bowl and leave the batter to rise for about 40 minutes.

5. Cut the butter into small pats and beat it with the currants into the batter.

6. Pour the batter into 6 to 8 large dariole tins or one ring-mould; the tins should be only half-full.

7. Prove the batter until doubled in size.

8. Bake the babas in small tins for 15 to 20 minutes, the savarin in one tin for 30 minutes until very light and crisp on top.

9. Turn them out of the tin and prick them all over with a skewer, then baste them with the hot syrup.

10. Serve them cold with whipped cream or 'mock' cream or with fruit salad.

26

SCONES, CAKES

Scones are very plain, very light cakes which take their name from the town of Scone in Scotland. They were probably all cooked originally on a girdle over a peat fire; nowadays, although girdle scones are still made, scones are usually baked in a hot oven. They are meant to be eaten with butter, preferably hot from the oven and certainly newly baked or toasted.

Although they should be very light it is important that too much baking-powder should not be added as it leaves a dry or acid taste due to a residue of tartrate or phosphate. Very good scones may be made using sour or butter-milk with equal quantities of bicarbonate of soda and cream or tartar instead of baking-powder. The lactic acid takes the place of some of the acid in baking-powder and has the added advantage of softening the gluten in the flour.

Basic Recipe for Scones   *12 scones*

Oven 450° F. Gas No. 8-9
Baking time   7 to 10 minutes

½ lb. plain flour
2½ to 3 level teaspoons baking-powder ⎫with fresh milk

or ½ lb. plain flour
1 level teaspoon bicarbonate of soda ⎫ with sour milk or
1 level teaspoon cream of tartar ⎭ butter-milk

or ½ lb. self-raising flour
½ level teaspoon salt
1-2 oz. fat
1-2 oz. sugar (optional)
¼ pint milk
1 egg (optional)

General Method

1. Heat the oven; lightly grease a baking-tray or heat it later.
2. Sieve the flour with other powder ingredients.
3. Rub in the fat, aerating the flour at the same time.

4. Make a deep 'well' in the flour, pour in almost all the liquid and mix to a soft, spongy dough with a palette knife.

5. On a floured surface, knead the dough very lightly until it is just smooth. Divide the ½ lb. into two and lightly knead each piece to a ball; flatten each to ¾ inch thick and cut each round into 6 triangles.

6. Heat the baking-tray in the oven.

7. Brush the scones with beaten egg for a glossy crust or with flour for a soft one.

8. If possible leave the scones to rest for 15 to 20 minutes before baking them (see Experiments, p. 151).

9. Bake the scones at the top of the hot oven until well-risen and brown.

Kind of scone		Variations of basic recipe
Sweet:	Brown	Use all wholemeal or ½ wholemeal and ½ white flour.
	Fruit	Add 1 to 2 oz. chopped dates, or currants or sultanas.
	Treacle	Add 1 to 2 tablespoons treacle or syrup and if liked ½ teaspoon ground ginger.
Savoury:	Cheese	Add 1½ to 2 oz. grated cheese, brush the tops with egg or milk. Cheese scones cut in fingers can be used for savoury sandwiches.

Girdle Scones   *12-16 scones*

To cook them: a girdle or solid electric hot-plate
Cooking time   12 to 15 minutes

Basic scone recipe with the higher proportion of baking-powder.

1. Clean the girdle or hot-plate by scouring it with salt and clean, soft paper then dusting off all the salt.

2. Heat the girdle on moderate heat the hot-plate at low.

3. Make the scone dough a little firmer than for oven-scones.

4. Divide it as before but roll the rounds to ¼ inch thick and cut them in 6 to 8 triangles; dust them with flour.

5. Test the heat of the girdle or hot-plate by holding the hand ½ inch above it, for the correct heat the palm should feel a comfortably warm glow.

6. Put the scones on the dry, hot surface one at a time, rather slowly and cook them for 7 to 8 minutes on each side.

When ready they should be golden-brown on both sides and slightly springy when pinched.

Serve them hot, if possible, in a folded table-napkin.

Scotch Pancakes or Dropped Scones *24-30 scones*

To cook them: a girdle or solid electric hot-plate
Cooking time 5 to 6 minutes

> ½ lb. flour, self-raising, with 1 level teaspoon baking-powder
> *or* ½ lb. plain flour with 3 level teaspoons baking-powder
> 2 oz. caster sugar or golden syrup
> 2 oz. fat 1 egg
> about ½ pint milk

1. Clean and heat the girdle as for Girdle Scones.
2. Have ready a piece of raw meat-fat impaled on a skewer for greasing the girdle.
3. Sieve the flour with the dry ingredients, rub in the fat.

Add the egg and ¾ of the milk, and mix all to a thick batter adding as much milk as needed. The batter should just settle to its own level.
4. Test the girdle as for girdle scones and grease it; the grease should give off a very light haze.
5. With a tablespoon pour neat rounds of batter, rather widely spaced, on to the girdle.
6. The batter should rise and, when the bubbles break the surface, the scones must be turned with a palette knife and cooked on the other side. Both sides should be golden and the scones should be spongy.

Keep them warm in a clean tea-towel till all are cooked.

Baking-Powder Rolls *8-12 rolls*

Oven 450° F. Gas No. 8-9
Baking time 10 to 15 minutes

> ½ lb. flour, self-raising
> *or* ½ lb. plain flour and 2½ level teaspoons baking-powder
> 1 level teaspoon salt   ¼ pint milk, milk and water, or
> ½ to 1 oz. margarine   water

These are made like scones but shaped like milk rolls.

Divide into 8 or 12 pieces, roll these into round balls or into finger-thick rolls which can be coiled, knotted or twisted (see Figs. 67, 68). Brush the rolls with beaten egg or milk, or, for soft rolls brush them with flour. Bake them on a hot, dry baking-tray until they are brown and crisp.

Norfolk or Suffolk Rusks

Oven 400° F. Gas No. 7
Baking time 15 to 20 minutes with extra time to dry

½ lb. plain flour
2 level teaspoons baking-powder } *or* ½ lb. self-raising flour
½ level teaspoon salt   1 oz. sugar (optional)
2 to 4 oz. margarine or butter   1 egg
a little milk if necessary

1. Grease a baking-sheet.
2. Sieve the flour and other powdered ingredients.
3. Rub in the fat.
4. Mix a dry dough, rather softer than short pastry, using a very little milk if needed.
5. Knead the dough very lightly and roll it to ½ inch thick. Cut it in 1½- inch to 2-inch rounds.
6. Bake them until they are risen and golden-brown.
7. Take them from the oven and split them in halves by pulling them apart. Meanwhile reduce the oven heat to 300 to 325° F. Gas No. 1 or 2.
8. Put them back in the cool oven to dry till they are crisp.

Note. These are rather short scones that are dried until crisp and may be stored in a tin for several weeks. They are served with butter as are scones.

Spiced Tea Bread (*baking-powder*)

Oven 350° to 375° F. Gas No. 5-6
Baking time ¾ to 1 hour

½ lb. plain flour
2½ level teaspoons baking-powder } *or* ½ lb. self-raising flour
½ level teaspoon salt   2 to 3 oz. margarine or cooking
3 oz. brown sugar   fat
½ to 1 level teaspoon mixed   1 egg
spice   1 tablespoon black treacle
under ¼ pint milk

Additions: 4 oz. dates, raisins or sultanas or 2 oz. chopped walnuts

Grease a ½-lb. size bread tin or a trough tin 8½ by 4½ inches.

Sieve flour with powdered ingredients, add the sugar.

Rub in the fat, add the fruit or nuts.

Mix the egg, treacle and most of the milk and mix the cake to a sticky dough that will fall from the spoon when shaken; use more milk if needed.

Turn the mixture into the tin and bake it until well risen, brown and crisp.

Serve fresh, sliced and buttered.

CAKE-MAKING

For choice of ingredients see Chapter 6, Fats, p. 132. Flour, p. 149, 'Making Flour Mixtures Light'.

The Function of Different Ingredients Used in Cake-making

Flour forms the main structure or bulk of most cakes: for a light cake with a tender crumb a *weak flour* is needed, usually called 'Pastry' or 'Cake' flour but as this cannot always be bought a *home-made cake flour* is:

7 oz. plain flour, 1 oz. cornflour or custard powder to give ½ lb.

Self-Raising Flour gives good results with plain recipes, using up to half fat to flour, but for richer cakes the proportion of raising agent is too high, so plain flour is used and varying amounts of baking-powder are added; the richer the recipe, the less the amount of baking-powder.

Sugar of course sweetens a cake but it also makes it softer or more tender because, besides forming a syrup as it dissolves, it also softens the gluten of flour. The right proportion of sugar in a recipe helps the cake to rise but too much sugar softens the gluten so much that it cannot hold the risen shape of the cake which therefore sinks in the middle.

Golden Syrup may be used in place of a small proportion of sugar to keep a cake moist and tender, probably because it contains fructose which does not easily crystallize and therefore remains a syrup when the cake is baked. Some sugar turns to caramel where the cake is exposed to the dry heat of the oven and this in part accounts for the glossy, brown crust.

Fat makes a cake short or rich and helps to keep it from getting dry during storage. Butter and margarine give their own flavour to a cake.

Fat and Sugar can be made to hold air when they are creamed together. Caster sugar is used for this because the small crystals introduce air in tiny bubbles and, by the friction of their many sharp corners, soften the fat so that an air-in-fat foam is formed.

Fat and sugar are most often used in equal amounts: if sugar exceeds fat the cake will be more tender and spongy; if fat exceeds sugar it will be richer but closer in texture.

Eggs are extremely important in a cake mixture because of their great power of entrapping air, they also add fat and protein and give the cake a pleasant, yellow colour. The more eggs the lighter the cake will be and therefore the less baking-powder needed. The ability of eggs to hold fat in emulsion is also made use of in making richer cakes, see p. 437.

Liquid, as milk or water, produces steam during baking and therefore helps to raise the cake but it also develops gluten and therefore tends to toughen the cake: in general, the less liquid added the shorter and more tender will the cake be.

Flavouring is mainly a matter of personal choice but it is worth noting that essence, being volatile, tends to dry a cake and that the zest of lemon or orange rind, being oily, helps to prevent it getting dry during storage. Fruit, added for flavour, also keeps a cake moist and by introducing a little air and steam helps to make the cake rise.

Preparing Cake-tins (Fig. 71)

Grease all tins with a pure fat, free from salt, solids and water; white cooking fats or lard are suitable.

Melt the fat and use a brush for speedy, efficient greasing.

In addition to greasing:

For small plain cakes, no further preparation.

For large plain cakes and gingerbread, line the bottom of the tin with greased greaseproof paper.

For creamed small cakes, dredge the greased tin with flour and shake out any surplus flour, or use paper-cases.

For creamed large cakes, line the tin completely with greased greaseproof or, for heavily-fruited mixtures, cartridge paper, cut to fit the tin, see Fig. 71.

For *sandwich cakes or any cakes cooked in wide, shallow tins*, line the bottom
of the tin with greased greaseproof paper.

For *sponge cakes, small, in deep, fancy tins*, dredge tins with an equal
mixture of caster sugar and flour, knocking out any surplus.

For *Swiss Roll*, line the baking-sheet with greased greaseproof paper,
cut to fit the corners and to stand up 2 inches above the edge of the
tin all round, see Fig. 71.

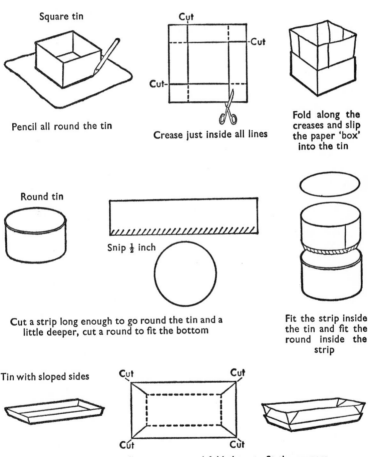

Fig. 71. LINING CAKE TINS

Preparation of Ingredients

Flour: Always sieve flour with any powdered ingredients such as baking-powder or spices, this mixes them thoroughly, breaks up any lumps and mixes in air.

Fruit: Cake fruit may be bought ready-washed, in packets, and costing more than the loose varieties.

To prepare fruit pick off all stalks, examining a small handful at a time. Wash it in a strainer by pouring boiling water through it. Dry it quickly by shaking off loose drops of water, then spreading it on a clean baking-tray and putting it into the pre-heated oven for exactly 3 minutes: this makes it plump and soft, or it can be dried more slowly for ½ hour or more in a warm place outside the oven. *Cool it* before use.

For a rubbed-in mixture the fruit need not be dried, as a fair proportion of liquid is usually added to give the right consistency.

Raisins may be bought 'seedless', 'seeded' or whole, unseeded—usually brown Valencia or purple Muscatel raisins.

To stone raisins use a small, sharp knife and have a basin of hot water at hand; wash one raisin, slit it open, prise out the seeds with the knife and put it on the tray for drying; rinse fingers and knife and continue the process.

Cherries. Wash these in boiling water and drain them, cut them in 4 then dry them; the syrup must be washed off to prevent them from sinking in the cake.

Candied Peel is usually bought ready chopped; orange, lemon or citron peel may be bought separately 'whole', really in half rinds, these must be emptied of sugar and shredded on a coarse grater or with a sharp knife and then chopped or, for speed, put through a mincer.

Lemon or Orange rind should be grated finely without using the white pith which is bitter.

Nuts: Almonds are blanched to remove the skins by covering them with cold water, bringing them just to boiling-point then draining them and slipping them out of their skins; they must then be dried.

Walnuts are not usually skinned. All nuts are chopped if they are to be mixed into the cake—left in halves for decoration on top.

Syrup or Treacle may be measured accurately if either the tin is stood in hot water to liquefy the syrup or the spoon is dipped in boiling water To weigh syrup the scale-pan should be floured and the syrup can then be rolled off it without sticking.

Baking Cakes

Kind of cake	Oven setting Electric	Gas No.	Time	Special points
Small plain	340° to 350° F.	4	15 to 20 minutes	Bake in upper half of oven
Small rich	325° to 340° F.	3-4	" " " "	" " "
Rock cakes	375° to 380° F.	6	15 minutes	Bake on top shelf.
Large plain	325° to 340° F.	3-4	1½ hours for ½ lb. size	Bake in the middle of the oven. As soon as cake begins to brown reduce heat by 25° F. or one Gas number.
Large rich or medium rich	325° to 330° F.	3	1½ to 2 hours for ½ lb. size	
Large, rich and heavily fruited	320° to 330° F.	2-3	2½ to 4 hours for ½ lb. flour, depending on weight of fruit	Bake in middle or lower half of oven. After 1 hour reduce heat by 25° F. or one gas number, and again after each successive hour.

To Test a Cake to Find if it is Cooked

1. It should look well risen and brown.
2. It should have begun to shrink very slightly from the sides of the tin.
3. It should feel as firm and springy in the middle as at the edge when pressed lightly with a finger.
4. It should smell cooked (raw cakes smell a little musty).
5. There should be no sound of bubbling when the ear is held close to the surface—only a faint ticking.

Never take a cake right out of the oven until it is fully baked or it will sink in the middle.

Cool cakes on a wire rack but do not hurry to remove large cakes from their tins—if left to cool a little in the tin they are less likely to break. Leave the lining paper on the cake until it is about to be cut or iced.

KINDS OF CAKES

Cakes are classified according to the method used for making them and this partly depends on the proportions of ingredients.

The methods are:

Rubbing-in Method

The fat is rubbed into the flour and this method is therefore only suitable for recipes with half or less than half, fat to flour.

Creaming Method

The fat and sugar are creamed together; this method is used for recipes with half, or more than half fat to flour.

Melting Method

The fat is melted with treacle, syrup and sugar for gingerbread which characteristically has a high proportion of sugary ingredients, mostly treacle or syrup.

Whisking or Sponge-cake Method

The eggs and sugar are whisked together for sponge cakes and Swiss roll in which the proportion of these ingredients to flour is high.

CAKES MADE BY RUBBING–IN METHOD

Basic Recipe

½ lb. plain cake flour
2-2½ level teaspoons baking powder } or ½ lb. self-raising flour
3 to 4 oz. granulated or brown sugar   ¼ level teaspoon salt
3 to 4 oz. fat—margarine or cooking fat
0 to 1 egg   ¼ to ⅛ pint milk
flavouring ingredients and/or dried fruit

General Method

1. Prepare the oven, wash and dry fruit. Prepare the tin (see p. 428).
2. Sieve together all powdered ingredients and flour. Add the sugar, this speeds up the rubbing-in of fat.
3. Rub in the fat with fingertips, aerating the flour at the same time.
4. Add the fruit if used.

5. Beat the egg and mix it with other liquid ingredients, keeping back some milk.

6. Check the recipe.

7. Make a deep hole or 'well' in the flour, pour in the liquid ingredients and mix the whole smoothly, adding more milk if needed.

8. *Consistency*. Rubbed-in cakes should be of a more or less stiff consistency; if baked in tins the mixture should fall from the spoon only when shaken hard; if baked as rock buns, on a baking-tray, they should be almost as firm as short pastry.

9. Bake the cake until it is well risen and brown.

10. Test it and cool it.

See charts on pp. 434 and 435.

MELTING METHOD FOR GINGERBREAD

Notes on Gingerbread. See p. 153 for use of bicarbonate of soda as a raising agent.

There is not a basic recipe for gingerbread, which can be made from many different recipes. The characteristics of gingerbread are a rich brown colour, a moist rather open texture and a sweet taste as well as the flavour of ginger.

The raising agent used in gingerbread is bicarbonate of soda in the proportion of 2 level teaspoons to 1 lb. flour; the mixture is a thick batter before cooking.

The weight of syrup, treacle and sugar usually equals that of the flour in a really moist, spongy gingerbread.

Because of the high proportion of sugary ingredients gingerbread is easily burnt; the oven heat must therefore be rather low, 325° F. or Gas No. 2. At this temperature the gingerbread does not set very quickly and opening the oven door during baking may cause it to sink in the middle.

To weigh treacle or syrup, first weigh the saucepan then weigh the syrup in the pan.

Parkin is a form of gingerbread made with $\frac{1}{2}$ to $\frac{3}{4}$ medium oatmeal to flour.

Rubbed-in Cakes ★

Name of cake	Additional ingredients to ½ lb. basic recipe	Variations of method
SMALL CAKES.	*Use* 1 *egg to* ½ *lb. in all small cakes. Make* 12 *to* 16 *small cakes*	
Chocolate	1 oz. cocoa but omit 1 oz. flour; ¼ teaspoon vanilla essence	Bake in bun-tins about 20 minutes.
Coconut Buns	2–4 oz. desiccated coconut	
Coffee Buns	2–3 level teaspoons instant coffee powder, vanilla essence	
Ginger Buns	1–2 level teaspoons ground ginger, 1 oz. 'chip' ginger	Use brown sugar.
Lemon Buns	rind and juice 1 lemon, add no milk	Cut in pieces, roll each to a smooth ball, brush with milk and dredge with sugar.
Raspberry Buns	rind of ½ lemon, or vanilla essence for flavour, 1 tablespoon raspberry jam. Add only 1 tablespoon milk, if needed, to make a soft, but dry, dough	Cut and shape the dough into balls. Make a hole in the top of each and fill it with jam; the edges may be pinched together if liked. Brush with milk, dredge with sugar. Bake on a baking-tray.
Rock Buns	2–4 oz. currants, sultanas and peel (as liked) ¼ teaspoon mixed spice or grated nutmeg (optional) Add as little milk as needed for a dry dough 'Rock' refers to the rough shape not the texture of these buns	With a spoon and fork divide the dough into 12 pieces and shape each into a 'rocky' cone on a greased baking-tray.
American Doughnuts	Use 2 oz. each fat and sugar and about 2 tablespoons milk for mixing to give a soft, dry dough. Caster sugar with a little powdered cinnamon to toss the doughnuts	On a floured board roll the dough ½ inch thick, cut out rounds 2 to 2½ inches across, then cut ¾-inch round from the centre of each. Fry them in deep fat at 330° F. or shallow fat that browns bread in 50 seconds. Fry them about 10 minutes in all, till firm.

★ See p. 432.

Name of cake	Additional ingredients to ½ lb. basic recipe	Variations of method

LARGE CAKES, WITH EGG.   *Use 6- to 7-inch round tin or 8½ by 4½-inch trough tin*

Chocolate cake	As small chocolate cakes, but for large cake use ½ fat and sugar to flour and add 1 tablespoon syrup	
Coconut cake	As small coconut buns, but use ½ fat to flour and an additional ½ egg	
Coffee cake	As small coffee buns, using ½ fat to flour 2 oz. chopped walnuts, 2 oz. sultanas (optional)	Bake at 340° F. Gas No. 4, reducing to 310° F. Gas No. 2 after 1 hour; 1½ hours in all.
Farmhouse Fruit cake	6-8 oz. mixed dried fruits, 1 oz. chopped peel 1 level teaspoon mixed spice or grated rind ½ lemon 1 tablespoon marmalade or golden syrup	
Fruit cake	Any one or two dried fruits can give a name to the cake, e.g. date, currant, sultana or raisin	
Seed cake	2 teaspoons caraway seeds, 2 oz. chopped peel	
Soda-Spice cake	4 to 8 oz. dried fruit, 1 level teaspoon mixed spice 1 level teaspoon bicarbonate soda instead of baking-powder; 1 tablespoon black treacle, sour milk, or sweet milk with 1 tablespoon vinegar to mix	Bake this cake slowly at 330° F. Gas No. 3, reducing it to 300° F. or Gas No. 1, after 1 hour.

LARGE CAKES, EGGLESS

Dorset Apple cake	½ level teaspoon ground cinnamon or ginger or grated rind ½ lemon. Additional ½ level teaspoon baking-powder, ½ lb. cooking apples or green gooseberries both prepared and chopped and mixed with the sugar 20 minutes before mixing the cake. Add no liquid as the juice that runs from the fruit makes the cake moist enough	Bake ¾ to 1 hour in an 8-inch sandwich-tin, sprinkle the top with sugar. Serve hot or cold and, if liked, split and spread with butter.
Vinegar cake	1 level teaspoon bicarbonate soda instead of baking-powder; ½ level teaspoon mixed spice 4 to 8 oz. dried fruit; 3 oz. sugar and 1 tablespoon syrup or treacle; 2 tablespoons vinegar and under ¼ pint milk	

Method for Gingerbread

Heat the oven, prepare the tin: for ½ lb. size use an 8-inch round tin or an oblong tin about 9½ by 6 inches—a shallow gingerbread is easier to bake. In a saucepan gently warm the fat, sugar, syrup and treacle until the fat is just melted: this mixture must not boil or the gingerbread will be hard. Cool the syrup mixture.

Sieve the powdered ingredients, make a well in them.

Mix the egg with about half the milk and pour this and the cooled liquid syrup mixture into the well.

Mix all the ingredients to a smooth, thick batter, adding more milk if necessary. Pour the mixture into the tin and bake it for ¾ to 1 hour for ½ lb. size.

Leave parkin to cool in the tin and mark it in squares when just firm. Gingerbread and parkin are both improved by storing them in a tin for at least a week, when the crust gets soft and the whole texture moist and spongy.

Two Recipes for Gingerbread

Ingredients	Gingerbread	Parkin
Flour	½ lb.	4 oz. with 4 oz. medium oatmeal
Bicarbonate of soda	1 level teaspoon	1 small level teaspoon
Ground ginger	1½ level teaspoons	1 level teaspoon
Margarine, cooking fat or lard	3 oz.	2 oz.
Brown sugar	2 oz.	4 oz.
Treacle and syrup mixed	6 oz.	4 oz.
Eggs	1 or 2 small	1 small
Milk	4 to 5 tablespoons	3 tablespoons
Optional, dried fruit, nuts, crystallized ginger	2 oz. sultanas or almonds 2 oz.	none none

See p. 457 for Gingernuts which are made from gingerbread recipe without eggs or milk.

THE CREAMING METHOD

General notes. For choice of ingredients see Chapters 6, 8, on Fats, Flour and 'Making Cake Mixtures Light'. Notes on the function and preparation of ingredients, pp. 427-30, apply of course to cake making by the creaming method but there are additional points to note.

Choice of ingredients. Butter gives a good flavour but needs rather hard work to cream it.

Cooking fats are very easy to cream but lack flavour. *A mixture of cooking-fat with either butter or margarine* is satisfactory. *Lard is not suitable*, being neither easy to cream nor well-flavoured.

Caster sugar is suitable because it makes creaming easy and encloses small, even air bubbles; icing-sugar may be used successfully when a very fine, close texture is required but granulated sugar is unsuitable because it gives a coarse uneven texture.

Temperature of ingredients. The fat and eggs should be at room temperature, that is about 60° F.; if fat is cold and hard much energy is wasted in beating it soft before it can be creamed with sugar and if eggs are very cold they do not easily emulsify the fat when they are beaten in. If an emulsion is not formed the mixture is said to be *curdled*, this does not spoil the cake but is disconcerting. *To prevent curdling*, as well as having the eggs at room temperature, each egg must be beaten vigorously into the well-creamed fat and sugar until the mixture stiffens.

To improve a curdled appearance a little of the flour may be beaten in with the egg.

General Method of Creaming

1. Light the oven, prepare the tin (see p. 428), wash and dry any fruit to be used. In cold weather warm the bowl by filling it with boiling water, then draining and drying it, or by warming the sugar in the bowl above or below, but never in the oven; if the bowl is too hot the fat will melt and creaming will be impossible.

2. Sieve the flour with powdered ingredients; beat the eggs slightly.

3. Cream the fat and sugar together by working them vigorously round the bowl with the back of a wooden spoon or, for large quantities, with the hand. From time to time scrape the mixture down the sides of the bowl. Continue creaming until the mixture is white, 'fluffy' and looking like whipped cream, indicating that an air-in-fat foam has been produced.

4. Beat in any flavouring in the recipe.

5. Beat in the equivalent of one beaten egg at a time, continuing to beat after each addition until the mixture is quite smooth and has stiffened, indicating that an emulsion of fat with egg has been formed. Failure to beat each egg to this smooth, stiff consistency gives rise to a 'curdled' effect.

6. Stir in any fruit in the recipe before adding the flour, so that the flour is stirred as little as possible.

7. Sift half the flour once more, this time directly into the mixture and fold it in lightly.

8. When this flour is completely folded in add the liquid as in the recipe.

9. Sift and fold in the other half of the flour.

10. Spread the mixture evenly into the prepared tin and bake it.

Basic Recipes for Creaming Method

Ingredients	Plain recipe	Medium recipe	Rich recipe
Flour	½ lb. self-raising	2 oz. plain and 6 oz. self-raising	¼ lb. plain, ¼ lb. self-raising
Baking-powder	or ⎰ ½ lb. plain ⎱ 2 level teaspoons	or ⎰ ½ lb. plain ⎱ 1½ level teaspoons	or ⎰ ½ lb. plain ⎱ 1 level or none
Fat	4 oz.	5 to 6 oz.	8 oz.
Sugar	4 to 6 oz.	6 oz.	8 oz.
Eggs	2	3	4 to 5
Milk or water	2 to 4 tablespoons	1 to 2 tablespoons	1 to 0 tablespoons
Tin, for large cake:	7-inch round or 9¼ by 4½ trough	7- to 8-inch round	7- to 9-inch round
Bake at:	330° F. Gas No. 3, 1¼ to 1½ hours	330° F. Gas No. 3 for 1½ hours	320°-330° F. Gas No. 2-3 for 1½-2 hours

Some Recipes for Cakes made by Creaming Method

Name of cake	Additions to ½ lb. basic recipe	Special points
Cherry	3 to 4 oz. glacé cherries, 1 to 2 oz. peel (optional) grated rind ½ lemon or ¼ teaspoon vanilla	Plain or medium recipe
Chocolate	Replace 1 oz. flour with 1 oz. cocoa. Add ⅛ level teaspoon bicarbonate to the baking-powder, 1 tablespoon syrup in plain recipe only	
Coffee	2 to 3 level teaspoons instant coffee powder ¼ teaspoon vanilla, 2 oz. chopped walnuts	Medium or rich recipe Ice with coffee glacé or butter icing

Name of cake	Additions to ½ lb. basic recipe	Special points
Dundee	¾ lb. mixed currants, raisins and sultanas 2 oz. peel, 2 oz. cherries, 2 oz. ground almonds grated rind 1 lemon, only 1 level teaspoon baking-powder	Medium recipe. Cover the top with blanched and split almonds. Bake at 320° F. Gas No. 2 to 3.
Genoa	¼ lb. each of currants, sultanas, peel; 3 oz. cherries	As Dundee cake.
Ginger	½ level teaspoon ground ginger 2-4 oz. crystallized ginger	Medium or rich recipe. Ice with lemon glacé icing.
Lemon or Orange	grated rind of 1 lemon or 1 orange, the juice may be used for mixing instead of milk	Ice, if liked, with glacé icing (lemon or orange juice used to mix it).
Madeira	grated rind of 1 lemon, juice of 1 lemon to mix, if liked; a thin slice citron peel	Medium or rich recipe. Put the slice of peel on top.
Queen cakes, (small)	4 to 5 oz. dried fruits, e.g. cherries, currants or sultanas, grated rind ½ lemon or ½ teaspoon vanilla	Medium recipe. About 24 cakes baked in deep buntins or paper cases.
Seed	2 teaspoons caraway seeds, 2 oz. almonds, 2 oz. peel, 2 oz. cherries (if liked)	Medium or rich recipe.
Sultana	6-8 oz. sultanas, 2 oz. peel, grated rind ½ lemon	
Sandwich cake, plain	Use 4-6 oz. fat, 6 oz. sugar, 3 eggs to ½ lb. flour, grated rind ½ to 1 lemon or vanilla essence, 1½ level teaspoons baking-powder, 1 tablespoon milk	Bake in 2 7-inch sandwich tins for 35 to 40 minutes at 330°-340° F. Gas No. 3-4.
Victoria Sandwich	6 oz. fat, 6 oz. sugar, 3 eggs, 6-7 oz. flour, only 1 level teaspoon baking-powder, flavour as above, add no liquid	Bake as above. Sandwich these with jam, lemon-curd or butter icing and cover with glacé icing.
Walnut	2 oz. chopped walnuts, ½ teaspoon vanilla essence	Medium or rich recipe. Ice with white glacé or American icing, decorate with ½ walnuts.
Small cakes	Any of the above recipes can be cooked as small cakes, see Queen cakes	

TWO SPECIAL RECIPES

Birthday or Christmas Cake

> 10 oz. flour and ½ level teaspoon baking-powder
> *or* 8 oz. flour and no baking-powder

8 oz. caster sugar	1 level teaspoon cocoa
8 oz. butter	½ level teaspoon instant coffee
1 tablespoon black treacle	powder
4 to 5 eggs	½ to 1 level teaspoon spice if liked
2 oz. ground or chopped	½ lb. each of currants, raisins and
almonds	sultanas
grated rind of 1 lemon	2 to 4 oz. cherries, 4 oz. peel

> 1 tablespoon milk if 10 oz. flour are used

Bake in a 9-inch round or square tin lined with greased cartridge paper for 3½ to 4 hours beginning at 330° F. Gas No. 2-3

reducing to 315° F. „ „ 1 or 2 after 1 hour

again reducing to 300° F. „ „ ½ or 1 after second hour

Icing. ¾ to 1 lb. almond icing, see p. 448.
1 lb. royal icing, see p. 450.

Simnel Cake

Recipe as Christmas cake, omitting cocoa, coffee and treacle.

Almond icing: inside, ½ lb. (from ¼ lb. ground almonds)
outside, ½ lb. to ¾ lb., beaten egg to glaze

Glacé icing from 6 oz. icing sugar; sugar-eggs or glacé fruit to decorate. Half the cake mixture is spread in the prepared tin; the ½ lb. almond paste is rolled to a round the size of the tin, laid on the cake mixture and covered with the other half of the mixture.

The cake is baked as for Christmas cake with the almond icing inside. When cold the top is covered with the other amount of almond icing, decorated with a border of little balls of almond icing and brushed with beaten egg. It is then browned in a fairly hot oven for 10 to 15 minutes. When again cooled the centre is coated with white glacé icing, see p. 450.

Two Quickly Mixed Sandwich Cakes: One Stage Method

	Using 'ready-creamed' cooking fat	Using cooking oil (cotton-seed, maize or sunflower)
Flour	4 oz. self-raising, no baking-powder	5 oz. self-raising, no baking-powder
Baking-powder	or 4 oz. plain ⎱ 1½ level teaspoons ⎰	or 5 oz. plain 1½ level teaspoons
Fat or oil	4 oz.	7 tablespoons (3½ fluid oz.)
Caster sugar	4 oz.	4½ oz.
Eggs	2	2
Liquid	1 dessertspoon milk	1 dessertspoon
Salt	¼ level teaspoon	¼ level teaspoon
Flavouring	grated rind ½ lemon or ¼ teaspoon vanilla essence	grated rind ½ lemon or ¼ teaspoon vanilla essence

Method

Oven 325° to 350° F. Gas No. 3-4
Baking time 35 to 40 minutes

1. Grease one deep 8-inch sandwich tin or two 6- to 7-inch, line the bottom of the tin with greased paper.
2. Sieve the flour, salt, sugar and baking-powder.
3. Make a 'well' in the dry ingredients, drop in the unbeaten eggs, the fat, flavouring and milk.
4. Beat the ingredients together with a wooden spoon for 1 minute for fat, and 2 minutes for oil.
5. Bake the cakes in the middle of the oven.

WHISKING OR SPONGE CAKE METHOD

Basic Recipe, Sponge Cake

Oven 340° to 350° F. Gas No. 4
Baking time 15 to 30 minutes

2 eggs	2 oz. flour
2 oz. caster sugar	¼ teaspoon vanilla essence

Basic Method

1. Prepare the tins: 2 6-inch sandwich tins or 1 8-inch sandwich tin or 8 to 10 small tins (see p. 428).
   Heat the oven.

P

2. Spread the flour out on a plate or paper and warm it above or below, but not in the oven.

3. Put the eggs and sugar into a wide mixing-bowl for use with a hand-whisk or into a deep bowl for a rotary beater and set the bowl on a saucepan quarter-filled with boiling water with low heat under it—the water must not touch the bottom of the bowl.

4. Whisk the eggs and sugar together, at first very quickly till a froth is formed then steadily till they are pale, fluffy and showing a trail behind the whisk.

5. Take the bowl off the saucepan and continue whisking until the trail left by the whisk lasts for 3 seconds.

6. Sieve the flour, then sieve it again on to the surface of the egg-sugar foam, at the same time lightly folding it into the mixture. Add the vanilla when folding is nearly finished.

Stop folding as soon as all the flour is smoothly mixed into the foam.

7. Pour the mixture into the tins and bake the cakes at once. These cakes may be sandwiched with jam or butter-icing, iced or used as a base for a sponge-cake flan, or eaten with fruit.

Swiss Roll

Oven 400° to 425° F. Gas No. 7
Baking time   7 to 8 minutes

2 eggs	¼ teaspoon vanilla essence
3 oz. caster sugar	1 tablespoon warm water
2 oz. flour	*Filling:* 2-3 tablespoons jam

Method as for Sponge cake

1. Prepare and line a baking-tray 11 inches by 7½ inches, see Fig. 71.
2. Heat the oven.
   Warm the flour.
3. Whisk the eggs and sugar and fold in the flour as for sponge cake, adding the water and vanilla as the last flour is folded in.
4. Spread the mixture in the tin, pushing it well into the corners.
5. Bake the roll at the top of the oven.
6. While it is baking warm the jam in a basin over boiling water. Dredge a sheet of paper with caster sugar *or* wring a cloth tightly out of cold water.
7. When the roll is cooked turn it upside down on to the cloth or paper; with a finger dipped in water damp the edges of the paper and peel it off.

8. Trim the crisp edges off the cake, spread it with warm jam, leaving $\frac{3}{4}$ inch margins on 3 sides.

9. Mark one inch from the near, short end with the back of a knife, to begin the roll and, holding the paper or cloth, roll the cake as tightly as possible away from you. Hold the roll in shape for a second or two, then remove the paper and dredge the roll with caster sugar.

Butter icing or whipped cream may be used as a filling and if so the hot Swiss roll must be rolled without filling and left to cool. When cold it must carefully be unrolled, spread with filling and re-rolled.

Turn the Swiss roll on to sugared paper, remove the paper, trim off the crisp side edges

Spread the cake with jam and make a groove I inch from one end

Turn over the grooved end

With the paper, roll up the cake

Cool the roll on a cake rack

Fig. 72. ROLLING A SWISS ROLL

Chocolate Swiss Roll

Recipe as for Swiss roll, but remove one level tablespoon of flour and sieve with the flour one level tablespoon cocoa.

Filling: Butter icing from 2 oz. butter, flavoured with vanilla. Roll the Swiss roll while hot, leave it to cool then unroll, fill it then re-roll.

MISCELLANEOUS SMALL CAKES

Macaroons   *about 12*

Oven 330° to 340° F. Gas No. 3-4
Baking time   10 to 15 minutes

3 oz. ground almonds	1½ egg-whites
2 level teaspoons rice-flour	few drops almond essence
or ground rice	split almonds for the top
4 oz. caster sugar	rice paper

1. Heat the oven.
   Cut 2-inch squares of rice paper and put them on a dry baking-sheet.
2. Mix sugar, ground almonds and rice-flour.
3. Beat the egg-white slightly and stir it into the dry ingredients, adding only enough to make a sticky paste.
4. Shape the mixture into balls the size of small walnuts, using two tea-spoons.
5. Put each ball on a square of rice paper, put a split almond on top of each and flatten it slightly.
6. Brush the tops with white of egg.
7. Bake until golden, slightly crisp, but still soft in the centre.

English Madeleines   *10–12 cakes from 4-oz. flour*

Oven 340° to 350° F. Gas No. 4
Baking time   15 to 20 minutes

> Medium or rich creamed cake mixture
>
> *To coat:* $\begin{cases} \text{sieved jam} \\ \text{desiccated coconut} \end{cases}$
>
> *To decorate:* halved glacé cherries

1. Heat the oven, grease and flour deep dariole or Castle Pudding tins.
2. Make and bake the cakes and stand them upside down.
3. When cool brush them with warm sieved jam over top and sides.
4. When all are coated roll one at a time in desiccated coconut on a plate or paper.
5. Press half a cherry on each.

Note. French Madeleines are very rich cakes baked in small shell moulds.

'Melting Moments'

Oven 325° to 340° F. Gas No. 2-3
Baking time 25 to 30 minutes

> 4 oz. flour, plain ⎫
> 1 level teaspoon baking-powder ⎬ *or* 4 oz. self-raising flour
> 1 oz. rolled oats   ½ egg
> 3 to 4 oz. margarine   a few drops of vanilla essence
> 3 oz. caster sugar   *or* grated rind ½ lemon
> *To coat:* rolled oats
> *To decorate:* halved glacé cherries

1. Grease a baking-tray.
2. Follow creaming method, making a soft but not sticky paste.
3. Divide it into 8 pieces, dip the hands in cold water and roll the pieces into little balls.
4. Roll the damp balls in the rolled oats.
5. Place them 2 inches apart on the baking-tray and flatten each one a little.
6. Bake them; while still warm, press half a cherry on each.

Meringues

Oven 250° to 260° F. Gas No. ½
Cooking time About 2 hours

> 2 egg-whites
> 4 oz. caster sugar
> *To fill:* ¼ pint double cream, sweetened, flavoured and whipped
> *or* ¼ pint 'mock' cream
> *or* ice cream

For baking use an oven after other baking is finished or use a plate-warming compartment while the oven is in use.

1. Cut strips of greaseproof paper about 1½ inches wide and as long as the baking-tray.
2. Brush the underside of the baking-tray and the strips of paper with cooking-oil.
3. Have ready a large forcing-bag with a ½- to ¾-inch plain pipe and a caster-sugar dredger.
4. Sieve the caster sugar.

5. In a clean, dry bowl whisk the egg-whites until they stand up in stiff peaks.

6. Add 2 level teaspoons of caster sugar and continue whisking until the egg-whites are close, dry and firm—looking like cotton-wool.

7. With a metal tablespoon lightly fold in the rest of the sugar; at once put the mixture in the bag.

8. Pipe the meringue in little 3-tier cones or large stars on the paper (Fig. 73).

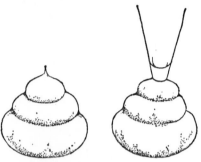

Fig. 73. PIPING MERINGUES

9. Dredge them at once with sugar and put them in the oven with the door ajar to dry without browning.

The strips of paper make it easy to remove some meringues as they dry or to change their positions.

10. When the meringues are firm, peel off the paper, press the middle of the underside gently with a thumb, put the hollowed meringue shell on the clean, upper side of the baking-tray and put them back to finish drying. When dry and cold, sandwich 2 shells together with whipped cream or ice cream.

Meringue shells may be stored in a tin for future use if they are quite dry.

Coconut Meringues or Pyramids

Oven 300° to 325° F. Gas No. 1
Baking time 35 to 40 minutes

2 egg-whites	4-5 oz. desiccated coconut
5 oz. caster sugar	rice-paper

Cut 1½ inch squares of rice-paper and put them on a dry baking-sheet.

1. Whisk the egg-whites as for meringues and fold the coconut in with the bulk of the sugar.

2. Pile the mixture in rough heaps on the rice paper.

3. Bake them slowly till crisp outside, slightly soft inside but not brown.

Nut Meringues

2 egg-whites	2 oz. chopped or milled nuts
4 oz. caster sugar	almonds, hazelnuts or walnuts
rice-paper	a few drops of almond or vanilla essence

Make them exactly as coconut meringues but bake them till fawn in colour. They may be sandwiched with coffee butter icing.

27

ICINGS

Almond Icing (*Almond paste or marzipan*)

½ lb. ground almonds	1 egg
¼ lb. caster sugar	¼ teaspoon vanilla essence
¼ lb. icing sugar	⅛ teaspoon almond essence
1 tablespoon lemon juice	1 teaspoon orange flower water

1. Sieve the sugars, and the ground almonds if they have any brown flakes. Mix these together, beat the egg.
2. Measure the flavourings into the dry ingredients then gradually stir in the beaten egg to make a soft paste. Almond icing gets stiffer after a short time and for covering a cake it must neither be sticky nor so dry that it cracks at the edges. Extra egg may be worked in later if it gets too dry.
3. Knead the paste until it is quite smooth.
4. If it is not to be used at once put the almond icing in a plastic bag to keep it from getting dry.

Apricot Glaze

½ lb. apricot jam	1 tablespoon lemon juice

1-2 tablespoons water (this must vary with the consistency of the jam)

1. Warm the jam with a tablespoon of water and rub it through a nylon or fine wire sieve.
2. Return it to the saucepan, add the lemon juice and bring it just to boiling-point.
3. Add more boiling water if the glaze is too thick; it should be quite sticky while still hot. Use it hot, to prepare cakes for icing or as a glaze finish.

American Icing

½ lb. granulated sugar	1 egg-white
⅛ pint water	

1. Put the sugar and water in a saucepan and warm them very slowly until the sugar dissolves. The syrup must not be stirred nor must it boil until the sugar is all dissolved or it will form new crystals which cannot be dissolved.

2. When the sugar is dissolved put on the lid and boil the syrup vigorously for 1 minute, to dissolve sugar left on the sides of the pan.

3. Remove the lid and boil the syrup to 240° F. or until a few drops in cold water can be rolled into a soft ball.

4. Whisk the egg-white till stiff then pour in the syrup in a steady stream, whisking hard all the time.

5. Whisk the icing until it cools and stiffens so that it only just stands up in peaks, then spread it very quickly on the cake as it sets at once

6. It is quite correct to have this icing rather rough, as if it is used while warm and smooth it runs off the cake.

Butter Icing

> 2 oz. butter
> 3-4 oz. icing sugar
> colouring if liked
> *Flavouring:*
> 1 oz. plain chocolate or 2 level teaspoons cocoa
> *or* 2 level teaspoons instant coffee powder
> *or* rind and juice of ½ lemon or orange
> *or* vanilla essence to taste

1. Cream the butter till it is soft, sieve the icing sugar and cream it with the butter till the mixture is white and soft as whipped cream.

2. *To flavour the icing* with chocolate, melt the chocolate with a few drops of water in a small saucepan.

With cocoa or coffee powder, blend the powder with 2 teaspoons of boiling water, beat the flavouring gradually into the icing.

To colour the icing add cake colouring from the point of a skewer.

Chocolate Icing

> 6 oz. icing sugar
> 1½ oz. plain chocolate
> *or* 1 tablespoon cocoa
>
> 1 to 2 tablespoons hot water
> ¼ teaspoon vanilla
> ¼ teaspoon butter

1. Sieve the icing sugar.

2. Break the chocolate into rough pieces or blend cocoa with a little

water, add 1 tablespoon water and the butter and warm the pan till the
chocolate is melted then beat it smooth and cool it a little.

3. Add the vanilla then stir in the icing sugar, thinning it if necessary
with more warm water, till it will coat the back of the spoon.

4. Use the icing at once while warm.

5. If it gets cold and too thick stand the saucepan in hot water and
beat the icing till it softens.

This icing must not be made really hot or it will be dull instead of
glossy.

Glacé Icing

½ lb. icing sugar   flavouring and colouring
about 2 tablespoons warm water or strained fruit juice

1. Sieve the icing sugar

2. Mix it with a little warm water or lemon, orange or pineapple juice,
beating it hard until it is of a consistency to coat the spoon thickly.

3. Pour and spread it over the cake.

Any decoration must be put on while the icing is still soft.

Royal Icing

1 lb. icing sugar, for soft icing to be kept, 2 to 4 teaspoons glycerine
2-3 egg-whites; for hard icing for piping, 2 drops acetic acid
for icing to be eaten fresh, 4 teaspoons lemon juice

Notes. For coating a Christmas cake, glycerine is recommended; for
piping, glycerine should not be added but acetic acid may be omitted;
lemon juice gives a pleasant flavour but makes the icing brittle and
hard when kept.

1. Sieve the icing sugar. Wring a clean cloth out of cold water.

2. Whisk 2 egg-whites a very little in a clean, dry bowl.

3. Work in about half the sugar and beat the icing vigorously until it
loses the yellow tinge of the egg-whites and looks quite white.

4. Work in more sugar and if necessary more egg-white until the icing
coats the back of the spoon and only slowly settles to its own level.

5. Cover it at once with the damp cloth and leave it to stand for about
10 minutes to allow bubbles to escape then bump the basin once or twice
on a pad of cloth to break out more bubbles. This icing can be run on to
a cake like glacé icing. For piping the icing must be stiff enough to
stand in peaks.

FILLINGS FOR SANDWICH CAKES

Butter Icing with Additions

2 oz. butter	flavouring as for butter icing
3-4 oz. icing sugar	*or* 2 tablespoons chopped nuts,
2 to 4 teaspoons boiling milk	glacé fruit or grated chocolate

1. Make the butter icing, beat into it gradually the boiling milk; this makes it smoother and makes it go further.
2. Add other ingredients and flavouring to taste.

Cream, Whipped and Extended

Whipped: Double cream, sugar and vanilla essence

1. Whip the cream lightly with sugar to sweeten and a few drops of vanilla. It must be whipped only until it will stand in smooth, soft peaks, whipping must then stop at once. The time needed varies very much with the age of the cream; when really fresh it may take several minutes; when 'aged' but still fresh it may stiffen after 2 or 3 strokes.
2. Put the cream in a really cold place until it is used.

Extended Whipped Cream

1 egg-white to $\frac{1}{4}$ pint double cream
1 level teaspoon caster sugar   1 teaspoon sherry *or* $\frac{1}{2}$ teaspoon vanilla essence

Put all the ingredients in a clean, dry basin, and whip them until they are stiff and doubled in bulk.

Confectioner's Custard

1 oz. butter	1 egg yolk
1 level tablespoon caster sugar	$\frac{1}{4}$ pint milk
1 oz. flour	$\frac{1}{4}$ teaspoon vanilla essence

1. Melt the butter in a small pan, stir in the flour and sugar.
2. Beat together the yolk and the milk and strain them into the pan.
3. Over moderate heat whisk the mixture till it justs boils. At once remove it from the heat and continue whisking for a minute.

4. Add vanilla essence and cover the surface with wet greaseproof paper to prevent a skin forming.

5. Chopped nuts or glacé fruits may be added as for Butter Icing with Additions.

Lemon Curd.   *1⅓ to 1½-lb. jam-jars*

3-4 oz. unsalted butter	2 to 3 lemons
3 eggs (or 4 yolks)	½ lb. granulated sugar

1. Melt the butter in a small thick saucepan or in a basin set over a saucepan of boiling water. Warm the clean, dry jars, scrub the lemons. Beat and strain the eggs.

2. Grate the rind of the lemons on a fine, stainless grater, squeeze and strain the juice and add them to the butter.

3. Add all the ingredients to the butter and juice and stir the mixture over the boiling water or slow heat until it turns cloudy and thickens to a thin coating consistency.

4. Pour the curd into warm jars, cover it as for jam if it is to be stored. The curd will keep for 2 or 3 weeks but after that time the flavour of the butter may be spoilt.

Mock Cream. I

2 oz. butter or margarine	½ oz. cornflour or custard powder
2 oz. caster sugar	(good weight)
vanilla essence or flavouring	¼ pint milk
as for Butter Icing	

1. Mix and cook the cornflour or custard powder and milk as for Cornflour Mould. If cocoa or instant coffee powder is used blend it with the dry, starchy powder.

2. Turn the mould at once into a mixing bowl, cover the surface closely with wet greaseproof paper and leave it to get quite cold.

3. Cream the fat and sugar thoroughly and add the essence.

4. Whisk the cold cornflour mould until it is soft and creamy, then whisk in a small teaspoonful of creamed fat and sugar at a time and continue whisking till all is mixed.

Notes. The separate parts of this cream may be prepared the day before use, but the finished cream must be used the day it is mixed or the emulsion may break up, giving it a 'curdled' effect.

This cream should not be stored in a refrigerator as the cold also gives it a 'curdled' appearance.

Mock Cream. II

    2 oz. butter or margarine   2-4 tablespoons boiling milk
    2 oz. icing sugar   vanilla essence to taste

Make this as Butter Icing, beating the boiling milk gradually into creamed fat and sugar.

Whipped Evaporated Milk as Cream

Chill the tin of milk overnight in a refrigerator.
or Boil the unopened can for 10 minutes in a saucepan of water then cool it completely.
or Add 1 teaspoon gelatine dissolved in 1 tablespoon warm water (see p. 409) to $\frac{1}{4}$ pint evaporated milk and leave the mixture to get quite cold.

Add to all the above a small teaspoon lemon juice and flavouring as needed. The milk may be whipped to a soft froth that stiffens when chilled.

To cover a Cake with Almond Paste (Fig. 74)

    $\frac{3}{4}$ lb. (total weight) almond paste will cover top and side of a 6-inch cake
    6 oz. (total weight) almond paste will cover top only of a 6-7-inch cake

1. Stand the cake on an upturned plate.
2. To get a smooth result quickly with the minimum of almond paste, turn the cake upside down and ice the bottom.
3. Brush the cake all over with hot apricot glaze, or white of egg.
4. If the top of the cake is to be covered fill up any hollows and level the curved edge with the paste.
5. Cut greaseproof paper patterns: 1 round, $\frac{1}{4}$ inch larger all round than the top of the cake; 2 strips for the sides, each $\frac{1}{4}$ inch wider than the depth of the sides and together $\frac{1}{2}$ inch longer than the circumference of the cake.
6. Divide the almond paste into two, one piece a little smaller than the other; knead the smaller piece to a ball; divide the larger piece again into two and roll each piece to a roll as long as the strips of paper.
7. Put each piece of paste on to its pattern and roll it to the exact shape; straightening or rounding the edges and pressing any cracks together.
8. Lift each strip on its paper and press it firmly on to the side of the cake

with the top edges level. Trim the join and press the edges neatly together.

9. Tuck the spare ½ inch underneath the cake and press it in place to anchor it.

10. Peel off the paper patterns.

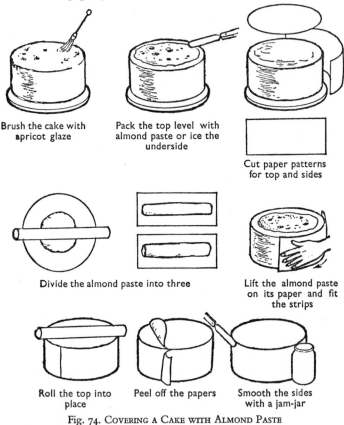

Brush the cake with apricot glaze

Pack the top level with almond paste or ice the underside

Cut paper patterns for top and sides

Divide the almond paste into three

Lift the almond paste on its paper and fit the strips

Roll the top into place

Peel off the papers

Smooth the sides with a jam-jar

Fig. 74. COVERING A CAKE WITH ALMOND PASTE

11. Lift the round of paste on its paper and press it on to the top. Roll it gently with a rolling-pin. The outer rim should cover the edges of the paste on the sides.

12. Peel off the paper and smooth the join with a palette knife. Check that sides are smooth and vertical and the top smooth and horizontal.

13. Leave the cake for 24 to 48 hours to dry the almond paste before covering it with Royal or American icing.

To Ice a Cake

Soft icing, glacé or chocolate

1. Split and fill the cake as required and stand it on a wire rack over a plate. It is easier to ice the sides if they are brushed with hot apricot glaze or hot sieved jam: this keeps loose crumbs from spoiling the icing and makes the icing stick to the cake smoothly.

2. Have the icing just stiff enough to coat the back of the spoon and to settle to its own level in the basin.

3. Pour the icing on to the top of the cake with a circular movement, quickly spread it to the edge and round the sides with a palette knife, work very lightly and stop smoothing as soon as possible to allow the icing to run level.

Instead of icing the sides they may be finished with browned chopped nuts or dried cake crumbs on either apricot glaze or butter icing.

5. If the top only is to be iced draw the palette knife firmly round the top edge as soon as the icing has covered the top. This removes any trickles from the sides and usually stops the icing running further.

To Decorate the Cake

1. The decoration must be put on while the icing is still soft.
2. Arrange the decoration on a plate before icing the cake and
3. Keep it as simple as possible.
4. Match or contrast the colour of the decoration to the icing.

Suggested decorations:

half walnuts or almonds or whole hazelnuts
halved glacé cherries
diamonds of angelica
chocolate drops or 'Smarties' or other small sweets
crystallized flowers
tiny fruits or flowers made of coloured almond paste
piped stars of butter icing (Fig. 75)

Marbled or Feathered Icing

1. When the glacé icing is mixed keep back a little (about 2 teaspoonfuls) colour this strongly or stir cocoa into it to darken it, adjust the consistency so that it only just settles level.

2. If chocolate icing is used mix a little white glacé icing for marbling.

3. Put the small quantity of icing into a greaseproof paper icing-bag, Fig. 75, and have ready a long needle or skewer.

4. Ice the cake and, while the icing is still soft, pipe straight lines across it about $\frac{1}{2}$ inch apart.

5. At once draw straight lines with the needle at right-angles to the lines of icing, backwards and forwards.

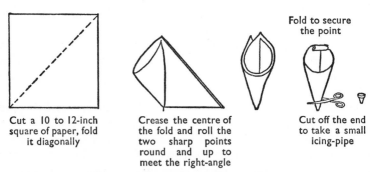

Cut a 10 to 12-inch square of paper, fold it diagonally

Crease the centre of the fold and roll the two sharp points round and up to meet the right-angle

Fold to secure the point

Cut off the end to take a small icing-pipe

Fig. 75. MAKING A PAPER FORCING BAG

To Ice Small Cakes

1. (a) For small cut shapes ice the whole slab of cake, decorate it at evenly spaced intervals and when the icing has set cut the slab into neat squares or fingers with a long knife dipped into hot water.

   (b) *Alternative Method.* Cut the cake into shapes and dip these into apricot glaze, by impaling one at a time on a fork.

2. Leave them to dry a little on a wire rack.

3. To ice them either spoon the icing neatly over each one or again impale them one at a time, dip them in the icing and slip them carefully off with another fork and so on to the wire rack. Éclairs and biscuits may be iced in this way, holding them with the fingertips and dipping their surface only into the icing (Fig. 59).

28

BISCUITS

Biscuits that Need No Rolling, Gingerbread Method'

Oven 325° to 340° F. Gas No. 2-3
Baking time 15 to 25 minutes

Basic Method
1. Grease the tins.
2. Use gingerbread method for mixing.
3. *To shape cookies and gingernuts.* Put the mixture in teaspoonfuls on a baking-tray, or cool it and roll it into balls the size of a small walnut and space them 3 inches apart as they spread during baking.

Flapjack. Press the mixture into a shallow tin, 8 inches square or 7 by 9 inches, and, while warm after baking, mark it into fingers about 1 by 3 inches; *or* press the mixture into 24 shallow patty-tins.
4. Bake the biscuits at 325° to 340° F. Gas No. 2 or 3 for 15 to 20 minutes, until golden and set; biscuits do not feel crisp until they are cold.

Some Recipes (about 24 biscuits)

Ingredients	Flapjack	Fruit cookies	Gingernuts	Oat cookies
Flour	—	4 oz. plain	4 oz. plain	2 oz. plain
Rolled oats	5 oz.	—	—	2 oz.
Baking-powder	—	1½ level tea-spoons	—	—
Bicarbonate soda	—	—	½ level tea-spoon	½ level tea-spoon
Brown sugar	2½ to 3 oz.	1 oz.	1 oz.	2 oz.
Margarine	2½ to 3 oz.	2 oz.	2 oz.	2 oz.
Golden Syrup	2 tablespoons	2 tablespoons	3 oz.	1 tablespoon
Flavcuring, etc.	—	2 oz. chopped dried fruit ⅛ teaspoon mixed spice or cinnamon	1 level tea-spoon ground ginger	¼ teaspoon vanilla essence

Brandy Snaps (or Wafers)

Oven 330° F. Gas No. 2-3
Baking time 7 to 10 minutes

2 oz. golden syrup
2 oz. margarine
2 oz. fine, brown sugar
1 teaspoon lemon juice

2 oz. flour
$\frac{1}{4}$ teaspoon ground ginger
$\frac{1}{4}$ teaspoon grated lemon rind
2 teaspoons brandy

1. Use the gingerbread method for mixing; oil the handle of a wooden spoon.
2. Drop small teaspoonfuls of the mixture, 4 inches apart, on a greased baking-tray.
3. Bake them in the slow oven until slightly set and golden-brown.
4. While warm lift them off the tin with a palette knife and roll them over the oiled spoon-handle. If they harden on the tray, put them back in the oven for a few seconds until they are soft enough to roll.
5. When cold they may be filled with mock cream or whipped cream, but they are delicious without this.

Biscuits Made by Rubbing In

Some Recipes

Ingredients	Almond biscuits	Apricot biscuits	Chocolate biscuits	Coconut biscuits
Flour	4 oz.	4 oz.	3 oz. 1 oz. ground rice	4 oz.
Baking-powder	—	$\frac{1}{2}$ level tea-spoon	$\frac{1}{2}$ level tea-spoon	—
Margarine	2 oz.	2 oz.	2 oz.	2 oz.
Sugar	1$\frac{1}{2}$ oz.	1 oz.	2 oz.	2 oz.
Egg	$\frac{1}{2}$ or 1 yolk	—	$\frac{1}{2}$ or 1 yolk	$\frac{1}{2}$ or 1 yolk
Other ingredients or special method	1 oz. ground almonds, 2 drops almond essence Brush with egg-white and dredge with caster sugar before baking	1 table-spoon sieved apricot jam	2 level tea-spoons cocoa $\frac{1}{4}$ teaspoon vanilla Sandwich with chocolate butter icing	1 oz. desiccated coconut $\frac{1}{4}$ teaspoon vanilla Roll in caster sugar

Basic Method

Oven 330° to 340° F. Gas No. 3-4
Baking time 10 to 15 minutes

1. Grease a baking-tray.
2. Follow the rubbing-in method.
3. Mix the ingredients to a dough a little softer than short pastry.
4. Roll it to $\frac{1}{8}$ inch to $\frac{1}{4}$ inch thick.
5. Cut into shapes with round or fancy cutters, or cut them into neat fingers, 1 by 2 inches; carefully lift the biscuits without spoiling their shapes. Prick them with a fork or skewer.
6. Bake them until set and pale golden, moving them to a cooler part of the oven if they are not quite firm in the middle.

Shortbread

Oven 330° to 340° F. Gas No. 3-4
Baking time $\frac{3}{4}$ hour for one cake; 15 minutes for fingers

4 oz. flour	4 oz. butter
2 oz. rice-flour or ground rice	2 oz. caster sugar
$\frac{1}{8}$ teaspoon salt	

Follow the rubbing-in method, but knead the dry dough until all the ingredients are mixed to the consistency of short pastry; do not oil the butter.

To shape a Large Shortbread

1. Knead the dough to a smooth ball, gently press and roll it to a round $\frac{3}{4}$ inch thick and keep the edges smooth and free of cracks.
2. Lift the cake carefully on to a square of greaseproof paper on the underside of a baking-tray to make it easy to slide it off when baked.
3. Neatly pinch the edge or mark it with a spoon-handle and prick the shortbread all over in a neat pattern.
4. In warm weather cool it before baking.
5. Bake it until firm and light golden-fawn in colour; if the shortbread colours before it is set move it to a cooler shelf in the oven or cover it with foil or paper.

A wooden shortbread mould may be used: dust it with flour, make sure that the dough is cool and firm, knead it into a smooth ball and lightly press it into the mould with a rolling-pin or the hand. Knock it out of the mould on to paper as above and prick it.

Shortbread Fingers or Shapes

1. Roll the dough ¼ inch thick for fingers or ½ inch thick for shapes.
2. Cut fingers 1 by 1½ inches, or small fancy shapes with cutters about 1 inch across.
3. Prick them neatly.
4. Bake them for 15 to 20 minutes until coloured light, golden fawn and firm.

Biscuits Made by Creaming

Follow the creaming method for mixing and the basic method for *Biscuits Made by Rubbing In* for rolling cutting and baking.

Some Recipes

Ingredients	Shrewsbury biscuits	Easter biscuits	Dundee biscuits	Piped biscuits
Flour	4 oz.	4 oz.	4 oz. 1 oz. rice flour	4 oz.
Butter or margarine	2 oz.	2 oz.	3 oz.	2½ to 3 oz.
Caster sugar	2 oz.	2 oz.	2 oz.	2 oz.
Egg	½ or 1 yolk	½ or 1 yolk	1 yolk	½ or 1 yolk
Other ingredients or special method	1 teaspoon grated lemon-rind *or* ¼ teaspoon ground cinnamon or caraway. Cut in large rounds, *or* Cut in 2-inch rounds, sandwich with jam and dredge the tops with icing sugar	¼ teaspoon ground cinnamon or caraway and 1 oz. currants	Roll to ½ inch, cut into fingers 1 by 1½ inches and roughen with a fork, drawn over them lengthways	¼ teaspoon vanilla essence or ¼ teaspoon ground cinnamon. Pipe as stars and finish, when cold, with glacé cherries or sandwich 2 with jam, or pipe as fingers and dip the ends in chocolate icing.

29

BEVERAGES AND BREAKFAST DISHES

BEVERAGES

Cocoa

To each breakfast cup of milk or milk and water:

- 2 level teaspoons cocoa
- 1 level teaspoon sugar or more to taste

or 1 tablespoon sweetened chocolate powder or flakes

1. Mix the cocoa and sugar.
2. Heat the milk and when it is only warm, sprinkle the cocoa and sugar into it, whisking it at the same time. Bring it to boiling-point and boil it for a minute to improve the flavour. Serve it hot.

Coffee

As the flavour of coffee is volatile it is quickly lost if ground coffee is left open to the air or if it is stored too long.

To get the best flavour from coffee:

1. Buy it freshly-ground, a week's supply only, vacuum-packed or, if it is packed in the shop, store the packet in an airtight tin.
2. Roasted coffee beans may be bought to be ground at home in a coffee mill, fresh for each brew.
3. Make coffee fresh for each meal as it loses its aroma if it is kept hot for long or if it is re-heated.
4. Wash the coffee-pot or other apparatus perfectly clean after each use and scald it and drain it dry.
5. Avoid using muslin for straining coffee as it absorbs the flavour of stale coffee; well-made coffee can be cleared without straining.

Proportions for Making Coffee

4 level tablespoons coffee to 1 pint boiling water

Black Coffee: 1 pint gives 3 teacups or 6 coffee cups
White Coffee: 1 pint coffee and ¾ pint hot milk gives 4 to 5 teacups
Serve Coffee: black, or black with cream; or white with hot but not boiled milk. Hand brown sugar with either kind.

Making Coffee

There are several different ways of making coffee and various types of coffee-making apparatus but all methods are designed to infuse the coffee for a few minutes and to clear it of all coffee-grounds.

Three good methods of making coffee follow.

The Jug Method

1. Find the capacity of a coffee jug and make it really hot by filling it with boiling water; empty this water out but keep the jug hot.
2. Measure in the coffee.
3. Add boiling water, $\frac{1}{3}$ of the jugful at a time; stir the coffee after each addition, wait 3 to 5 minutes between additions and make sure the water is boiling each time.
4. By the time the jug is full the coffee will be infused and the grounds will have settled to the bottom of the jug.

If the coffee is served at once it may be poured from the jug; if it must be kept hot for a few minutes it may be poured off into another hot coffee-pot.

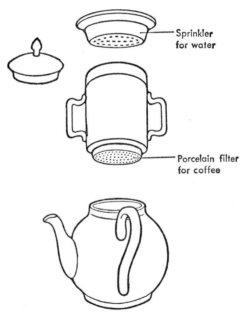

Fig. 76. Cafetiére Method of Coffee-making

Filter or Cafetiére Method (Fig. 76)

The coffee-pot for this method has a removable top section, perforated at the bottom, and a sprinkler cover below the lid; one type has a filter-paper over the perforations.

1. The coffee-pot is heated, the coffee is measured into the perforated section, the sprinkler top is put on and boiling water is poured in, a little at a time, until the lower part of the pot is full; the coffee-pot must be kept hot during this addition and the water must be boiling.

2. The perforated section is lifted off to serve the coffee in the jug section.

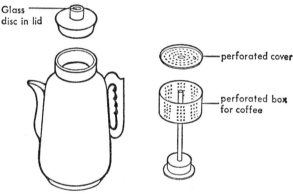

Glass disc in lid — perforated cover — perforated box for coffee

Fig. 77. PERCOLATOR METHOD OF COFFEE-MAKING

Percolator Method (Fig. 77)

The percolator consists of a tall coffee-pot with a perforated metal box to hold the coffee; the box fits under a glass lid and has a long tube passing through it from the bottom of the pot.

1. The measured coffee must only half fill the box as it will swell when water reaches it and if it is tightly packed water cannot percolate through it.

2. The measured water is poured into the coffee-pot; boiling water may be used if time is short, and the box of coffee is put in place with the glass lid shut.

3. The percolator is then heated slowly, on gas or electric top heat or by an electric element in the apparatus; as the water reaches boiling-point it passes up the tube and is sprayed through the coffee in the box.

4. Heating is continued until the liquid can be seen to be a deep brown,

showing that the coffee is strong enough, this is usually in 10 minutes after boiling-point is reached.

5. The box of coffee is lifted out of the coffee-pot before serving.

The 'Vacuum' Method (Fig. 78)

This type of coffee-pot consists of a glass flask, heated over its own methylated spirit lamp or electric heater, or over a gas-ring or electric hot-plate, and a funnel which fits through a rubber 'cork' into the flask. A glass stopper, roughened underneath, closes the upper part of the funnel but allows water to trickle through it to the flask below.

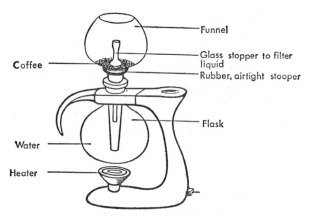

Fig. 78. VACUUM METHOD OF COFFEE-MAKING

1. The measured amount of boiling water is poured into the flask which is then heated.

2. The coffee is measured into the funnel and when the water again boils the funnel is fitted into the flask.

3. As the water boils it is forced up the tube into the funnel by the pressure of steam in the flask; by this means all but ¾ inch of water rises up and infuses the coffee in the funnel.

4. Stir the coffee in the funnel once or twice and after one minute stop heating the flask and stop stirring.

5. As the water cools slightly, pressure in the flask is reduced and the coffee can run back into it.

6. The funnel is removed and the coffee is served in the flask.

Notes. 1. It is important that the rubber stopper should fit tightly otherwise the pressure will not be sufficient.

2. A second infusion must not be made through the damp coffee as this makes an effective seal to the funnel producing too great pressure in the flask which may break.

Tea

Personal taste must determine how strong to make tea but a usual amount is: 1 level teaspoon for each person ⎱ allowing at least ¼ pint
1 level teaspoon 'for the pot' ⎰ water for each person

1. Fill the kettle with freshly drawn cold water and just before it boils scald the teapot and empty it.
2. Measure the tea into the heated teapot.
3. As soon as the water boils take the teapot to the kettle and fill it with boiling water.
4. Infuse small-leaf tea for 3 minutes, china tea and other large-leaf tea for 5 minutes. Have ready more boiling water, in a jug, to refill the teapot for second cups.
5. Serve tea with milk or thin slices of lemon and with sugar: guests should be asked which of these additions they like or, at a teaparty, milk, lemon and sugar may be handed separately.

BREAKFAST DISHES

The most important thing to remember when serving breakfast is correct timing, because, although there may be several different dishes to prepare this meal must be ready punctually so that the family can eat and enjoy it peacefully and still leave for work in time. Breakfast should of course be as well balanced as any other meal but the various items should be reasonably quick to prepare and to eat. Because of shortage of time in the morning breakfast is often, unfortunately, a hurried snack, and not at all well balanced, for example:

'*Continental*' *breakfast* usually consists of:

Tea or coffee
Rolls, toast or bread with butter and marmalade, jam or honey.

This meal obviously lacks Vitamin C and animal protein and can be improved by adding:

orange juice or grapefruit, for Vitamin C;
cheese, in the Dutch fashion, for animal protein

Neither of these need take long to prepare.

A Full or Cooked Breakfast

To the 'continental' menu may be added:

> Cereal or porridge with milk, or fresh or stewed fruit
> A cooked dish of:
>> Eggs—boiled, fried, poached, scrambled or as an omelet;
>> bacon with eggs, fried bread, potatoes, tomatoes or mushrooms;
>> sausages, liver, kidneys, usually with bacon;
>> smoked haddock or kippers or fried fresh fish or fish-cakes;
>> cold ham or cold boiled bacon;
>> in some parts of England, Welsh rarebit.

To serve a full breakfast punctually the timetable is usually:

1. Lay the table (often done overnight), put on the kettle.
2. Heat serving dishes and plates and collect everything needed for cooking.
3. Begin making porridge and coffee if these are to be served.
4. Prepare grapefruit or orange-juice, make toast and keep it hot in a toast-rack.
5. Cook the main dish and keep it hot.
6. Make the tea.

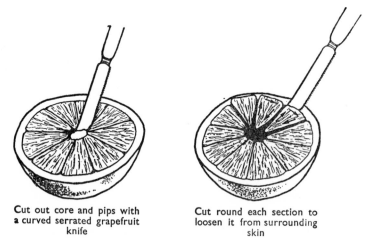

Cut out core and pips with a curved serrated grapefruit knife

Cut round each section to loosen it from surrounding skin

Fig. 79. GRAPEFRUIT—TO PREPARE

Recipes for Breakfast Dishes

Recipes for most of the dishes listed above will be found under subject headings; three special breakfast dishes are given below.

To Prepare Grapefruit (Fig. 79)

1. Scrub the rind.
2. Cut the fruit in half, remove all pips and with a special curved knife or with scissors cut out the core.
3. With a sharp knife loosen each cut segment all round, inserting the knife at the core-end of each and slipping it between skin and fruit, between rind and fruit and so round to the core again.
4. Sprinkle the fruit with a little caster sugar if liked, and serve it in a bowl or grapefruit glass with a teaspoon.

For a first course for dinner a cherry may be put in the middle of each half, but this is not usual for breakfast.

Porridge: I. Oatmeal   *2-3 helpings*

Cooking time   20 minutes

> 2 oz. medium oatmeal   1 level teaspoon salt
> 1 pint water or milk or milk and water

1. Use fresh oatmeal as, owing to its high proportion of fat, oatmeal, when stale, tastes rancid or bitter.
2. Soak the oatmeal in the water overnight.
3. Next morning add the salt and simmer the porridge for 20 minutes or until it has thickened; stir it frequently or use a double saucepan.
4. Serve the porridge very hot with milk or cream and salt or sugar or syrup.

II. Rolled Oats   *2-3 helpings*

Cooking time   10 minutes

> 2 oz. rolled oats to 1 pint water, milk or milk and water
> *or* 1 cup rolled oats to $2\frac{1}{2}$ cups liquid
> 1 level teaspoon salt to 1 pint

1. Boil the liquid, sprinkle in the rolled oats and stir them until the mixture begins to thicken, then simmer the porridge for 10 minutes.
2. Serve the porridge as for oatmeal.

Note. Rolled oats do not need as long cooking as oatmeal, nor do they taste bitter when stored because they are heated between hot rollers during processing.

Muesli or Swiss Breakfast Dish

No cooking

To each helping:

> 2 rounded tablespoons rolled oats
> 2½ tablespoons milk or water
> 1 teaspoon honey
> 1 tablespoon cream or top of the milk
> 4 oz. shredded or crushed raw fruit, e.g. apples, soft dessert fruits
> juice of ½ orange or lemon
> *or* 1 tablespoon blackcurrant or rose-hip syrup
> *Optional:* 1 tablespoon chopped nuts

1. Soak the rolled oats overnight in the milk or water.
2. Next morning grate the apple, mix in all the ingredients adding extra fruit juice or honey to taste.
3. Serve the muesli cold.

Note. This dish is much nicer than it sounds and is a pleasant, balanced breakfast, particularly attractive in hot weather.

30

SICK-ROOM COOKERY

REFRESHING DRINKS

Barley Water, Clear

2 oz. pearl barley   rind ½ lemon
1 quart water   juice of 1 to 2 lemons
sugar or glucose to sweeten

1. Blanch the barley, strain it and simmer it in the quart of water for 1 or 2 hours with the lemon rind, peeled thin.
2. Cool it.
3. When cold add the lemon juice and sugar to taste and strain it. Make only enough for 1 day unless it can be kept in a refrigerator.

Quickly made Barley Water

½ oz. 'patent' barley or 'cream of barley'
1 quart boiling water
lemon and sugar or glucose as above

1. Mix the powdered barley with a little cold water, stir into it the boiling water, turn it into a saucepan, add the lemon-rind and bring it to boiling-point.
2. Leave it to cool then add lemon juice, sugar or glucose and strain it.

Blackcurrant Drink

2 tablespoons blackcurrant jam
or 1 tablespoon blackcurrant syrup
½ pint boiling water
lemon juice to taste

Pour boiling water on to the jam, stir it well, add lemon juice to freshen the flavour and drink it hot. It may be strained but this wastes some of the jam.

    This is pleasant as a 'nightcap' for a patient with a sore throat.

Lemonade or Orangeade

1 lemon or 1 orange and a little lemon juice
½ pint water, sugar or glucose to taste

Scrub the orange or lemon and peel the rind with a vegetable peeler.

Pour ½ pint boiling water on to the rind, cover and cool it. When cold, add the juice and glucose or sugar to sweeten. Strain and serve it cold or it may be served hot as soon as it is mixed.

MILK DRINKS

Cup of Arrowroot

2 level teaspoons arrowroot
a breakfast cup of milk
1 teaspoon sugar or 2 teaspoons glucose
1 teaspoon brandy (if this is allowed by the doctor)

1. Mix the arrowroot with a little cold milk in the cup.
2. Boil the rest of the milk, stir it quickly into the arrowroot and milk and continue stirring till it thickens.
3. Add the sugar and brandy and serve it at once before a skin forms on top.

Egg Flip

1 egg ½ teaspoon sugar or 1 teaspoon glucose
¼ pint milk 1 teaspoon brandy (if allowed)

1. Separate yolk from white of egg and whisk the white till frothy.
2. Heat the milk till it steams and beat into it the yolk, then fold in the white while it is hot.
3. Add the brandy and sugar.

Milk Shake

a glass of cold milk
1 tablespoon blackcurrant syrup
or 1 tablespoon rose-hip syrup
a little lemon juice to taste
or the juice of 1 small orange
sugar to taste

1. Add lemon juice to the syrup to taste or sweeten the orange juice if necessary.
2. Quickly stir the two liquids together and serve the drink at once.

Savoury Milk

>   a cup of hot milk
> $\frac{1}{4}$ teaspoon Marmite, Bovril or other meat or yeast extract

1. Boil the milk and stir the extract into it until it dissolves.
2. Serve it hot or cold.

SAVOURY DISHES FOR A PATIENT ON A LIGHT DIET

Fish Custard   *1 helping*

Oven 325° to 350° F. Gas No. 3-4
Cooking time   30 minutes

> $\frac{1}{4}$ lb. white fish, e.g. plaice, sole or haddock or cod
>   salt and pepper $\frac{1}{4}$ pint milk
>   a little grated lemon rind   1 yolk or 1 small egg
>   1 teaspoon chopped parsley

1. Grease a $\frac{1}{2}$ pint oven-ware cup or pie-dish
2. Have the fish filleted and remove the skin.
3. Cut the fish in neat pieces or fold or roll small fillets, season the pieces lightly and put them in the dish.
4. Beat the egg, heat the milk till it steams, stir it on to the egg, add the parsley, lemon-rind and a little seasoning.
5. Strain the custard over the fish.
6. Bake the custard till just set, standing the dish in a tin of water if the oven is in use at a higher temperature than 350° F.

Liver Fricassée   *1 helping*

>   2 to 3 oz. raw calf or lamb liver
> $\frac{1}{4}$ pint white coating sauce
>   salt, pepper, lemon juice
>   1 tablespoon cream (if liked)
>   chopped parsley and sliced lemon

1. Have the liver sliced by the butcher.
2. Remove the skin and any blood-vessels.
3. Grill the liver until it is only just brown outside and still spongy.
4. Make the white sauce and season it to taste.
5. Chop the liver roughly, add it to the sauce and heat it gently till any red juice turns brown but do not boil it. Serve it garnished with chopped parsley and lemon.

Tomatoes Stuffed with Liver   *1 helping*

Oven 325 to 350° F. Gas No. 3-4
Baking time   15 to 20 minutes

1 to 2 firm, ripe tomatoes	1 teaspoon breadcrumbs
2 to 3 oz. raw liver	salt and pepper

1. Cut a neat round from the top of each tomato, scoop out the juice and seeds.
2. Grill the liver as for fricassée and chop it fine.
3. Mix liver and tomato pulp and add crumbs to soak up the juice. Season the mixture to taste and pack it into the tomatoes.
4. Bake the tomatoes in a greased tin or oven-ware dish till they are just soft.

Stewed Sweetbread   *1 helping*

¼ lb. sweetbread (calf's or lamb's)	2 teaspoons arrowroot or corn-flour
¼ pint milk or water	*or* 1 tablespoon flour
salt, pepper and lemon juice to taste	slices of lemon
	1 tablespoon cream

1. Blanch the sweetbread then put it into cold water. This will set the fat hard and it can be pulled away without cutting the skin.
2. Put the sweetbread in a small pan or casserole, just cover it with milk or water and stew it with the lid on for 1½ to 2 hours until quite soft.
3. Mix the starchy powder with a little cold milk.
4. Strain the sweetbreads, thicken the cooking liquid with the blended starch, season it and stir in the cream at boiling-point but do not cook it any more.
5. Coat the sweetbread with the sauce and garnish with lemon.

Other dishes suitable for patients on a light diet or convalescing will be found under subject headings (see also p. 179).

INDEX

Q

C